Self and Interpersonal Insight

INDUSTRIAL AND ORGANIZATIONAL PSYCHOLOGY SERIES

Editors

Cary L. Cooper

Neil Schmitt

Self and
Interpersonal Insight

How People Gain Understanding
of Themselves and
Others in Organizations

MANUEL LONDON

State University of New York at Stony Brook

New York   Oxford
OXFORD UNIVERSITY PRESS
1995

Oxford University Press

Oxford   New York
Athens   Auckland   Bangkok   Bombay
Calcutta   Cape Town   Dar es Salaam   Delhi
Florence   Hong Kong   Istanbul   Karachi
Kuala Lumpur   Madras   Madrid   Melbourne
Mexico City   Nairobi   Paris   Singapore
Taipei   Tokyo   Toronto

and associated companies in
Berlin   Ibadan

Published by Oxford University Press, Inc.,
200 Madison Avenue, New York, New York 10016

Library of Congress Cataloging-in-Publication Data
London, Manuel.
Self and interpersonal insight : how people gain understanding of
themselves and others in organizations / Manuel London.
p. cm.—(Industrial and organizational psychology series)
Includes bibliographical references and index.
ISBN 0-19-509077-2
1. Psychology, Industrial.   2. Social perception.   I. Title.
II. Series.
HF5548.8.L59   1995   94-49381
158.7—dc20

1 3 5 7 9 8 6 4 2

Printed in the United States of America
on acid-free paper

For Jared Michael London

Preface

My interest in interpersonal insight arose from two streams of research and practice. One was my work on career motivation theory and its tie to the design of career development programs (cf. London, 1983; London & Stumpf, 1986; London & Mone, 1987). The idea to study career motivation stemmed from the research of Douglas Bray and Ann Howard at AT&T, who showed that young managers in the late 1970s and early 1980s were as competent but not as motivated to advance as those entering the company twenty to twenty-five years earlier (Howard & Bray, 1981). Shortly after I joined AT&T in 1977, Doug Bray, then director of the company's Basic Human Resources Research Group, asked me to help develop an assessment center to study career motivation. Bray and I began by reviewing the literature and developing a set of career motivation dimensions based on relevant personality variables, needs, and interests. We categorized these dimensions into three domains: *resilience* (the extent to which people resist career barriers and work disruptions), *insight* (how realistic people are about themselves and their careers), and *identity* (the extent to which people define themselves by their work). Insight was viewed as a prerequisite to the development of meaningful career identity—meaningful defined in terms of career goals that matched available opportunities and that reflected the individual's strengths, weaknesses, and ability to learn. The key questions surrounding the concept of insight were how do people develop an accurate picture of themselves and a realistic perception of their environment, and what types of support can facilitate this process? (For an explanation of career motivation see London, 1983. For recent research, see London, 1993, and Noe, Noe, & Bachhuber, 1990. For descriptions of the career motivation assessment center, see London and Bray, 1983, and London, 1985a.)

The second stream of research on person perception was stimulated by Milton Hakel's employment interview studies at the Ohio State University where I was a graduate student. I first examined the effects of information order and favorability on impression formation. In subsequent research I studied the role of the rater in performance appraisal. My research in this area with Richard Klimoski found that the rater's position (e.g., supervisor, co-worker, or self) biased the ratings both in the structure of items and in the favorability of the ratings (Klimoski & London, 1974). During the mid-1980s I was asked to develop upward feedback programs at AT&T. This stemmed from management's increasing awareness of how changing business needs were affecting expectations for employees' development, the importance of the manager's role as coach and developer, and the need for managers to have feedback from their subordinates about how well they carried out this role. This led to research on variables that affect agreement between how managers see themselves and how they are perceived by their subordinates (Wohlers & London, 1989; London & Wohlers, 1991; Wohlers, Hall, & London, 1993). I continued this research after becoming a faculty member and director of the Center for Human Resource Management at the State University of New York at Stony Brook in 1989. This later research considered subordinates' reactions to the upward feedback process and their use of the feedback for their career development (Smither, Wohlers, & London, 1992; Smither, et al., 1993). I also worked on guidelines for implementing upward and 360-degree feedback (London, Wohlers, & Gallagher, 1990; London & Beatty, 1993). (See Chapter 5 for details about the role of insight in judging the performance of others and Chapter 10 for a review of the research on upward and 360-degree feedback and the implementation guidelines.)

In this book I integrate major cognitive processes to form a four-step model that will help us understand how people attain insight about themselves and others. The four steps include (1) receiving information about oneself or others (called *reflected feedback*), (2) integrating and reconciling the information with other information (*categorization*), (3) interpreting the information (*attribution*), and (4) incorporating the outcome into perceptions about oneself and others (*cognitive reevaluation of self-concept*). I define insight as that point at which an attribution turns into a reevaluation of oneself or others. I apply this model to the development of important interpersonal processes—specifically, one-on-one relationships, group dynamics, and negotiations. I show how human resource executives can use this process to understand how interpersonal situations operate and can be improved. As such, I describe how human resource programs can be designed so that they deliberately enhance self- and interpersonal insight.

Thus, my goal is to draw on social psychological theory and research to answer the following:

- How do we develop awareness of ourselves?
- How do we gain insight about others?
- How do self- and interpersonal insight affect behavior?
- In what situations is insight important?
- What affects insight? What facilitates insight development and emergence?
- Are there ways to enhance insight and thereby improve decision quality?
- When and how do people disclose information about themselves to others?
- To what extent do people try to manage the impressions others have of them? How do they do this?

- Is there a way to induce interpersonal insight?
- Can people be trained to be more aware of others—that is, be more insightful?

I attempt to answer these questions by examining insight from individual and work-group perspectives. I consider the meaning of insight in terms of self-awareness, awareness of others, and awareness of interpersonal relationships between two people and within groups. Cooperation and conflict resolution are considered. Theories of social and cognitive psychology are used to explain how insight emerges, how it develops, and how it affects behavior. Agendas for theory-testing research, measurement, and training evaluation are suggested.

The book is intended for students, researchers, and practitioners interested in improving organizational effectiveness through interpersonal dynamics. Organizational, social, and industrial psychologists as well as their students will appreciate the book's theoretical foundation, review and integration of a broad literature, and ideas for research and practice. The book could be a supplement for psychology and management courses in group dynamics and behavior, career development, communications, human relations, and organizational change and development. Human resource professionals will learn about facilitation and training programs that are based on cognitive processes. Such programs can help employees understand how their self-awareness develops and influences their behavior, and how their perceptions of others influence their success in groups and negotiations.

Stony Brook, N.Y.   M.L.
September 1994

Acknowledgments

I am grateful to my colleagues who influenced my thinking about insight processes and collaborated on the research and development of programs. These included Drs. Douglas Bray, Milton Hakel, Ann Howard, Richard Klimoski, James Smither, Stephen Stumpf, and Arthur Wohlers. I especially appreciate my colleagues at Stony Brook who took the time to read and discuss my ideas on person perception and social information processing applied to models of insight formation. In particular, I want to acknowledge Drs. Robert Boice, Jeff Casey, Gerrit Wolf, and Joseph Pufahl for their enthusiasm and encouragement. Gerrit Wolf recruited me to Stony Brook, and I will always be grateful to him for the opportunity to reenter the academy. His friendship and entrepreneurial spirit have been an important source of encouragement for me. My faculty and administrative positions at Stony Brook, most recently as deputy to the president of the university, helped me understand new dimensions of organizational behavior, enhancing my own and others' interpersonal insight during times of change and tight resources. I am grateful to Dr. Stan Altman and President John H. Marburger for this opportunity. I also appreciate Dr. Jennifer Clarke's help in identifying meaningful quotes to open the chapters.

Finally, there is no way I can repay my wife, Marilyn, and sons, David and Jared, for their never-waning love. In the language of this book, they are a meaningful and unavoidable source of feedback. They don't allow me to categorize their input arbitrarily or make faulty external attributions. Their cues are direct and sincere. The result is always worthwhile. This book is dedicated to Jared. His artistic creativity, musical talent, and desire for fun are a joy and a model. Never reticent in expressing his expectations and evaluations, he helps me to learn and grow.

Contents

Self and Interpersonal Insight

Introduction

This book explores the meaning of insight as a way to enhance individual and interpersonal effectiveness. How we view ourselves and others influences our behavior. It affects the extent to which we cooperate with others to accomplish tasks and how we work with others to resolve conflicts and negotiate agreements. Recognizing how interpersonal insights develop and influence behavior should contribute to effectiveness in one-on-one situations, groups, and negotiations.

How we view ourselves and others is important to the effectiveness of key interpersonal relationships. However, individual biases often obscure information processing and bog down organizational initiatives. Unfortunately, human resource programs often do not take these cognitive processes into account.

Consider problems faced by many human resource (HR) executives, such as communicating organizational strategies and performance expectations, designing interventions that improve cooperative relationships and promote conflict resolution, and encouraging employee development in directions important to organizational effectiveness and individual goals (London, 1994). Too often, programs that address these issues occur in isolation. They are based on what the organization wants to accomplish or on what's popular (Johns, 1993). They are based on economic and sociological models that drive efforts to improve quality, reduce costs, or develop a strong organizational culture. Or they are based on theories of individual motivation, group dynamics, or organizational processes (e.g., about leadership or structure). What is missing from these programs is how people process information, apply it to themselves, and learn about social interactions that are the foundation of organizational functioning and success. This cognitive approach adds another dimension to understanding how individuals react to the work environment. It is an approach that cuts across a variety of human resource efforts aimed at enhancing organizational functions.

This book bridges two areas—what we know about social cognition and what we know about industrial and organizational psychology. It recognizes that the underlying cognitive processes common to key interpersonal situations in organizations can help link, integrate, and create more effective human resource programs. Social information processing can affect individuals' self-image, behavior, and quality of interpersonal relationships. Human resource programs such as assessment, feedback, and training can be improved by building on how we process information about ourselves and others.

Cognitive information processing has been applied to performance appraisal (e.g., Ilgen, Barnes-Farrell, & McKellin, 1993). Other human resource programs, such as self-assessment, attitude surveys, feedback, and development planning, assume cognitive processes occur, but they usually do not delineate them. That is, the cognitive components and their relationships are not used as a basis for program design. Also, the programs do not recognize how the underlying cognitive components are related to interpersonal dynamics.

Here I combine an understanding of how we perceive others and ourselves with an analysis of situational conditions that are so important in organizations. Both cognition (thought) and emotion are relevant to our attainment of interpersonal insight. It follows that insight is critical to how interpersonal situations develop. Thus, I have suggested ways in which insight may be fostered in organizations as a way of avoiding and resolving conflicts, stimulating cooperation and productive work relationships, and fostering career development and motivation.

This book describes appraisal and feedback processes that can enhance not only self-awareness but also the perceptions of others. Insight assessment centers, behavioral simulations, computerized assessments, self-diagnostic methods, and employee attitude surveys are just some of the tools that can enhance insights about oneself and others. I also present ways to capture and track employees' reactions to major organizational and career changes and review methods for facilitating team development. We look at problems that emerge in management teams, and how feedback and joint discovery of impediments improve group functioning. Common breakdowns in interpersonal relationships are explored, and ways to overcome them are suggested.

Throughout the text I try to show how research informs practice, and vice versa. I recognize that practitioners and researchers have different needs. Most practitioners probably have little prior background in the theories of social cognition, such as image theory. My goal is to demonstrate how these theories are important to the design and implementation of human resource programs that involve interpersonal judgment, such as 360-degree feedback. Some practitioners may find the discussion of laboratory studies involving students to be unimportant. However, laboratory experiments are often used by social, industrial, and organizational psychologists to control for unwanted effects and ensure that significant effects are resulting from the variables being manipulated. This concern for reliability and internal validity may sacrifice generalizability. But the assumption is that social psychological experiments reveal generically applicable principles of perception and behavior—especially when results from several studies are taken together. I suggest where such results indicate the need for more research in real-world settings.

Just as practitioners should be open to the value of basic research, researchers should recognize practitioners' needs for general guidance. Some of the material in later chapters of the book may seem basic and not directly relevant to their research interests. I have tried to address researchers' concerns by indicating areas of practice where basic research is needed to prove the validity of human resource programs.

Outline of Chapters

In Part I we explore the meaning of insight. We look not only at the cognitive processes underlying the formation of insight but at how insight affects performance judgments. Chapter 1 begins with some definitions and examples of insight. The chapter looks at the importance of self-awareness to interpersonal relationships, career development, self-disclosure, and how we want others to see us (impression management).

Chapter 2 offers a theoretical foundation for understanding the development of insight. The importance of feedback about oneself and information about others is highlighted. Then, cognitive processes are examined as a basis for insight. These involve collecting information about oneself and others, processing these images by categorizing them into already formed impressions, or creating new explanations for behavior, and changing the images. The chapter considers factors that influence the extent to which we see ourselves the way others see us. Emotional and cognitive barriers to accurate perceptions and attributions are explored as well.

Chapter 3 focuses on self-awareness and self-image. Aspects of identity include self-confidence, self-efficacy, need for achievement, and internal control. Aspects of self-management include how we present ourselves to others, regulate our behavior, form expectations, set goals, and track accomplishments. Self-assessment processes are suggested, such as feedback seeking and self-evaluation.

Chapter 4 applies the processes described in Chapter 2 to how we perceive others—their characteristics, behavioral tendencies, competencies, and accomplishments. These include supervisors' appraisals of their subordinates' performances and employment interviewers' perceptions of applicants. We will consider why some people are more insightful than others, and discuss observation skills, self-monitoring, and empathy.

Chapter 5 integrates rating and feedback processes, building on concepts described in the earlier chapters. It considers how we perceive others and how feedback from others influences our self-perceptions. Emphasis is placed on 360-degree feedback programs in organizations, which provide managers with ratings from multiple viewpoints—subordinates, supervisors, peers, and customers. Drawing on image theory, the chapter considers factors that influence ratings and reactions to feedback. The perceptual process model shows the mutual interrelationships between self-image and goals, the situation, and acceptance of feedback from others.

Part II focuses on interpersonal insight applied to the development of relationships, group dynamics, and negotiations. Chapter 6 applies the preceding discussion of how we gain insights about others to the development of interpersonal relationships. Relationships evolve from first acquaintance to being able to predict others' behaviors and reactions. The chapter suggests how interpersonal insights emerge and contribute to the development of the relationship.

Chapter 7 shows how group development is affected by the interpersonal insight of its members. In large part, group interactions depend on the demands of the task. For instance, some tasks require sequential interaction whereas others require synchronous interaction. Group members' awareness of each other and the task produces work relationship patterns. New groups form these patterns quickly and maintain them over time, even after task requirements change. Newcomers to ongoing groups quickly gain an understanding of the prevailing interpersonal dynamics. Their success in contributing to the group depends on these insights and the insights of the group members to each other's capabilities and willingness to adapt.

Negotiations are another type of group effort involving two or more opposing parties or teams. Negotiations and conflict resolution are vital in many aspects of organizational dynamics, including labor–management bargaining and cooperation, sales, finance, and intergroup work relationships. Chapter 8 applies concepts of insight emergence to negotiation processes and effectiveness. Interpersonal insights affect how and when information is revealed, interests and preferences are divulged, and offers are formulated and presented. Negotiators' observation skills, biases, and experiences with alternative negotiation strategies and bargaining partners are insight-related components that influence these negotiation processes.

Part III outlines ways to enhance interpersonal insight. Chapter 9 reviews insight induction techniques, such as self-assessment, survey feedback, assessment centers, computerized assessment, socialization processes, retraining, and observation skills training. While these are commonly used techniques in organizations, they are not necessarily designed specifically to improve self- and interpersonal insight. The chapter shows how the components of information processing described in this book can guide the design of these methods to enhance insight.

Chapter 10 covers processes by which managers receive feedback from their subordinates (called upward feedback ratings) or from subordinates, peers, supervisors, and customers (360-degree feedback). It reviews why these have become popular and valuable techniques for supporting employee development in organizations. Methods for developing these feedback programs are described.

The concluding chapter outlines directions for research and practice. Potentially important topics for research include identifying cues and clues in interpersonal perceptions and determining the effects of task demands, rule and role clarity, self-disclosure, and self-monitoring on insight. Alternative measurement methods are considered. Directions for practice entail designing and testing new insight-induction techniques and training programs to enhance interpersonal interactions.

The Resource Guides appended to the book as addenda to Chapters 9 and 10 outline human resource programs grounded in the importance of self- and person perception. These include processes for career development, self-evaluation, survey feedback, a developmental assessment center, socialization for new employees, and 360-degree feedback. The guides demonstrate how these programs can be tailored to maximize the insight we gain about ourselves and others. The guides show how self-assessment, situational analysis, internal attributions, and self-evaluation can be designed into career development programs and other human resource programs and performance improvement processes.

I

Theoretical Perspectives:
A Cognitive Model of Insight

selfimage {
= service provider
= teammate

performance { Adapting new performance expectations
judgment relationships

1

The Meaning of Insight

No deep insight into human minds is possible without unconscious comparisons with our own experiences.

Dr. Theodor Reik, *Listening with the Third Ear*

The evidence in studies of creative people is that they get their important insights on those particular problems on which they have wrestled with perseverance and diligence, even though the insight itself may come at a moment of lull.

Rollo May, *Man's Search for Himself*

This book is about self-insight and interpersonal insight—that is, how we see ourselves and others. The book addresses how such insights form, how they affect our behavior in organizations, and how they can be developed to improve the quality of our decisions and the effectiveness of our actions. The book organizes and integrates interpretations of insight in organizational contexts with applications to self-awareness, performance judgment, and the development of relationships between two people, within groups, and between negotiating parties.

This introductory chapter explores the meaning of self- and interpersonal insight. I describe insight in terms of the cognitive processes people use to interpret social information, the recognition of insight, and its effects on decision making and behavior; I discuss both applications of insight to social situations and means of inducing insight.

The Meaning of Insight and Insight Processes

Webster's defines *insight* as "the power or act of seeing into a situation; the act or result of apprehending the inner nature of things." This suggests several related concepts and their definitions. *Intuition* is immediate apprehension or cognition—quick and ready insight. *Awareness* is sensitivity to, and recognition of, information or cues about oneself, others' behaviors and attitudes, or events. Other associated terms include *attribution* and *prediction*.

Insight is often used in conjunction with the idea of a sudden and surprising experience (an "aha" or "now I see" occurrence).

The multiple connotations of insight are captured in the philosophy of the Lyubavitsher movement—a Jewish sect founded in the eighteenth century in the town of Lyubavitsh, Russia. The Lyubavitshers speak of three segments of intellect: knowledge, understanding, and wisdom (Bishop, 1985, p. 273). Knowledge suggests facts. Understanding refers to interpretation of facts to form meaning. Wisdom refers to the depth, clarity, importance, and practical value of the interpretation. These are interrelated concepts. They imply an incremental or developmental sequence, with understanding resting on a foundation of knowledge and wisdom requiring an advanced level of understanding.

Issues of self-knowledge, personal identity, and knowledge of other persons have long occupied philosophers, among them Descartes, Locke, Berkeley, Hume, Kant, and Wittgenstein, and probably countless others. (See Vohra, 1986, for an overview.) These philosophical issues merged with concepts of insight, which in turn helped form the foundation of cognitive psychology discussed throughout this book. As one philosopher stated, insight is "an illuminating moment in which previous thinking falls into perspective and sensitive spontaneity undergoes an effortless change" (Lonergan, 1957, p. 203).

We use the term *insight* in different ways. For instance, we use it to refer to someone's ability ("She is insightful") and to describe an idea ("This is a real insight"). We use it to refer to the process of acquiring understanding. Insights may be about intentions (what you are planning), reasons (why you are performing this action), states (how you feel), and problem solving (how you do this) (Bowers, 1984; Reilly & Doherty, 1992).

Self-insight refers to how completely and accurately we know ourselves. Similarly, *interpersonal* insight refers to how well we know others. Self-insight and interpersonal insight allow us to judge ourselves in relation to others to determine, for example, whether we are "on the same wavelength" or behave in ways that are "in synch" with others. Insight refers to interpreting actions and behaviors—what Meryl Louis (1980) and Karl Weick (1979) call "sense-making." An insight may be a realization of errors in perceptions or judgment. As such, it could lead to the elimination of an error or "oversight." Alternatively, an insight may be a creative or novel idea. Insight implies perception, accuracy, immediacy, novelty, and pertinency— seeing or realizing something that wasn't evident before, something about the inner nature of the object. Another interpretation of insight is the realization of something that is both new and different.

The process of gaining insight involves imputing meaning to a body of facts or attributes. Moreover, accuracy is implied. That is, insight is not a matter of simply attending to and reporting objective information but a matter of making judgments about the inner, and not readily observable, nature of things. Insights imply something more than information that is available to anyone. They go beyond tacit knowledge—knowledge of the environment that makes the formulation of pictures and words possible (Gibson, 1982; Reed, 1991). Accuracy is problematic because there is usually some ambiguity or difficulty in verifying the insight. A criterion for accuracy is interpersonal agreement about the insight—that is, people agree that the insight is correct. Another criterion for accuracy is the consistency of the judgment with prior behavior patterns of the individual or other individuals in similar situations—for instance, realizing that the way others behave is the standard and expected mode of group behavior. Another view of accuracy may be convergence between decisions based on insights and optimization models applied to variables with known values (i.e., people as "intuitive statisticians"). (Accuracy will be discussed further in Chapter 4 in relation to rating processes.)

Insights require information processing, including integration, interpretation, and recollection. What seems to be a sudden, immediate, and new idea that pops out of nowhere is likely to result from an incubation period during which information is collected and processed (Perkins, 1981). (This process is described in the next chapter.) Understanding self- and interpersonal insight requires determining how we process social information. Such information may be derived from self-reflection, observation of behavior, or written or oral information about our own or others' actions.

Thus, insight is an amalgam of concepts referring to individual differences (elements of personality and skills), ways people seek and interpret information, and the outcome of information seeking—that is, realization or awareness and its content, clarity, and practical impact for decision making and behavior.

Theoretical Perspectives

Several theoretical perspectives explain how we interpret information to form insights. Insight formation rests on perceptual and cognitive processes. These encompass the social psychological processes of impression formation, person perception, social information processing, and impression management. Impression formation is "the process of perceiving pieces of information about an individual (e.g., prior expectations, verbal and nonverbal behaviors) and integrating them into some coherent summary impression" (Copeland, 1993, p. 118). People's behavior is in part motivated by their concerns about how others see them and their desire to influence these impressions. A better understanding of insight offers a variety of organizational applications and directions for extending and testing theories of person perception and the development of interpersonal relationships.

Social cognition research is concerned with how people make sense of themselves and others. It focuses on mentalistic explanations, thought processes, and social behavior and perceptions (Fiske & Taylor, 1991, p. 553). To some degree, cognitions cause, and are affected by, affective responses, attitudes and attitude changes, and behavioral strategies. However, cognitions, affect, and behavior are fairly autonomous and often fail to predict each other, at least in a simple way (Fiske & Taylor, 1991, p. 554). On the one hand, cognitions simplify the way people perceive the world by allowing them to categorize information so that it provides sufficient explanation and understanding. On the other hand, motivation to resolve inconsistencies and comprehend unusual and unexpected occurrences leads to attributions of causes and reevaluations of oneself and others.

Perceptual Psychology

An early theoretical foundation for understanding insight stems from perceptual psychology (Snygg & Combs, 1950; Combs, Richards, & Richards, 1988). This field holds that the awareness and intensity with which events are experienced is a function of the person and the situation. Our first awareness of events is generally vague and undifferentiated. This perception becomes more differentiated over time as we understand better the nature of the object we are perceiving in relation to its context or field. "The factors which appear to determine the nature and extent to which an event is differentiated are the need of a person and the opportunities for differentiation that are available" (Combs, Richards, & Richards, 1988, p. 31). For instance, self-efficacy may be a need. To quote Combs again, "Out of all the things we *might* perceive, we perceive what is meaningful to us and what helps us to maintain the organization of our phenomenal field and thereby to satisfy our fundamental need" (p. 61; italics in the original).

Perceptual psychology suggests that some people are more insightful than others because they have wider or richer phenomenal fields and a lower need for self-defense. "They are capable of seeing relationships not seen by others. Their more efficient perceptions make it possible for them to penetrate more effectively to fundamental premises while others are sill muddling about with more superficial techniques" (Combs, Richards, & Richards, 1988, p. 273). Combs describes this as a "reservoir of positive perceptions and the ability to accept new experiences" (p. 272).

A Cognitive Perspective

Psychology rests on the study of cognitions, attitudes, emotions, and behavior. Different fields in psychology have concentrated on one or another of these approaches. The approach I take to insight in this book is largely cognitive in nature. That is, it focuses on a representational view of the mind that indicates how information is categorized and interpreted. This is a helpful way to view interpersonal insight for several reasons. Cognitivism provides a working model of our minds that parallels reality (Craik, 1943; Johnson-Laird, 1983). The perceiver reconstructs basic information, each piece of which may be meaningless in and of itself. Cognitivism offers a stability and predictability of the world order "by reducing unique, disorderly, and contextualized events and actions to decontextualized regularities" (Shotter, 1991, p. 68; see also Billig, 1987, Snyder, 1981, and Mills, 1940). It provides a concrete way of conceptualizing and categorizing information and explaining how it is used. This suggests that people are rational in their perceptual and interpretive processes. Moreover, it suggests that people can be trained to be better observers and processors of information.

Sinnott (1993) interpreted how cognitive science is applied to self-knowledge that is based on social–cognitive experience and skills that arise from interpersonal experience. People face and solve problems by confronting multiple conflicting ideas about what is true. These ideas are often contributed by others. People realize that "truth" rests within their own minds, and they act within the limits of others in their social system. To quote Sinnott,

> [W]e can never be completely free of the built-in limits of our system of knowing and . . . we come to know that this very fact is true. This means that we take into account, in all our decisions about truth, the fact that all knowledge has a subjective choice component and therefore is, of necessity, incomplete. So, any logic we use is self-referential logic. Yet we must act, and do so by making a lower level decision about the higher level rules of the game (nature of truth), then play the game by those rules. Sooner or later, we come to *realize* that this is what we are doing. We then can consciously use self-referential logic. (Sinnott, 1993, p. 163; italics in original)

Beyond Cognitivism

There are other approaches to human perception and decision making that are broader and more inclusive than cognitivism. The literature on the philosophy of psychology indicates that broader approaches may be more fruitful in improving our understanding of interpersonal perception and relationships than a pure cognitive framework. Consider the following views (adapted from Shanon, 1991, pp. 240–250):

- People form, manipulate, weigh, and evaluate perceptions and ideas. This is what is meant by cognition.
- Cognitive activity is a large neural-like associative network. Patterns of brain activity parallel cognitive models. While this might seem to be an academic distinction, at some time in the future, behavioral-neural science and technology may provide a more accurate and complete picture of thought processes than models of perceptual process and judgment.
- Thinking consists of verbal-like expressions that spontaneously pass through people's minds. It can be described in terms of mental events, such as occurrences of "realization," "understanding," and "insights" that are associated with observable events in the environment. This theoretical perspective may be the closest to what I mean in this book by the development of self- and interpersonal insight.

- Statements of thought impute meanings to the thinker and the object of the thought, such as the recognition of a desire or the attribution of a reason for an observed behavior. This is also consistent with the views in this book.
- Phenomena are consciously experienced, without theories of their causal explanation such as motivations and desires. Also, there are no underlying structures or behavior-generation mechanisms. The subject's statements of thoughts are all we need to study. This is termed *phenomenology*.
- Cognition is rooted in action and its locus is in the external environment, either biological or sociocultural. Cognitive social psychologists have tried to extend the information-processing paradigm from the realm of individual, mental behavior to the realm of interpersonal, social behavior.
- Reports and models of cognitive process are irrelevant. The focus should be entirely on behavior and the relationships between events and behavior. This is behaviorism.

Shanon (1991, p. 257) predicts that rather than studying the underlying mechanisms of mind, psychology will eventually study the structural constraints of cognitive expression, their progression in time, the functions they perform, the situational dependencies associated with them, and the history of their evolution in cultures and societies.

Thus, insight can be explained by different psychological mechanisms. While the approach I will take here is primarily cognitive, I see the importance of understanding behavioral tendencies, individual characteristics, social situations, and situational conditions. The next section extends this idea by considering how emotions affect self- and interpersonal insights.

Judgments of Emotions

Forming judgments about oneself and others is not simply a cool, calm, and rational process. It entails feeling emotions in ourselves, feeling emotions as we observe others, and making inferences about the emotions others are feeling (empathy). This raises questions about how judgments of emotions arise and relate to other judgments that we make about ourselves and others (e.g., attributions of motives, personality, abilities, and interests). Judgments of emotions do not occur in isolation from these other types of judgments. Instead, an event or series of verbal and nonverbal behaviors may be classified in terms of a profile of attributes. Thus, the cognitive evaluation (i.e., categorization) of an event may include an emotional component (Johnson-Laird & Oatley, 1992). For instance, achieving a goal, or seeing someone achieve a goal, perhaps making an important sale, or receiving a promotion at work may be associated with an emotional response of happiness, satisfaction, or possibly envy. The emotion or set of emotions serves not just an *informational function* but a *control function* (Johnson-Laird & Oatley, 1992). It may alert us to a problem, a dangerous situation, or maybe just to the contingencies that can lead to positive emotion in the future, such as what one has to do to be promoted.

Emotions and associated personality characteristics (e.g., arrogant, quarrelsome, warm-agreeable, gregarious) are evident from nonverbal as well as verbal behavior. Gifford (1994) found that people's self-assessments are moderately related to reliably scored nonverbal behaviors (e.g., $r = .40$). People are better at decoding nonverbal behaviors. That is, their assessments of others correlate highly with reliably scored nonverbal behaviors (e.g., $r = .78$). Not surprisingly, Gifford also found that self-assessments agree more highly with others' assessments when people use nonverbal cues that appropriately reflect a disposition than when they use inappropriate cues. Of course, misinterpretations of cues can lead to conflict. Behaviors that are perceived to be arrogant or cold can lead to negative responses, which in turn generate surprise as well as negative emotions and behavior in kind, thereby damaging a developing relationship.

Research suggests that we use a set of basic emotions to structure our perceptions of others and ourselves. Johnson-Laird and Oatley (1989) identified five emotions in this set: happiness, sadness, anger, fear, and disgust. Ekman (1992) suggested that this set may be much larger, including (in alphabetical order) anger, awe, contempt, disgust, embarrassment, enjoyment (which encompasses amusement, contentment, relief, and accomplishment), excitement, fear, guilt, interest, sadness, shame, and surprise. While emotions are evident in behavior and expressions, these physical links are not universal. They vary by culture (Russell, 1994). Thus, understanding sociocultural conditions is necessary to capture how people convey emotions in themselves and how they attribute emotions to others.

Emotions and cognitions are reciprocally related. (See a review by Fiske & Taylor, 1991, pp. 409–461.) Feelings seem to "color almost everything that we experience and do" (Isen, 1984, p. 226). Feelings seem to lead automatically to compatible thought and behavior. Thus, emotions may cause cognition in that the affect (e.g., anger or sadness) causes a search for an explanation or interpretation (Schachter, 1964; Sinclair et al., 1994). Moods may evoke or thwart cognition, as when happiness leads one to think about ways of helping others while anger leaves one blind to another's positive behaviors or attributes. Not reaching a goal may initiate disappointment as well as a search for reasons (Mandler, 1990). Emotions may interrupt goals and lead to a change in priorities. In interpersonal relationships, the more people are interdependent, the greater the potential for interruption of the relationship, leading to emotional distress and causing rationalization and a search for the facts (cf. Berscheid, Snyder, & Omoto, 1989). The situation and accompanying emotion may affect attributions. Serious conflicts result in a greater attribution of mood than simple conflicts. For instance, sad people attribute real-life conflicts more to internal, stable causes and do so more for serious conflicts than for simple conflicts (Forgas, 1994).

Cognitive structures may influence emotion. For instance, feelings may become associated with cognitive schemas. When a perception evokes a schema, the associated affect also emerges, as when one meets one's new boss for the first time and feels apprehension. In general, as people appraise their situation, they determine its meaning. This, in turn, may incite emotion, as when employees who just received a raise seek to compare themselves with others to determine equity. The same raise, then, may result in the recipient's feeling satisfied or dissatisfied.

Person Perception

Research on person perception since the late 1950s has attempted to examine the elements of social perceptions (Cronbach, 1958). The concept of "person perception" was used by Tagiuri and Petrullo (1958) to mean apperception and cognition. They proposed applying the term person perception

> whenever the *perceiver regards the object as having the potential of representation and intentionality.* . . . As a physical stimulus a person is, of course, not different from other stimuli. In the sense that, through information gained via perception, we infer properties and potentialities of the object that are not immediately given, persons are doubtless special objects, for persons have psychological properties. Indeed, when we speak of person perception or of knowledge of persons, we refer mostly to the observations we make about *intentions, attitudes, emotions, ideas, abilities, purposes, traits*—events that are, so to speak, inside the person. We make these observations as we follow, among other things, the *actions* of persons, but we formulate the actions in terms that are strictly psychological. We seldom describe the sheer sequence of bodily movements of a person; rather, we say that a person is friendly, fearful, boastful, hesitant, aggressive. (p. x, italics in original)

The conditions of perceptions form the basis for the interaction between one person and another. Each person in an interaction has a "phenomenal representation of the environment" (Tagiuri & Petrullo, 1958, p. xi). Each makes known to the other that she is sensitive to the other. This becomes a "mutually shared" field of interaction between persons, which, according to Tagiuri and Petrullo, is the prerequisite for all true social processes.

Perceptual and cognitive processes of insight include how people seek and interpret feedback about themselves and information about others. Sometimes information is interpreted in terms of preexisting categories. In such cases, preexisting judgments are confirmed and insights do not arise. Other times the information is used to reevaluate one's own or others' abilities and behavioral tendencies. In these cases, insights emerge and are used to reframe judgments about others and suggest new behavioral strategies. Interpersonal behaviors are a function of cognitive and biological mechanisms. Just as mammals, such as chimps and dolphins, form teams and synchronous behavior displays that have survival functions, people develop ways of reacting to each other, cooperating, and synchronizing their behavior. Chapter 2 offers a model of the cognitive processes underlying self- and interpersonal insight and their situational antecedents and behavioral consequences.

Applications

This book focuses on how self- and interpersonal insight contribute to self-development, performance judgments, and interpersonal relationships. In the process, it considers barriers to insight, including stereotypes, judgment errors, and defense mechanisms. Self-assessment tools and training usually are a part of interventions that focus on self- and interpersonal insight.

Career Development

Experts in career theory have long posited that self-knowledge helps people plan their careers and make decisions about themselves that will lead to positive outcomes. Insights about what we are like—that is, our interests, desires, personalities, and behavioral tendencies—drive the goals we set for ourselves and the extent to which we exert energy to accomplish these goals. Self-insights refer to the conception we have of our goals (their clarity and specificity) and of how others are likely to react to us. Insight into the social and organizational context affects both the goals we set for ourselves and our ability to change direction in response to the environment.

Self-Assessment.   Recognizing the importance of self-insight, career development programs usually include self-assessment tools. These methods may ask individuals to rate themselves on a host of behavioral statements and skill dimensions. They may also request participants to collect information from others by, for example, asking for feedback from supervisors and subordinates. The purpose is to help individuals understand themselves in relation to career opportunities and work demands. This should result in setting more meaningful goals—goals that are realistic given the environment and the individual's capabilities and interests.

The Role of Feedback.   Managers, human resource experts, and psychologists have long recognized the value of feedback as a basis for development (London, 1988). People need information about themselves in order to form realistic impressions that guide behavior. Feedback motivates and directs behavior by serving either as an incentive for future performance goals or as a reward or punishment for behavior that has already occurred. It keeps goal-directed behavior on course, increases error detection, and demonstrates behaviors that contribute to successful performance (Nadler, 1979). Feedback is likely to be perceived more accurately and to be accepted when it occurs soon after the behavior, when it is specific, positive, and frequent, and when the source of the feedback is credible (i.e., is viewed by the recipient as having expertise, familiarity with the situation, trustworthiness, or power to influence valued outcomes; Ilgen, Fisher, & Taylor, 1979).

Feedback Seeking.   Ashford and Cummings (1983) argued that people seek feedback while negotiating their organizational environments in pursuit of their goals. Feedback seeking occurs by actively monitoring the environment or by active inquiry. The feedback reduces uncertainty by determining whether one's behavior is accurate. Feedback signals the relative importance of various goals, creates the feeling of competence, allows self-evaluation, and provides the chance to defend one's ego. However, the motivation to seek feedback may be mixed. On the one hand, feedback may be useful for correcting errors and reducing uncertainty. On the other, it may be dysfunctional if it threatens one's self-esteem. Ironically, low performers who need the feedback the most may be the most reluctant to seek it. Thus, in seeking feedback, one takes into account the possibility of losing face, the amount of effort required to obtain the information, and the likelihood that clear, salient information will be forthcoming. Chapter 3 discusses the cognitive and behavioral processes underlying the development of self-insight.

People are more willing to give feedback when the recipient can use the information to change behavior, the recipient is dependent on the source of feedback (as would be the case for a subordinate who is dependent on the supervisor), the source is responsible for providing information, and there are positive norms in the organization for giving feedback (Larson, 1984). The process of giving and receiving feedback increases the salience of the information and the importance of the process itself. Moreover, feedback that has positive effects increases the control and power felt by both the source and the recipient.

Performance Evaluation.   Many organizations have performance evaluation processes that collect information from different sources—supervisors, co-workers, subordinates, or customers and then report the results to the target manager (Tornow, 1993). Known as 360-degree feedback, these multisource rating programs provide managers with information about how others see them on behavioral dimensions that are important to the organization. Having information from multiple sources is valuable because we don't behave the same way with everyone and because people vary in the perspectives they have of us. Implementing a 360-degree feedback program requires determining what types of behaviors should be rated and helping recipients of the ratings interpret the results to shape strategies for development.

Other methods have been used to provide people with better information about themselves. Supervisors are trained in how to give meaningful feedback in a nonthreatening, constructive way. Assessment centers with various behavioral simulations provide participants with objective and comprehensive information about their managerial and interpersonal skills. The assessors (often managers) and assessees (employees being evaluated for managerial positions) learn to be better observers of themselves and others.

We often evaluate ourselves and others in relation to comparisons and existing frames of reference. For example, information we have about others' salaries will affect how we evaluate our own salary. Stereotypes we hold about gender and racial groups influence the information we observe and how we interpret it. We all use stereotypes to make information processing easier. For instance, meeting people for the first time requires attending to what they are saying and forming an impression about them. When a label is used to describe someone (e.g., "She is a doctor"), the impression-management task is easier, although not necessarily more accurate (Macrae, Milne, & Bodenhausen, 1994). These frames of reference are often barriers to accurate perceptions and lead to erroneous conclusions about our own or others' abilities. Chapters 4 and 5 examine how we perceive and evaluate others.

Interpersonal Relationships

Next, consider how self- and interpersonal insight contribute to the development of interpersonal relationships.

The "Johari" Window.   An early interpretation of the importance of self- and interpersonal insight to one-on-one and group interactions was conceptualized by Joseph Luft and Harry Ingham in the model they referred to as the *Johari Window* (Luft & Ingham, 1955; Luft, 1969, 1970). Their four-quadrant model shown in Figure 1.1 illustrates relationships in terms of awareness. This graphic model suggests that our knowledge of self and others is in part inferential and that in some cases others may be better able to evaluate our frame of mind and our behavior than we can ourselves. The

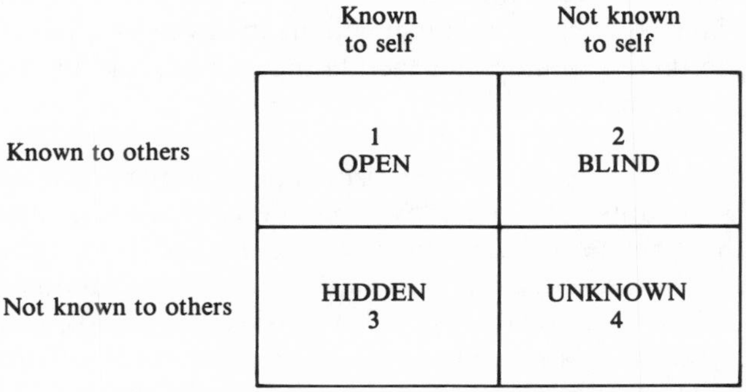

	Known to self	Not known to self
Known to others	1 OPEN	2 BLIND
Not known to others	HIDDEN 3	UNKNOWN 4

FIGURE 1.1   The Johari Window. (From Luft, 1970, p. 11.)

size of the quadrants changes relative to each other as people learn about themselves and others. In a new and unfamiliar social situation, quadrant 1 in Figure 1.1 is initially very small. There is likely to be little free spontaneous interaction. Over time, however, we feel more comfortable and become able to express ourselves freely and perceive others as they really are. The hidden area (quadrant 3) shrinks as we feel less compelled to hide or deny things we know or feel, and correspondingly, quadrant 1 increases. Quadrant 2 shrinks slowly because of psychological defense mechanisms that make us blind to ourselves in certain areas (those that threaten our self-concept). But at times self-insight may come about suddenly. Quadrant 4 changes even more slowly, although interventions (see, for instance, Chapter 9) can enhance self- and interpersonal insight.

The Johari model further suggests that the quadrants change in accordance with several principles:

- A change in any one quadrant will affect all other quadrants.
- Threat tends to decrease awareness; mutual trust tends to increase awareness.
- Forced awareness (exposure) is undesirable and usually ineffective.
- Interpersonal learning means a change has taken place so that quadrant 1 is larger and one or more of the other quadrants has grown smaller.
- Working with others is facilitated by a large enough area of free activity. An increase in quadrant 1 means more of the resources and skills of the (group) can be applied to a task.
- The smaller the first quadrant, the poorer the communication.
- There is universal curiosity about the unknown area, quadrant 4, but this is held in check by custom, social training, and diverse fears.
- Sensitivity means appreciating the covert aspects of behavior, in quadrants 2, 3, and 4, and respecting the desire of others to keep them so (Luft, 1970, p. 15).

Thus, the Johari Window is a heuristic model aimed at helping people understand their insensitivity. It gives us a way of interpreting how and what we know about ourselves and others, which suggests at least three areas of application: interpersonal insight can help us in developing interpersonal relationships, in understanding and facilitating groups, and in resolving conflicts through negotiation.

One-On-One Relationships.   Interpersonal insight means understanding interpersonal situations. This includes perceptions of how we relate to others and how others relate to each other. These may be boss–subordinate relationships, customer–supplier relationships, group relationships, or the negotiation relationship of the opposing parties. This book examines how perceptions of these relationships emerge. Sometimes these perceptions develop slowly as we work more closely with people and get to know them better. Other times, interpersonal judgments may emerge quickly and early on in a relationship, rapidly affecting the course of the relationship. Chapter 6 examines the association between interpersonal insight and the development of relationships between two people.

Understanding Group Dynamics. These days, a considerable amount of work is accomplished in groups. These groups may be task forces that have clear objectives and involve people from different specialties to solve a particular problem. They may be quality improvement teams or quality circles that are formed to identify ways to improve productivity. They may be process teams that coordinate the work of people from different areas in the production of a product or service. They may be self-managing work groups that require group members to formulate their own goals, work schedules, and job structures. These team efforts vary in the type and extent of coordination they require. Sometimes the work must be sequenced, with the product of one person's work needed before another person can do his or her job (e.g., assembly tasks). Other times the work is synchronous, with team members doing different tasks simultaneously (e.g., military flight crews and orchestras). The tasks require that team members know each other well. They must know what to expect from each other and how each person contributes to the team. Such insights are likely to affect the group's success.

Interpersonal insights should help participants become productive group members and effective negotiators. This may mean realizing and meeting others' expectations so behaviors are coordinated. This applies to cooperative groups (task forces, quality improvement teams, self-managing work groups), performance ensembles (flight teams), and partnerships (law firms, businesses). In Chapter 7, we consider how group members' insights affect group processes.

Conflict Resolution and Negotiation. Negotiation teams also require self- and interpersonal insight. For example, in labor negotiations, team members must understand each other's objectives as well as the objectives of the opposing party. Such insights are based on past experience, communication, and trial and error as issues are put on the table and offers are made. Insights about conflicts and negotiations include understanding mixed motives and opposing strategies. Sometimes negotiators perceive the process as a win–lose situation (that is, giving in to an opponent's demand means losing something). At other times, negotiators may perceive the process as a win–win situation (that is, they try to identify solutions in which both parties can be winners). This frame of reference is likely to influence the negotiators' beliefs about each others' likely reactions to different outcomes. Also, negotiators try to influence others' perceptions of them by their verbal and nonverbal behavior, the amount of information they divulge, and how they express and react to alternative offers. Chapter 8 considers these influences in more detail.

Interventions to Improve Insight

Many exciting, new methods are available to help sensitize people to the meaning of interpersonal insight, improve the accuracy of person perceptions and self-awareness, and, as a result, enhance interpersonal effectiveness. These include self-assessment tools and feedback based on performance in simulations and actual work situations. Organizations support these programs because they recognize the value of having information from diverse sources—the individual, the supervisor, the co-worker, and so on. The complexity of work today suggests that the traditional, single source of feedback—typically, the once-a-year supervisor performance appraisal—is insufficient to guide an employee's development. The pace of change and the complexity of tasks and interpersonal situations necessitate that we pay attention to our capabilities in relation to what's required of us. In addition to 360-degree feedback ratings, other methods for insight development include insight assessment centers, self-assessment methods, training in observation skills, and training in providing meaningful feedback to others. These and other techniques are examined in chapters 9 and 10 and in the Resource Guides at the end of the book.

Conclusion

This chapter has described the multiple meanings of self- and interpersonal insight. Insights are complex associations of ideas that emerge from our processing social information. Insight is important to knowing about ourselves and others and to the development of effective interpersonal relationships.

This introductory chapter suggests the following conclusions:

1. Insights about ourselves and others are key to understanding behavior and decisions.

2. While we could try to ignore the "black box" of our minds by taking a purely behaviorist perspective, we can better understand and predict behavior from a more comprehensive, multiple-paradigm perspective. Such a perspective argues for capturing what people are thinking about themselves and others and determining the antecedents and consequences of these thoughts.

3. Distinctions can be made between the source of self- and interpersonal insights, the content of the insights, and the effects of the insights.

4. Sources of insight may be external (e.g., observations or information, statements from others) or internal (predispositions to pay attention to certain information or to interpret information in one way or another).

5. Insight emergence is not just a cognitive process. Behavioral and emotional components can be integrated with a cognitive interpretation for a more complete psychology of self- and interpersonal insight.

6. Understanding insight formation and use will help us understand important interpersonal processes—the development of relationships between

two people, the interaction among members in cooperative groups, and the behaviors and reactions of parties engaged in conflict and negotiation.

7. Insights can be induced by providing information (such as performance feedback), encouraging self-assessment, and training people to be aware of errors in perception and judgment.

Chapter 2 offers a deeper view of the components and processes of insight formation and associated situational and individualistic variables.

2

Person Perception:
Theoretical Perspectives

Be sure to keep a mirror always nigh
In some convenient, handy sort of place,
And now and then look squarely in the eye,
And with thyself keep ever face to face
John Kendrick Bangs

This chapter examines the cognitive processes underlying the formation of self- and interpersonal insights. We look at the importance of various sources and types of information, especially the effects of feedback about one's performance in establishing self-insight. Drawing largely on cognitive theories of information processing that are supported by research, I suggest how people acquire information about themselves and others, process this information by forming their interpersonal insights, and then use the information to guide decisions and behavior.

Forming an Insight

Insight formation entails three primary processes: (1) information reception or perception, (2) encoding or interpretation, and (3) recall and use (e.g., in evaluating oneself and others or in deciding to take an action; Ilgen, Barnes-Farrell, & McKellin, 1993). Together these are potentially overlapping and continuous processes. For instance, part of information interpretation may be seeking new or confirmatory information. Feedback from the use of information is likely to help verify the value of the insight and adherence to it (or belief in it).

Retrospective and "Real-Time" Information Processing

Information acquisition and interpretation vary in duration. In some cases they require substantial retrospection and consciousness (i.e., awareness of one's cognitions and sensations) as information is recalled, perceptions are interpreted and categorized, and alternative attributions are considered. In other cases they are rapid and unconscious (i.e., not available in the immediate field of awareness). Indeed, sometimes they occur in "real time"— almost concurrent with observed behavior and feedback reception. This becomes important in understanding the emergence of insight from observations of behavior patterns between two or more individuals.

Mental Processes: Conscious and Unconscious Insights. Some insights are "aha" experiences that are explicitly recognized. They may even be startling. However, they may be a sudden recognition of concepts that have been building over time. For instance, you "know" something about yourself or someone else, but you don't conceptualize and formulate it unless asked for an assessment (e.g., "How are you at card games?" Or "Can we trust Joe to negotiate for us?").

The notion of insights in "real time" suggests that insights result from *mental leaps* that are instantaneous and somehow partly unconscious. As described by Perkins (1981) in his analysis of insight and creativity, "mental leaps usually (1) achieve an insight quickly, without conscious thought; (2) achieve an insight toward which there has been no apparent progress; (3) achieve an insight that otherwise would seem to require considerable ordinary conscious thinking, if ordinary thinking would help at all" (p. 41). A related view is that mental leaps depend on unconscious thinking. The mental leap occurs when the result of that thinking suddenly becomes conscious. However, Perkins (1981), using a diary method, found that such mental leaps are rare. Rather, there is almost always some focusing on a significant clue or other stepwise progression before a solution emerges. Further, insights don't require extended thought that might have occurred unconsciously over a long period. Perkins (1981) believes that nothing special marks the mental processes involved in insight. They are the same processes of recognizing and realizing that mediate ordinary acts of quick identification and understanding.

Now consider the processes of incubation, noticing, and intuition.

Incubation. Thoughts may incubate over time until something happens to jog our memory and combine information to form an insight. A change of situation or simply the passing of time while doing other things may lead to insights.

Noticing. The term *noticing* implies that we recognize something that we were not looking for or at directly. That is, the recognition occurs with little attention and intention. Relevant features of our environments are noticed spontaneously. To notice something is an accomplishment, which may be valuable in the sense that something that was overlooked is now recognized (Perkins, 1981, p. 78). The act of noticing can be supported by the context, in the sense that the observer notices things relevant to the activity under way.

However, we may notice something out of context; for example, in a setting removed from the problem, something may occur to us for the first time that is very relevant to work in progress. Such a breakthrough can also occur when one sets a project aside for a while and then returns to it with a fresh eye for strengths and weaknesses. As such "insights do not occur complete but in consequence of brief sequences of thought" (Perkins, 1981, p. 82). The out-of-place recognition or fresh perspective initiates a sequence of new thoughts initially outside the dominant frame of reference.

Intuition.   While insight generally applies to the processes of observation and realization or recognition, intuition refers to the judgment process—that is, combining insights and other information to make a decision or draw a conclusion. Intuition might also be used to refer to what we know about something—what we reasoned was or is the case. As such, intuition and insight are overlapping constructs. Judgments are intuitive when there are no conscious reasons for it (Perkins, 1981, p. 105).

Behling and Eckel (1991) described intuition as a personality trait, an unconscious process, a set of actions, and a distilled experience. They concluded that traits (i.e., characteristics that refer to being "intuitive") apply to the individual's preference for deciding intuitively, not his or her ability to decide well. Intuition as a set of actions suggests that the constituent behaviors of intuition are observable, but this does not address the quality of the actions (the likelihood that they will lead to successful outcomes). Intuition as unconscious process connotes that intuitive judgments are superior to analytical ones. But this suggests that people must be willing and able to listen to the "promptings of their inner voice" (Behling & Eckel, 1991, p. 53). As distilled experience, intuition is simply "analyses frozen into habit and into the capacity for rapid response through recognition" (Simon, 1987, p. 45, cited in Behling & Eckel, 1991, p. 53). In some areas of the decision maker's experience, the decision can be made rapidly on the basis of a few pieces of information and will be of equal or higher quality than analytical decisions. These alternative views of intuition have implications for training, as we will see in Chapter 9. For instance, role playing could enhance intuition by providing experiences that help a person decide rapidly on the basis of limited information.

Barriers to Insight.   Judgment biases may prevent insight formation. Examples of these biases are overconfidence, confirmation bias (interpreting information in a way that confirms expectations), hindsight bias (exaggerating felt insights and preventing new, revised, and more accurate insights), and avoidance of cognitive dissonance through false attributions (making an inaccurate judgment to avoid admitting a mistake) (Russo & Schoemaker, 1992). Such biases become self-perpetuating and increase over time even when a person does not have evidence to support the bias (Hill et al., 1989). The operation of these biases is at the level of perception and interpretation of information in the decision process. This suggests that some thoughts we take to be insights are not. It also suggests the possibility of failing to recognize the salience of perceptions as an insight. (Chapter 9 describes ways to overcome judgment biases through feedback and observation training.)

So far, this chapter has considered the process of forming insights. Next, consider the content and sources of the information on which insights are based.

Feedback Content and Sources

Cognitive feedback is the process of providing people with information that allows them to compare their judgments with various cues about the way things really are. There are three types of information (after Balzer, Doherty, & O'Connor, 1989; Balzer et al., 1992):

1. *Task information* provides data *about the environment*. This includes information about another person. This might be information about what another person does well. Or it could be information about relationships between behavioral indicators and later performance. Such information is meant to be an aid in making judgments by clarifying available information and showing how this information is related to criteria that are important to the decision. For instance, interviewers might be given information about relationships between applicants' background characteristics (e.g., holding leadership positions) and their later performance on the job. The information would be meant to improve interviewer recommendations. Or supervisors may be given information about subordinate capabilities, task requirements, and levels of performance. The information would be meant to assist in improving the accuracy of later performance appraisal judgments. In another example, supervisors might be given information about how others view them (in the case of 360-degree feedback programs) and what other managers have done with information when it is discrepant. This would be meant to enhance the supervisors' use of the information in formulating development plans.

2. *Cognitive information* is feedback about one's cognitive strategies. This is information about *how a person incorporates information about environmental characteristics in making actual decisions*. Here the goal is to help people understand how they integrate information to form judgments. For instance, interviewers would receive information about their decisions. This might be correlational data on the relation between applicant characteristics and the interviewer's accept or reject decisions. The intention would be to help the interviewers understand the success of their judgment processes and how they make decisions (i.e., the weights they give to different applicant characteristics). The interviewers would then presumably be able to improve their decisions by paying more attention to cues they ignored previously or by taking more care in general in an effort to improve their success ratio. Similarly, subordinates making upward ratings of managers may be given information about their judgments in the past and some

objective characteristics of the managers. This would be meant to help the subordinates pay attention to the full range of information or incorporate information they had ignored in making their decisions.

3. *Functional validity information* refers to feedback in relations between the environmental results and the person's judgments. The intention is to show decision makers *how the components of their judgments contributed to the success of their decisions.* For interviewers this would be information on the rate of success of the applicants they hired (e.g., the percentage remaining with the firm after one year). For subordinates it might be relations between their upward judgments and top executives' opinions of the managers. Or it might be data on relationships between their upward ratings and objective information about the work group's prior performance. Again, the intention would be to help the judges, in this case subordinates, to recognize their prior success rates.

Thus, task information addresses the environment while cognitive information and functional validity information show judges how they use information. Cognitive information shows how the decision maker combines data, and functional validity information shows how judgments relate to decision success. Varying combinations of these types of feedback could lead to different levels of improved judgments. Decision-making research has shown that task information is most important to improving the accuracy of judgments (i.e., the extent to which judgments reflect reality) and the validity of judgments (the extent to which judgments relate to making successful decisions) (Balzer et al., 1992). Receiving cognitive and functional validity information is also valuable as long as task information is present. This implies that environmental data should be collected, analyzed, and provided to people making interpersonal judgments. Sometimes the information is available naturally, as it might be for interviewers observing what happens to the people they hire or for subordinates observing what happens to the managers they rate. However, such information is not necessarily collected systematically in a way that allows decision makers or raters to draw accurate conclusions about their judgment processes. Indeed, misinterpretations are likely because people want their decisions to be successful. Consequently, organizations should systematically collect such data. This may require establishing new data collection mechanisms, analyses, and report procedures.

Consider how data that are not collected systematically or data that people are not trained to use could lead to biased or inaccurate perceptions. A problem with providing cognitive feedback may be "hindsight bias"—the tendency of decision makers to say "I knew it all along" after discovering the outcome of an uncertain event (Schkade & Kilbourne, 1991). When decision makers retrospectively exaggerate the degree to which they foresaw an outcome, they may ignore the new information because they "knew" it already or make the new information consistent with what they thought they knew earlier. Hindsight bias may be reversed by heightening demands to use feedback or by focusing attention on the possibility of the bias (Sharpe & Adair, 1993).

Thus, although different types of information may have different value depending on the perceiver, this does not address *how* information is processed. The next section returns to the discussion of insight formation begun at the outset of this chapter to understand theories of information processing that underlie self- and interpersonal insight.

Toward an Information-Processing Model

Cognitive functions refer to "symbolic processes that require some form of transformation of a past or present sensory input" (Murphy & Zajonc, 1993, p. 724). Insight formation involves a number of processes, including receiving information about oneself or others, integrating and reconciling the information with other information, discounting and discarding data, interpreting the information, and adding meaning. These components of the insight formation process are outlined in Figure 2.1. The results of the insight include desires and goals that direct behavior. An insight may take the form of values, motives, goals, desires, or preferences. It may be recognition of stimulus–response contingencies ("if . . . , then . . ." propositions). It may be an understanding of response mechanisms by which such contingencies are established (that is, how "if, then" occurrences are created). In addition, it may be an understanding of mechanisms by which values are generated.

Theories that explain how people react to feedback about themselves and others should help us understand interpersonal insight development. Such theories describe how we interpret feedback by categorizing it or making judgments about it that affect attributions of ourselves or others. The following section, from London (in press), outlines a four-step sequence of (1) receiving and reflecting on feedback, (2) categorizing it, (3) if ready categories

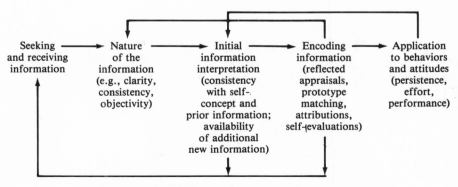

FIGURE 2.1   Insight acquisition and development.

do not apply, making attributions, and (4) if internal attributions result, altering the evaluation we have of ourselves and/or others. An internal attribution means that the cause of the behavior is attributed to characteristics internal to oneself or to others as opposed to the situation. The insight is the reevaluation of our self-concept or our concept of others. These four stages form the basis for insight formation discussed throughout the rest of the book.

Insight Formation as a Sequential Process

Insight formation can be thought of as a sequential process involving receiving information about oneself and/or others (called reflected feedback), integrating and reconciling the information with other information (categorization), interpreting the information (attribution), and incorporating the outcome into perceptions of oneself and others (cognitive evaluation). These components of the insight formation process are outlined in Figure 2.2. Each of these components is described in the following.

Reflected Feedback.   Psychologists and philosophers recognize that people derive information about themselves and others from what others say and do (Stryker & Statham, 1985; Vohra, 1986). According to this "symbolic interactionist" perspective, self-concept forms by using interpersonal feedback as a mirror (Felson, 1985; Jussim, 1991). In this sense, one's interpretations of others' evaluations are referred to as "reflected appraisals." Feedback may be formal, for instance, performance appraisal ratings and feedback sessions with one's supervisor, or informal in the sense of information sought deliberately or obtained in the course of events. People begin to "internalize" this information (i.e., make it part of their self-concepts) by judging its accuracy and realism.

Subjective feedback adds information beyond that available from objective feedback. Objective feedback is quantitative information about the level of a performance without any explicit evaluation of that performance. Sometimes objective feedback is communicated interpersonally, as when a super-

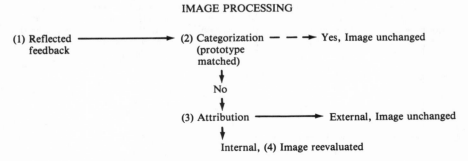

FIGURE 2.2   Information processing components.

visor meets with a subordinate to review errors of communication in a memo written by the subordinate.

Reactions to feedback about oneself are likely to depend on the favorability of the feedback as well as whether it is objective or subjective (i.e., derived from someone else's opinions of us). Jussim et al. (1992) found that interpersonal feedback was more influential when the favorability of objective feedback was moderate than when it was high or low. Further, subjective information was more likely to affect one's self-concept when available objective information was ambiguous or did not provide a clear view of the level of performance. This suggests that information about self or others is evaluated based on such self-imposed criteria as accuracy and realism. Objective feedback carries more weight than interpersonal (subjective) feedback. However, interpersonal feedback carries more weight when objective feedback is not available or is ambiguous, inconsistent, or for other reasons not to be trusted.

Categorization and Attribution Processes. Once performance feedback is internalized, it must be interpreted in relation to our current beliefs (DeNisi, Cafferty, & Meglino, 1984). This occurs through the processes of categorization and attribution. Images of our values, goals, and plans frame our perceptions and guide our decisions. Information that is consistent with preexisting images is accepted automatically. Inconsistent information causes us to reinterpret the information and/or alter our frames of reference—the way information is stored, recalled, and interpreted. A person's perceptions of appropriate and expected behavior guide the integration and interpretation of information. Inconsistent information may be ignored or denied; if it is sufficiently strong, it may break the frame of reference and cause reinterpretation.

Image theory holds that the perceiver performs a test to determine the value of the information in relation to preestablished categories and the value of likely alternative attributions (Beach, 1990; Mitchell & Beach, 1990). Automatic (unconscious) categorization occurs when the feedback can be easily categorized based on prior experiences, expectations, or the nature of the information (e.g., its clarity and objectivity). Motowidlo (1986) proposed that information is not stored in purely descriptive form but is transformed and stored as either positive or negative evaluative impressions. People develop a similar sense of how to interpret and categorize others based on commonly used adjectives, such as *conscientiousness* and *agreeableness*. Associations among these adjectives are learned over time and influence the way we structure our perceptions of one another (Barrick & Mount, 1991, 1993; Bruner & Tagiuri, 1954; Kelly, 1955; Cronbach, 1955; Norman, 1963; Schneider, 1973; Hakel, 1974; Scheier & Carver, 1983). Langer (1989) refers to "mindless" information processing in which there is a state of reduced awareness and lack of attention to detail. Zalesny and Ford (1990) call this weak or automatic processing.

The categories into which information is automatically processed have been variously called schemas, scripts, plans, categories, implicit theories, prototypes, and heuristics (Wofford, 1994). The concept of schema is the heart of cognitive science (Arbib & Hesse, 1986). Schemas or scripts are cognitive memory structures that consist of "objects, events, roles, conditions, sentiments, and outcomes that occur in a sequential pattern in familiar tasks and situations" (Wofford, 1994, p. 181). Strategy structures are components from scripts that apply in unfamiliar situations. The process of confronting an unfamiliar task and testing the applicability of other scripts is called *strategy processing* (Wofford, 1994). This may lead to new scripts. Experience with particular situations leads to having more scripts to apply to these situations. Wofford (1994) found that the number of scripts a person has available to solve job problems is related to the frequency with which such problems occur. People draw on readily accessible scripts to handle minor problems and adapt strategy structures to handle major problems. These problems demand more mindful cognitive processing.

Mindful or controlled categorization occurs when decisions are problematic in some way, for example, when information is inconsistent or ambiguous (Fiske, 1982; Fiske & Neuberg, 1990; Fiske et al., 1987; Kulik & Ambrose, 1993). Mindful and automatic judgment are different aspects of the same process (Kruglanski, 1992). Mindful processing means that more information will be considered, that the criteria for evaluation will be judged more deliberately, and that a conscious attribution of internal or external causality will result. Some people are more motivated than others to engage in effortful cognition. Individuals with a high need for cognition engage in extensive issue-relevant thinking when formulating a position on an issue and tend to have a strong correspondence between their attitudes and their behavior (Cacioppo et al., 1986). (Research on need for cognition has focused on motivation to think about issues, for instance, political concerns. However, need for cognition may also suggest a tendency to avoid mindless categorization when it comes to evaluating oneself and others.)

When feedback cannot be assigned easily to a category, new information may be sought, with selective attention given to information that confirms a likely opinion. Feedback that cannot be categorized leads people to determine causes for the feedback (Cronshaw & Lord, 1987). These causes may be internal (i.e., we attribute the feedback to our own behavior) or external (i.e., we attribute the feedback to the situation, perhaps to the unreliability of the source). Moreover, people tend to avoid negative feedback and seek positive feedback (cf. Heider, 1958; Yammarino & Atwater, 1993). Positive feedback tends to be processed "mindlessly" while negative or mixed feedback tends to be processed "mindfully" because it commands attention (Fiske, 1993; Dunegan, 1993). Insight recognition arises as information cannot be categorized and attributions are made to interpret the information.

People quickly fall into categorizations about their self-efficacy as a task becomes familiar; they are more aware of their cognitive processing on unfamiliar tasks than on tasks that are familiar. During skill acquisition, people report reductions in their cognitive processing for doing the work and forming judgments of their self-efficacy (Mitchell et al., 1993). That is, they report moving from a more effortful cognitive process (one that is more complex and comprehensive) to a less effortful (simple and quick) cognitive process.

According to image theory, feedback that matches expectations is categorized unconsciously or automatically. This yields an automatic judgment that is consistent with the expectation. Feedback that is unique, unusual, counterintuitive, or unexpected signals the need for a conscious or deliberate attribution. Information that sets oneself or others apart from the norm is likely to result in an internal attribution—making a judgment about one's own self-efficacy or that of others (Heider, 1958).

Category- Versus Feature-Based Processing. During categorization, people engage in the relatively automatic process of trying to associate a target person with a social category. During this *category-based processing,* once the target is categorized, the perceiver need only obtain the appropriate evaluation that fits the category. Thus, it is a simple cognitive process. If the target cannot be matched to a social category, information about the target is encoded separate from the social category (Kulik & Ambrose, 1993). This requires more controlled and time-consuming processing, requiring the perceiver to retrieve specific information about the target and evaluate each of the target's features. This *feature-based processing* requires the perceiver to combine the evaluations of these features to form an overall evaluation. While category-based processing is easier, it is more difficult for the perceiver to derive an accurate evaluation of the target. Indeed, the category affects the further interpretation of the target's features (Fiske & Neuberg, 1990).

Thus, there is a continuum of processing modes. At one extreme of the continuum, people are motivated to process all information as carefully and accurately as possible. At the other extreme, people are motivated to process information rapidly and rely on social categories for evaluation (Fiske & Neuberg, 1990; Kulik & Ambrose, 1993). The situation, including the mode of information and instructions or incentives for accurate evaluations, may influence which end of the continuum is most likely to occur (Copeland, 1993). For instance, some stimuli are more likely than others to elicit category-based processing. Features that are distinct, such as race, are likely to do so. The more ambiguous or complex the information, the more likely it will be to induce feature-based processing (Kulik & Ambrose, 1993). (Image theory and research on the effects of information and rater instructions on processing modes are described in more depth in Chapter 5.)

Cognitive Evaluations. Insights develop and are internalized through the process of cognitive evaluation. This is the process of drawing a conclusion about some aspect of ourselves or others. This explains how performance feedback influences intrinsic motivation. So, for instance, positive feedback influences our feelings of mastery, which in turn affect the goals we set for ourselves (Deci & Ryan, 1990). Applied to perceptions of others, observations of another's performance lead to conclusions about that individual's competence.

While this process is sequential, it is not simply linear. Over time, people may reconsider their initial reactions, recategorize feedback, or make new attributions. This may occur if they are asked to think about the information, for instance, in rating their reactions to it or in making a revised self-rating.

These cognitive processes can be extended by understanding dynamics that affect them. Social information processing, control, social comparison, and prospect theories and the role of emotions provide this further understanding.

Social Information Processing

Social information-processing models propose that social information affects perceptions, attitudes, and behaviors (Salancik & Pfeffer, 1978). As interpreted by Zalesny and Ford (1990), social information (e.g., the opinions of one's co-workers) will affect an employee's perception of the job or task characteristics. These perceptions, in turn, affect the employee's job attitudes. In addition, the process of "social reality construction" (e.g., the recognition of norms and other social comparison information that guide the employee's interpretation of behavior and events) influences how the environment is perceived. Social information processing (e.g., attributional biases, cue detection accuracy, and evaluation of response outcomes) causes behaviors associated with social adjustment (for instance, behaviors that demonstrate self-confidence and social status among peers). This developmental aspect of social information processing has been linked to adjustment in children (Crick & Dodge, 1994).

Behavioral linkages represent information from the social context that justifies behavior (Zalesny & Ford, 1990). Self-observations of behavior affect the employee's attitudes (e.g., saying, "I did this, therefore, I must believe thus and so"). The behavior provides information on which to form attitudes and, as such, is an attributional process. Social information may also influence behavior directly, as when the opinions of others guide what we do. Moreover, behaviors partially influence the social construction of reality, as when norms form as a result of our actions. Information from the social context may influence attitudes directly, and these attitudes may then affect behavior; thus, attitudes may affect behavior and vice versa. Attitudes "provide the link between information and behavior and between perceptions and behavior" (Zalesny & Ford, 1990, p. 219). The effects of social influence on perceptions and attitudes depend on the encoding and judgment processes discussed earlier. "Regardless of whether people are actively involved in creating their reality or are recipients of a reality created by others, it is how they *perceive* (i.e., encode and evaluate) that reality which has consequences for their reactions to it" (Zalesny & Ford, 1990, p. 225).

Information processing varies in depth (Zalesny & Ford, 1990). There may be a deliberate and extensive processing of information, or much less cognitive effort may be extended in the development of attitudes and judgments. Such shallow information processing corresponds to the image theory and categorization processes discussed previously. Deep processing causes stronger attitudes to form, which in turn have a stronger influence on the construction of social reality, the weight given to social information, and behavioral change. Such situational determinants of depth of processing include a persuasive communication or rewards that increase the personal relevance of information (e.g., favorable upward feedback ratings lead to rewards). These situations create the need to pay increased attention and devote more thought to interpreting perceptions (Fiske, 1993). The amount of time available for a response to feedback is likely to influence the depth of information processing that occurs. Stronger attitudes are likely to form as a feedback process is used over time. The relevance of the process and opportunities for behavior change will be more evident as employees have more experience with the program. The next section provides a theoretical explanation for feedback seeking and interpretation.

Control Theory

Control theory explains how feedback results in behavior change. Perceptions of outcomes, for instance, the outcomes of negotiation or performance appraisal, may be affected by initial expectations. Control theory holds that behavior is not a result of antecedent causes in the environment. Rather, people seek to control the types of stimuli they perceive so that the stimuli match internally held standards. They alter their behavior to achieve this control (Nelson, 1993; Powers, 1973a, 1973b; Carver & Scheier, 1981, 1982). According to Nelson, "Sensed deviations from a particular standard motivate a person to perform a behavior to change the environment, with the goal of causing the perceived environmental stimuli to match the standard" (1993, p. 121). A feeling of discomfort, or, in the extreme, a feeling of stress, results from a discrepancy between the way things are and the way things should be (Edwards, 1992). Control theory posits that people compare outcomes to referents or standards that lead to positive or negative discrepancies of differing magnitude. The discrepancies influence affective and behavioral reactions (Kernan & Lord, 1991; Lord & Hanges, 1987; Conlon & Ross, 1993). Rice, McFarlin, & Bennett (1989) found that discrepancies between desired levels and actual levels of a variety of job "outcomes" (e.g., pay, promotion, commuting time, conversation time with co-workers and supervisors) were determiners of satisfaction with these job facets (Conlon & Ross, 1993). Moreover, these discrepancies may be the basis for goal improvement. Performance feedback or information about how others performed establish standards for comparison, which can become goals for doing better.

Control theory holds that people engage in a continual process of matching their behavior to a goal. Discrepant feedback causes them to reduce the discrepancies (Carver & Scheier, 1981; Brief & Hollenbeck, 1985; Ashford, 1989). Thus, people set standards, obtain feedback, detect discrepancies, and attempt to reduce discrepancies. They also determine whether the standards they have chosen can be accomplished. In addition, they develop an ability to assess their behavior in a manner consistent with how others perceive and evaluate it (Ashford, 1989).

Social Comparison Theory

Social comparison theory holds that people evaluate their opinions and abilities through comparisons with others, especially others who are similar to themselves (Festinger, 1954; Brewer & Weber, 1994). Individuals are especially motivated to make such comparisons when they are uncertain about the level of their ability or the correctness of their opinions. People with similar characteristics tend to become models of effective behavior or appropriate attitudes (Berger, 1977; Goethals & Darley, 1977). In addition to using social comparisons to gain accurate information, people use them to cope with threats to their self-esteem (Gibbons & Gerrard, 1991). In such cases, they seek downward comparisons, contrasting themselves with others against whom they look good. While such comparisons may make them feel better about themselves, they neither provide a constructive direction for improvement nor motivate improvement. The result is just as dysfunctional as upward comparisons—that is, comparing oneself to others who are so advantaged that they set standards one cannot possibly attain. Thus, people may use social comparisons for a number of different reasons, including obtaining an accurate self-evaluation and for self-enhancement; moreover, the comparison may be with others who are similar or different. Comparison tendencies are highly variable from one individual to another and depend on the overall psychological context affecting the judgment of self or others (Kruglanski & Mayseless, 1990).

Feedback from others can make self-evaluations easier by establishing norms and providing information that is valued because it comes from others who are important to us or who set standards for us. The feedback may be in the form of direct input from others about our behavior (i.e., someone expressing an opinion), perhaps resulting from our seeking the feedback, or it may be indirect (e.g., data about our own performance along with the results achieved by our peers). Alternatively, feedback may take the form of observations of another's behavior or outcomes that are relevant comparisons to our own.

Information about others and feedback from others about ourselves help us interpret behavior, form expectations for appropriate behavior in relation to the situation, and establish behavior strategies (Wofford & Goodwin, 1990). Feedback and comparative information help determine the likely success of various behavioral alternatives—whether one should try harder, volunteer for a special assignment, or pay attention to the needs of one customer versus another. Feedback can stem from many sources in the environment, which raises the possibility of conflict among evaluators and the importance of interpreting such feedback. Disagreements among raters may occur because one or more raters are simply inaccurate or because they have different perspectives and different criteria for evaluation. Knowing these criteria and differences in behavior standards might make the information more useful in guiding behavior in different circumstances. As the next section demonstrates, how these criteria are framed (whether in a positive or negative light) affects how they are interpreted by raters.

Prospect Theory

Prospect theory, from which control theory is derived, holds that potential outcomes are evaluated in relation to some reference point or "frame" (e.g., past feedback). As such, the identical outcome may be perceived in different ways by different individuals (Kahneman & Tversky, 1979; Larrick, 1993; Tversky & Kahneman, 1979). A lower expectation leads to more positive evaluations of an outcome than would occur if the same outcome was viewed from a position of heightened expectations (Conlon & Ross, 1993). As applied to negotiations, informing negotiators that they are bargaining over expenses (losses) rather than profits (gains) creates a frame through which proposals are viewed (Bazerman, Magliozzi, & Neale, 1985). When losses are expected, the offer of a gain takes on a more positive light than it would if a gain is expected.

This applies to decisions to engage in and pursue social relationships. Such a decision may be guided by the expected return from the relationship, whether that return is social, emotional, or monetary. The decision may be influenced by the desire to avoid unpleasant psychological consequences that occur when a relationship turns out poorly. The choice can be threatening because a poor outcome can undermine one's sense of competence and sociability.

Effects of Framing on Cognitive Processing and Emotions

A reason for framing effects is that people react less strongly to potential gains than to potential losses. Framing alters people's affective state such that a negative frame engenders negative affect and a positive frame engenders positive affect (Kahneman & Tversky, 1982). The pleasure of winning is less than the displeasure of losing equivalent amounts (Tversky & Kahneman, 1981; Dunegan, 1993). A related reason, or a result of this differential weighting, is that cognitive processing is less thorough and systematic when incoming information is positive. Conversely, cognitive processing is more deliberate and careful when information is negative (Dunegan, 1993; Klein, 1989; Kulik & Ambrose, 1993; Wofford & Goodwin, 1990).

Dunegan (1993) found that the way problems are framed may bias not only perceptions of the problem but also the decision maker's mode of cognitive processing. He varied the frame of research and development funding decisions by telling managers how many prior projects had been successful or unsuccessful. The results confirmed the framing effect. Negatively framed alternatives were allocated fewer funds than their positively framed counterparts. Moreover, characteristics of controlled thinking occurred when information was negatively framed, while characteristics of automatic processing occurred when information was positively framed. In particular, perceptions of the problem that suggested deliberate processing (e.g., perceptions of risk, importance of the problem, feelings of control, responsibility, and disappointment in the alternatives) predicted the funding decision after a negative frame but not after a positive frame.

Framing may also affect a decision maker's perception of project images. In a second study, Dunegan (1993) used image theory to propose how framing affects reactions to perceptions of a project's progress. Image theory predicts that managers' decision making will be automatic and intuitive unless there is a significant incompatibility between a decision maker's current image of a project and the conception of the future state to which he or she aspires (its "trajectory image"; Beach & Mitchell, 1990). A positive bias toward projects leads to feelings that current and trajectory images will remain compatible. Dunegan's study of college students considering the research and development funding problem replicated the results of his first study and supported the image theory hypothesis. That is, when the project's performance record was framed in a negative way, decision makers perceived the current and trajectory images to be significantly less compatible than when the same information was positively framed.

Framing may affect managers' reactions to feedback and consideration of alternatives for development in similar ways. Negative feedback and/or negative framing of the likely success of developmental opportunities may lead to more deliberate decisions but also more negative ones. The negative frame puts people on alert but makes them more pessimistic—perceiving greater risk and feeling more disappointed in the alternatives. Such perceived characteristics of the problem weigh more heavily in making a decision. Moreover, decision makers with a negative frame may have more difficulty conceptualizing "how they get there from here" or understanding how their current conception of their job or career matches where they want to go.

Performance standards are a means of measuring and evaluating performance and a basis for feedback. How standards are framed is likely to affect employees' motivation to perform and reactions to feedback. Positively framed performance standards (e.g., percent accuracy) are likely to be more motivational than negatively framed standards (e.g., number of defects)

(Bobko & Colella, 1994). Also, standards framed in terms of changes in individual performance are likely to be more motivational than minimal or absolute standards of performance (Bobko & Colella, 1994). A negative frame makes it more difficult to take advantage of developmental opportunities—to participate in them or to devote energy to them. The implication is that performance feedback should be framed in a positive way, as should explanations of the likelihood of success from positive opportunities. This does not mean misleading the individual but rather stating the same thing in a positive light, similar to saying the glass is half full rather than half empty (Dunegan, 1993).

While framing may influence reactions to decision alternatives, some people are more likely to be negatively disposed than others. For instance, according to a cognitive theory of depression, unhappy individuals have dysfunctional thoughts that undermine self-worth (Beck, 1987; Burke, Brief, & George, 1993; Judge, 1993; Judge & Locke, 1993). We might expect, then, an interaction between dysfunctional thought patterns tied to depression and framing. Mano (1994) found that people who were in an aroused, pleasant state (measured by a questionnaire asking about mood) were higher in risk taking than those who were in an aroused, unpleasant state. When individuals in a pleasant state were asked how much they would pay for lotteries (a response frame that emphasized gains), they indicated they would be willing to pay more than did people in an unpleasant state. When individuals in a pleasant state were asked how much they would pay for insurance to protect themselves against losses (a response frame that emphasized negative outcomes), they indicated they would be willing to pay less than did people in an unpleasant state. Thus, the effects of reference frame may depend on an individual's emotional state. (See Chapter 1's discussion of the relationship between cognition and emotions.) This suggests that supervisors should be attentive to such attitudes and moods in their subordinates and be especially careful about framing feedback and decision alternatives.

In addition, as stated earlier in this chapter, goals influence frames of reference. For instance, a goal may influence the meaning of a frame by defining the nature of the loss. Loss is whatever results from not achieving a goal. Information that is framed in a way that is incongruent with the goal leads to discomfort, and this highlights the possibility of a loss. Consider two alternative information frames: describing a manager's job performance in positive terms (e.g., percentage of subordinates rating the manager favorably) versus describing job performance in negative terms (percentage of subordinates rating the manager unfavorably). If the question is asked whether to retain or lay off the manager, the negative information frame focuses attention on losses (i.e., the "danger" of keeping a low-performing manager), which in turn would lead to a greater likelihood that the manager would be dismissed than if the information is framed positively. If the company's goal is to save as much as possible in salary expenses, this increases the likelihood that the manager will be dismissed regardless of the information frame. The negative information frame would be consistent with this goal. A positive information frame would be inconsistent with the goal and cause a loss (keeping too many people) to loom large. Under this condition, the positive information frame would result in a higher likelihood that the manager would be dismissed than the negative information frame. If the goal is to avoid disrupting a manager's career and life whenever possible, there would be a lower likelihood that the manager would be dismissed regardless of the information frame. This goal would be consistent with the positive information frame but inconsistent with the negative information frame. The negative information frame would highlight the loss (in this case the danger of disrupting a manager's life), thereby lowering the likelihood that the manager would be dismissed. Research is needed to test the effects of such interactions between goals and information frames on decisions. This is important because the way information is framed, for instance, in performance feedback and assessment reports, may influence the subsequent decisions people make about themselves and others.

Framing and Self-Esteem

Decisions must be analyzed both in terms of what the individual has to gain and in terms of the effects of the choice on the decision maker's self-esteem (Larrick 1993). This is more than making decisions based on the anticipated positive or negative outcomes. It involves the joy of winning or the loss of face, humiliation, or other negative emotions resulting from failing. As described by Larrick, "People respond to the emotional consequences of making a decision that come from self-awareness and a sense of agency: feelings of success and failure, elation and disappointment, efficacy and impotence, rejoicing and regret" (1993, 443–444).

The tension between motives to avoid making poor decisions and making positive decisions drives decision makers toward a specific level of risk taking. Situational and personality factors lead to motivational concerns as people strive to maximize their expected outcomes and maintain a positive self-image. These emotional components are often ignored in economic and cognitive decision theories (Larrick, 1993). Important decision consequences to consider include the following:

- feelings that arise from learning that a decision has turned out poorly, such as failure, regret, and disappointment
- feelings that arise from publicly made decisions, such as embarrassment and pride
- feelings that arise from how outcomes are distributed among people, such as envy and gloating (adapted from Larrick, 1993, p. 448)

This suggests the influence of emotions on social information processing and insight formation.

Affect, Cognition, and Awareness

As indicated in the previous chapter, emotions are intertwined with cognitive processes. An affective reaction alone, however, does not require much in the way of cognitive processing. Murphy and Zajonc (1993) demonstrated that minimal stimulus input produces affective reactions. People develop affective preferences for various stimuli with minimal but repeated exposure. These preferences occur even when the individuals cannot recognize specifics of the stimuli. This suggests that simple affective qualities of stimuli, such as good versus bad or positive versus negative, are processed more easily than cognitive aspects of the stimuli, such as their specific characteristics. Impressions and judgments may be influenced by emotion-laden stimuli presented outside of conscious awareness. Thus, affect may actually precede and thus alter subsequent cognitions (Murphy & Zajonc, 1993).

In actual experience, cognitive processes and affective experiences occur together. Thus, affective reactions to feedback (e.g., feelings of anger or resentment accompanying negative feedback) can be separated from recollection of the content of the feedback. Both types of responses should be recognized, and their effects on each other considered. That affect may arise quickly and precede cognition suggests that feelings or emotional reactions to events may come before cognitions; as such, they have the potential to influence cognitions, such as recognizing the favorability of information and ways to react to it. The extent to which the reaction is constructive (e.g., take action to correct negative feedback) may depend on the affect or mood that precedes it. Negative emotions may block cognitions of the behavior—essentially restricting cognitive processing as a defense mechanism. Interventions that maintain focus on self-awareness may be needed to prevent this blocking (cf. Heatherton et al., 1993). These processes may occur differently depending on the individual's level of self-esteem. Self-esteem may interact with affect to influence reactions such that those with low self-esteem may be more receptive to negative feedback (cf. Aspinwall & Taylor, 1993).

See sect through other

Conclusion

This chapter has described cognitive components and processes of insight formation. Several theoretical perspectives are involved. Reflected feedback implies that the mind acts as a mirror to reflect information about oneself and others. Information that matches expectations (prototypes) is easily categorized and can be processed without much deep thinking. Information that diverges from expectations or is sudden and unusual requires an attribution; this is a slower, more deliberate cognitive process. When self-perceptions are involved and the information is negative, we tend to search for an external attribution—one that suggests the cause is due to something other than ourselves. When this is not possible (that is, the information does not match environmental characteristics), we tend to attribute the cause to ourselves. Positive information is more likely to be attributed to ourselves. However, if there is some reason that makes this unrealistic (e.g., we lack the skills to be solely responsible for an accomplishment), an external attribution will emerge. Internal attributions may change our self-image through the process of cognitive evaluation. *The cognitive evaluation is the insight.*

Social information processing suggests how our attitudes, including our self-image, are influenced by our view of social reality or, more specifically, by what others say about us. Furthermore, our attitudes are justifications of behavior as much as causes of behavior. Control and social comparison theories suggest the relevance of comparative information for setting standards, evaluating information by comparing it to these standards, and using the discrepancy to set goals. How we interpret these standards and opportunities for future rewards depends on our frame of reference (prospect theory). A lower initial expectation will lead to more positive evaluations; a higher initial expectation will lead to being more critical. Affect or mood may further predispose an individual to be more attentive. Negative attitudes may block information perception or cause inappropriate or inaccurate categorization of information. Positive moods, too, may result in overlooking salient information or making instant categorizations. The perceptions may remain unconscious until a later time when a sudden jolt causes more thoughtful evaluation.

These ideas suggest the following conclusions about the formation of interpersonal insights:

1. Even if insights occur quickly, they emerge from a complex cognitive process that is influenced by many potential factors internal and external to the individual.

2. Insights may get sidetracked or lost as information is processed. Tendencies to categorize information and avoid new attributions make insight formation, especially self-insights, a chancy process. Maybe that is why insights seem so "insightful" when they occur: we are surprised at the "sudden" realization.

3. Attitudes about ourselves and others (the result of cognitive evaluation) do not always emerge from observation of our own and others' behavior—at least not directly. Our perceptual processes are influenced by our frame of reference. This includes our disposition as well as social information.

4. We have a common set of categories for evaluating ourselves and others. Providing information in these categories may help people to more accurately sort information and make accurate attributions. The less ambiguous the information, the less likely we are to ignore it.

5. Social information is powerful. Sometimes we are more readily influenced by what others tell us to believe than by our own values and observations.

6. Comparative information is important to us in understanding our own behavior and the behavior of others. It motivates us to calibrate the meaning of events, set standards or goals, and change our behavior.

7. Time is important for digesting information. Feedback that seems to be ignored or rationalized may be processed slowly or be integrated with new information. This suggests that programs to provide performance feedback shouldn't expect much the first time around. They may require repetition (e.g., administering 360-degree feedback surveys annually or even quarterly) before people begin to "see" the value of the results. (Changes in self-ratings and improvements in agreement between our self-ratings and others' perceptions of us indicate this is the case. See, for instance, London & Wohlers, 1991.)

8. The way problems are framed may bias not only perceptions of the problems but also the decision maker's mode of cognitive processing. Cognitive processing is less thorough and systematic when incoming information is positive but more deliberate and careful when information is negative. Negative feedback or negative framing of the likely success of developmental opportunities may lead to more deliberate decisions but also to more negative ones.

9. The processes that describe self-insight also apply to insight about others, but people may have less vested interest in evaluating others than they do in evaluating themselves. People are heavily invested in their self-concepts, and their self-esteem may influence cognitive evaluations. Therefore, information-processing biases may be more influential in self-evaluation.

The following three chapters apply these ideas to examine more deeply the emergence of insight about oneself and others. The next chapter focuses on self-assessment and self-image. Chapter 4 applies the cognitive processes discussed here to interpersonal insight. This is followed by a chapter on how self-assessment and social context influence evaluations of others and the acceptance of feedback from others—that is, the reciprocal processes of giving and receiving feedback.

3

Self-Assessment and Self-Image

Who in the world am I?
Ah!, that is a great puzzle.
Alice's Adventures in Wonderland

In their text on developing management skills, Whetten and Cameron (1991) argue for the importance of self-assessment as a foundation for self-learning. They quote Brouwer (1964, p. 156) who wrote: "The function of self-examination is to lay the groundwork for insight, without which no growth can occur. Insight is the 'Oh, I see now' feeling which must consciously or unconsciously precede change in behavior." Whetten and Cameron believe that we cannot develop new capabilities until we know what level of capability we currently possess.

However, Whetten and Cameron acknowledge a paradox: self-knowledge can sometimes inhibit personal improvement rather than facilitate it. People frequently evade personal growth and new self-knowledge (Maslow, 1962). They resist acquiring additional information in order to protect their self-esteem. Seeking feedback carries the risk that new information will be negative or that it will lead to feelings of inferiority or weakness. As a result, feedback is often avoided.

Three biases in self-knowledge are pervasive among the average normal adult, at least in North American culture: (1) the tendency for judgment and memory to be focused on self, the tendency to perceive oneself as effective in achieving desired ends and avoiding undesired ones, and the tendency to resist cognitive change (Greenwald, 1984, p. 139).

Individuals may also not believe they have changed, when they actually have. This is because people perceive their initial attitudes to be similar to their current ones—an implicit judgment they make about the stability of their own personality (Ross, 1989, cited in Fiske Taylor, 1991, p. 501). While people expect their attitudes and behavior to be stable, they can change as the situation changes (Greenwald & Pratkanis, 1984). This change may occur slowly as they become inured and committed to new attitudes through subtle persuasion. They may perceive a sudden insight about themselves, but that insight emerges from a gradual process that transforms an attitude.

The desire for self-knowledge is a prerequisite for, and motivator of, growth and improvement. But self-knowledge may also lead to stagnation, because we fear to know more possibly negative things about ourselves (Whetten & Cameron, 1991, see p. 53). Yet if feedback is verifiable, predictable, and controllable, people are less likely to deny it. Such information may come through a testing process from reliable authoritative sources (e.g., assessment centers) or by using reliable self-assessment instruments.

In the early 1990s, the AT&T Company developed an assessment center for midlevel, high-potential managers. The assessment process was called "Insight," and it was used solely to give the participants developmental feedback on their managerial skills and related behaviors. The results of the center are not used to make decisions about the managers. Other similar assessments, such as the Center for Creative Leadership's "Looking Glass," provide similar developmental information. (The Center for Creative Leadership, headquartered in Greensboro, North Carolina, conducts management training and research on leadership topics.) Such assessments sometimes supplement performance information through the use of simulations that try to capture real problems and settings. The participants' subordinates, peers, and supervisor then rate the performance. Such combined feedback is meant to be a guide for career development. (Techniques for enhancing insight are discussed in detail in Chapters 9 and 10.)

In this chapter I examine the ways self-insights emerge and develop to form *self-schemas*—the concepts we have about ourselves and how situational factors affect self-assessment. I consider the accuracy of our insights into and evaluations of others to determine how much we really know about our own judgment processes. We then consider the agreement between our self-perceptions and how others see us. I review research on the extent to which self-perceptions relate to, and are affected by, others' perceptions of us. Individual characteristics affecting self-ratings and the tendency to avoid negative feedback are discussed. Self-regulatory mechanisms that increase self-awareness and insight are described. These include self-affirmation, self-monitoring, self-protection, and self-handicapping. Finally, I explore the relationship between self-insight and goal setting.

Self-Schemas

Several authors have conceptualized the meaning of a self-concept and self-schema.

> The self-concept is the more or less organized perceptual object resulting from present and past self observation. . . . [It is] what a person believes about himself. The self-concept is the map which each person consults in order to understand himself, especially during moments of crisis or choice. (Raimy, 1948, cited in Combs et al., 1988, p. 161)

Beliefs about self
mnp → idea of self

(1) Beliefs about self
(2) certainty of the beliefs
(3) Importance of the Beliefs

[T]he self-concept is at once an attitude, an attribution, and a set of schemas. It is both cognitive and affective, both stable and unstable, both verifying and enhancing. (Pelham, 1991, p. 518)

For Pelham (1991), the self-concept contains three essential components: people's beliefs about themselves, the certainty of these beliefs, and the importance of these beliefs. Emotional and motivational factors determine the importance we attach to these beliefs. In contrast, *what* we believe is determined by information we have available. Emotive (emotional and motivational) processes are hedonistic, giving way to people's tendencies to believe that what they are good at and are rewarded for is what is important. A particular self-view may be important because of its relevance for personal goals and ambitions.

Ross (1992) defined self-schema in terms of categories and prototypes. The self-schema is "an organized cluster of all the information people possess about themselves: their characteristics, attributes, features, skills, social standing, occupation, family status, and gender—in short, all of their ideas about who and what they are" (Ross, 1992, p. 24). Ulric Neisser (1994) proposed that each of us has an "ecological self" based on our immediate situation in the environment and an "interpersonal self" established through social interactions.

Forming a Self-Schema

The schema develops over time as a result of the individual's experiences. As such, memory is an important aspect of self-schema evolution. Information that has personal relevance is easier for people to store and retrieve. Moreover, new information can be interpreted more easily if it fits into the self-schema. Thus, we are inclined to recall information about ourselves especially if it supports our preestablished self-conception. We respond more quickly to information that is consistent with this self-concept (Markus & Smith, 1981). People interpret a behavior or characteristic as descriptive of them by recalling an instance of similar behavior or behavior that reflects the characteristic (Bem, 1972, as reviewed by Ross, 1992, p. 26). If an applicable instance of the behavior is not found immediately, we keep on searching our memories until we are sufficiently convinced that the behavior or characteristic is "not me."

Person perception involves categorizing observations and evaluating them. We evaluate our experiences, for example, determining whether we like them or not or whether we are good at something or not. We interpolate this into a more general statement about ourselves—for instance, "I am the type of person who likes, and is good at, 'x'" (Ross, 1992, p. 39). The self-concept becomes more complex and differentiated as we increase our experiences and as successes reinforce prior observations and conclusions. When we look at ourselves, we see strengths and weaknesses (Markus & Kunda, 1986). Of course, people differ in the weights they give to different aspects of the self. Physical appearance may be important to some people while status or position are more important to others.

A Developmental View. While a review of personality and adult development theories is beyond the scope of this book, a selective look at the ideas of one theorist, Erikson, is valuable because he ties the development of self-schema to psychosocial development (Smelser & Erikson, 1980; Bee, 1992). Moreover, he believes that this development continues over the entire life span. According to Erikson, the emergence of a sense of self-identity results from successfully resolving a sequence of "crises" or "dilemmas" as new relationships, tasks, and demands arise. Thus, self-perception is intertwined with the development of key interpersonal relationships in one's life. These include personal and work-related relationships. Here are the dilemmas associated with different age-related stages of life:

- The *identity versus role* dilemma during the teenage years involves achieving a sense of occupational competence and career goals.
- The *intimacy versus isolation* dilemma between the ages of approximately nineteen and twenty-five entails the immersion of self in the sense of "we." Successful resolution means the development of high-quality, intimate relationships, while failure results in suffering feelings of isolation.
- The *generativity versus stagnation* stage during early and middle adulthood suggests that each adult must discover a way to satisfy the need to be generative. This means supporting the next generation, for instance, through mentoring relationships at work. It requires turning outward from oneself toward others.
- The *ego integrity versus despair* stage occurs after about age fifty. Here people try to accept themselves as they are.

Self-Disclosure   Self disclosure - unknown self

Self-insight can occur through self-disclosure—the process of opening up to others to discuss aspects of the self that seem ambiguous or unknown. Self-disclosure is a means of seeking feedback. It provides a basis for others to react to us and to provide their view of the accuracy of the disclosed information. In addition to being a stimulus for feedback, self-disclosure results in social support and commiseration (Pennebaker, 1990). This can also foster self-insight by creating a comfortable environment for frank discussion. However, self-disclosure does not necessarily lead to self-insight. Although some people may find value (catharsis) in the process of confiding in others, these individuals may not be able to attend to others' reactions to their disclosures.

Actually, people draw conclusions about others based on their comments about other people as well as themselves. Listeners think about why the information was conveyed, and they draw conclusions about the speaker.

So, for example, a person's unfavorable statements about another may be recalled because they violate norms of politeness and say more about the speaker's likableness than about attributes of the person to whom the comment referred. On the other hand, a person's self-descriptions that are highly favorable are recalled because they violate the normative expectations to be modest (Wyer et al., 1994).

Some people follow others' leads in self-disclosure by disclosing more to others who are self-disclosive. They show a high desire to please (Ross, 1992, p. 65). Other people are focused on their own thoughts and feelings, but they may reciprocate their partner's level of self-disclosure in order to do the socially correct thing and not to be shamed or embarrassed. They want to be agreeable and polite by doing the socially correct thing—that is, talk about themselves to the extent that others do. Still other people are unconcerned about the impression they make on others and have no need to reciprocate to others' disclosures. Consequently, their own disclosures are unaffected by what others say about themselves.

Some people take longer to reciprocate others' self-disclosures and have more difficulty deciding what to say. They want to both make a good impression on others and remain sensitive to internalized social norms. This should make them more self-disclosive. However, their attention is divided. They are attentive to their own thoughts, motives, and feelings as well as to those of others. Social norms may dictate that it is improper to talk about intimate matters with a relative stranger and that being polite to such a person is important as well. So they are stymied and have difficulty responding in kind to another person's self-disclosure, especially if the disclosure reveals intimate information (Ross, 1992, pp. 66–68).

Situational Effects on Self-Assessments

The way people structure their perceptions of both themselves and others is situationally based. Stated another way, the insight people have about themselves and others depends on the situation—how it affects what is important and how characteristics relate to one another. People change their personality test scores when they want to or are instructed to create certain impressions (Schmit & Ryan, 1993). For instance, being a job applicant creates demand effects that result in the individual's desire to make a good impression on all fronts or to convey an impression that is more complex than may be the case in other situations. As such, applicants respond to particular personality items in different ways depending on their interpretation of the item in relation to performance demands (Hakel & Schuh, 1971; Schmit & Ryan, 1993).

The commonly used personality adjectives mentioned in Chapter 2 (e.g., conscientiousness and agreeableness) are reliable elements of our cognitive schemas some of the time but not necessarily all the time (Smith & Kihlstrom, 1987). Situational conditions activate various schema that influence how we structure perceptions of ourselves and others (Fiske & Taylor, 1991). We might use these adjectival factors to describe ourselves to strangers in a way they can easily understand. However, a self-serving bias and the desire to demonstrate performance capabilities may result in a more complex self-description in job applicant or performance appraisal situations. *Insight : negative information cannot be attributed to situation*

Cognitive Bases for Insight Emergence

The theoretical concepts of social cognition introduced in Chapter 2 can be applied to explain the emergence of self-insight. The feedback we perceive stems from the cues we receive about our behavior such as other's reactions to us. If the information matches a prototype, it may reinforce preestablished self-perceptions but may be unlikely to cause a new self-insight. If the behavior is unique or variant from our self-perceptions, an attribution is required. Internal attributions are likely when the information is positive and cannot be attributed readily to the situation (Heider, 1958; Cronshaw & Lord, 1987). An internal attribution may also occur if the information is negative and cannot be attributed to the situation. The result is a change in perceptions of self-efficacy that in turn affects behavior and attitudes (effort, performance, motivation). Thus, feedback that provides information about the viability of performance strategies or effort expenditure required for task performance will increase self-efficacy (Gist & Mitchell, 1992).

Phenomenologically oriented psychologists argue that a person's own reality is all that matters (Rogers, 1959). In other words, if someone says she is happy, then she is (Ross, 1992, p. 79). However, self-awareness may be inaccurate for a number of reasons. Illusions can be self-serving, making us appear more skilled, intelligent, and moral than we really are (Ross, 1992, p. 80). Memory can be distorted by recalling positive information about ourselves more readily than negative information. Such distortions are not necessarily undesirable or unhealthy. Indeed, healthy, well-adjusted people generally hold positively biased illusions about themselves, whereas individuals with low self-esteem hold more realistic self-evaluations (Campbell & Fehr, 1990). *Self enhancement bias*

Thus, some people are more inclined to self-enhancement bias than others. Self-deprecating behavior is associated with low self-esteem, while self-enhancing behavior is associated with high self-esteem (Jones et al., 1981). Overestimation of one's performance (i.e., self-ratings higher than peer or assessment staff ratings) have been found to be positively related to measures of narcissism (John & Robins, 1994); the latter refers to having a grandiose sense of self-importance and a tendency to exaggerate accomplishments and talents. Self-enhancing behavior strengthens our self-perception. Self-deprecation would be discrepant behavior for an individual with high self-esteem; lowering one's self-image is a way to reduce this dissonance.

One way to conceptualize the degree of self-insight we have is to consider how much we know about the way we make interpersonal evaluations. That is, do we recognize the criteria we apply and how we combine these criteria in evaluating others? This question is considered in the next section.

Self-Insights about How We Evaluate Others

Considerable research suggests that people have few or no accurate insights about their judgment policies when it comes to evaluating others (Slovic & Lichtenstein, 1971; see a review by Reilly & Doherty, 1992). In these studies subjects are asked to make a series of judgments based on receiving quantitative information on a set of descriptive attributes. Subjects might receive job candidates' résumés that are constructed with certain information varying the number, type, and favorability of the attributes. The subjects are asked to make an accept or reject decision for each candidate. In this way an objective set of weights can be derived in a regression analysis that predicts the judgments based on the attributes. Lack of insight into evaluation criteria is evidenced by low relationships between the attributes subjects say are important in evaluating the candidates and those that are derived objectively in the regression analysis. Low insight is likely because culturally assigned rules govern how we think we make judgments and do not reflect actual statistical weights in models of judgment processes (Nisbett & Wilson, 1977). Individuals' descriptions of how they make judgments, therefore, do not help others learn how to make evaluations, but statistical information about how individuals form judgments is helpful in learning how to make evaluations (Summers, Taliaferro, & Fletcher, 1970).

While people may have little insight into their judgment processes, this doesn't mean they lack insight altogether. People are able to accurately express the overall importance of attributes (Surber, 1985). Reilly and Doherty (1992) suggest that findings of poor insight may be due to the research methods used (e.g., the use of statistical importance measures as criteria for insight when those measures are unstable, the use of artificial or contrived judgment tasks that provide subjects with only limited information, or simply inappropriate or inaccurate ways of measuring insight into judgments). Also, there are different types of insights, such as insights about intentions, reasons, states, and problem solving (Bowers, 1984). Further, there may be some situations in which people have more insight than others, for instance, after repeated practice in similar situations with clear criteria for the quality of the decision (e.g., as an experienced recruiter or employment interviewer may have). Another reason for negative results about interpersonal insight is that people may not operate under sets of consistent rules or diagnostic principles when making judgments.

Despite these potential barriers, people do have reasonable interpersonal insight. For example, the way people think they make decisions changes after they receive feedback about their actual decisions (Reilly & Doherty, 1989). People can even identify their own policy when given a choice among alternatives. This suggests a high degree of interpersonal insight (Reilly & Doherty, 1989).

In a study of female college students making judgments of the desirability of potential roommates, Reilly and Doherty (1992) found that two weeks after making their judgments a significant number of students could select their own policies from the set calculated from their own and their peers' judgments. Not unexpectedly, recognizing one's own pattern of judgment weights was more difficult when others' patterns were similar. Also, it was easier to recognize one's judgment pattern when there were more cues or attributes for each judgment (more information about each roommate). This may be because having more information is somewhat overwhelming and may cause judges to focus on a limited number of attributes and ignore others. These subjects would then have an advantage in recognizing their own judgment policy because of a clear presence or absence of highly weighted attributes.

Asking subjects about how they made their judgments revealed that many of them who accurately identified their objective policies indicated they would search for their most important attribute and cross out all policies that did not use this attribute. Subjects were also able to accurately recognize their policies even when the attributes were correlated in the experiment, although it was easier to do so when the attributes were independent.

Reilly and Doherty (1992) suggest that people who cannot recognize their own policies should be helped by receiving information about their cognitive system—for instance, explaining to them how the objective weights were derived and how they represent their cognitive processes. When the values of attributes were constructed so that the attributes were correlated, the roommates received higher mean ratings. This occurred even though there was no actual difference in mean attribute levels between conditions with independent and correlated attributes. However, correlated attributes presented a picture that is closer to what the subjects expected. That is, the built-in relationships were more consistent and matched expectations about "what goes with what." This suggests that the intercorrelations produced stronger judgments that are not necessarily deserved. Thus, insight about interpersonal judgment processes may be fairly high. Moreover, it seems that people can recognize their own judgment processes.

Recognition of how we evaluate others is one indicator of insight. Another is the extent to which our self-perceptions match how others see us. This is discussed in the next section.

Agreement between Self- and Others' Perceptions and the Value of Feedback

The extent to which self-ratings diverge from others' ratings suggests a gap that has diagnostic value. The "others' ratings" could be from subordinates, peers, superiors, or customers—that is, the entire 360-degree range of feedback sources. This assumes that the others are credible and trustworthy sources of information. It also assumes that averaging ratings across multiple raters produces reliable and valid information. This is not always the case, since some raters may inflate their ratings and others may provide inconsistent feedback. Also, people behave differently with different people. Nevertheless, self–other agreement may suggest directions for development. In general, people are likely to recognize the need for change when both self and other (e.g., subordinate) ratings are on the low side (Yammarino & Atwater, 1993). However, behavior change may be needed when self-ratings are higher than others' ratings. In this case, categorization processes and the tendency for external attributions or other defense mechanisms (such as denial) may prevent performance improvement. Indeed, the person may try harder to manage others' impressions through explanation and self-disclosures that try to rationalize his or her viewpoint to others.

McCall and Lombardo (1983) found that inflated self-evaluations were associated with career derailment; they reported that managers who agreed with their co-workers' assessments of them were more likely to be promoted. Yammarino and Atwater (1993) argued that managers' performance will be higher when their self-other agreement is high than when it is low. People who rate themselves higher than others rate them tend to produce poor organizational outcomes, for instance, because of poor supervisor–subordinate relationships or misunderstanding customer or co-worker expectations. Those who rate themselves lower than others rate them have mixed performance results. They may be interested in self-development, but they are unlikely to try difficult tasks or aim for high achievements. They tend to have low aspiration levels (Bandura, 1982).

Individuals with low self-insight (those who rate themselves higher or lower than others rate them) may misdiagnose their strengths and weaknesses. Further, they may be less likely to use information about themselves to change their self-perceptions and alter their behavior (Ashford, 1989). However, feedback can reduce inaccurate self-perceptions. Negative feedback is likely eventually to lower inflated self-perceptions and improve leadership performance (Atwater, Roush, & Fischthal, 1992). Since our self-concept affects how hard we work, inaccurate self-judgments are likely to lead to setting goals that are too low (in the case of people who underestimate their capabilities) or too high (in the case of overestimaters). Individuals with inflated self-perceptions will not see the need for training or for changes in their behavior.

Failed leaders are more likely to be individuals who overestimate their performance, believing their capabilities are higher than others recognize them to be (McCall & Lombardo, 1983). For instance, consider the case of a stunned and bewildered top executive who was fired without warning. He had believed that his greatest strength was interpersonal relationships, which to him meant forming advisory groups to give the appearance of participative management and being vindictive to co-workers who crossed him in some way. To him, this was demonstrating he was boss; to others, his actions were seen as threatening and mean. The chief executive officer put up with the numerous complaints about the executive for several years in an effort to be supportive of the executive's tough decisions, but ultimately recognized the need to face up to the "problem" executive.

Accuracy of Self-Assessment

In general, three types of agreement relationships are possible in considering accuracy of self-assessments (Ashford, 1989):

1. Agreement between self-ratings and "metaperceptions" (the individual's beliefs about how others view his or her behavior)
2. Agreement between self-ratings and others' ratings
3. Agreement between perceptions of others' assessments and others' actual assessments

There tends to be a modest to strong correlation between individuals' perceptions of themselves and the way they assume others see them (Ashford, 1989). There is less agreement between actual ratings by others and self-ratings. There is some relationship between the way people believe others see them and the way they actually do see them. In general, people tend to assume a greater similarity between their self-perceptions and the way they think others see them than is actually the case (Schrauger & Schoeneman, 1979; Mabe & West, 1982; Ashford, 1989). Overall, the data do not support the idea that self-appraisals are a reasonable substitute for traditional supervisory ratings.

Other ways to evaluate self-assessments than agreement with co-workers should be considered. Co-workers might agree with self-evaluations, but the individual's objective performance might not. The observer could be overly influenced by the individual's impression management and fail to observe behavior accurately. On the other hand, some people know more about themselves and their own performance than others do, resulting in low self–other agreement but accurate self-evaluations (Ashford, 1989).

While people generally overestimate their performance, their self-assessment is important to them and to the organization. Individuals need to make sense of their environments and the requirements and decisions imposed on them. As such, they want to be accurate. Self-delusion only goes so far if events do not coincide with one's self-concept.

How We Think Others See Us

After reviewing the literature, Shrauger and Schoeneman (1979) concluded that people's self-perceptions agree substantially with the way they believe others see them. Agreement between their self-perceptions and the way they are actually viewed by others is much lower, however. Self-perceptions do change with direct feedback as well as other means of social interaction. Shrauger and Schoeneman also considered how people react to discrepant information about themselves:

> Although judgments that match an initial self-perception may do little more than fortify this perception, judgments that are at variance frequently set up some dissonance or tension that requires cognitive reappraisal. There is an

implicit disagreement between symbolic interactionist and self-attribution theories as to how such discrepancies areresolved. The symbolic interactionist view implies that such discrepancies are typically dealt with by changing one's self-perceptions, whereas self-attribution theories suggest that people have a reasonably clear and stable picture of themselves and may not readily conform to the discrepant appraisal of another individual. (p. 567)

Summarizing the recent literature on self–other perceptions, Kenny and DePaulo (1993) concluded that people determine how others view them (called *metaperceptions*) not just from the feedback they receive from others but from their own self-perceptions. Specifically, they found that people overestimate the degree of consistency in the ways that others view them. Other research discovered that people who are more self-centered are likely to believe that others see them as they see themselves (Fenigstein & Abrams, 1993). Self-focus or public self-consciousness is positively related to the assumption of shared perspectives. Also, people are better at understanding how others generally view them than how they are uniquely viewed by specific individuals (Kenny and DePaulo, 1993). This is consistent with Wohlers and London's (1989) finding that self–subordinate agreement in upward ratings is higher when subordinate ratings are averaged than when agreement is determined separately for each subordinate and then averaged across subordinates.

Kenny and DePaulo (1993) reasoned that people should be highly motivated to discern others' impressions of them when they believe that valued outcomes will be determined by how others view them. Thus, supervisor ratings take on significance when the ratings will be used for salary increase and/or promotion decisions. However, this does not mean that the metaperceptions will be accurate.

> To learn something about a person's view of another person by looking into his or her eyes, there must be something there that is not misleading and not so subtle that it is likely to be missed. . . . The question of interest is whether people attend to, and process insightfully and evenhandedly, information about how others view them that is available during ongoing social interactions. (Kenny & DePaulo, 1993, p. 146)

Kenny and DePaulo (1993) concluded that feedback is less important to self-perceptions than individuals' self-analysis: "People can, without looking at the behaviors or the reactions of others, examine their own behavior and imagine how the other person may view it. . . . people observe their own behavior in order to discern what others may be thinking of them" (pp. 146–147).

Self-perceptions occur in different ways that operate at different times (Kenny & DePaulo, 1993). Some people have strongly held beliefs about their own personalities. They believe that others will perceive immediately these aspects of their personalities regardless of how they and the observer actually behave in a social interaction. As such, in perceiving how others see them, they see what they expect to see. People observe their own behavior and try to determine how others view them. People judge their own behavior and then assume that others will see that behavior in the same way. Also, people observe their own behavior in order to determine what impressions others may be forming of them on the basis of the behavior. Such observations do not necessarily change self-perceptions but do influence how people believe others view them. There may be times, then, when people's self-perceptions do not match beliefs about how others view their behavior.

When there is a link between self- and metaperceptions, self-perceptions affect metaperceptions rather than vice versa. This is contrary to the symbolic interactionist view, which holds that people's perceptions of themselves stem from their beliefs about how they are viewed by others (Kenny & DePaulo, 1993). Over time, and after many interactions, people's self-perceptions influence how others actually see them, rather than the reverse. This is less likely to occur, however, when people show they are unsure of themselves. Showing evidence of low self-confidence weakens the impressions that people try to convey of themselves.

In rating others, people are able to perceive meaningful differences among individuals—differences that other people also see. Kenny and DePaulo (1993) found that people are able to attend to available data and make an evaluation with which others will agree. They also found, however, that people have trouble perceiving differences in how they are seen by other people, with one reason for this being that people are invested in their self-concepts and in the perceptions that others have of them. This exceeds any concern they might have about how they view others. When they have information about how others see them, they interpret the information to be consistent with what they expect or want to see. This is in the short run. In the long run, consistent feedback from others might change one's self-image. This may occur faster if the source of feedback is also the source of rewards.

This suggests a process by which others' views of us affect our self-image (symbolic interactionism). Once established, self-observations influence how we believe others see us. This belief about how others see us may be shaped, in turn, by information about ourselves from others especially if there is good reason to attend to the feedback (as there would be if the feedback has positive or negative consequences). As Kenny and DePaulo (1993) concluded, "Occasionally, then, people do look to others for feedback and thereby catch a glimpse of how others really do view them" (p. 159).

An implication of this discussion is that organizational feedback programs, such as upward or 360-degree feedback that are conducted solely to provide developmental information to managers, should not be expected to have much success in changing self-views or behavior the first time they are administered. Over a number of administrations occurring annually or more often, however, they may become more salient and less threatening and subject to denial. Although this may take several years to accomplish, the results may have a meaningful effect even after one administration especially when the results are consistent (e.g., subordinates agree with each other). Also, the procedure is likely to be valuable the first time simply because it highlights the managerial behaviors that are important to the organization and on which managers should be evaluating themselves (e.g., elements of boss–subordinate relationships). This may cause greater attention to how well the associated behaviors are conducted (e.g., spending time with subordinates to discuss their career development).

Inaccurate or incomplete feedback can have negative outcomes. Mild feedback to overestimaters will perpetuate the inaccurate self-image and maintain poor work behaviors. Similarly, feedback that is not specific and clear in its evaluation will not change self-perceptions of those with low self-esteem.

Individual Characteristics Affecting Self-Ratings

A variety of individual difference variables may influence self-ratings, including personality and ability (Yammarino & Atwater, 1993). An example is self-esteem (leading to leniency bias) and self-awareness (leading to incorporating information about oneself from comparisons of one's behavior with that of others). People who are high in cognitive complexity make better use of feedback cues. People who are higher in intelligence, internal locus of control, and achievement status provide more accurate self-evaluations (Mabe & West, 1982). Various biases in self-ratings include leniency, attributions of good outcomes to self and poor outcomes to external factors, and the desire to make a good impression. Leaders who are introverts have more accurate self-perceptions of their leadership style compared with their supervisors' ratings of them (Rousch & Atwater, 1992). Self-ratings tend to be lower for more successful than for less successful leaders (Bass & Yammarino, 1991).

Others' perceptions are also affected by similar personality, ability, and bias factors (Yammarino & Atwater, 1993). The accuracy of ratings from others is likely to be higher the more familiar the rater is with the person rated and the more similar the rater and ratee are in background and demographic characteristics (e.g., education, race, and gender). The role of the rater also affects ratings (Klimoski & London, 1974). For instance, supervisor and peer ratings are more likely to agree with each other than with self-ratings (Harris & Schaubroeck, 1988). However, this may depend on the nature of the ratings. Subordinates have firsthand experience about the manager's performance in boss–subordinate relationships while supervisors only observe these relationships and may not be present when interactions with subordinates occur. Agreement between self–subordinate ratings tends to be higher when subordinates have similar roles and hence similar interactions with the supervisor as they do in line units (Wohlers, Hall, & London, 1993). Also, self–subordinate agreement tends to be higher in organizations that foster supportive relationships (Yammarino & Dubinsky, 1992).

In summary, while self-ratings tend to be inflated, the preceding findings indicate that self–other agreement can be high under some conditions. Also, some individuals have a tendency to deflate their self-perceptions.

Self-Awareness and the Effects of Negative Feedback

Low self-awareness can limit the effects of negative feedback. People who fail at a task and who are made to observe or reflect on their feedback, thereby creating high self-awareness, are likely to be more attentive to avoiding failure in the future. A study of dieters demonstrated this point. Dieters who received negative feedback on a problem-solving task were likely to maintain their diet (eat less or no ice cream when offered as much as they wanted) if the feedback was accompanied by observing themselves failing on a videotape (Heatherton et al., 1993). Subjects who received similar feedback but who were distracted by an unrelated video (one on bighorn sheep) in between the feedback and the offer of ice cream ate more ice cream. Receiving no additional information in between feedback and the treat had the same effect as the distraction.

Generalizing from this study, negative feedback per se does not necessarily lead to a constructive response. Indeed, it may lead to a defensive or self-defeating response (i.e., going off the diet). A constructive response requires highlighting self-awareness. This suggests that feedback alone may not be sufficient to induce reflection and action to change behavior. Methods may be necessary to encourage self-reflection. Self-assessment guidelines, help in interpreting feedback results, or even watching videos of oneself participating in a task or exercise may generate self-awareness. Not providing such guidance may eliminate the potential positive effects of the negative feedback or might even lead to a defensive backlash that causes the individual to exhibit more of the behavior that led to the poor performance to begin with.

An open question is why heightened self-awareness doesn't produce more emotional distress and, in turn, increase, rather than decrease, emotional behavior? Failing on a task that is highly ego-relevant should, by itself, lead to a state of high self-awareness. This should cause one to feel more incompetent or deficient—an aversive state that people want to escape (Heatherton et al., 1993). The counterproductive escape from high self-awareness is achieved by a cognitive restriction that increases the negative behavior. An intervention that prevents this restriction, thereby maintaining and enhancing self-awareness, results in a decrease or elimination of the negative behavior.

The notion of cognitive processes that restrict or enhance self-awareness implies that we control our openness to new ideas about ourselves. The next section examines the importance of self-regulatory mechanisms to self-insight.

Self-Regulation

Social learning suggests that people learn from observing others as well as from direct experience (Bandura, 1977). We observe behaviors that are rewarded or punished and the conditions under which these behaviors occur. That is, we come to know when we are likely to be effective (Thornton & Byham, 1982, p. 412). As such, we are able to regulate our self-awareness and behavior. We guide our actions, set our own standards, act, and administer rewards and punishments to ourselves.

A Control Theory Explanation for Self-Regulation

Behavior is self-regulating in that people actively engage in self-correcting behaviors to maintain a perception of the environment that matches a standard (Carver & Scheier (1981, 1982; Nelson, 1993). According to control theory, described in Chapter 2, behavior allows us to regulate our perceptions to match standards. The standards may be imposed by external sources (e.g., job requirements set by one's supervisor) or by oneself (e.g., the minimum standard of living one desires) (Nelson, 1993). Feedback allows people to adjust their behavior so that their perceptions match their standards. Standards fall into a hierarchy (Powers, 1973a, 1973b). The idealized image one has for oneself is at the top of the hierarchy (Nelson, 1993). Next come principles or prescriptions for general behavior, such as honesty and kindness, followed by standards for behaviors themselves, such as sitting down with subordinates to discuss their career plans. People are concerned about their ideal self (their hopes and wishes) and what they believe they ought to do (their sense of duty and responsibility) (Higgins et al., 1994). While this hierarchy of standards guides our behavior, we are not always self-focused. Out attention is usually focused on our environment, and we only periodically note how well our behavior matches the relevant standard for that behavior or its conformance with our higher standards such as our principles or our idealized self-image (Nelson, 1993). Moreover, when we realize that our behavior cannot match a standard, we don't keep trying indefinitely but tend to disengage from the self-regulatory process after repeated negative feedback (Carver et al., 1983).

Control theory indicates how people regulate their perceptions and behavior by studying their goals. We can determine the level in the hierarchy at which people focus their attention and regulate their behavior (Nelson, 1993). Interventions can set adaptive and realistic standards. Also, feedback mechanisms can focus attention on the self. For instance, guidelines for using feedback can help people interpret the results in line with reasonable standards.

Mechanisms for Self-Regulation

Several mechanisms, described in the following, allow us to engage in this self-regulation process. These include self-affirmation, self-monitoring, self-protection, and self-handicapping.

Self-Affirmation. A self-affirming, image-maintaining process begins with any event that threatens the image, such as negative judgments (Steele, Spencer, & Lynch, 1993). This rationalization and self-justification process occurs through constant interpretation and reinterpretation of one's experiences until the image is restored. The intention is not to dismiss every threat that comes along but rather to address those that are significant, as long as the overall image of self-integrity is maintained. Individuals with high self-esteem have favorable self-concepts and an overall sense of self-integrity. As a result they tend to rationalize an esteem-threatening decision less than those with low self-esteem (Steele, Spencer, & Lynch, 1993). High-self-esteem individuals have more resources and more routes to affirmation than people with low self-esteem.

Self-Monitoring. Some individuals are highly attuned to what the external environment requires and expects of them. Labeled *self-monitors,* these "aware" individuals are able to vary their behavior to meet the needs of the situation (Snyder, 1987; Anderson, 1990). Self-monitors are guided by group norms, roles, and other features of the social situation. In contrast, low self-monitors are guided primarily by internal, dispositional features such as attitudes, values, and other personality traits. Consequently, low self-monitors display their attitudes and values consistently from one situation to another. High self-monitors display a variety of behaviors, adjusting their behavior as they move from one situation to another (Caldwell & O'Reilly, 1982).

Self-awareness is simply being aware of oneself. It is "a situational variable because both its focus and magnitude vary as a function of the situation in which the person happens to be at the moment" (Ross, 1992, p. 53). Self-monitoring refers to comparing, checking, and adjusting one's own behavior against an external or internal standard. External standards usually involve the expectations or reactions of other people, while internal standards involve one's own concerns and values.

Snyder's (1974; Snyder & Gangestad, 1986) self-monitoring scale assesses how a person behaves in social situations. High self-monitors indicate statements such as the following are true of them:

"I can make impromptu speeches even on topics about which I have almost no information."
"I guess I put on a show to impress or entertain others."
"In different situations and with different people, I often act like very different persons."
"I may deceive people by being friendly when I really dislike them."

Low self-monitors reject these statements and consider the following ones self-descriptive:

"I find it hard to imitate the behavior of other people."
"In a group of people I am rarely the center of attention."
"I am particularly good at making other people like me."

Self-Protection Mechanisms. Davey (1993) identified three cognitive appraisal strategies whose function is to change the meaning of a stressor. *Threat devaluation* is rationalizing that the information or situation is not really threatening. Examples of threat devaluation include telling oneself it is not worth getting upset about the situation or that "I can put up with this problem as long as everything else in my life is okay." *Positive reappraisal* is finding a positive side to the information or situation. Examples include changing something about oneself, rediscovering what is important in life, or believing one has changed or grown as a person in a good way. The third strategy is *denial*. Examples are refusing to believe that something has happened, pretending that something hasn't really happened, or saying to oneself that "this isn't real." Threat devaluation and positive reappraisal can result in a constructive focus on a problem, while denial is a way to avoid, or disengage from, a problem. Devaluating a threat is most likely to be used by people who feel they have control over situations. In contrast, denial is more frequently used by individuals with poor problem-solving confidence who believe they have little personal control over problems.

People use self-protection mechanisms to reduce threats to their self-concepts and maintain and restore beliefs about their capabilities (Wohlers & London, 1989; Bandura, 1982; Tesser & Campbell, 1982). An example is requesting distorted information, such as asking for praise ("Did I do okay?") or saying things that make others feel compelled to say good things about one's performance. Thus, people who use self-protection mechanisms will have less insight into their competencies. This lower self-awareness. Concomitantly, having less basis for self-definition will lead to lower feelings of self-worth (Maddi, 1980).

In their study of variables associated with self-awareness (defined in terms of agreement between self-perceptions and others' perceptions), Wohlers and London (1989) identified four general self-protection mechanisms: *denial, giving up, self-promotion,* and *fear of failure.* They found that co-workers' ratings of managers' use of self-protection mechanisms were negatively related to self-awareness measures. The following characteristics of each of these factors include items that reflect self-protection and its inverse:

Denial

- Reacts negatively to feedback.
- Blames others for failure.
- Never admits mistakes.

- Inhibits other's performance.
- Accurately perceives one's own performance. [inverse]
- Frequently asks for feedback. [inverse]
- Gives credit where it is due. [inverse]
- Accurately perceives other's performance. [inverse]
- Accurately describes events. [inverse]

Giving Up

- Abandons difficult tasks.
- Avoids being compared with better performers.
- Tunes out others who perform better.
- Would leave a job because co-workers perform better.
- Negative feedback lowers performance.
- Dislikes better performers.
- Tries hard on difficult tasks. [inverse]
- Sticks to tasks until succeeds. [inverse]

Self-Promotion

- Makes sure others know about successes.
- Asks for praise.
- Concerned about status symbols.
- Talks about own good performance.
- Makes others feel compelled to say good things about his or her performance.
- Does not admit one's own contribution to a group's success. [inverse]

Fear of Failure

- Points out own strengths when criticized.
- Afraid of failure.
- Gets upset by own poor performance.
- Tries to prevent others from doing well.
- Tries to convince others they are wrong.
- Tries to raise others' opinions of self.
- Downplays own weaknesses.
- Concerned about making the "right" career moves.

Self-Handicapping. People seem to make self-attributions based on the hedonistic desire to enhance pride in cases of success and avoid shame in cases of failure. They also seek to enhance potential success and to discount potential failure. This is accomplished by self-handicapping strategies that protect self-esteem (Jones & Berglas, 1978, described by Ross, 1992, p. 113). Self-handicapping is avoiding diagnostic information about one's own characteristics and capabilities. People who do this don't want to know precisely what they can do best and so act in a way that obscures making self-attributions. An example is an employee who stays up late preparing for an important presentation. If he does not do well, he can attribute this to being tired rather than to his poor presentation ability. If he does well in spite of the handicap of fatigue, it will enhance his self-esteem all the more. The paradox is that the handicap decreases the likelihood of success.

Self-handicapping is typical of people who are low in self-esteem (cf. Snyder, 1987). Self-handicapping is particularly likely when individuals are unsure about the outcome of an evaluation and do not know how their performance will affect the results (Tice & Baumeister, 1990). Trying hard and avoiding a handicap will not do as much to enhance one's self-esteem as doing well with the handicap. But as indicated, the handicap decreases the likelihood of doing well. Thus, people with low self-esteem maintain their self-image by creating a handicap especially when they know they could do well (for instance, after receiving favorable preliminary feedback on a task such as being told, "It looks like you're doing a fine job on the project!"). On the other hand, high-self-esteem individuals create a handicap in order to protect their high self-esteem unless they have received favorable preliminary feedback. Such feedback demonstrates that they can indeed do well on the task, and so they try all the harder, no longer needing the handicap to protect the image they present to themselves and to others.

Self-handicapping has elements of both self-presentation and self-protection (Tice & Baumeister, 1990). High-self-esteem individuals may use self-handicapping to impress others in case of success and protect their image in case of failure. Low-self-esteem individuals use it to avoid success, especially when they begin to realize that success is possible. When success is in sight, then failure would require a painful, negative self-attribution.

Thus, self-regulation affects the degree to which we open ourselves to new achievements. Self-protection and handicapping protect our self-esteem and perhaps prevent our realizing our full capabilities, suggesting that self-insight influences our desires for achievement and the goals we set for ourselves. This is discussed in the final section.

Self-Insight and Goal Setting

Our self-insight affects our expectations about how well we can perform in a given situation, and this performance expectation, in turn, affects the goals we set for ourselves. Making judgments about future performance depends on self-insight about capabilities and on knowledge about performance requirements and conditions (Locke, Motowidlo, & Bobko, 1986). Predicting our future performance is often a private task—something we do on our own as we undertake various endeavors. On many occasions, however, we may be asked by another person, such as a supervisor, to judge how well we can do on a particular task. Private and public performance judgments occur as we set performance standards or goals. For instance, this might be how well we will do on an athletic task such as our golf game. Or it may be a personal objective, such as weight loss. It could also involve a level of job performance, such as how successful we will be if we accept a particular job or undertake a certain initiative, such as an investment banker pursuing a new client.

The judgment of a future goal involves estimating how well we expect to do on a given task, while a self-set goal is the level of performance for which we will strive (Henry & Sniezek, 1993). In making judgments of expected performance, we try to be as accurate as possible. When we set a goal, we try to maximize our level of performance; that is, the goal affects our motivation for doing better. We may set a goal based on our expected level of performance (e.g., "I can do that") or a higher level of performance (e.g., "I can do better").

Language is important here. In making a performance judgment, we specify what we anticipate we can do (e.g., "I *expect* that I will finish the task tomorrow"). In setting a goal, we indicate what we will attempt to accomplish (e.g., "I will *try* to finish the task tomorrow"). Saying what we *hope* to do implies elements of what we expect to do and what we want to do. But we may hope for things that are beyond our control. Stating what we *can* do indicates capabilities but not necessarily willingness, motivation, or expectation about what will happen (Henry & Sniezek, 1993).

These are subtle differences but important ones in terms of how our self-insight guides our expectations and commitments. Clearer self-insight is likely to lead us to more definitive and accurate statements of our capabilities and expectations. Moreover, self-efficacy and goal setting are related, with higher levels of perceived capability leading to more challenging yet realistic goals (Bandura, 1977).

Perceptions of self-efficacy (i.e., general confidence in being able to improve) predict people's performance as they learn a task (Mitchell et al., 1993). After people become more familiar with the task, goals are more predictive of performance than self-efficacy. Therefore, self-efficacy has a motivational function on unfamiliar tasks. Once people are experienced with the task, they base their expected performance on prior performance.

Henry and Sniezek (1993) studied situational factors that affect judgments of future performance. In particular, they examined performance judgments under varying conditions of monetary rewards and perceived internal control over performance. Subjects were confident, expected high levels of performance, and tried hard when they perceived high levels of internal control and when monetary rewards would result.

Self-Denying Prophecies

Self-denying prophecies change people's behavior to shift the outcome of their actions in the direction opposite that of the prophecy (Hurley, 1993). They are the counterparts to self-fulfilling prophecies (e.g., a manager treating a subordinate in such a way that the subordinate's behavior fulfills the manager's expectations; cf. Rosenthal & Rubin, 1978). Self-denying prophecies start with a negative prophecy and produce a positive outcome. Neg-

ative feedback is tantamount to a negative prophecy; it generally lowers motivation, especially for low-self-esteem individuals who are willing to believe
negative prophecies about themselves (Brockner, Derr, & Laing, 1987). Self-
denying prophecies occur when the individual sets goals and acts to disprove
a negative expectation—that is, to ensure that the negative prophecy does
not come true. Hurley (1993), studying students performing a clerical task,
found that the anticipation of negative performance motivated high-self-esteem individuals to perform better.

Conclusion

Everyone has a self-schema—a picture of themselves in relation to the environment. This may include what others think about them, their capabilities
to perform various tasks under different circumstances, and their feelings
(likes and dislikes, emotional states, and personality tendencies). The self-
schemas derive from the reflection and attribution processes described in
Chapter 2. People have different self-schemas to match different situations.

Self-insight motivates personal and professional growth. It is the basis
for establishing realistic goals. As a result, career development programs
often begin with self-assessment. (See Chapter 9 for examples.) Such prods
seem to be necessary to encourage people to attend to feedback and reflect
on it. Many people prefer to ignore information about themselves as a means
of self-affirmation or self-protection; others, however, are keenly attuned to
the external environment and are able to relate their capabilities to opportunities.

This chapter has reviewed individual characteristics that prompt people
to be more self-aware. Self-monitoring increases self-insight while self-protection and self-handicapping decrease it. Several conclusions about self-
insight emerge from this discussion:

1. Self-insight is important for personal and professional development. It
motivates performance by establishing realistic expectations.

2. Inaccurate or insufficient self-knowledge (low self-insight) will reduce
expectations or interfere with setting realistic goals. Overestimating capabilities can lead to disappointment, and underestimating them can lead to
low achievement.

3. Self-reflection needs to be encouraged. For many individuals this
means overcoming a natural resistance to self-knowledge. It requires creating a reason for increased attention to one's own performance and to performance feedback. It also requires overcoming proclivities to ignore or mis-
interpret such feedback.

4. Situational demands reflect how we structure self-assessments. The
structure of self-assessments is more complex when the situation calls for
it. Thus, general self-descriptions will follow a common structure that others
can easily understand. When self-descriptions have possible consequences,

however, as they do for job applicants, people try to structure an ideal image that matches situational requirements.

5. Self-disclosure is a means to test reactions to self-concepts. However, some people avoid self-disclosure just as they avoid direct feedback. Social norms of reciprocating self-disclosure statements promote self-reflection. However, some people are more likely than others to respond to these norms—for instance, people who monitor the environment and are aware of their public selves are more likely to be self-disclosive.

6. Self-protection mechanisms, such as denial and self-promotion, insulate the individual from meaningful feedback and self-insight. Self-handicapping is a proactive strategy that establishes an external excuse for failure. In these situations, self-protection takes precedence over succeeding.

7. Our perceptions of how others view us are largely a function of our self-observations.

8. Feedback from others, especially those who control valued outcomes, is likely to affect our self-image.

9. Self-insight establishes a success cycle. Realistic expectations and openness to evaluating performance increases self-insight, which further enhances goal setting and performance.

10. Negative feedback may engender a self-denying prophecy—that is, motivate goals and actions that reverse the negative feedback.

These ideas about self-insight are developed further in the next chapter, which considers insights about others, in particular, processes for how people categorize information about others based on social information and individual biases. This leads to the discussion in Chapter 5 of the interrelationship of self–other perceptions, feedback processes, and impression management behaviors.

4

Interpersonal Insight

The subtlest and most pervasive of influences are those which create and
maintain the repertory of stereotypes. We are told about the world before we
see it. We imagine most things before we experience them. And those pre-
conceptions, unless education has made us acutely aware, govern deeply the
whole process of perception.

Walter Lippmann *Public Opinion*

This chapter considers how people form impressions of others. I begin by
reviewing how early social psychologists viewed person perception and individual characteristics affecting interpersonal judgment. I then apply the
cognitive mechanisms of insight emergence (feedback, categorization, attribution, and evaluation) discussed in Chapter 2 to perceptions of others' behavior. The underlying process of forming impressions of others is similar
to that of forming self-impressions, as described in Chapter 3. Here, I review
recent research on gathering and integrating information, and drawing conclusions about others. Attention is given to variables affecting perceiver accuracy and the effects of social context on perceptions. These concepts are
then applied to important organizational decisions involving interpersonal
insight—performance appraisal and interviewer judgments.

Person Perception

Early theory and research in person perception provide a foundation for
understanding interpersonal insight. Bruner and Tagiuri (1954) grouped person perception research into three categories: the recognition of emotion in
others, the accuracy of appraisals of other personalities, and the process by
which personality impressions are formed. Building on this idea, Heider
(1958) considered conditions that permit us to become aware of others' perceptions, intentions, desires, pleasures, abilities, and sentiments. He distinguished between cognition and perception. The term *perception* goes beyond the cognition of raw material to include an understanding, awareness,
meaning, or recognition of an object. Perception is "all the different ways
we have of getting to know the environment, from direct perception to ex-

Perception—getting to know the environment

plicit inference" (p. 27). An important judgment that we make about ourselves and others is attributing the cause of behavior to internal (stable) or external (environmental or situational) factors.

Misperceptions are conditions that impede our recognizing cognitive errors (Heider, 1958, pp. 53–55). Such conditions include erroneously thinking that behavior is stable across situations, assuming that another person's situation is the same as our own, and having insufficient or inadequate data to form a meaningful judgment. Heider argued that person perception is a function of the knowledge the parties have of each other. Moreover, he referred to the possibility of insight as a skill:

> Phenomenologically oriented psychologists in particular have stressed that for one person to be in contact with another and to perceive and react to the other's sentiments and wishes, it is not enough that he is exposed to certain stimulus configurations. A general readiness to perceive psychologically is necessary; this receptivity makes possible the arousal of such percepts as "he is angry," or "he wants to tell me something." *As we know, people vary widely in such social-psychological perceptivity* (p. 57; italics added)

Heider also believed that "knowledge about organismic factors enables the person to improve perception by affecting the functioning of the sensory tool" (p. 67). (Sensory organs refer here not only to physical organs of perception, such as eyesight, but also to psychological factors, such as motivation, beliefs, mental set, and judgment.) Thus, Heider suggested that people can become more insightful.

In addition, Heider outlined five conditions of perception: (1) the object, (2) mediating conditions for establishing contact between person and object (e.g., clarity and position of the object), (3) factors within the perceiver, (4) conditions behind the conditions of perception (how one happened to see something, whether one searched for it, whether one accidentally stumbled upon it), and (5) the perceiver's egocentric cognition (perceiving what one wants and seeing oneself as the focus of others' actions). Despite the reference to perceptiveness as, in part, an individual difference variable, Heider did not identify what individual differences affect perceptiveness. Rather, he treated perceptiveness as the intersection of cognitions and volition.

> Since one's idea includes what "ought to be" and "what one would like to be" as well as "what is," attribution and cognition are influenced by the mere subjective forces of needs and wishes as well as by the more objective evidence presented in the raw material. Especially important is the point of view adopted—whether one perceives and interprets according to one's own outlook or whether one is able to assume the position of the person who is the source of the action. (p. 118)

The notion of perceiving and interpreting according to one's own outlook suggests that individual characteristics may influence perceptions of others.

Individual Characteristics Affecting Interpersonal Insight

Our skills and personality tendencies may influence how we perceive other individuals. This section discusses observation skills, self-monitoring tendencies (our sensitivity to the environment), and empathy as individual difference variables influencing person perception.

Observation Skills

Boice (1983) examined the concept of observation skills, considering in particular skills of good observers, situational factors that facilitate observation, and programs for the training of observational skills. Boice indicated that observation requires being able to discern and distinguish between person, situation, and person-by-situation effects. Some people are better observers than others because of their skills. These include the ability to monitor cues in various situations and the role of cognitive memory.

Boice noted that while good observers can be defined in terms of directly observed and measured skills, some traits might prove useful. An example might be an index of anxiety, such as impassivity, that characterizes social skills individuals exhibit across most social situations. Good observers are high in experience observing, similar in characteristics to the observed, intelligent, high in self-awareness, high in cognitive complexity, and socially intelligent (Boice, 1983). The ability to make swift and accurate judgments of others is not equivalent to a profound understanding of them, but it is effective in predicting their most likely behaviors.

Self-Monitoring

As discussed in Chapter 3, self-monitoring addresses how people relate to the external environment. It also addresses insight into others' behaviors. High self-monitors (SMs) tend to have insight into others' actions. For instance, high SMs are more accurate than low SMs in judgments of actors' emotions, and high SMs are also more accurate in displaying arbitrarily assigned emotions (Snyder, 1974). Anderson (1987; Anderson & Thacker, 1985) found that being high in self-monitoring facilitates the job effectiveness of people in gender-nontraditional occupations such as men in nursing or women in management. Such individuals must perform their work effectively, but they must also demonstrate that they are legitimate occupants of their work roles. Thus, compared with people in traditional jobs, they benefit greatly from the adaptive self-presentation skills of high self-monitoring.

Empathy

Empathy, accurately perceiving how another person is feeling, derives from the cognitive ability to take the perspective of another or to understand someone's structuring of the world without necessarily adopting that same perspective (Stinson & Ickes, 1992). This allows the empathizer to remain at a social distance from the individual observed. It requires being able to distinguish the external situation and the past experiences of the target. Stinson and Ickes (1992) believe that although the cognitive ability of the perceiver may be a necessary condition for empathic accuracy, it is not sufficient in and of itself. They tested the hypothesis that well-acquainted partners are more accurate than strangers in inferring the content of thoughts and feelings. In unstructured interactions male friends were found to be more accurate than male strangers in inferring each other's thoughts and feelings. Plausible reasons for this difference were that friends interacted more and exchanged more information, had more similar personalities and therefore more rapport with each other, and had more detailed knowledge of each other's lives. The study showed that friends did indeed interact more and were more similar in their sociability than the strangers; however, these differences did not account for the friends' greater empathic accuracy. Instead, this was primarily attributable to a difference in knowledge structures, namely, the friends' ability to accurately read their partners' thoughts and feelings about imagined events in another place or time.

Emergence of Insights about Others

Just as people have self-schemas (as described in Chapter 3), perceptions of others are guided by schemas. Fiske and Taylor (1991, pp. 143–146) formulated research-based principles about how schemas apply to perceptions of others—especially first impressions. Schemas form around roles (e.g., "office manager," "chief executive officer") and subtypes (e.g., male versus female). People rely on visual, physical cues that are easily perceived, such as age, race, and sex. Early information is likely to produce relevant schemas such that the first information received causes one to draw conclusions that color later perceptions. Cues that set a person apart from others are likely to prompt a schema—for instance, a woman manager in a male-dominated firm is likely to be gender-stereotyped. People use schemas that they are already primed to use, as when they get in the habit of categorizing others (e.g., the high-achieving manager categorizing others as "competent" or "incompetent"). People use schemas that match their current feelings, so individuals in a good mood tend to see good sides of others. Finally, people use schemas to describe others who control their outcomes—that is, those in a position of power. Thus, people may have difficulty overcoming evaluation apprehension and developing a close working relationship with a top executive.

While schemas influence person perception, people may use more mindful evaluation rather than automatically categorizing people into schemas. To use the language of the cognitive theories of person perception outlined in Chapter 2, reflected information stems from observation of others and others' self-disclosures. Both observations and self-disclosures may be affected by one's own and others' attempts at impression management. The observer will categorize the information if it matches a schema or prototype; if it does not, the observer will make an attribution to the individual or the situation. Attributions of others may be influenced by characteristics of observers. For instance, observers who want to enhance their own self-image may be prone to negative attributions of another's abilities. Ultimately, perceptions of the other person's efficacy will influence evaluations of the individual (e.g., in performance appraisal) and various behaviors (e.g., trusting the individual to accomplish a key task).

Cognitive Models of Performance Appraisal

Theory and research on performance appraisal during the last decade have attempted to translate principles from social cognition and cognitive psychology to understanding rater judgment processes. This focus was a switch away from an earlier focus on developing psychometrically sound rating scales. Ilgen, Barnes-Farrell, and McKellin (1993) reviewed the literature on how people gather, store, and retrieve information about social stimuli for the purpose of rating performance. They concluded that research has helped to guide the design of rating tasks and has led to an increased understanding of rater characteristics that may facilitate more accurate ratings; they predicted that future contributions to the design and operation of appraisal systems are likely to come from research in three areas: "(1) the investigation of the content of cognitive variables, (2) the identification of work group and organizational factors that influence these variables, and (3) the design of appraisal systems that incorporate cognitive principles" (p. 362).

For instance, conditions in the rating environment are likely to influence ratings. So rating inflation can be predicted from the extent to which raters feel they can be open and honest when rating their subordinates (Padgett & Ilgen, 1989). This depends on the rating purpose and method—for instance, using the information for development only rather than for making salary decisions. Other relevant conditions include the extent to which ratees discuss their ratings with others, the extent to which raters document their ratings or other measures of ratee performance, and the extent to which raters desire to be liked by the ratees (Ilgen, Barnes-Farrell, & McKellin (1993). So cognitive variables need to be viewed within the broader rating context in order to more fully understand appraisal processes.

Situational Constraints and Performance Judgments. Sanders (1993) developed a decision model of performance judgments to illustrate how they are influenced by situational constraints. When performance is observed and compared with preconceived impressions, raters determine if their expectations were violated or met. If they were met, automatic processing and categorization occur and the situation is not considered. If expectations were violated, controlled processing occurs and people feel uncertain (cf. Vallacher, Nowak, & Kaufman, 1994). Three decision points then arise in processing information (from Sanders, 1993): (1) Is there reason to search the situation? If yes, then the rater proceeds to the second question. (2) Can the situation be viewed as a cause of the performance observed? If yes, the third question arises. (3) Is the performer expected to deal with the situational constraints? If no, then the rater attributes the performance to the situation and evaluates the performance in relation to a standard that takes the situation into account.

Raters may be unlikely to consider the situation in the first place because their attention is focused on the performer, under the assumption that behavior is intentional. This is especially likely if the performer is experienced (Sanders, 1993). On the other hand, if the raters are themselves experienced on the job, they are likely to be aware of constraints that affect performance and consider elements of the situation in evaluating performance.

If the situation is seen as a possible cause of behavior, raters will use available information and their own experience and judgment to decide what happened. They will also take into account the reasons people give for the performance—for instance, what the subordinates say was important. Subordinates' statements, however, may be inaccurate, as in the case of a subordinate who is reluctant to blame the situation for a mistake. Or a subordinate who does blame the situation may be perceived as covering up incompetence or low effort. Moreover, the rater is likely to view the performer as the cause of poor performance when the negative outcome is serious rather than mild (Mitchell & Wood, 1980) or when the subordinate is perceived to have little control over the situation (Murphy & Cleveland, 1991).

People pay attention to the consistency of information and are likely to make errors when information does not "fit" expectations. Barnes-Farrell, L'Heureux-Barrett, and Conway (1991) studied the effects of job and task gender type on the accurate evaluation of task performance. Employee behaviors for male-typed tasks were appraised more accurately when presented in the context of a male-typed occupation, and behaviors for female-typed tasks were appraised more accurately in the context of a female-typed occupation. Worker gender did not influence the accuracy of performance ratings.

Social and situational factors shape rater cognition and evaluation. As described by Judge and Ferris (1993), "Performance rating is a process with multiple social and situational facets that need to be considered simultaneously" (p. 80). Judge and Ferris (1993) showed that the supervisor's rating of a subordinate's job performance will be higher when:

- The supervisor has more opportunity to observe the subordinate—because close observation will motivate higher performance.
- The supervisor has a low span of control—because the supervisor has more opportunity to know and work with the subordinate.
- The supervisor has more experience—because supervisors have learned that unfavorable ratings are not worth the trouble they cause

and because they realize that ratings are not error-free and so subordinates deserve the benefit of the doubt.

• The supervisor believes the subordinate's self-perception is favorable and the supervisor feels pressure to conform to the subordinate's wishes.

• The supervisor likes the subordinate—because it would be cognitively inconsistent to give a low rating to a person one likes. Supervisors tend to like subordinates with whom they have a close working relationship, perhaps because they know them better. Also, supervisors tend to like subordinates who are similar to themselves—similar in terms of key demographic characteristics such as age, race, and gender.

The Effects of Motivation on Rater Accuracy.   Rater motivation can increase rater accuracy by increasing the extent to which stages of cognitive processing in appraisal (attention, encoding, recall, and integration) are controlled rather than automatic. Salvemini, Reilly, and Smither (1993) reached this conclusion in a study that offered a monetary reward to those who made the most accurate ratings. One-third of the raters were offered the incentive prior to observing performance of ratees on a videotape, another one-third were offered the incentive after viewing the tape but before making the ratings, and the remaining one-third received no incentive offer. Another variable—raters' having information about the ratee's prior performance—was added to the study because previous research indicated that ratings are biased in the direction of past performance (cf. Smither, Reilly, & Buda, 1988). Raters who were motivated to provide accurate ratings were better able to rank order ratees both across and within performance dimensions. The most accurate ratings were provided by raters who were informed about the incentives before viewing the ratees' job performance samples. The incentive alleviated the biasing effects of prior information.

Salvemini, Reilly, and Smither (1993) explained that knowing about the incentive before observing performance allowed greater accuracy because it affected the full realm of cognitive processes required in performance appraisal—attending to, encoding, and recalling specific behaviors for specific candidates on specific dimensions. Learning about the incentive after the observations occurred affected only the recall and integration stages of person perception. Automatic processing was likely during the attention and encoding stages in that information about past performance resulted in loss of finer-grained information about the ratee. Without the incentive, raters with knowledge of the ratee's prior performance are more likely to attend to, encode, and recall ratee behavior that is consistent with the prior performance. Interestingly, this is a process of differential attention rather than differential interpretation of the same behaviors. Other research has shown that raters who were told that a ratee's prior performance level was poor were more likely to report having observed poor behaviors that did not occur than were raters who were told that prior performance was good (Buda, Reilly, & Smither, 1990).

Insight Into What Is Important In Our Decisions. People's beliefs about their own decision making are important if they take them into account in making decisions. One type of belief is the relative importance of the factors entering into a decision (Goldstein & Mitzel, 1992). What people say about the relative importance of dimensions that affect their judgments may tell us something about their cognitive processes and the way they formulate and structure beliefs. This is the extent to which people have insight into their own decision making.

Understanding people's insights about their insights is important because people are often asked to describe to others what is important to them. This may occur when we ask others to make decisions for us (e.g., a chief executive officer appointing a search committee to fill a critical position in the organization). Statements about what is important to us are valuable if we actually use (i.e., base our decisions on) criteria that we say are important. Goldstein and Mitzel (1992) studied people who were required to process information about another person's relative importance judgments and make inferences about the other person's decisions. They found that people are able to abstract and generalize others' relative importance judgments from information about their decisions. Further, people do not interpret other individuals' relative importance ratings as a reflection of more general attitudes because they expect relative importance ratings to be related to the person's ordering of preferences. Also, people do not discount perceptions of others' relative importance ratings when they are inconsistent with previous decisions.

Accuracy in Performance Ratings

In the first chapter I suggested that one defining element of insight is accuracy. That is, when we believe we have an insight, we assume that the insight has a basis in reality and tells us something about what is true. If we learn otherwise in testing the insight, then the insight is lost to us. Appraisal processes also assume that our interpersonal judgments are accurate—or at least can be made more accurate with the right support. Many variables may be barriers to accurate appraisals, such as the biases we hold and the availability of information. Nevertheless, considerable research has tried to determine variables affecting the accuracy of interpersonal judgments and has tested methods to improve rater accuracy. Some of these variables are considered in the following.

Memory and Judgment

Woehr and Feldman (1993) extended the research on information processing in performance appraisal by examining the relation between memory and judgment processes. Traditionally, performance appraisal researchers assumed that performance judgments are based on memory for specific behaviors (Feldman, 1981), thus, as memory improves, judgmental accuracy should also improve. However, performance appraisals may be based on previously formed judgments rather than on memory for specific information. The extent to which memory and/or judgment is important may depend on the nature of the information-processing task (Hastie & Park, 1986).

One important task characteristic affecting judgment is the purpose of the rating. If the goal is to evaluate others, judgments are likely to be formed as the behavior is observed. As a consequence, later evaluations would not depend on memory for specific behaviors but on previously formed judgements (Woehr & Feldman, 1993; Lichtenstein & Scrull, 1987). Memory will play a role, however, if memory for specific behaviors is highly accessible. If an evaluative objective does not precede information presentation, then subsequent evaluations are likely to be based on memories of specific behaviors. As explained by Woehr and Feldman (1993),

> [I]t may be difficult to keep people from making evaluative judgments, especially in contexts in which evaluations are relevant to a particular outcome. It is not likely that individuals habitually access memory when making evaluations. Rather, they use the most readily accessible information that is diagnostic of the required judgment, typically previously formed evaluations. (p. 240)

Woehr and Feldman's (1993) research suggests that evaluation causes people to make early judgments that may be only slightly related to actual observed behaviors. However, this early judgment bias may be minimized if the rating tasks ask the rater to recall behaviors before making an evaluation; in this case, memory is more likely to drive judgment rather than vice versa. Thus, the purpose for the rating may be as important, if not more so, to rater accuracy as the format for the ratings and the nature of the questions asked. This will become important in Chapters 5 and 10, which discuss the purpose of ratings, for instance, whether upward and 360-degree feedback should be used to guide development or to make salary and promotion decisions about individuals.

Toward a Definition of Judgment Accuracy

Understanding insight goes beyond a consideration of cognitive processes in observing, encoding, storing, retrieving, and evaluating social information. The *correctness* of the ultimate judgment is a critical factor in the meaningfulness of an insight. (See Zalesny & Highhouse's [1992] review of accuracy in performance evaluations.) Different types of accuracy occur at different stages of information processing (Lord, 1985). Behavioral accuracy implies faithfully encoding and recalling specific observed behaviors. Classification or inferential accuracy occurs when raters simplify and integrate behavioral observations into appropriate categories or overall impressions.

In considering whether judgments are right or wrong, it is necessary to compare them with external criteria; two such criteria are agreement with others, particularly experts, and the ability to predict behavior (Funder, 1987). These two measures of accuracy should be interrelated because experts, by definition, are those who have been trained and have experience making correct judgments. Experts may disagree, however, if differences occur between raters in task or situational characteristics. Also, characteristics of the rater may affect recall and judgment processes (e.g., the extent of experience or the rater's similarity to the ratee; cf. Chapdelaine, Kenny, & LaFontana, 1994).

Zalesny and Highhouse (1992) examined these two measures of agreement (agreement with expert ratings and ability to predict behavior) in a sample of student teachers and school administrators (the experts) evaluating the performance of a focal teacher. Student teachers observed a videotape of a teacher's performance and then rated the teacher on a variety of performance items reflecting four dimensions of performance—specifically, instructional methods, classroom management, personal and professional qualities, and interpersonal relationships. Accuracy as agreement was the absolute difference between the average expert ratings across the performance measures and the average student teacher ratings. Accuracy as ability to predict behavior was the relationship between the student teachers' prediction of behavior after viewing a large portion of the tape and the teacher's actual behavior in the last part of the tape.

The study found that predictive accuracy was significantly related to accuracy as agreement with experts on the performance dimension most closely associated with the behavior predicted. That is, agreement with experts on the teacher's classroom management was related to predicting how the teacher in the videotape would discipline a student. Raters who viewed their own teaching attitudes as more similar to those of the teacher in the tape were higher in both accuracy measures than were raters who viewed themselves as dissimilar in attitudes, perhaps because perceived similarity (measured after performance was evaluated) caused the raters to pay more attention to the behavior. In addition, the two accuracy measures were more highly related when the raters were asked to predict behavior before making an evaluation than when making the evaluation first.

This suggests that the evaluation interferes with rating accuracy. This may occur because processing and ordering information may cause raters to ignore some information when they are asked to predict behavior. Making a prediction before an evaluation may aid recall of specific information related to the particular behavioral prediction. Another conclusion is that perceived similarity enhances rating accuracy.

Accuracy Measures

Lord (1985) conceptualized the following three types of judgment accuracy:

Behavioral Accuracy. A rater observes, accurately recalls, and correctly recognizes particular behaviors in another. This means that the proportion of items correctly identified ("hit rates" in the language of signal-detection theory) will be greater than the proportion of items falsely recognized as having been exhibited by the subject ("false alarms") for all types of items rated.

Classification Accuracy.   A rater correctly recognizes that a ratee behaved consistently with a performance level for a particular dimension of performance, such as "poor organizational skills"; the rater correctly recalls the dimension but does not necessarily recall the specific behavior. In the language of signal-detection theory, high hit rates and high false alarms occur for prototypical behaviors (those that reflect common, expected, or stereotypic behavior). Low hit rates and high false alarms occur for antiprototypical behaviors because such behaviors are not expected, receive inordinate attention, and can lead to wrong conclusions.

Rating errors, such as leniency and halo, may account for poor classification accuracy. There are three types of rater halo (after Fisicaro & Lance, 1990; and Lance, LaPointe, & Fisicaro, 1994): *General impression* is the tendency of a rater to allow overall impressions of a person to influence judgments of that person's performance along several conceptually independent dimensions of job performance; *salient dimension* is the influence of a rater's evaluation on one dimension to influence the rater's judgment of the individual on other dimensions; *inadequate discrimination* is a rater's inability to discriminate among conceptually separate and potentially independent aspects of a ratee's behavior.

Lance, LaPointe, and Stewart (1994) tried to determine whether rating contexts could be manipulated that favored the operation of the three types of halo error models. The results showed the general impression error occurred in spite of experimental conditions designed specifically to induce other forms of halo rater error (e.g., instructions to pay attention to lecturers' speaking ability as a way to accentuate the salience of this dimension of lecturing performance, or rearranging behavioral examples of dimensions to be congruent and incongruent with the dimension as a way to induce inadequate discrimination). The finding of the stability of the general impression model suggests that halo rater error is a unitary phenomenon that should be defined as "the influence of a rater's general impression on ratings of specific ratee qualities" Lance et al., 1994, p. 332).

Decision Criteria Accuracy.   A rater judgment is consistent with the actual performance but the evaluation includes the rater's performance standards (e.g., leniency). Lenient standards would suggest high hit rates and high false alarms for all ratings. Stringent standards would suggest low hit rates and low false alarms for all ratings—because nothing is good enough, even when positive behaviors occur.

Another way to view accuracy is in terms of the *inferences* made about the information observed (Nathan & Alexander, 1985). This suggests the importance of accurately classifying performance levels and correctly perceiving factors that affect performance (Ilgen, Barnes-Farrell, & McKellin, 1993).

Trying to Improve Rater Accuracy

The previous sections describe the meaning of judgment accuracy but say little about the rating format. Typically, performance judgments are made on fairly simple rating scales. Several performance dimensions might be rated, for instance, quality and quality of performance, or the dimensions might be more behavioral and specific, such as "meets objectives" or "works with subordinates to set performance goals." The item rated might be stated in terms of behavioral expectations, such as "the manager could be expected to provide subordinates with sufficient training." Ratings are on a numerical scale, such as 1 = low to 5 = high. Therefore, the feedback would be actual ratings, in the case of supervisor judgments, or average ratings across subordinates, in the case of upward ratings. Given the subjectivity of the rating process, however, the likely disagreement among raters, and the sensitivity of ratees to feedback, psychologists have tried to improve the accuracy and precision of the rating process. Although a review of rating methods is beyond the scope of this book, I will provide one recent example that relies on the rater's cognitive ability to discriminate differences within and between ratees.

The Distributional Rating Form. This process was developed to reflect the idea that each ratee's performance may vary throughout the rating period while the performance assessment occurs at one point in time. A distributional rating format asks the rater to indicate the percentage of the ratee's time that is described by each performance level. The method is based on the general idea from cognitive psychology that people are capable of detecting variability in a distribution and providing fairly accurate ratings of this variability (Holland, Holyoak, Nisbett, & Thagard, 1986).

In a test of such a scale, Steiner, Rain, and Smalley (1993) had college students rate an instructor's videotaped performance. When rating the instructor's confidence in what he was saying, the ratee indicated the proportion of time the instructor's confidence was poor, average, and good (say 20, 50, and 30 percent, respectively). Such ratings provide richer information than simpler rating formats (Steiner, Rain, & Smalley, 1993). In particular, they yield both central tendency and dispersion indexes unlike a typical rating method that asks the rater to provide a single rating on each performance dimension. (See Chapter 9's discussion of training methods to improve rater accuracy.)

The Employment Interview

So far this discussion has centered on performance appraisal judgments and ratings. The employment interview is another important applied context for interpersonal insight, the success of which rests on the interviewer's insight about the interviewee. The goal of the employment interview is to select candidates who will be successful on the job. Success may be defined as ability to get along with others in the organization, stay with or show loyalty to the organization, perform well on the first job, and/or learn what is needed to assume new responsibilities at higher organizational levels. Therefore, the interviewer may be required to make a complex prediction based on multiple criteria. Also, the interview is a two-way street in that the applicant selects the organization at the same time the organization, represented by the interviewer, selects the applicant. In this section I concentrate on the interviewer's interpersonal insight, although I recognize that the interview is a dynamic process during which the interviewer affects the applicant and the applicant affects the interviewer.

Several interviews may occur at different stages of the employment decision (for instance, a college senior may have an initial on-campus interview with company recruiters followed by an on-site interview or series of interviews). Often, the interview is a final hurdle, one that involves eliciting and analyzing considerable information about a job candidate. Sometimes the interview is conducted by a panel or selection committee. Other times, there is a series of interviews; the interviewers later meet to combine information, discuss their perceptions, and achieve agreement. This process allows the individual interviewers to check their judgment against that of others—their perceptions of the candidate and the importance of the different information.

Unlike performance appraisal, the interview requires making a judgment after only a short time. Considerable research has been conducted to explain person perception processes in such a situation (see Eder, Kacmar, & Ferris, 1989). This includes understanding the effects of interviewer and applicant characteristics on decisions, relevant preinterview impressions, the interview context and purpose, process dynamics including impression formation and information processing, and interview outcomes. Relationships among these components are depicted in Figure 4.1.

A thorough review of each component of this model is more than I can cover here. (Interested readers are referred to Eder & Ferris, 1989.) Rather, I will focus on the process elements involved in insight formation, specifically, cognitive attribution processes, impression management, and the use of structured interviews to enhance the accuracy of interview judgments.

Attribution Processes

Herriot (1989) outlined how Heider's (1958) model of attribution and Kelley's (1967) covariation principle apply to the interview. Interview information (including the interviewee's verbal and nonverbal behavior) is categorized and attributed to a cause based on three forms of covariation: consensus, distinction, and consistency. Interviewee behavior will be attributed to the situation if other people tend to behave in the same way in a given situation (consensus), if the interviewee is unlikely to behave in the same way in other situations (distinctiveness), and if the interviewee usually behaves in this way in the interview situation (consistency). All three prin-

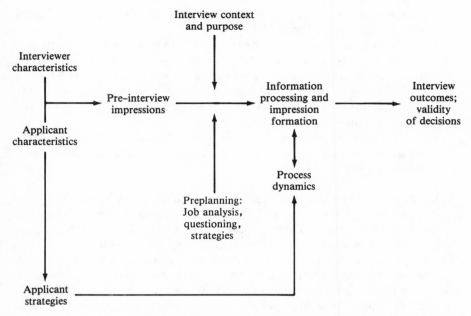

FIGURE 4.1   A framework for understanding interview processes. (Adapted from Eder, Kacmar, & Ferris, 1989, p. 30.)

ciples are likely to apply to the way people usually dress for an employment interview. We expect standard business dress; if a person comes dressed casually, we are likely to impute poor judgment or sloppy habits to the interviewee (because people don't come dressed to interviews this way, and we surmise that the interviewee is likely to behave in the same way in other situations).

People do not collect much evidence about covariation before they make attributions (Kelley, 1972); instead, they make snap judgments without much investigation (for instance, finding extenuating circumstances for an interviewee wore shorts). Moreover, people are not very good at perceiving covariation and may apply causal reasoning that does not even fit the evidence. Herriot (1989, pp. 99–100) reviewed this literature and identified the following biases:

- *Self-serving* bias where desirable outcomes are attributed to oneself and undesirable ones to the situation (as when interviewers congratulate themselves upon punctual completion of an interview but blame applicants for running over).
- *False consensus* bias, where we suppose that most people share our expectations, beliefs, and attitudes (as when the interviewer believes that everyone thinks an applicant should never ask a question until

invited to do so at the end of the interview, and considers applicants who violate this as "brash").

- *Actor–observer divergence,* where people tend to attribute their own actions to the situation but when the same actions are carried out by other people attribute them to those people's dispositions (as when an applicant coughing nervously at the start of the interview attributes this behavior to the situation while the interviewer attributes it to the applicant's anxious disposition).
- *Fundamental attribution error,* where people underestimate the situational factors and overestimate the dispositional ones in their evaluation of another's behavior.

Cognitive and motivational explanations underlie these biases. The need to maintain one's self-esteem is likely to cause self-serving bias. False consensus may result from trying to appear "normal" to oneself or others (Herriot, 1989). A cognitive explanation is that actors pay attention to their environment while observers pay attention to the actor. For instance, research has shown that when actors are made to watch themselves on video, they make more dispositional attributions than situational attributions. When observers are shown the actor's point of view on video, they make more situational attributions (Storms, 1973).

Impression Management

Copeland (1993) has described self-presentational motives as "concerns associated with managing one's image, one's appearance in the eyes of other people, or one's self-perception" (p. 119). Another motive is interaction facilitation, which centers on having pleasant interactions with others. In the employment interview, interviewers' perceptions of applicants are positively related to applicant perceptions of interviewers (Macan & Dipboye, 1990). This suggests that applicants evaluate interviewers in terms of the extent to which the interviewers are favorably or unfavorably disposed toward them (Liden, Martin, & Parsons, 1993). Moreover, interviewer dispositions toward applicants are related to interviewers' judgments of the applicants (Phillips & Dipboye, 1989).

Interviewers do not merely assess applicant behavior but also they affect it (Liden, Martin, & Parsons, 1993). Applicants adjust their behavior during the interview depending on how the interviewer appears to be reacting toward them. Individuals reciprocate behavior during an interaction (cf. Street, 1986; Liden, Wayne, & Stilwell, 1993). That is, they adjust their behavior to make it similar to the other person's. For instance, one person's smiling and making eye contact begets similar behavior in the other person. (This is termed *synchrony* by Matarazzo & Wiens, 1972; it is similar to the concept of *synchronicity* used by McGrath to refer to group behavior, described in Chapter 7.) In the employment interview, warm interviewers who smile and maintain eye contact cause applicants to behave in ways that generate a more favorable impression (Liden, Martin, & Parsons, 1993).

Applicant characteristics will also drive positive applicant behavior. Applicants who are high in self-esteem express confidence in having the abilities needed for a job (Liden, Martin, & Parsons, 1993), and they are better able to interpret interviewer behaviors than are applicants with low self-esteem, who are less inclined to believe they are the cause of interviewers' exhibiting positive cues. That is, the interviewee with low self-esteem is likely to attribute favorable interviewer behavior to the interviewer or the environment rather than to their own behavior or performance during the interview. Applicant self-esteem interacts with interviewer behavior in such a way that interviewers who exhibit cold behavior have a more negative effect on the behavior of applicants with low self-esteem than on the behavior of applicants with high self-esteem.

This phenomenon has implications for the validity of the interview. That interviewers' behavior affects applicants suggests that interviewer evaluations may have little to do with the job performance capabilities of the applicant. Interviewers should be trained to understand their potention effects on applicants' behavior.

Structured Interviews

Continuing the preceding line of reasoning, traditional interviews poorly predict actual job performance (Janz, 1989). This may occur because of a weak link between the interviewer's ideas of what is important and what is actually important for job performance. For example, an interviewer may try to assess the applicant's technical competence, but probing the applicant's typical experiences and opinions may not reveal elements of technical competence at all. Interviewer biases and applicant–interviewer impression-management processes are other reasons for low interview validity.

Personnel psychologists have attempted to overcome these difficulties by structuring interviews to elicit relevant behaviors and avoid erroneous interviewer judgments. This shows that the accuracy of person perception and interpersonal judgment can be controlled and enhanced. One approach is the *patterned behavior description interview* (Janz, Hellervik, & Gilmore, 1986), which focuses on determining what the applicant has actually done in the past, not on the applicant's opinions or generalities. The goal is to systematically collect information about *credentials* (objective verifiable information about the applicant that predicts performance) and *behaviors* (detailed accounts of actual events and decisions from the applicant's job and life experiences). Credentials can be efficiently collected from background or biodata forms. The interview can be used to collect behavioral descriptions. This means staying away from surface descriptions of experiences (such as usual duties, capabilities, responsibilities, or practices) and opinions (applicants thoughts about their strengths, weaknesses, plans, goals, and intentions) (Janz, 1989).

A patterned behavior description interview starts with a situation and asks the applicant to recall the most satisfying, most disappointing, most frustrating, or most recent time in the applicant's past that was similar to the situation. The goal is to determine what the applicant did when faced with a series of situations that are relevant to the job.

A variation on the patterned behavior description interview is the *situational interview* (Latham, 1989). Here the applicant is asked, "What would you do if . . . ?". The intention is to derive behavior expectations—what the applicant would be expected to do in a series of critical incidents derived from job analyses. A scoring guide is developed to strengthen agreement among interviewers on what constitute excellent, acceptable, or unacceptable responses to each question. Research on the situational interview reveals high agreement between interviewers, undoubtedly a result of the scoring guide (Janz, 1982). Patterned behavior description interviews that do not use such a guide result in lower interviewer agreement than do traditional interviews. Predictive validities are high because the performance appraisals used as criteria, similar to the situational behaviors, are realistic and concrete behavioral measures (e.g., supervisors using behaviorally anchored rating scales rather than generalized judgments of overall performance) (Latham, 1989).

Conclusion

This chapter has examined how people form impressions of others. Drawing from Heider's early work on person perception, the perspective of the observer ("the eye of the beholder") was deemed critical to understanding how people form insights about others. Individual characteristics affecting interpersonal insight include observation skills, self-monitoring (referring to environmental sensitivity versus self-focus), and empathy. Insights about others emerge from observation of others and from others' self-disclosures.

Cognitive models of person perception applied to the performance appraisal and interview processes suggest the following conclusions:

1. People pay attention to the consistency of information and are likely to make errors when information does not "fit" expectations (for instance, in the case of gender-inconsistent information).

2. People have insight into their own decision making, and they take their beliefs about their own judgment processes into account in making judgments. Moreover, people are often asked to describe to others what is important to them as a means of conveying the reasoning behind their judgments.

3. The purpose of the rating influences memory and judgment processes. If the goal is to make an evaluation, judgments are likely to be formed as the behavior is observed. Thus, later evaluations do not depend on memory for

specific behaviors but on previously formed judgments. As such, processing and ordering information may cause raters to ignore some information when they are asked to predict behavior.

4. Rating accuracy may be conceptualized in a number of ways (e.g., behavioral, classification, and decision-criteria accuracy).

5. Social and situational factors shape rater cognition and evaluation. For instance, appraisals will be more positive when the supervisor believes the subordinate's self-perception is favorable or the supervisor likes the subordinate.

6. Rater motivation, which may be induced by monetary incentives for increased accuracy, increase rater attention, encoding, recall, and integration.

7. Attribution and impression-formation processes and perceptual biases influence interviewer perceptions and judgments. Methods for structuring the collection and analysis of interview information reduce interviewer bias and increase the validity of the interview.

The next chapter applies cognitive processes to how managers receive and interpret performance feedback and how co-workers form perceptions of each other.

5

Perceptual Processes in Giving and Receiving Performance Feedback

> Of course, *understanding* of our fellow-beings is important. But this under-
> standing becomes fruitful only when it is sustained by sympathetic feeling in
> joy and sorrow.
>
> Albert Einstein, *Ideas and Opinions*

This chapter integrates the perceptual processes discussed in the last two
chapters. It deals with how we perceive others and how feedback from others influences our self-perceptions. I draw on image theory, introduced in
Chapter 2, to integrate cognitive, interpersonal, and organizational dynamics that affect ratings and reactions to feedback. I use applied performance
programs, such as 360-degree feedback, as a way to understand underlying
psychological processes. Building on the cognitive processes introduced in
Chapter 2 and used as a basis for understanding self- and interpersonal insight described in the last two chapters, I present a model that recognizes
the parallel information processing of raters and ratees. Components of the
model include rater and ratee self-image and goals, the interpersonal performance environment, and the nature of the rating or feedback program (e.g.,
whether the rating program is for development, evaluation, or both). Outcomes of the model include rater image formation and evaluation and ratee
acceptance and behavioral reactions to feedback. Finally, I propose ways to
study and enhance image accuracy and avoid image distortion.

360-Degree Feedback

In many organizations today, performance appraisal is not the responsibility
of just the immediate supervisor. In the process known as *360-degree feedback,* alternatively called *multisource ratings,* ratees, usually managers, are
evaluated by their subordinates, peers, and supervisors (possibly including
higher-level supervisors along with the immediate supervisor) and maybe by
others as well, such as customers or suppliers who are internal or external

to the organization. Therefore, we need an approach to perceptual processes underlying performance judgments that is general enough to account for multiple sources of information.

The 360-degree feedback process differs from typical performance appraisal in several ways. Information is provided from multiple sources as a way to give the manager more relevant information than would be available from the supervisor alone. As such, the manager has considerably more information available to interpret and integrate than is usually obtained from supervisor feedback. Unlike performance appraisal, the ratings are usually made anonymously. In addition, the information is often intended to serve as guidance for development rather than as an evaluation for placement, promotion, or salary treatment (although 360-degree ratings are used for these purposes in some organizations). Further, the manager is usually asked to provide self-ratings. The feedback report generally consists of item-by-item results for subordinate, supervisors, and peer ratings (averaged for each rater group), the self-rating, and possibly normative data (how, on average, other managers are perceived by their supervisors, peers, and subordinates). The range of ratings may also be reported (e.g., lowest and highest rating received from subordinates).

Thus, 360-degree ratings add a complexity from the raters' and ratees' perspectives that goes beyond traditional supervisor performance appraisal. They impose considerable demands on person perception and information processing, involving issues of self-disclosure, impression management, integration of information, and career development.

In the following sections I present an overview of information processes involved in performance evaluation and reactions to feedback. I examine the image-formation process from the raters' and ratees' viewpoints. Then four moderating conditions are examined: the raters' and ratees' self-concepts and sense of self in relation to others (e.g., similarity to others and perceived fairness of treatment), the raters' and ratees' impression-management tendencies, the interpersonal performance environment, and the assessment situation.

An Information-Processing Model

Figure 5.1 is a two-stage sequential model that describes the parallel perceptual and interpretive processes of the sender and receiver of performance information. Say the focus is the performance of a manager. The sender of information (the rater) forms an image of the manager's behaviors, which is then translated into an evaluation when ratings are made. The receiver of the feedback (the manager) judges the acceptability of the information, and this judgment in turn yields emotional or behavioral reactions and presumably plans and actions for development. Ideally, the information will confirm the effectiveness of past behaviors and/or provide directions for behavior change and performance improvement.

RATER

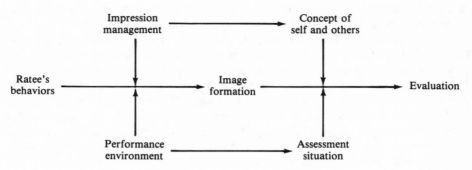

RATEE (THE MANAGER)

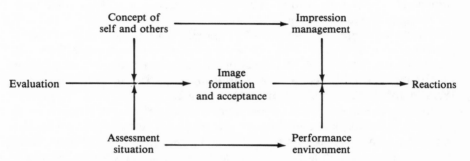

FIGURE 5.1   An information-processing model for 360-degree feedback based on image theory.

Image perception and acceptance are attribution processes that describe how the manager matches the information against expected or accepted prototypes and ascribes internal or external causality. The rater's image formation and evaluation and the ratee's image acceptance and reactions are moderated by environmental conditions and individual characteristics. These moderators enhance the image (increase its accuracy) or distort the image (create an unrealistic or inaccurate conceptualization). The moderators addressed here show how environmental and individual variables may influence image formation, evaluation, and reactions. Other variables may also be relevant, however, and should be included as the model is further developed.

Consider the rater. Perceptions of the manager's behavior are moderated by the rater's impression-management tendencies and the interpersonal performance environment. The latter includes organizational culture, role clarity, job structure, and interpersonal relationships that affect the availability of information and the importance of the manager's behavior to the rater. Once an image is formed, it is translated into an evaluation at the time ratings are made or when there is an informal opportunity to communicate an impression and provide feedback. The relation between the image and the evaluation will depend on the assessment situation and the rater's self-concept. The assessment situation establishes the conditions under which the ratings are made. In the case of 360-degree feedback, the rating process influences whether the image will be conveyed accurately or be distorted, for instance, because of the particular behaviors rated, the rating scale, and the anonymity of the rating. The rater's self-concept will also influence the image–evaluation relationship. For example, the desire to convey a certain message or impression will be likely to affect the evaluation.

In the case of the manager being rated, feedback from multiple sources may be perceived selectively or integrated in a way that makes sense to the manager. The acceptance of the information will depend on the assessment situation and the manager's self-concept and sense of self in relation to others (e.g., similarity to others and need to be fair to others). The assessment situation includes the people who provided the ratings, their importance in relation to the manager, the format for the reporting (e.g., how much information is provided), and the agreement among the raters (evident from information on the range of ratings on each item). Acceptance of information also depends on the extent to which the information is consistent with one's self-concept and/or willingness to accept inconsistent information. Once the information is integrated into one's self-concept, the resulting reactions are affected by the desire to create a certain impression and by the performance environment (the extent to which changing behavior fits with the role and work requirements).

This model is applicable to traditional performance evaluation provided by the supervisor. It also applies to the raters' roles and perspectives in 360-degree feedback and the ratees' reception of different sources of information.

The Image-Formation Process

Image theory, usually applied to decision making, argues that images of values, goals, and plans frame our perceptions and guide our decisions (Beach, 1990; Mitchell & Beach, 1990). When events and alternatives are consistent with our frames of reference, then decisions are made automatically. When inconsistencies (e.g., "frame-breaking" changes) occur, we apply various heuristics to reinterpret the situation or alter our frames of reference.

Performance evaluation requires that raters encode and decode information. Encoding, or the representation and storage of information (DeNisi, Cafferty, & Meglino, 1984), involves categorizing information and making causal inferences. Raters (including self-raters) encode information about the manager from direct observation, indirect information (e.g., what others say about the manager), comparisons with observations of other managers, and comparisons to prototypes of what a manager should be and do. Decoding occurs when the subordinates are asked to make their ratings.

Image theory can explain the encoding processes that occur for ratings of oneself and others. Also, image theory can explain how managers encode (perceive and interpret) the 360-degree feedback results. The manager's self-perceptions and raters' schemas of appropriate and expected managerial behavior guide the integration of information about the manager's behavior and rating process. Information is interpreted in terms of these schemas. Inconsistent information may be ignored or denied; if it is sufficiently strong, it may break the frame of reference and cause a reinterpretation of oneself or of the manager who is being evaluated.

Images are the rater's values or prototypes about a desirable rating in comparison with the manager being rated. Image alternatives that are incompatible with the rater's values, goals, or plans are rejected. Self-ratings, therefore, are unlikely to be low, since such a rating would generally be inconsistent with one's self-concept and desire to view oneself as an effective individual. Extreme judgments are likely to be viewed as exceptions. Their appropriateness will depend on their match to general feelings about the manager and the extent to which the manager fits a prototype (one's sense of what a manager should be or what everyone says the manager is). Images that are not incompatible with this image are accepted.

Cognitive processes come into play when something exceptional is encountered. For instance, raters may not believe that the ratings will be anonymous. If the 360-degree feedback process, when first introduced, is incompatible with the organizational culture (e.g., subordinates and peers are rarely asked for their opinions), then the whole process may be viewed as an exception demanding attention, for instance, by asking oneself or others such questions as: "Will anyone really look at my ratings?" or "Does it matter what I say?" or "Suppose this really makes a difference?"

Another form of exception may stem from the manager being rated. If the manager's behaviors are clearly exceptional (highly positive or negative) and can be attributed to the manager rather than to the policies or situation in the organization (i.e., other managers do not behave the same way), then the rater will form specific goals or intentions, and the rating process becomes a plan to implement these goals (e.g., communicate a poor evaluation). Alternatively, the content of a specific item may be an exception; the item may evoke recall of an unusual behavior, or it may not be familiar at all.

In processing such exceptions, the rater performs a "profitability test" (to use the language of image theory). Raters may search their memories for concrete examples. (The rater may have an opportunity to document these recollections in a written comments section of the rating report.) Cognitive and social perception processes that have been applied to performance appraisal (e.g., Feldman, 1981; DeNisi, Cafferty, & Meglino, 1984) apply to this recollection and interpretation process. These include categorization and attribution.

Categorization and attribution operate in the following way here. Judgments of others stem from observations of, and experience with, the person who is judged (Funder & Colvin, 1988). The closer the relationship, the more information the rater has to recall and integrate. However, information processing (e.g., attention, categorization, recall, and integration) occurs by means of automatic or controlled categorization processes (Feldman, 1981). Automatic (unconscious) categorization occurs when ratees can be easily categorized based on observable characteristics. For instance, raters gravitate to information on performance dimensions that are viewed as important to the job and organization (e.g., knowledge, productivity, and attendance). Experienced raters seek this information earlier in the rating process, and they gather more information on these dimensions than on others (Werner, 1994).

Controlled (conscious) categorization occurs when decisions are problematic, for example, information is inconsistent, ambiguous, or unusual. In such cases the decisions are based on internal or external attributions of causality. Unusual or distinctive conditions that vary with the occurrence of an event are perceived as a cause of the event. These events may be situations and tasks (e.g., unusually high work demands) or people (whose behavior departs from what others do). When behavior covaries with the event, then observers attribute the event to the individual. When the actor has been categorized previously, then new observations that could be attributed to either the individual or the situation are likely to be attributed to the individual, discounting the situation.

Prototype matching assigns a person to a particular category. When ratees cannot be easily assigned to a category, conscientious observers may establish impressions by seeking new information, with selective attention to information that confirms a likely opinion. Alternatively, raters may reconstruct past information. Information is selectively integrated, resulting in a positive or negative evaluation (Cronshaw & Lord, 1987). While infrequently occurring behaviors that disconfirm an image of the manager may be ignored, behaviors that are aprototypical may lead raters to determine the locus of causality for the behavior. When subordinates see that peers of the manager behave the same way as the manager, subordinates are likely to attribute the behavior to external causes. When the manager behaves differently from others, the behavior is likely to be attributed to internal causes, and more extreme ratings will be provided.

Category-based processing occurs in performance appraisal when a manager considers a subordinate to be a good performer. The request to evaluate the subordinate elicits traits that are typical of good performers, not necessarily an accurate description or judgment of the subordinate's behavior. That is, the judgment is biased toward the category evaluation (Feldman,

1981; Kulik & Ambrose, 1993). More difficult feature-based processing is necessary when the manager cannot make a category match. This is more likely to result in a more accurate rating because it requires more deliberate attention to, and integration of, information about the subordinate (Favero & Ilgen, 1989).

The Receiver of Feedback

Turning to managers as receivers of feedback, several elements of feedback are relevant to how they react to performance results. The most obvious is favorability of the ratings. Positive reactions to feedback are more likely when the results are favorable. Others are agreement between the manager's self-ratings and the others' ratings, agreement among the others' ratings, extremity of ratings, and differentiation among items or dimensions (i.e., the extent to which favorability or agreement varies by item or sets of items); these are discussed in the following. Another pertinent variable is the inclusion of norms as part of the results (i.e., how other managers, on the average, were rated on each item). Such information provides an anchor for the manager's self-evaluation and self-regulation (Earley & Erez, 1991). Norms can influence an individual's self-efficacy expectations, personal goals, and performance. When norms are not provided, information for comparison will not be readily available, and how others are rated is less likely to be salient.

Consider agreement between self- and others' ratings, using subordinate ratings as an example. Managers may behave differently with different subordinates, especially if the subordinates' task requirements and capabilities vary. If self-ratings are inflated, as is commonly the case (Farh, Dobbins, & Cheng, 1991), and ratings from others are more accurate, then disagreement is likely between subordinate and self-ratings; therefore, it is important to understand disagreement between the manager and subordinates. Self–subordinate agreement may be a function of organizational and biographical variables, as reported earlier. Managers cannot easily discount the results when there is high agreement among subordinates. However, low agreement among subordinates provides an opportunity to discount results. (Agreement in ratings has been measured by differences between the manager's self-rating and the average subordinate rating and by an index called *pattern agreement*—the correlation across items between the average subordinate ratings and the self-ratings; Wohlers & London, 1989; London & Wohlers, 1991. See Chapter 3's review of this topic that includes the suggestion that agreement between self- and others' ratings is likely to be associated with higher performance—an argument made by Bass & Yammarino, 1991, and Yammarino & Atwater, 1993.)

The results of 360-degree feedback may be subject to several rating artifacts. For instance, extreme means for subordinate ratings will be associated with decreased variability (increased agreement) among subordinates. Differentiation among items will be associated with less agreement among subordinates because of increased variance likely for items that are rated in the center of the scale. Despite these possible artifacts, several areas for investigation arise. For instance, we would want to know whether higher agreement among subordinates is associated with higher agreement between self- and subordinate ratings. Also, we would want to know whether higher agreement among subordinates results in greater attention from the manager, especially when the subordinates' ratings disagree with the manager's self-ratings. Such questions link the results to the manager's encoding process in evaluating 360-degree feedback.

How a manager encodes 360-degree feedback results depends on rating scale characteristics and the amount of information presented. As such, the encoding process may require judgments of means, variances, and probabilities of accuracy in relation to the manager's self-concept. Managers are likely to make two probability judgments in receiving 360-degree feedback: the probability that the information received is true and the probability that the information can or will have some instrumental outcomes. One instrumental outcome is the extent to which the information can be used to guide behavior change. Another is the probability that the results will have some positive or negative consequence, such as more or less merit pay. In addition, the results may affect the subordinates if, for instance, the group members receive copies of the feedback report or if the subordinates surmise the results and feel the manager's reaction is not what they wanted.

Interpreting 360-degree feedback is likely to be a process of image matching and confirming, especially when the feedback is ambiguous or detailed. Managers who believe that a rating result is common (received by their coworkers) will attribute the behavior to external factors. The less common or more extreme the rating and the more it fits a prototype, the more internal attributions are likely. When the feedback is exceptional (unusual) or self-perceptions differ from subordinate perceptions, the manager will search for a way to categorize and attribute the cause of the behavior. Categorization will increase internal attributions. Exceptional behavior that is not exhibited by other managers will be attributed to internal factors. Inconsistent feedback provides an opportunity for selective interpretation and external attribution of extreme ratings, for instance, attributing the feedback to the source (e.g., disgruntled subordinates or jealous peers).

The use of 360-degree feedback should improve *resolution* and *calibration* skills in making subsequent judgments (Sharp, Cutler, & Penrod, 1988). Resolution is the manager's ability to discriminate correct from incorrect judgments by differentially assigning confidence levels to accurate and inaccurate judgments. Calibration is the ability to assign appropriate probability levels to judgments about the likelihood of an answer being correct. Overconfident managers are likely to assign greater probabilities than are warranted by available information, and underconfident managers are likely to assign lower probabilities than are warranted.

Judgments of confidence in the information are important in believing the feedback and acting on it. The more managers participate in 360-degree feedback programs, the more experience they have in understanding the accuracy of the information. Also, the better they know their subordinates (e.g., the closer or longer they work with them), the more confidence they should have in their subordinates' judgments. Frequency of evaluation may influence perceived fairness and accuracy of a performance evaluation (Landy, Barnes-Farrell, & Cleveland, 1980).

Effects of Rater Agreement on Reactions to Feedback. Agreement among the raters providing feedback is likely to be important in how managers feel about the feedback and the extent to which it influences their self-image. Casey (1993) conducted a laboratory study of how people react to consistent and inconsistent feedback from others. Student subjects were asked to suppose how a hypothetical manager would feel receiving feedback from two supervisors. The feedback was manipulated to be either the same (i.e., consistent) or different. Moreover, it was varied to be higher or lower than the hypothetical manager's self-assessment. The mixed feedback included one supervisory rating that was higher than the manager's self-assessment and one that was lower, such that the average of the two supervisory ratings equaled the self-assessment. The consistent feedback was equal to, higher, or lower than the manager's self-assessment. The subjects thought that the manager would be happier with equal feedback as long as it was the same as or higher than their self-assessment. However, they felt that the manager receiving mixed feedback would have a higher postfeedback assessment.

Casey (1993) used prospect theory's concept of loss aversion to explain why people prefer the consistent information. (Prospect theory was introduced in Chapter 2 as an explanation for how people frame perceptions of loss and gain.) In the mixed-feedback condition, people's aversion to negative information may have outweighed their satisfaction with the positive information. However, when it came to reevaluating one's self-assessment, the ambiguity in the mixed feedback provided justification for, or at least allowed, self-enhancement. The finding of higher satisfaction with consistent information was not due merely to subjects preferring unambiguous feedback since they preferred mixed feedback when their self-rating was equal to and higher than the others' ratings.

Casey (1993) suggested that the affective reaction to feedback may occur at a different time than the revision of one's self-assessment. While the subjects seemed to believe that people avoid feedback that is lower than their self-assessment even when another opinion is more positive, this may be an initial and transient reaction; once this emotion is absorbed and there is a chance for reevaluating one's self-image, self-enhancement takes hold. At this point the subjects may presume that the managers ignore the feedback that was lower than their self-assessment (or attribute it to external causes) and accentuate the rating that was higher than their self-assessment (or attribute it to internal causes).

Thus, receiving consistent information, or at least information that suggests agreement among raters, is important to avoiding biases that may affect reactions to the feedback and later revision of self-image. More research is needed to understand the sequential process by which people react to feedback and use the information to revise their self-image. However, in relation to the cognitive model of self-assessment outlined in Chapter 2, Casey's (1993) intriguing findings suggest that the initial categorization of information may be altered later, after the individual gives it some thought. This does not mean that the information will be perceived accurately. The initial bias in favor of consistent information, because of an aversion to loss occurring with the mixed feedback, gives way to feeling the need for an attribution. The attribution process is then biased in favor of the more positive feedback. The self-enhancement bias was less likely to occur when the feedback was consistent, even when the initial self-rating was fairly high.

Note that Casey's study asked subjects to think about how they view others who are receiving feedback. This may be typical of situations in which we are discussing how acquaintances are likely to react to information about themselves. Research is needed to understand the cognitive evaluation sequence over time as people receive feedback about themselves. Further, research is needed to test the effects of rater agreement (e.g., degree of variance) on reactions to, and use of, the feedback.

Acceptance and Use of Feedback. Feedback acceptance refers to the recipients' evaluation of the accuracy of the feedback. Feedback acceptance is important because it can lead to setting meaningful, realistic goals that, in turn, improve performance (Ilgen, Fisher, & Taylor, 1979; Taylor, Fisher, & Ilgen, 1984). Feedback acceptance is especially important when objective performance information is not available.

DeGregorio (1991) investigated the effects of congruence between external feedback and self-assessments of performance on feedback acceptance. Feedback acceptance was higher when external feedback was more favorable than self-assessment and lower when the external feedback disagreed with the self-assessment. Also, self-assessment carried more weight than external judgments of performance in influencing overall performance judgments after all information was received. Other research found that perceived fairness and accuracy of performance evaluation is associated with trust in the source (Fulk, Brief, & Barr, 1985).

Managers who are high in self-confidence are likely to be low in evaluation apprehension and ego protection. As a result, they are likely to welcome 360-degree feedback. In general, people who are high in self-esteem rate themselves high in performance, especially when the appraisal is done on ambiguous performance dimensions (Harris & Schaubroeck, 1988; Farh, Dobbins, & Cheng, 1991). People often have a self-serving bias, so they tend to take credit for success and attribute blame to external causes (Levy, 1991). However, people who are high in internal control are likely to make more accurate attributions and be willing to attribute negative events to themselves and attribute positive events to others when appropriate. Those low in internal control and self-confidence are more likely to rate themselves leniently and protect themselves from criticism (Levy, 1991; Yammarino & Atwater, 1993). Thus, self-confidence and internal control become a foundation for seeking and receiving accurate information about oneself.

Insight about oneself and the environment stems from accurate interpretation of feedback. Individuals who are high in self-confidence and self-insight are likely to engage in self-assessment and self-regulation, as discussed in Chapter 3. Those who are low in these characteristics are likely to deny or avoid negative feedback and, in general, try to control the feedback they receive. Managers' tendencies to seek negative feedback can increase the accuracy of their understanding about how others evaluate their work (Ashford & Tsui, 1991). Also, seeking negative feedback can enhance the source's opinions of the manager's overall effectiveness, while seeking positive feedback can decrease the source's opinions.

Feedback Seeking

As indicated in Chapter 3, people engage in self-regulating behavior. Feedback seeking is an important part of the process of self-regulation (Ashford & Tsui, 1991). Self-appraisal requires information seeking (Klimoski & Brice, 1991); feedback seeking can be a means of collecting accurate information. In terms of the Johari Window, described in Chapter 1, it is a way to increase quadrant 1 (the area of information that is known to both self and others). However, feedback seeking can also be a way to manage others' impressions. As such, there are three motives for feedback seeking: to obtain useful information, to protect one's ego or self-esteem, and to control how one appears to others (impression management; Ashford & Cummings, 1983; Morrison & Bies, 1991). Feedback seeking may be a joint process in that a performance review discussion may be initiated by the manager or by the subordinate in the process of seeking feedback (Klimoski & Brice, 1991). In either case, the discussion involves an exploration and analysis of performance information.

People weigh various costs and benefits when deciding whether to ask an individual for feedback. Morrison and Vancouver (1993) investigated what determines the decision to ask a particular source for feedback. They considered multiple dimensions that might influence the choice—in particular, the source's expertise, accessibility, quality of the relationship with the individual, and reward power (the source's ability to affect positive and negative outcomes). Sixty-four undergraduate students reviewed sixteen written scenarios that asked them to imagine that they were working on a draft paper and were considering asking someone for feedback. The potential feedback source was then described, with the description varying on the four dimensions. The results showed differences across the participants in the importance of three of the four variables to the decision. Students with high need for achievement and self-esteem chose sources high in expertise and relationship quality. Those with high performance expectations chose sources high in reward power.

Karl and Kopf (1993) asked whether individuals who need to improve the performance the most will volunteer to receive videotaped feedback. They studied ninety undergraduate students who gave an oral presentation. Those who needed to improve their performance the most were least likely to seek feedback. Those who chose not to receive feedback were also lower in self-esteem and self-efficacy.

Rater-Ratee Similarity

Perceptual psychology, introduced in Chapter 1, explains why people vary in their perception of the same phenomenon. Since people do not have identical perceptual fields, they will not necessarily impose the same meanings and interpretations on their perceptions. However, the more they have in common, the more likely they are to see things the same way (Combs, Richards, & Richards, 1988). Social comparison theory, described in Chapter 2, suggests that people evaluate their opinions and abilities by comparing themselves with others, particularly those who are similar to themselves (Festinger, 1954).

Just being told about how similar our attitudes are to others' attitudes can influence our attraction toward others even when we have no explicit information about others' attitudes. College students who were informed that their attitudes were similar to a stranger's rated themselves more attracted to the stranger than those receiving no information about the stranger's attitude similarity (Hoyle, 1993). Students who were told their attitudes were dissimilar to the stranger's were least attracted to the stranger.

The similarity between the manager and subordinate may determine the closeness of the relationship that develops between them. Similar people see each other as more attractive and likable than dissimilar people (Byrne, 1971). Also, similarity may increase self-disclosure, which in turn may influence agreement between self-ratings and subordinate ratings. Self-disclosure has been related to similarity in race (Ridley, 1986; deJung & Kaplan, 1962). Race may also affect the level of ratings. In studies of performance appraisal, black raters rated black ratees higher than white ratees while white raters rated black ratees lower than whites (Hamner et al., 1974; Bigoness, 1976a, 1976b). In their study of 360-degree feedback ratings, Wohlers, Hall, and London (1993) found higher agreement between manager self-ratings and subordinate ratings for same-race than different-race manager–subordinate dyads.

Another potentially relevant variable is age. Older people disclose more about themselves to others, especially to other older people, than do younger people (Brown, 1989). However, older employees are often rated more negatively than younger employees (Rosen & Jerdee, 1988), perhaps because of stereotypes about the age-appropriateness of different jobs. Older workers may not be rated as highly as younger people on the same jobs (Cleveland & Landy, 1983; Cleveland & Berman, 1987; Lawrence, 1988). Wohlers, Hall, and London (1993) found that managers over age fifty-five rated themselves more favorably than their subordinates rated them.

Gender is another likely important variable. Females disclose more about themselves to others than do males (Taylor, 1979, p. 127; Rosenfeld, Civikly, & Herron, 1979). Reisman (1990) found that females were perceived by young adults as more self-disclosing of their feelings and problems than men. London and Wohlers (1993) discovered that subordinates' ratings were more likely to agree with female managers' self-ratings than with male managers' self-ratings, regardless of the subordinate's gender.

In other research males disclosed more to females and females disclosed more to males than did either males or females to those of the same gender (Brooks, 1974). In another study men did not feel as close to same-gender friends as did women, and men believed that they would be more open to females than to males (Reisman, 1990). We would expect that higher self-disclosure by managers to opposite-gender subordinates would lead to higher self–subordinate agreement than would occur for same-gender boss–subordinate pairs.

How people are treated can bias their perceptions of others. In the case of employment selection, women who knew they were selected for a job based on preference for their gender rather than merit were more likely to react negatively to women applicants for entry-level positions (Heilman et al., 1993). Apparently, being selected based on gender weakens regard for one's own and others' accomplishments. Gender-based preferential selection results in negative perceptions of others' competence when individuals (women or men) lack confidence in their ability (Heilman, Lucas, & Kaplow, 1990).

Perceptions of Fairness

Another dynamic in 360-degree feedback ratings is procedural justice. Norms of reciprocity may evolve among work-group members, with the implicit assumption that managers will evaluate each other favorably. For example, subordinates who receive favorable ratings may feel obliged to rate the manager favorably, or the subordinates' evaluation of the manager may be favorably biased when the subordinates receive a favorable performance evaluation. Midlevel managers usually participate in the 360-degree feedback process by rating their bosses in addition to rating themselves and receiving feedback from their subordinates. The manager's values may create a "Golden Rule" response set (i.e., "Rate others as fairly as I want to be rated," or "Rate others as highly as I want to be rated"). Raters may feel morally obligated to rate themselves and their boss against the same standard. Thus, applying image theory, raters may have an image for the fairness and/or appropriate favorability of the ratings. This may temper (inflate) their ratings of their bosses. It may also decrease the leniency of self-ratings.

The first part of this chapter presented an information-processing model that explains the formation of images about oneself and others. Acceptance of feedback was linked to objective aspects, such as rater–ratee similarity, that characterize the relationship between the observer and the receiver of feedback. The next section considers how people attempt to manage impressions others have of them.

Impression Management

Rating practices may be a form of impression management (Villanova & Bernardin, 1989). A subordinate's defensive tactics may deflate ratings in order to attribute his or her poor performance to the manager, or may inflate ratings in order to maintain a friendship with the manager. Assertive tactics may deflate ratings to demonstrate the subordinate's independence of the manager, or may inflate ratings to comply with the manager's expressed desire for favorable 360-degree feedback, perhaps to demonstrate the excellence of the work group compared with other groups in the department. These tactics may become long-term strategies to maintain favorable treatment from the manager or demonstrate the manager's lack of ability.

People use self-descriptions of their personal characteristics and feelings to influence how others see them. In part, people disclose more about themselves to others they know well. So, for instance, we would expect that managers disclose more about themselves to in-group members (those members of the work group who have a close working relationship with the supervisor) than to out-group members (Graen, 1976). However, as suggested earlier, some people provide accounts of events in ways that enhance the desirable implications of the events for themselves. Subordinates' impression-management attempts may increase managers' performance ratings of them (Wayne & Kacmar, 1991). Managers may also try to affect the impressions their subordinates and co-workers have of them, especially if 360-degree feedback occurs regularly. Given the importance of people viewing managers favorably because of their visibility within the organization (Wortman & Linsenmeier, 1977), managers are likely to attempt to portray themselves as favorably as possible to subordinates. Managers are most likely to convey a favorable impression to subordinates with whom they are familiar and feel comfortable. Some managers behave in ways that communicate favorable information about themselves to all subordinates, trying to create and maintain a public image that is consistent with their ideal self (Baumeister, 1982).

Impression management includes the behaviors people exhibit and the process of self-disclosure to create and maintain desired impressions (Gardner, 1991). Morrison and Bies (1991) examined impression management in the feedback-seeking process and found that feedback seeking depends in part on the effects of asking for information on the individual's public image. For instance, they proposed that asking for information will be positively related to the probability that the message will enhance one's public image. This guides when to ask for information (e.g., sooner after a favorable event than an unfavorable event, and when the source is in a good mood), whom to ask (e.g., good performers ask sources who have high reward power and poor performers ask sources who have low reward power), and how to ask (e.g., phrase feedback requests in ways that focus the source's attention on favorable aspects of the performance). Concern for what others think will be greater when the seeker is dependent on the source for feedback and rewards, when feedback is public, and when a formal performance evaluation is imminent. Also, according to Morrison and Beis (1991), situational ambiguity and propensity to engage in social influence will be positively related to impression management.

Impression management may be assertive (such as ingratiation, intimidation, or self-promotion) or defensive (such as apologies, restitution, and disclaimers) (Kumar & Beyerlein, 1991; Tedeschi & Norman, 1985, Wayne & Kacmar, 1991; Gardner, 1991). Indirect impression-management tactics may be attempts to connect oneself to (or separate oneself from) an event or another person (e.g., "boasting"—linking oneself to a favorable event; and "burying"—disclaiming a link to an unfavorable event; Cialdini, 1989; Gardner, 1991).

Ferris, Judge, Rowland, and Fitzgibbons (1994) distinguished between job-focused influence tactics (e.g., "Try to make a positive event that you are responsible for appear greater than it actually is") and supervisor-focused influence tactics (e.g., "Praise your immediate supervisor on his or her accomplishments"). They found that employees engage in influence tactics directed at the supervisor when the subordinates and supervisors work in close proximity. Job-focused influence tactics did not depend on distance. Supervisor-focused tactics (essentially ingratiation behaviors) lead to higher supervisor affect for the subordinate; however, job-focused tactics (essentially self-promotion of one's competence), lead to lower supervisor affect toward the subordinate. Ferris et al. (1994) surmised that job-focused tactics are less situationally appropriate than supervisor-focused tactics. Impression management is discussed further in the next chapter, which addresses the development of interpersonal relationships.

Confirmation Bias

Expectancy confirmation is a bias that causes one to behave in a way that confirms expectations or simply to interpret information in a way that confirms expectations (Copeland, 1993; Jussim, 1991). This is how stereotypes influence people's perceptions. However, the expectancy confirmation process can be weakened by motivating people to achieve goals that are counter to expectancy confirmation. Alternatively, expectancy confirmation can be strengthened by motivating people to form quick or unchanging impressions. This has implications for improving rater accuracy, and it suggests the potential value of insight training (Chapter 9).

People who are motivated to form stable, predictable impressions will use social information to develop impressions that confirm their preinteraction expectations (Copeland, 1993; Snyder, 1992; Snyder & Haugen, 1990; Snyder, Tanke, & Berscheid, 1977). People who consciously try to be accurate in forming an impression of another individual will be less biased in information gathering than are people who are trying to form a rapid impression (as a manager might in evaluating a job candidate during an employment interview) (Copeland, 1993; Neuberg, 1989). Thus, stability of impression differs from accuracy. Training, or simply instructing, someone (e.g., a manager or an interviewer) to form stable, predictable impressions is likely to result in the perceiver merely confirming his or her initial expectations. This is less likely if the perceiver is asked to form an accurate impression.

Thus, there are different ways to improve accuracy of perceptions and avoid expectancy confirmation. In general, the preceding discussion suggests that the images conveyed depend on the intentions of the individual observed as well as the observer. The following section extends the discussion to the effects of the situation on impressions and ratings, as referred to in Figure 5.1.

The Interpersonal Performance Environment

As stated earlier, the performance environment includes the organization's climate, role clarity, task interdependence, and work-group relationships. Organizational climate connotes the favorability of the relationships in the organization—for instance, the extent to which people cooperate, communicate, and work effectively with each other and with those outside the organization (Reichers & Schneider, 1990; Beyer, 1981). The results of 360-degree feedback can be viewed as a measure of climate. At the organizational level of analysis, culture and climate set the frame for 360-degree feedback. For instance, asking subordinates for input on the manager's performance may be consistent with the organization's values and decisions (e.g., in a participative culture with open and honest communication), or it may be an unusual intrusion (e.g., in a staid, hierarchical structure with clear roles and boundaries between organizational levels).

Another frame established by the organization may be prototypical managerial behaviors—those that are expected, desired, and rewarded in the organization. Prototypes of leaders include behaviors such as delaying action, planning, emphasizing group goals, coordinating the group's activities, and letting group members know what is expected of them (Cronshaw & Lord, 1987). Aprototypical behaviors may include worrying over other group members' ideas, wanting one's own way on issues, being confused about an issue, refusing to explain actions, and letting other group members decide what to do (Cronshaw & Lord, 1987). The prototypical manager may be a reflection of the organization's need for leadership. As such, the prototype may be deliberately established and encouraged by the organization when, for instance, top executives describe desired leadership behaviors and reward these behaviors by promotion and merit pay. On the other hand, the organization may give little attention to the prototypical manager, and typical behavior may show little attention to the quality of boss–subordinate relationships. Thus, 360-degree feedback ratings may be made in relation to a frame of reference (shared expectations) of desired or typical managerial behavior.

Managers seem to define performance more broadly than do performance appraisal systems. That is, in addition to seeking information about dimensions that are defined as important to the job and the organization, such as productivity and knowledge, managers also seek information about dimensions that go beyond role requirements, for instance, evidence of dependability, following rules, cooperation, and extra effort (Werner, 1994). Moreover, ratings on these extra-role behaviors result in halo because they weaken differentiation among all the performance dimensions (Werner, 1994). Thus, information about behaviors that are aprototypical (that is, somehow special or unusual) influence perceptions of behaviors on prototypical areas of performance.

Opportunity to Observe

Close supervision is likely to be required when subordinate tasks are interdependent. The close working relationships among subordinates and peers and the attention they receive from the manager increase opportunities for raters to observe the manager in the same context. This is reinforced by a mutual dependence between raters and the manager (Thompson, 1967; Galbraith, 1977). For instance, the subordinates may depend on the manager for direction, and the manager depends on subordinates for work-group outcomes.

In a study of upward feedback, London and Wohlers (1991) demonstrated the potential importance of job structures and organizational context to agreement between managers' self-ratings and subordinates' ratings of the manager. Agreement was higher in line units than in staff units. An explanation may be that subordinates' jobs were similar in the line units, and so the manager behaved similarly with most subordinates. In staff units, subordinates' jobs were dissimilar, requiring different types of manager–subordinate interactions, depending on the job demands. Other research on 360-degree ratings found higher self–subordinate agreement in military and large corporations than in government/nonmilitary and small private corporations (Wohlers, Hall, & London, 1993). This may be because the manager–subordinate relationship is highly structured in military and large corporations but less so in other government agencies and in small private firms.

Interpersonal relationships provide a frame for expected behaviors and reactions. Managers may establish an environment of frequent and open communication, sharing of personal information, close friendships, and cooperative working relationships. In such an atmosphere, 360-degree feedback probably occurs naturally, and a formal 360-degree feedback process facilitates or complements the relationships. Alternatively, the work-group or particular manager–subordinate relationships may be characterized by distant and formal relationships, which are antithetical to 360-degree feedback.

Theory on role development in work groups suggests that differential relationships may emerge between the manager and subordinates or peers, forming an in-group and out-group. In-group members have higher-quality social exchanges with the manager and with each other than do out-group members (Graen, 1976; Graen & Scandura, 1987). People are likely to divulge more about themselves and try to convey more positive impressions about themselves to those they know well or work with more closely (e.g., in-group members) than to those they do not. People tend to perceive out-group members as more homogeneous than in-group members (Linville, Fischer, & Salovey, 1989). Therefore, ratings of the manager by out-group raters may reflect stereotypes rather than actual behavior and self-disclosed information. In-group ratings may be subject to less restriction of range and may more closely reflect actual behavior and self-disclosed information about the manager than do ratings by out-group subordinates.

The heterogeneity of work-group members and the favorability of relationships in the work group may also influence 360-degree feedback ratings. An examination of group heterogeneity with respect to age, tenure, education level, and a variety of career experiences found that group dissimilarity was related to turnover, and that reliance on internal recruitment predicted subsequent team homogeneity (Jackson et al., 1991).

So far, the discussion of the environment has focused on the work context. Another situational factor in the information-processing model, described next, has to do with the context for the ratings and the actual results.

The Assessment Situation

The effects of the assessment situation refer to how the rating and feedback processes are developed and introduced, the extent to which providing the ratings is viewed by the rater as potentially threatening, the clarity of the feedback report, and the use of group ratings. A brief review of these features of the assessment situation is provided here; more specific information and guidelines about the design and content of the 360-degree feedback process are covered in Chapter 10.

Involving employees in the design of the feedback process should enhance their interest in providing useful ratings. For instance, employees may be involved in writing items that are important from their perspective (e.g., suggesting items that are important to boss–subordinate relationships in the organization). This should ensure the relevance of the items. Moreover, participation in the development of the process should enhance the employees' commitment to it and increase their conscientiousness in making the ratings.

From the manager's perspective as recipient of information, knowing that co-workers were involved in the design of the process should increase the salience of the feedback.

The uses and consequences of the feedback should be clear. In some cases the information is meant only for development purposes. That is, the manager receives a feedback report and perhaps attends a general debriefing session describing the format of the report and potential application of results. However, it is up to managers to synthesize their results, draw conclusions, and formulate development plans. There is no requirement to share the results with higher management. In other cases the results may be available and used by higher management to make salary or promotion decisions about the manager.

In 360-degree feedback, raters should understand that their ratings will be anonymous. Data should not be collected or reported unless there is a sufficient number of subordinates or peers to guard the confidentiality of the rater. This is especially important when the feedback report includes the range as well as average ratings separated by subgroup (results from peers differentiated from subordinates). Four or five raters are generally a sufficient number within each subgroup.

Klimoski and Inks (1990) investigated whether knowing the subordinate's self-rating and anticipating giving face-to-face feedback to the subordinate affected the favorability of the rating. They found that supervisors (students participating in a work simulation) who anticipated sharing face-to-face feedback with a subordinate rated the subordinate's performance significantly more positively than did supervisors who received no self-assessment information. This suggests the importance of social pressure implied by future face-to-face interaction.

Another social force may be that supervisors tend to provide ratings that correspond to the subordinate's self-image. In addition to the earlier finding on the effects of anticipating face-to-face feedback, Klimoski and Inks (1990) reported that supervisors who received knowledge of a favorable self-assessment rated their subordinates significantly more positively than those receiving low self-assessment information. When no self-assessment information was available, supervisors rated their subordinates less positively than did those receiving high self-assessment but less negatively than did others who received low subordinate self-assessments. Meyer (1991) recommended that self-assessments be used at the start of the performance feedback session as a way of defusing the subordinate's defensiveness. This would be problematic if subordinates purposely distorted their self-assessments in a positive direction in the past and noticed a favorable effect upon the rater (Klimoski & Inks, 1990). Klimoski and Inks (1990) suggest that more accurate self-assessments might be expected if the performance feedback is for developmental purposes and the supervisor is acting as coach.

Modes of information about a subordinate's performance are likely to differ in the degree to which they produce distinct features that result in category-based processing. The more ambiguous and complex the information, the more likely it will defy categorization and produce feature-based processing requiring attributions and evaluations of the target. Kulik and Ambrose (1993) tested this idea by varying two modes: computer performance monitoring (CPM), which presents descriptions of performance results, often in quantitative terms (e.g., statistics about output, such as number of words typed by a secretary), and visual data, such as observations of actual behavior (recorded on videotape for purposes of the study). Undergraduate students were given information about a secretary interacting with others. The subjects obtained both CPM and visual information, each source providing either positive or negative information, resulting in a 2 (mode of information) × 2 (favorability of information) research design. Category-based processing was evident from faster response time to questions about the secretary and less accurate recall. Controlled, feature-based processing was evident from the reverse.

The study found that category-based processing occurred for positive visual information while feature-based processing occurred for negative visual information. CPM information did not influence the type of information processing. A follow-up study suggested that CPM data are not viewed as strongly as visual data, especially if the information is negative. Thus, negative visual information resulted in more controlled processing. Visual data span a larger number of dimensions than CPM data; negative information cued the need for more attention, and subjects were reluctant to use less demanding processing strategies that may not provide a fair evaluation of negative information. These findings allay some fears that CPM systems data (i.e., computer reports of units produced) will outweigh other information in a performance appraisal. In fact, the reverse may occur, although not if subjects have to justify their evaluations or provide face-to-face feedback (Klimoski & Inks, 1990). Kulik and Ambrose (1993) suggest that when CPM data are used, pains should be taken to ensure their vividness, for instance, with color graphics, to avoid raters' tendency to make categorizations.

Mode of information may interact with individual characteristics to influence reactions to feedback. Ellis and Kruglanski (1992) found that people with high self-ascribed authority benefited more from experientially based information than those with low self-ascribed authority. They studied 105 female college students participating in learning mathematics through an experiential method involving active participation in the learning process versus traditional instructor-led training. Those who believed they were authorities on the topic were more receptive to learning through participation.

The rating format is another situational factor. The last chapter described distributional scales that ask the rater to indicate the percentage of the ratee's time that is described by each level of performance (Steiner, Rain, & Smalley, 1993). The measures generate central tendency and dispersion indexes of performance. An open question is whether such an evaluation procedure and the richer, yet more complex, feedback information produces different reactions than traditional rating methods. The differentiation in ratings may be more fine-tuned and possibly more accurate than simpler rating methods, but there is also room for more disagreement among raters. Research is needed to examine various indexes of agreement and the effects of agreement on the ratee's attitude to feedback results from such a rating method in comparison with other evaluation methods. This suggests considering another situational factor, the clarity of report format.

Report clarity is likely to affect how well the ratees understand the results. The reports can become complex when they include average scores, ranges, and norms for subordinate, peer, and self-ratings. These may be provided for each item or for groups of items based on factor analysis. The methods used for grouping items into factors or scales should be made clear. Orientation programs may be needed to explain the report format and guide managers in its use.

Peer group discussions of subordinates' performance may be a way to clarify the rater's image of the ratee and increase rating accuracy. Martell and Borg (1993) compared performance ratings made by interacting groups to ratings by individuals. Students rated written vignettes of police officer performance. Ratings were made on a behavioral checklist during a twenty-five-minute rating process (group discussion or individual rating). Groups did not differ from individuals when the rating occurred immediately following observation of performance. After a five-day delay, however, groups remembered the behaviors more accurately than did individuals. Groups showed greater response bias in that they applied a more liberal decision criterion than did individuals. The study suggests that group discussion can be a way to help raters recollect behaviors contributing to performance. Organizations often use groups of peer managers to rank and rate the performance of subordinates in their units. The peer group acts as a check to ensure that behaviors are recalled and performance ratings are defended. Organizations may do well to require peer group discussions before individual ratings are made as a way to enhance recollection and reduce rating errors. (Chapter 7 addresses how interpersonal insight operates in groups.)

Last but not least, the organization's reward system should be structured to reward supervisors who make accurate appraisals, give constructive feedback, pay attention to their subordinates' development, and pay attention to their own development. In this way employee development becomes a key element of effective management tied to the organization's strategies (London & Mone, 1994). Support for employee development should be incorporated into the measurement and appraisal system, including subordinate ratings of managers' support. Directions for development should stem from the organization's goals and job requirements and an evaluation of employees' skills and abilities. A research challenge is to determine ways to evaluate and track rater accuracy, perhaps by correlating performance appraisals with objective measures of performance.

Conclusion

As 360-degree feedback grows in popularity, research will be needed to improve and facilitate the process. The information-processing model presented in this chapter describes the parallel perceptual and interpretive processes of the sender (the rater) and the receiver (the manager) of performance information. The sender of information forms images of the manager's behaviors, which are then translated into evaluations when ratings are made. The receiver of the feedback evaluates the acceptability of the information, which in turn yields emotional and/or behavioral reactions, including plans for development. The manager matches the information against expected or accepted prototypes and ascribes internal or external causality. The manager's image formation and evaluation and the rater's image acceptance and reactions are moderated by environmental conditions and individual characteristics. These moderators enhance the image (increase its accuracy) or distort the image.

The discussion of the moderators of agreement and acceptance of feedback, including impression management, confirmation bias, and factors in the performance and assessment situations, suggests the following:

1. Raters are more accurate when they are self-confident, are similar to the ratee, and believe in norms of reciprocity and fairness; managers see themselves more accurately when they are self-confident, similar to the rater, and have a sense of procedural justice.

2. Raters distort their ratings when they use the feedback process to manage impressions and/or confirm expectations. Managers distort feedback when they try to manage rater's impressions of them, confirm expectations, and avoid self-disclosure.

3. Raters are more accurate and ratees are more accepting of feedback when the organization's climate is participative, clear expectations for managerial behavior are established, roles are clear, tasks are interdependent, and work-group relationships are favorable and promote self-disclosure.

4. Raters are more accurate and ratees are more accepting of feedback when employees are involved in the design of the feedback process, the uses and consequences of performance evaluations are clear, ratings are anonymous and not threatening, raters are accountable for giving face-to-face feedback, the information is complex or negative and prompts feature-based processing, the report format is clear, and ratings are derived from group discussions.

These points establish an agenda for research on 360-degree feedback and other rating processes. Research is needed on different types of feedback processes (e.g., different methods of design and implementation and different rating and reporting formats). Differences between use for development and for evaluation should be studied. Investigations of feedback in different organizational cultures are needed, determining the short- and long-term effects of feedback on work group relationships and organizational culture. The effects of varying interpersonal relationships and characteristics on rater agreement and manager acceptance of feedback should be studied. Also, research is needed on image formation and acceptance processes. In particular, managers' self-concepts and raters' prototypes of managers and leaders should be identified. Ways to clarify and differentiate these images should be investigated (e.g., by involving subordinates, peers, customers, and managers in generating relevant behaviors to be rated). Practitioners should experiment with interventions to improve the acceptance of 360-degree feedback processes and results. The long-term effects of 360-degree feedback on management style and behavior change should be investigated. Finally, multiple criteria of feedback success should be measured, including employees' acceptance of the process, managers' acceptance and use of results, changes in managers' behavior, and changes in work-group and organizational relationships. Additional needed research specifically on 360-degree feedback is outlined in Chapter 10.

Part II of this book examines how self- and interpersonal insights are important to the development of interpersonal relationships. Chapter 6 describes how relationships develop between two people in an organization, with special emphasis on the boss–subordinate relationship. Chapter 7 considers relationships within cooperative work groups. Chapter 8 covers relationships between individuals engaged in negotiation and conflict resolution.

II

Insight and Important Relationships

6

Interpersonal Relationships

In truth we talk only to ourselves, but sometimes we talk loud enough that others may hear us.

Kahlil Gibran, *Sand and Foam*

This chapter extends the last two, which looked at person perception and rating processes. Here we explore how interpersonal relationships emerge and how they depend on person perception processes and attempts to manage impressions.

The Development of Relationships

People develop through their relationships with others (Fogel, 1993). While people learn from observing others or even from reading about them, and some people believe these are as important as learning directly from others (Joplin, 1993), here I address learning that occurs in the development of strong interpersonal relationships. Such relationships develop through communication that requires achieving a "consensual framing" of discourse and behavior. This is a negotiated process where by "individuals dynamically alter their actions with respect to the ongoing and anticipated actions of their partners" (Fogel, 1993, p. 34). Consensual frames are episodes of shared activity through which relationships emerge, preserve themselves, and change over time. These frames, which become the interactions people get used to doing with each other, are patterns of mutual expectations and desires. "Relationships develop unique consensual frames because each of the individuals has a preference or desire for the exploration of certain kinds of information themes" (p. 109). The partners co-create consensual frames that define the relationship. In turn, this defines the environment and is a learning experience for each partner—especially if one partner is junior to another. (Fogel applies his thesis to parent–infant development.) While consensual frames become stable, some are characterized by inventiveness and creativity, thereby maintaining a "mutually engaging process that embodies the seed of change" (p. 114). Others are characterized by rigidity, sameness, and obligation. Relationships encompass varying combinations of each of these processes, and the unique combination creates differences between relationships. However, rigidity eventually leads to dissolution of the relationship while creativity leads to its development.

Insight into interpersonal, dyadic relationships requires understanding consensual frames—the mutual expectations people have for each other's goals and behaviors. Expectations depend on the type of relationship. For example, social relationships differ from work relationships. Comparing the two, Gabarro (1990) noted the importance of task achievement, task instrumentality, and task-specific competence to work relationships and the importance of affect and self-disclosure to social relationships. Further, he listed the following dimensions of social relationship development that suggest the emergence or evolution of deeper insight over time:

Openness and self-disclosure
Knowledge of each other
Predictability of other's reactions and responses
Uniqueness of interaction
Multimodality of communication
Substitutability of communication
Capacity for conflict and evaluation
Spontaneity of exchange
Synchronization and pacing
Efficiency of communication
Mutual investment

The effectiveness of this evolution depends not on two people exhibiting each type of exchange but rather on how well they deal with problems and dilemmas that arise from deeper interpersonal involvement (Altman & Taylor, 1973). Dyadic relationships develop through both overt interpersonal behaviors and internal subjective processes (including attribution, assessment, and expectations) which take place before, during, and after exchanges. People evaluate interactions over time to see if further involvement is desirable. Applying social exchange theory, the development of interpersonal relationships depends on the expectation that continued interaction, mutuality, and commitment will be more rewarding than weakening or discontinuing the relationship. The processes involved in continued interaction include selective self-disclosure, exploration, testing, and negotiation (Gabarro, 1978, 1979, 1990).

Judgments of instrumentality and effectiveness are related to the development of interpersonal relationships. Mutuality of expectations evolves from (1) expectations about what the task is and what the outcomes of the joint endeavor should be, (2) expectations about how the two parties should actually work with each other (which include assumptions about process as well as responsibility), and (3) expectations about how the two people work singly and independently on the joint task. Thus, Gabarro (1990) concluded:

> [T]he task-salient aspects of mutuality include not only expectations about outcomes but also about interpersonal processes involving interdependence, autonomy, and individual influence, which are in turn affected by each person's assumptions about trust and power within a relationship. (p. 101)

Further, he stated that relationship building needs

> considerable internal subjective work by each party, involving attributional processes, the formation and revision of individual expectations, and evaluative processes of the type described by social exchange theorists. To work actively toward developing shared expectations therefore requires a clear communication of initial expectations, where possible, and the exploration and testing of any differences in expectations. (p. 102)

Expectations stem from the way we evaluate relationships. Generally, people evaluate relationships based on four dimensions: *benign-positive* (meaning that a relationship will definitely have a positive effect), *challenge* (that the relationship can be influenced to make it positive), *irrelevant* (that there will be no lasting impact from the relationship), and *threat* (that the relationship will have a negative outcome; Lazarus & Folkman, 1984). Goals for the relationship are then set based on the most likely outcome. Another element to relationship expectations is exchange—that is, what we expect in return. This is discussed in the next section under exchange relationships.

Emergence of Insight into Relationships

The major theoretical components of how we develop insights about interpersonal relationships involve an interchange between self- and other-perception. Information input starts a cycle of self- and other-disclosure, reflected appraisals, and mutual reinforcement. This is likely to be moderated by interpersonal similarity along a number of dimensions, such as race, gender, socioeconomic background, and work experience. Patterns of behavior are recognized and categorized. Some match expectations from previous experience, norms of socially acceptable behavior, or behavior expected given the task demands. Others require interpretation and result in attributions. This happens over time as causal inferences are tested. (These processes were outlined in the last chapter.) The interpersonal relationship develops as these processes progress or deteriorates as these processes fail. As Gabarro (1990) suggests, a well-developed relationship will be characterized by spontaneity of exchange, synchronization and pacing, efficient communication, and mutual investment.

The interpersonal affect that emerges from long-term interactions be-tween the rater and ratee may influence raters' cognitive processes. More specifically, interpersonal affect may influence components of the rater's cognitive processing (i.e., information acquisition, encoding, recall, and weighting). Robbins and DeNisi (1994) found that affect-consistent perfor-mance and affect-inconsistent performance were perceived by raters as more meaningful and weighted more heavily than affect-neutral perfor-mance.

> Raters may readily interpret affect-consistent information as meaningful or diagnostic in order to provide support for previously held attributes based on affect. In fact, raters may use affect consistency, rather than simply good or bad performance, as the criterion for diagnosing performance information. The finding that affect-inconsistent performance was also perceived as more meaningful than was affect-neutral performance . . . suggests that encoding of schema-incongruent material may require extra processing time in order to causally link the material. . . . The neglect of affect-neutral items during the encoding and weighting process may also be a result of not giving an equitable amount of attention to all performance information. In other words, a rater's perception of meaningfulness may depend not on whether the per-formance is good or bad in general, but on whether it taps an affect-based schema. (Robbins & DeNisi, 1994, p. 350)

Person perception dynamics influence supervisor–subordinate relation-ships and appraisals. These social cognitions are influenced by our social milieu and the reference groups to which we belong and aspire (Sherif, 1976). Barnes-Farrell (1993) felt that age disparity between supervisor and subor-dinates was particularly likely to affect person perceptions. A supervisor would be likely to view subordinates who were similar in age to the super-visor as "my kind of people" and subordinates who were younger or older as "that kind of people." There are a number of possible underlying reasons for this age effect. Age may be important to performance perceptions be-cause of stereotypes (e.g., "Older people don't work as hard as I do"). But the basic reason may be dissimilarity—that is, the "similar-to-me" error of social impressions in work contexts (Rand & Wexley, 1975).

In two studies of performance ratings, Barnes-Farrell (1993) found ad-vancing worker age did not necessarily affect evaluations of a worker's worth and potential within the organization. However, boss–subordinate age disparity was negatively related to promotability ratings. As a result, sub-ordinates who are substantially different in age from their supervisors may experience more barriers to career advancement than subordinates who are similar in age to the supervisor. While age should not be used to make as-signments of subordinates, Barnes-Farrell (1993) concluded that training programs might minimize the effects of age disparities on ratings and treat-ment of employees by making supervisors aware of this bias.

Competence in interpersonal relationships is central to emerging de-mands on leaders and managers. Conger (1993) argues that managing successfully in highly competitive, global environments and an increasingly diverse workforce requires a new set of leadership skills. Managers need to be strategic opportunists capable of managing highly decentralized organizations. They need to be interpersonally competent, community builders (pulling everyone together for a special initiative or project), and sensitive to issues of diversity. These skills require being able to establish a vision, enlist others' support, and empower others to act in ways that help achieve the vision. Understanding interpersonal relationships is key to these dimensions of leadership.

Exchange Relationships

Mutual exchange relationships occur when both parties give and receive something of value (Organ, 1988). Blau (1964) distinguished between economic and social exchange. Economic exchange involves (1) transactions of goods or services that have value independent of the two parties involved, (2) both parties understand their obligations to each other, (3) the tying of the exchange is explicit (e.g., when certain outcomes will be received in exchange for what behaviors, goods, or services), and (4) the conditions of the exchange are enforceable. For instance, the exchange may entail behavior for money (e.g., a certain level of sales for a predetermined level of compensation).

While economic exchange is based on explicit obligations, social exchange is based on implicit obligations and trust (Blau, 1964). The value of the exchange may depend on the identities and status of the two parties relative to each other. Such a social exchange occurs between a supervisor and subordinate, with the supervisor providing the subordinate with choice assignments or opportunities for career development and simply spending more free time with the subordinate.

Developing the social exchange relationship requires knowing something about the other party—what the other party needs and values and the social processes the party can benefit from and enjoy. For instance, individuals may value information, influence, favors, or just friendship. Each party has expectations about how he or she can benefit and what must be rendered in return, although these expectations and the timing of their delivery are not specified. Neither party knows the extent of the other's expectations and whether they have been fulfilled.

Norms of reciprocity guide the social exchange by imposing implicit standards about when and how the receiver of benefits must repay the donor in some way (Gouldner, 1960). People want to reciprocate those who benefit them (Bateman & Organ, 1983). People who feel they are benefiting from a relationship will try to provide something in return, and this fosters the relationship (Greenberg, 1990). The fairness of the exchange can affect its continuation and growth. One possibility is an inequitably low return. If an extension of friendship (e.g., an invitation to dinner) is not reciprocated, the friendship will not grow. Another possibility is an inequitably high return, which would be problematic if the receiver could not afford to reciprocate in kind. For instance, a friend might stop calling after a really big favor, such as finding the friend a job or donating blood to save the friend's life—something that cannot easily be repaid or that can never be repaid even with a host of small favors.

Graen and his colleagues (e.g., Graen, 1976; Graen & Scandura, 1987) developed leader–member exchange (LMX) theory to capture the idea that leaders differentiate among their subordinates. Low LMX is characterized by defining role relationships and exerting downward influence. High LMX is characterized by mutual trust, respect, liking, and reciprocal influence (Liden, Wayne, & Stilwell, 1993). This exchange relationship positively influences many organizational outcomes, such as tenure in the organization, performance evaluations, frequency of promotions, and receiving desirable work assignments. Duarte, Goodson, & Klich (1994) found that telephone company supervisors rated the performance of subordinates in high-quality leader–member exchange relationships high, regardless of the subordinates' objectively measured performance, whereas they rated the performance of subordinates in low-quality leader–member exchange relationships consistent with their objective performance.

The quality of LMX arises early in the life of the supervisor–subordinate relationship. Liden, Wayne, and Stilwell (1993) studied 166 newly hired employees and their immediate supervisors in a wide range of nonacademic university positions (e.g., librarian, admissions counselor, secretary, and computer programmer). They examined the extent to which LMX was predicted by expectations, perceived similarity, liking, demographic similarity, and performance. Supervisors' and subordinates' expectations of each other assessed in the first five days in the life of the dyad predicted LMX at two weeks, six weeks, and six months following the first day of the dyads' existence. Expectations predicted perceived similarity, and liking from both the supervisors' and subordinates' perspectives predicted LMX at most time periods. Actual demographic similarity between supervisor and subordinate was not significantly related to LMX. Performance ratings were not as important to LMX as were the affective variables. The new hires might have been especially sensitive to the leader's influence, making perceived similarity and liking especially important to the evolution of the relationship. Also, supervisors may be particularly attentive to the new subordinate who is also newly hired. This is a chance to acclimate the subordinate to the organization as well as the work group—to mold expectations and enhance commitment to the supervisor and to the organization.

Internal Models of Authority

People develop internal models of their relationship to authority figures. Such models emerge during childhood and adolescence and affect later work relationships. Building on this concept, Kahn and Kram (1994) identified three internal models of authority: *dependent* (which emphasizes hierarchical roles of superior and subordinate), *counterdependent* (which undermines hierarchical roles), and *interdependent* (which acknowledges interdependencies between roles and the desirability of collaborative relationships). Kahn and Kram (1994) proposed that relationships between supervisor and subordinate will be undermined when both parties hold dependent or counterdependent internal models of authority; both will deny their personal responsibility and expertise. In general, Kahn and Kram (1994) argued that when supervisor and subordinate bring different internal models of authority to the relationship, they are likely to experience interpersonal conflict, dissatisfaction, and difficulties with task performance. People with dependent authority models are likely to actively seek mentoring relationships. However, they are unlikely to be successful in reducing their dependence and redefining the relationship as the benefits of mentoring are expended. Those who are counterdependent are likely to avoid mentoring relationships and the intimacy and personal learning that go along with them. An effective leader–member exchange, to use Graen's term, requires that both parties have interdependent models of authority. In this case, according to Kahn and Kram (1994), "both parties are willing to share relevant personal dimensions, to acknowledge and work with hierarchical/status differences created by the formal roles they occupy, and to collaborate regarding both task accomplishment and personal learning" (p. 36).

Caregiving Relationships

The organizational context may require mutually supportive relationships between supervisor and subordinate. Such relationships are particularly important in caregiving organizations, such as hospitals, schools, and social service agencies. Primary caregivers frequently experience burnout as they exhaust or build up the emotional resources necessary to perform their jobs (Cherniss, 1980). Although this can also occur in other high-demand work situations, the emotional requirements in human service work make caregivers especially vulnerable to burnout.

Support from co-workers, especially one's supervisor, replenishes employees' emotional reserves. Kahn (1993, p. 546) identified eight behavioral dimensions of caregiving within organizations:

Accessibility: Remain in other's vicinity, allowing time and space for contact and connection.
Inquiry: Ask for information necessary to probe the other's emotional, physical, and cognitive needs; probe other's experiences, thoughts, and feelings.
Attention: Actively attend to other's experiences, ideas, self-expressions; show comprehension with verbal and nonverbal gestures.
Validation: Communicate positive regard, respect, and appreciation to other.

Empathy: Imaginatively put self in other's place and identify with other's experience; verbally and nonverbally communicate experience of other.

Support: Offer information (about salient issues or situations), feedback (about other's strengths or weaknesses), insights (about caregiving relationship), and protection (from distracting external forces).

Compassion: Show emotional presence by displaying warmth, affection, and kindness.

Consistency: Provide ongoing, steady stream of resources, compassion, and physical, emotional, and cognitive presence for other.

Kahn (1993) also identified three patterns of organizational caregiving: (1) *flow* (caregiving that flows from supervisors to subordinates during role-related interactions), (2) *reverse flow* (subordinates giving unreciprocated care to supervisors), and (3) *barren* (a mutual lack of caregiving between supervisors and subordinates, which leads people to emotionally withdraw from one another). The particular pattern that emerges depends on the level of staffing (understaffing increases work load pressures, leaving little time for caregiving within the organization), the executive director (who establishes expectations by modeling caregiving), and covert organizational dynamics (for instance, splitting the caregivers off from the rest of the organization, leaving them few outlets for painful emotions and anxieties).

Thus, interpersonal relationships involve an interchange between social perceptions, dependencies, and requirements. Mutual disclosure, evaluation, and reinforcement contribute to the development of dependencies and the emergence of functional or dysfunctional relationships. The next section explores aspects of the communication process by which people convey information about each other and, in the process, express and fulfill their needs and expectations.

Impression Management and Relationship Development

Relationships develop as people manage the impressions they have of each other. Writing about the "art of impression management," Gardner (1992) emphasized that managers need to be skilled in the "stagecraft" of organizational life. This means being able to act their own roles effectively and be discerning reviewers of others' performance. Gardner identified several impression-management strategies: ingratiation, intimidation, exemplification (i.e., being a role model of exemplary behavior and dedication), supplication (supplicants try to have others pity them and help them with their troubles), and face-saving. These strategies are not necessarily negative. We all manage impressions of ourselves every day as we try to put our best foot forward. And impression management works. For instance, Gardner's literature review indicates that people who are skilled at ingratiation are better liked and receive more pay raises and favorable performance appraisals than their co-workers. However, Gardner warned that ingratiation may backfire if motives to ingratiate are so transparent that supervisors see through the act. This could tarnish a manager's reputation. Gardner offered the following recommendations for using impression management:

1. Be aware of your impression-management behavior and the image you project.
2. Size up your audience and the situation (how the people with whom you interact may influence your performance).
3. Recognize the dangers of the strategy you have chosen.
4. Perform (impression management is not a substitute for high performance—indeed, demonstrating excellence is the surest way to make a good impression).
5. Be yourself (don't try to be something you are not because people will see through the facade).

Further, Gardner suggested the following recommendations for those on the receiving end of impression management (i.e., the supervisor, co-worker, or customer):

1. Be aware of your personal characteristics and the situational features that make certain types of impression-management strategies more likely (for instance, status differences).
2. Minimize personal, situational, and organizational features that foster undesirable performance (e.g., situations in which resources are scarce or performance requirements or standards are ambiguous).
3. Look for ulterior motives and avoid being overly influenced by dramatic behavior.

Impression-Management Cues

A manager's nonverbal behavior may affect a subordinate's judgments. These include such characteristics as eye contact, facial expression, interpersonal distance, gestures, physical attractiveness, and paralinguistic cues (Reilly, Warech, & Reilly, 1993; Gifford, 1994). Some nonverbal cues are inherent in a person's being, such as race and gender, while other nonverbal cues are more transitory and susceptible to direct manipulation, such as gestures, eye contact, and interpersonal distance (Reilly, Warech, & Reilly, 1993). Many such variables are under the control of the manager and may be used to manage impressions (Wayne & Ferris, 1990). They may do this through physical appearance, overt behavior, verbal descriptions of one's own or other's attributes, or verbal descriptions of explanations for behavior (Tedeschi & Reiss, 1981). Impression management is a way to gain social approval. Indeed, high need for approval has been shown to be related to a person's motivation to manage impressions others have of them (Leary, 1983).

Supervisor ratings are likely to be higher when subordinates try to manage the supervisor's impression (Wayne & Kacmar, 1991). Impression-management behaviors include saying things that enhance others and/or oneself, opinion conformity, and doing favors. In general, supervisors tend to be less critical of subordinates who use impression management than of subordinates who do not (Dobbins & Russell, 1986).

Reilly, Warech, and Reilly (1993) distinguished between the *ability* to manage impression and the *motivation* to manage impressions. This distinction can be understood by two eight-item scales (based on a factor analysis of a larger set of items drawn from Leary, 1983; Lennox & Wolfe, 1984; and Gangestad & Snyder, 1985). I list the items here to help convey the meaning of impression management:

Motivation to Manage Impressions

1. I am highly motivated to control how others see me.
2. I feel there are many good reasons to control how others see me.
3. Controlling others' impressions of me is not important to me. [inverse]
4. In social situations, one of my goals is to get others to form a certain kind of impression of me.
5. I never try to lead others to form particular impressions of me. [inverse]
6. I don't try to control the impression others have of me when I first meet them. [inverse]
7. I try to affect others' impressions of me most of the time.
8. At parties and social gatherings, I do not attempt to say or do things that others will like. [inverse]

Ability to Manage Impressions

1. When I feel that the image I am portraying isn't working, I can readily change it to something that does.
2. Even when it might be to my advantage, I have difficulty putting up a good front. [inverse]
3. I am not particularly good at making other people like me. [inverse]
4. In social situations, I have the ability to alter my behavior if I feel that something else is called for.
5. I feel a bit awkward in company and do not show up quite so well as I should. [inverse]
6. I have trouble changing my behavior to suit different people and different situations. [inverse]
7. Once I know what the situation calls for, it's easy for me to regulate my actions accordingly.
8. I have found that I can adjust my behavior to meet the requirements of any situation I find myself in.

After formulating these items, Reilly, Warech, and Reilly (1993) examined the relationships between managers' ratings on the ability and motivation to manage impressions and self, subordinate, and peer ratings of performance and ratings derived from an assessment center. Ability to manage impressions was positively related to supervisor ratings. There was higher agreement among subordinates for managers high in ability to manage impressions, perhaps because these managers exerted a greater consistency in self-presentation than those low in ability to manage impressions. However, there were lower relationships between subordinate and supervisor correlations and subordinate and peer correlations for managers high in ability to manage impressions, possibly because those low in this ability were less likely to present themselves differently to different sources. Self-ratings were more closely related to others' ratings for managers who were high in impression-management ability. This may have been due to these managers' greater insight and objective realism. The study also revealed that managers with high motivation to manage were likely to receive lower peer ratings. Currying favor and other behaviors associated with high motivation to manage impressions may have generated a "backlash" effect against the target individual by peers. One other important finding was that impression management was not related to the assessment center ratings. This suggests that impression-management behaviors did not have time to work in the assessment center or that the structured nature of assessment center exercises did not allow impression management.

The extent to which one tries to manage another's impressions of oneself may depend on the possible consequences. If another's impressions matter, as they usually do in a supervisor's performance appraisal, then managing the supervisor's impression is important. If ratings are for developmental purposes alone, as they might be for subordinate ratings in an upward-feedback process, then the target of the ratings may not try to influence subordinates' impressions. This may change if upward feedback were to become a regular part of the appraisal process (Reilly, Warech, & Reilly, 1993).

Impression Management and Feedback Seeking

Ashford and Northcraft (1992) found that people seek little feedback when being observed and when they respond to situational norms regarding the appropriate frequency of feedback seeking. These authors argued that feedback might occur more frequently in organizations if people did not feel constrained in seeking feedback. The felt constraint comes from perceived impression-management costs associated with asking, "How am I doing?" Seeking feedback may be viewed as a sign of insecurity, uncertainty, lack of self-confidence, or incompetence. Thus, feedback seeking is inherently tied to impression management. People believe there are costs to seeking feedback, and, in turn, they develop negative impressions of others who ask for feedback.

Impression management can result in costs and benefits. Employees try to manage supervisors' impressions of them because supervisors control important rewards, such as pay raises and promotions. Ways to create a favorable impression include setting higher public goals and providing excuses and apologies for poor performance. Employees will also try to repair tarnished impressions using similar tactics.

Ashford and Northcraft (1992) tested the hypothesis that having an audience present, especially observers who are charged with evaluating the employee, will create self-presentation motives and decrease feedback seeking. In general, people will avoid seeking feedback when they are being observed. The audience will increase feelings of anxiety and nervousness that arise because of the perceived risks to a favorable evaluation. However, if there are cues that norms favor asking for feedback, then feedback seeking will be enhanced. Such norms would be evident from talking to, or observing, others. On the other hand, if norms suggest feedback seeking is inappropriate, it is less likely to occur. The effects of norms and audience on feedback seeking is magnified for people who are "publicly conscious"—that is, susceptible to feelings of being observed when in the presence of others and sensitive to how others react to them.

Ability to Manage Impressions

Effective impression management requires increasing the benefits of managing impressions and reducing or minimizing the costs. Skill in impression management requires having sophisticated knowledge of the various behaviors that are likely to be interpreted favorably by the average perceiver (Schneider, 1981; Ashford & Northcraft, 1992).

Some variables lessen the negative effects of feedback seeking. For instance, being a new employee may alleviate the need to maintain a totally self-assured image (Ashford & Northcraft, 1992). New people are expected to appear uncertain and lack confidence. If instead a new employee exhibits confidence, this would be distinctive, and the unexpected behavior would be attributed to the employee's nature. For instance, telling co-workers about "what a good job I did" would be seen as negative behavior, especially for a new employee. On the other hand, leaders or experienced employees who seek feedback would be seen as weak or unable. However, asking co-workers for feedback can be viewed as collegial, which is consistent with what we expect from co-workers. As such, feedback-seeking would not be viewed as negatively when it comes from peers rather than from supervisors or experienced subordinates. Now if an employee has a reputation as an effective performer, then asking for feedback will carry fewer costs; the seeking will be a sign of self-confidence. The same behavior from average performers, though, may be a sign of insecurity; Ashford and Northcraft (1992) found that people who have a strong reputation for excellent performance are seen more positively (with more favorable personal characteristics and performance potential) when they seek feedback.

This section has emphasized the role of impression management in interpersonal relationships. The premise is that people try to affect how others view them, and, indeed, they may do so successfully. Next, we will consider how the extent to which people agree on their performance judgments affects their perceptions of each other.

Agreement between Performance Evaluations and Interpersonal Attitudes

Interpersonal insight extends far beyond what gets evaluated and discussed in a performance appraisal process. However, performance appraisal is a common and important process that reveals insight. Moreover, as noted by Steiner, Rain, and Smalley (1993), the performance appraisal task is not an easy one: "Raters are faced with observing, storing, recalling, integrating, and judging the effectiveness of behaviors for a number of ratees. Finally, they must translate this judgment onto a rating scale" (p. 438). Given this complexity, there is likely to be considerable disagreement between individuals in evaluating the same performer. However, the extent to which they agree may influence how they view each other. Hence, the performance appraisal process is important for understanding interpersonal insight.

Supervisors' and subordinates' reactions to each other are influenced by the extent to which they agree about the subordinates' performance. This is particularly important because people are not likely to agree with their supervisor about their performance. Self-ratings tend to be inflated (cf. Zammuto, London, & Rowland, 1982; see also Blakely's, 1993 review of the literature). There is evidence, however, that younger subordinates are more conservative in their self-ratings than their supervisor's ratings of them (Ferris et al., 1985). Such discrepancies in ratings may be due to a number of factors, such as attending to and weighting performance dimensions differently (Blakely, 1993). Regardless of the reasons, the discrepancies may affect how supervisors and subordinates view each other and how this perception affects changes in performance perceptions.

Performance feedback may affect the subordinate in several ways. Negative feedback is likely to lead to resentment and defensiveness, while feedback that is ambiguous or overly positive or the absence of feedback may not impair subordinate performance (Ilgen, Fisher, & Taylor, 1979; Blakely, 1993). In a study of the effects of performance rating discrepancies on supervisors and subordinates, Blakely (1993) randomly assigned people to supervisor and subordinate positions and provided them with bogus feedback about performance on an in-basket task. Feedback given to subordinates was manipulated to be either higher or lower than the self-rating. Also, in half the cases, the subordinate was told the supervisor attributed the subordinate's performance either to the situation or to the subordinate's capabilities. Subordinates were more satisfied with the feedback and their supervisor when the supervisor ratings were higher than the self-ratings. The supervisor's attribution for the performance did not affect the subordinates' reactions.

A second phase of the study provided bogus subordinate self-ratings that were either higher or lower than the supervisors' ratings (Blakely, 1993). Also, in half the cases, the supervisors were told the subordinate would contest a discrepant supervisory rating. Supervisors who were told that their subordinate's self-ratings were higher than their own ratings modified their initial ratings, gave larger raises, and were less desirous of discussing the appraisals with subordinates. The subordinate's willingness to contest a discrepancy did not affect supervisors' responses.

This was a laboratory study which did not have the richness of organizational settings or a future for the supervisor–subordinate relationships. Willingness to contest a discrepancy and the supervisor's reason for the performance might be more important in actual organizations. Nevertheless, the study was sufficiently realistic to improve our understanding of interpersonal evaluations.

Other research has found that supervisors are influenced by subordinates' self-ratings (e.g., Farh, Werbel, & Bedeian, 1988). This is especially problematic because some subordinates tend to systematically evaluate their own performance lower than others. This is true of women, who are more critical of themselves than are men (cf. Deaux, 1979). Also, as indicated earlier, younger subordinates tend to be more conservative in evaluating their performance, perhaps because of their inexperience and their desire not to appear to be self-serving (Ferris et al., 1985). Self-ratings may be of little value other than for development if individuals use the ratings to manage others' impressions of them (Campbell & Lee, 1988).

Supervisors may be influenced by subordinates' self-judgments because they want to avoid confrontation (Blakely, 1993); thus, supervisors are more lenient when they know the subordinates see themselves as high performers. Supervisors should be taught how they may be influenced by subordinate's self-descriptions. In particular, they should be taught to recognize how their anxiety about confrontation influences their performance appraisal ratings (Blakely, 1993).

So far, this chapter has examined the effects of impression management and performance feedback on interpersonal attitudes. Other factors that influence the perceptions people have of one another are preexisting stereotypes, expectations, and models (prototypes) of effective behavior. As discussed in Chapter 2, insights form when observations are not easily categorized and an explanation (attribution) must be found.

Stereotypes, Expectations, and Prototypes

Supervisors are expected to be leaderlike. Subordinates are expected to be deferential. Peers are expected to act collegially (Ashford & Northcraft, 1992). Behavior that is inconsistent with these roles is distinctive and likely to be attributed to the individual's true nature. For instance, a subordinate who is undeferential would suggest an underlying character epitomized by uncooperativeness, lack of motivation, or other negative traits and behavioral tendencies.

Fiske (1993) argued that stereotypes result from and maintain one person's control over another. They are especially important to first impressions that guide subsequent interactions. She conceptualized stereotyping as "a category-based cognitive response to another person" (p. 623). Descriptive stereotypes anchor perceptions. People may feel implicit pressure to behave in ways that meet others' expectations derived from stereotypes. The stereotype constrains behavior by anchoring the interaction. Prescriptive stereotypes act as a fence that is more explicitly controlling in that it tells how certain groups *should* think, feel, and behave.

In general, stereotypes are more likely to affect judgments when stimuli and criteria are ambiguous, as is the case in judging interpersonal skills. Stereotypes are less likely to affect behavior when the stimuli are concrete, such as the number of units produced. Further, stereotypes are likely to be applied when the perceiver has little reason to pay attention. This comes into play in supervisor–subordinate relationships. People pay attention when they need each other to achieve their goals. Since subordinates depend on supervisors, they are likely to be diligent in paying attention and avoiding stereotypes when asked to provide upward ratings. However, supervisors rating subordinates is another story, since supervisors do not need to pay the same sort of attention to subordinates. As a result, their judgments of subordinates' behavior may be superficial and susceptible to stereotyping. Thus, according to Fiske (1993), attention

> determines who has detailed knowledge of whom and who stereotypes whom. The power*less* are stereotyped because no one needs to, can, or wants to be detailed and accurate about them. The power*ful* are not so likely to be stereotyped because subordinates need to, can, and want to form detailed impressions of them. The powerless need to try to predict and possibly alter their own fates. They may have fewer competing demands on their attentional capacity. And to the extent that a low personal need for power happens to coincide with a low-power position, they may be less motivated to stereotype.
>
> . . . the powerful are victims of stereotypes too. . . . if the powerless stereotype the powerful, it simply does not matter as much; it demonstrably does not limit their behavior as much, . . . nor, by definition, control their outcomes as much. It is more an irritation than a fundamental threat, except when subordinates are given the power to evaluate, vote on, or otherwise judge those in power.
>
> . . . the powerful are motivated by what they perceive to be acceptable, according to the norms, and by their own self-concepts. (pp. 624, 627; italics in original)

According to Fiske's (1993) formulation, stereotypes (whether of women, African Americans, or ethnic or religious groups) support discrimination. That is, when stimuli are ambiguous and there is little reason for attention (e.g., the perceiver is in a more powerful position than the individual being evaluated), stereotypes are likely to arise.

Curtailing Stereotyped Thinking.   Fiske (1993, p. 627) recommends ways to avoid the stereotyping that is typical of powerful people evaluating others who are less powerful. These techniques include the following:

- Make accessible the supervisors' sense of responsibility as a means of increasing their attention. For instance, they could be reminded of their humanitarian and egalitarian values.
- Remind supervisors that they view themselves as fair-minded and careful people. This will work best for people whose natural proclivity is to treat people as individuals rather than as categories.
- Remind the powerful about appropriate norms for equal opportunity and avoiding discrimination. This works best for people whose natural proclivity is to treat people categorically. Such individuals can be influenced by information about the appropriateness of norms in the situation.
- Remind people about their own public accountability, fear of invalidity, and desire to be accurate.
- Make the organization's values evident and salient—that is, tie them to rewards (such as an award for managers who exemplify equal employment opportunity in their hiring practices and policies for employee treatment).

Interventions to Control Confirmation Bias.   The last chapter described confirmation bias as the motive to behave in such a way toward other people that their reaction confirms our expectations of them (Copeland, 1993). People who are motivated to form stable, predictable impressions are especially prone to this bias, whereas people who are motivated to evaluate others as accurately as possible will avoid the bias. Another motive that avoids expectancy confirmation is trying to facilitate a social interaction—to make it as pleasant as possible and avoid uncomfortable exchanges (Copeland, 1993). Snyder and Haugen (1990, cited in Copeland, 1993) found that people who were instructed to get along well with their target partner avoided behaviors and cognitions that confirm their expectancies. Trying to ingratiate oneself with others (be liked by them) has the same effect of dampening expectancy confirmation.

Yet another factor that lessens expectancy bias is the relative power of the perceiver and the target, consistent with Fiske's (1993) argument about the importance of power relationships in performance evaluations. When a perceiver can affect whether the target individual receives a positive outcome, the perceiver is motivated primarily to acquire knowledge about the target and the target is motivated to obtain the positive outcome (Copeland, 1993). In this case the perceiver is likely to confirm preinteraction expectations. (This is similar to the supervisor's appraising and affecting outcomes for subordinates.) However, when the target controls the positive outcome for the perceiver (as when subordinates rate the supervisor in an upward-feedback process), the perceiver (supervisor) is motivated to facilitate a favorable interaction and avoids expectancy confirmation. Moreover, a highly structured task that keeps the perceiver too cognitively and behaviorally busy to engage in expectancy confirmation will lessen this bias.

The importance of power relationships in reactions to feedback was also discovered by Ellis and Kruglanski (1992). They found that individuals with a high perceived authority gap between themselves and external communicators benefited more from information that the communicator provides than did individuals with a low perceived authority gap. Information derived from personal experiences is more meaningful to people with high self-ascribed authority than to those with low self-ascribed authority, as mentioned in the last chapter. Thus, mode of learning is likely to be differentially effective depending on the individual's motivation and feelings of authority in relation to the source.

Conclusion

This chapter has considered the perceptual and cognitive processes that underlie the relationship between two people. Such relationships emerge over time as the parties develop deeper insights about each other and as consensual themes emerge and stabilize in varying combinations of spontaneity and rigidity. Initial openness and self-disclosure give way to the capacity for conflict and evaluation, spontaneity of exchange, synchronization, and ultimately mutual investment. The effectiveness of this evolution depends on how well each party deals with problems and dilemmas that arise from deeper interpersonal involvement.

Conclusions derived from this chapter explain factors affecting interpersonal perception and involvement.

1. Interpersonal relationships develop through an interchange between self- and others' expectations and perceptions. The degree of mutuality in expectations about the task and internal models of authority and caregiving affect how two parties (e.g., supervisor and subordinate) work with each other.

2. Interpersonal relationships are influenced by impression-management strategies such as ingratiation, intimidation, supplication, and face-saving. Impression-management behaviors include saying things that enhance others and/or oneself, opinion conformity, and doing favors. Impression management is a way to gain social approval. High need for approval is positively related to a person's motivation to manage impressions others have of him or her.

3. A distinction can be made between the *ability* to manage impressions and the *motivation* to manage impressions. Employees try to manage supervisors' impressions of them because supervisors control valued rewards

such as pay raises. Ways of creating a favorable impression include setting higher goals and providing excuses and apologies for poor performance.

4. Effective impression management requires increasing the benefits and minimizing the costs of managing impressions. Skill in impression management requires having sophisticated knowledge of the various behaviors that are likely to be interpreted favorably by the average perceiver.

5. Agreement between the supervisor and subordinate about each other's performance is important because it influences how supervisors and subordinates react to each other. However, employees are not likely to agree with their supervisor about their performance, since self-ratings tend to be inflated.

6. Supervisors' ratings of their subordinates may be influenced by the subordinates' self-judgments because supervisors want to avoid confrontation. Supervisors are more lenient when they know that their subordinates see themselves as high performers.

7. Supervisors should learn how they influence subordinates' self-descriptions. In particular, they should be taught to recognize how their anxiety about confrontation influences their performance appraisal ratings.

8. Stereotypes result from, and maintain, one person's control over another. As such, stereotypes promote discrimination. When the stimuli are ambiguous and there is little reason for attention (e.g., the perceiver is in a more powerful position than the individual being evaluated), stereotypes are likely to arise. Therefore, supervisors are likely to stereotype and hence discriminate unfairly against subordinates based on characteristics that have nothing to do with job performance.

I have considered the association between person perception, interpersonal attitudes, and the development of relationships between two people. However, intensive and complex interpersonal dynamics and work demands often take place in groups. The next chapter explores person perception within cooperating work groups, and the subsequent chapter explores perceptions of people attempting to resolve conflict.

7

Group Development

When Crew and Captain understand
each other to the core,
It takes a gale and more than a gale
to put their ship ashore.
Rudyard Kipling, *Together,* stanza 2

The ideas about insight into dyadic relationships discussed in the last chapter can be extended to understand how group members gain insight about cooperative group work processes and how this insight affects their contribution to the group. While the same underlying processes of social cognition that apply to dyadic relationships also apply to group dynamics, the group process imposes increased task and interpersonal demands. There is a qualitative difference between dyadic and group interaction. Group task demands and member interaction impose requirements for sensitivity, responsiveness, and participation in relation to simultaneously occurring stimuli from multiple sources. Research on group dynamics suggests that group situation and task demands speed up relationship development, especially when the group needs to act quickly. Groups are important to organizations. They occur in the form of project task forces, quality circles, and quality-improvement teams—hence, the importance of examining the effects of self- and interpersonal insight on group process and performance (Hackman, 1990; Saavedra, Earley, & Van Dyne, 1993). This chapter tries to capture how group members gain insight into emerging group processes, for instance, how newcomers to established groups recognize group interaction patterns and identify ways they can contribute to the group effort.

Perceptual psychology suggests the value of groups for discovering new meanings from old experiences. As described by Combs, Richards, and Richards, "This often happens in some kinds of group discussion . . . [during which] . . . members discover that their perceptions of things which have happened to them in the past have changed as a result of bringing them out in the open where they can be explored subject to the impact of other personalities and other ideas" (1988) (p. 288). The Johari Window (Luft, 1970), explained in Chapter 1, proposes the importance of group interaction to learning about oneself and others. Moreover, it implies that group development does not occur until the members are sufficiently comfortable with themselves and others to share their feelings and behave like themselves. As the information known to self and others increases (quadrant 1 in the model), the group will be more productive. Luft (1970) believed that "learning about group processes as they are being experienced helps to increase awareness for the group as a whole as well as for individual members" (p. 15). Enhancing members' understanding of group process can enhance their insight about themselves and other group members.

> An enlarged area of free activity among the group members implies less threat or fear and greater probability that the skills and resources of group members can be brought to bear on the work of the group. The enlarged area suggests greater openness to information, opinions, and new ideas about each member as well as about specific group processes. Since the hidden or avoided area is reduced, less energy is tied up in defending this area. Since more of one's needs are unbound, there is greater likelihood of satisfaction with the work and more involvement with what the group is doing. (Luft, 1970, p. 16)

In this chapter I suggest that group members' interpersonal judgments affect decision processes and outcomes, and I explore how group members form insights into group work processes. I consider how individuals recognize interaction patterns among group members. Feedback, member expectations, and perceptions of group effectiveness are important for group members to become engaged in the group process. I examine the performance effects of task interdependence and directing goals and feedback to individual group members rather than the group as a whole. I describe interventions for enhancing group outcomes through group composition and structure. I also investigate requirements for group problem solving in relation to the emergence of group identity and ways to improve group functioning. Interventions that encourage member self-reflection and feedback help reduce biases of group members toward each other. Finally, I consider ways in which group members recognize multiple viewpoints and thereby use intragroup conflicts for group development.

Group Interaction Patterns

McGrath (1991; Kelly, Futoran, & McGrath, 1990; Kelly & McGrath, 1988; Kelly & McGrath, 1985) called the temporal coordination of group interaction *entrainment*. This term, borrowed from biological science, refers to the fact that some biological and behavioral processes are captured and modified by powerful (internal or external) cycles or pacer signals. Circadian rhythms are examples of entrainment. As applied to work groups, entrainment refers to the effects of time pressure on production rate and quality between and within work groups. Entrainment is the establishment of patterns of communication and interaction and the rate and quality of task performance.

Entrainment processes encompass the group's communication pattern as well as the group's productivity. The patterns include speech and silence, non-verbal expression, and features of the content of the interaction (McGrath, 1990; Gifford, 1994). These variations in patterns of entrainment arise partly through differences in perceptions and expectations that accompany different task conditions (e.g., experiences of different forms of task difficulty and different levels of time pressure; McGrath, 1990). Environmental cues include time lags in response, differential participation of potential sources, certainty or uncertainty about one's audience, and other situational elements. For new groups, cues about roles and behavioral patterns are embedded in the face-to-face group interactions as the group members discuss how to proceed. For newcomers to an existing group, similar cues are embedded in the verbal and nonverbal behavioral patterns of group members as they carry on the task.

The ways in which group members attempt to influence the group affect how they are perceived. Driskell, Olmstead, and Salas (1993) found that group members who exhibit behaviors that imply ability or task competence—high task cues—are perceived by fellow members as more competent and influential than those who are low in task cues. According to their definition, high task cues include a well-moderated voice tone, rapid speech, few verbal disfluencies, a steady gaze, and fluid gestures. Low task cues include a wavering voice, slow speech, numerous stumbles and hesitancies, limited eye contact, and a slumped posture.

In contrast, attempts to influence or control fellow members through threat, tenseness, and emotion (dominance cues) are ineffective in gaining status and influence and result in negative reactions from others (Driskell, Olmstead, and Salas, 1993). High dominance cues include a loud, tense voice; a glaring stare; knitted brows; intrusive, pointing gestures; and muscle tension. Low dominance cues include a soft, fearful voice; averted eye contact; lifted eyebrows; and nervous, submissive gestures. Driskell, Olmstead, and Salas (1993) found that their results held regardless of the gender of the group member attempting to influence the other and the gender of the other group members. Thus, behavioral cues, including voice and movement, can affect group members' perceptions of each other—that is, the entrainment process in McGrath's (1990) language.

Synchronization

Group member synchronization, that is, alignment of behaviors, is induced by the entrainment process of establishing behavior patterns. Synchronization occurs rapidly, unlike the slow development of dyadic relationships depicted in the last chapter. McGrath argued that patterns of entrainment vary with group, task, and situational conditions, such as time pressure. Synchronization is established rapidly. Once established, the pattern continues even when the situation changes.

Determinants of synchronization patterns include time deadlines and demands for quality rather than quantity of output. Kelly and McGrath (1985) found that groups that were assigned a tight deadline early in their limited experimental "lives" continued to work at a fast rate but with low quality and with an interaction pattern that was highly task-focused. The pattern continued on later trials even though they no longer had the tight deadline. Conversely, groups that began working against a less stringent deadline worked at a slower rate but with higher quality and with an interaction pattern that was more interpersonally focused. This pattern continued on later trials despite shorter deadlines. Under task conditions for which early trials yielded an experience of qualitative difficulty, groups tended to slow down on later trials and thereby may have increased the quality of their work (Kelly & McGrath, 1985).

In summary, McGrath and his colleagues showed that group members quickly discern interaction patterns and cues. They develop a flow of interaction to suit the situation and absorb new members in this pattern. Further, the pattern is maintained for a time even after the situation changes and another pattern would be more effective or productive.

Interpersonal Insight in Groups

While McGrath and his colleagues studied entrainment emergence and continuity in groups, they did not investigate how members gain the insights needed for entrainment to occur. The theoretical perspectives that explain interpersonal insight first outlined in Chapter 2 can be applied to how group members gain insights needed for entrainment. Reflected feedback helps individuals position themselves in the group. They compare information to the schemas or scripts they have about how the group should behave. Group members have common scripts about appropriate group behavior (Gersick, 1988). These scripts provide a way to categorize information and initiate habitual routines. As a result, different task groups exhibit similar patterns of behavior (Gersick, 1989). Group members may elicit feedback that helps them understand the scripts in progress. Alternatively, the feedback may be offered as the group gets under way or when a newcomer enters the group. Such feedback would deal with how the individual could fit into the group process based on members' views of the individual's knowledge, skills, and abilities. The feedback provides information for social comparison (Barr & Conlon, 1994). The feedback might come from group members' past interaction with the new member. Members' perceptions of current group behaviors might lead to recognition of a gap in the group's performance capabilities (for instance, "We need someone to do 'x'"). Group members may explicitly state their expectations. Feedback may come from supervisors or trainers about how the group performed and what the group might do to perform better (Earley, 1994).

Similar to McGrath, Gersick (1988) found that groups form behavioral patterns, a pace of work, and assumptions early in their lives (e.g., during the first meeting of a project team). This framework may seem to hinder the group's progress over time because the interaction pattern and assumptions limit using new information that is acquired over time. However, Gersick (1988) discovered that usually at about the midway point toward a deadline, the group makes a paradigm shift in its plans, the attention paid to different information, and the way work gets done. This enables the group members to capitalize on their earlier gradual learning, and, as a result, the group make significant advances toward its goal. Apparently, the alarm elicited by an approaching deadline causes group members to realize that old perspectives are no longer viable. This prompts them to search for, and be willing to accept, new ideas. Thus, members need to perceive that the scripts have to change and that they can participate in changing them. The group members experience this formative change together.

Cognitive evaluation suggests that the individual group member judges group feedback in relation to his or her existing conception of self-efficacy in similar situations. Or if the situation is novel, the individual forms a judgment of self-efficacy that he or she will test. The individual's image of the situation and group member relationships will guide the establishment of his or her ability to be effective in the group. That is, the member develops a sense of "group-specific self-efficacy." This will emerge quickly if the group situation matches existing prototypes, categories, or roles, such as "leader," "resource," and "producer." Group members individually make attributions as to whether the work requires using special skills or abilities (i.e., whether they bring unique value to the group), whether they are merely "cogs in the wheel" directed by situational demands, or whether they don't fit in at all.

Emergence of Insight Into Group Dynamics. The processes involved in developing insight into interpersonal relationships described in the previous chapter are magnified in the emergence of understanding cooperative group processes and entrainment. Group members both seek and convey expectations and reactions. They do so explicitly and implicitly. Behaviors evolve into discernible patterns of interaction. Some of these patterns are categorized easily as socially acceptable and expected; as such, they are readily adopted by the group members. When unusual patterns of behavior are required by the task or evolve because of the unique experience of group members, participants need to make attributions to themselves and others as to who is in control, what needs to be done, and the nature of role assignments. This entails the processes of leadership emergence and clarification of, and agreement to, roles and tasks. As McGrath (1990) articulated, the group needs to attend to production, member support, and group well-being as goals and methods are chosen, conflicts are resolved, and outcomes are produced. The result is a synchronization of behavior to match task demands.

Group Members' Cognitions

The frame of reference held by each group member may influence group outcomes. The discussion of prospect-theory in Chapter 1 showed that people tend to avoid risks when decision alternatives are framed in terms of gains but tend to seek risks when alternatives are framed in terms of losses (cf. Tversky & Kahneman, 1981). A possible explanation is that people react more strongly to potential losses than to potential gains because the displeasure of losing is greater than the pleasure of winning equivalent amounts (Tversky & Kahneman, 1981; Dunegan, 1993). While in some cases group members may enter the group with similar ideas about how the group should proceed (Gersick, 1988), in other cases the members may have different perspectives on the task. Consider a business meeting that contains members from different divisions of the firm, such as sales, production, finance, who may view the problem under consideration very differently. Tindale, Sheffey, and Scott (1993) examined the question of whether the group members must obtain a common perspective before reaching consensus on a single alternative. The researchers expected that the first stage of group problem solving would be a chance for the members to discuss and agree on relevant problem dimensions (after Maier, 1970). As group members gain feedback on the group process, they realize and discuss their different cognitive decision processes. The discussion leads to a cognitive organization of the task, which is shared by all group members (Doise, 1978).

Testing this, Tindale, Sheffey, and Scott (1993) manipulated group members' initial frame of reference prior to entering a group discussion by framing the problem in terms of potential gains (e.g., how many people could be saved by a particular means of combating a disease) or losses (e.g., how many people could die as a result of adopting a particular alternative)—the same procedure used by Tversky and Kahneman (1981) in studying individual decisions. Tindale, Sheffey, and Scott assembled groups with varied compositions: three gain-oriented and one loss-oriented member (3–1), two gain-oriented and two loss-oriented members (2–2), and one gain-oriented and three loss-oriented members (1–3). They found a postgroup discussion choice shift toward the risky alternative in the 2–2 and 1–3 composition conditions. That is, when the majority of members framed the problem in a manner consistent with the riskier alternative, the group process strongly favored that alternative. However, changes in members' preferences were not related to changes in members' frames of reference, suggesting that the group members did not change their cognitive frames even though the group composition affected the group's and each individual's preferences.

Group composition affected the outcome via the decision scheme used by the group. When the frame was unevenly balanced (i.e., the 1–3 and 3–1 groups), a majority rule or equiprobability scheme (any alternative brought up in group discussion is equally likely to be chosen by the group) tended to define the group response. When the frame was evenly balanced (the 2–2 groups), a proportionality scheme applied (the probability of a group choosing a particular alternative was equal to the proportion of members favoring the alternative).

These results demonstrate that group members' cognitive frames of reference are important to the group composition, but their frames of reference do not necessarily change as a result of the group process and outcome. The study also suggests that frames of reference can be manipulated readily and have an effect on work groups. Organizational interventions (e.g., communications about organizational strategy and likelihoods of success) can affect employees' frames of reference. However, accentuating the positive may cause more conservative behavior by individuals. Even if everyone does not have the same outlook, group decisions may be swayed when half or more of the people have a positive outlook and hence are averse to loss or risk. This may suit the organization's purpose if the goal is to stay the course and not take risks; if, however, the goal is to encourage proactive behavior, then framing issues in terms of losses may be beneficial.

Internal Authority Models

The last chapter described Kahn and Kram's (1994) conceptualization of dependent, counterdependent, and interdependent internal models of authority that characterize how individuals approach supervisor–subordinate relationships. These models are individual tendencies that develop during childhood. The match of models between individuals in a dyadic, authority relationship will influence the effectiveness of the relationship. These characteristics may also influence team effectiveness. Specifically, Kahn and Kram (1994) proposed that group members with dependent models of authority will want direction and support from the leader, and they will fail to recognize their own and their peers' potential to control outcomes. Counterdependent group members will distance themselves from formal team leaders and resist the authority of their peers while attempting to exert influence over the group. Interdependent group members will achieve team objectives by effectively using resources within and outside the group.

Cultural Diversity of Group Members

Group members are sensitive to their differences. In particular, the cultural diversity of group members influences the effectiveness of group process and performance, at least during the initial stages of the group's life. In a study of thirty-six student groups by Watson, Kumar, and Michaelsen (1993), homogeneous groups (those whose members were all from the same nationality and ethnic background) and culturally diverse groups were assessed after five, nine, thirteen, and seventeen weeks. Group process was defined as the actions of group members that affect other members over time. The group process measures used in the study asked members to evaluate interaction behaviors taking place during decision making and problem solving. This process survey was administered immediately after the groups' completion of each of four case analyses. Performance measures were instructor analyses of each case completed in terms of the range of perspectives shown in evaluating the situation, the number of potential problems identified, the generation of multiple alternatives, and the quality of the recommended solution. Process and performance measures were significantly interrelated for both homogeneous and culturally diverse groups at all four time periods. Homogeneous groups were significantly higher on all process and performance measures. These differences dissipated over time until by the seventeenth week either there were no significant differences or there was higher performance for the culturally diverse groups in the case of range of perspectives and alternatives generated.

This study had several advantages over previous research. It examined performance on a series of complex problem-solving tasks that were important to group members (a structured analysis of cases that described situations common in "real-life" companies). It employed a longitudinal design. In addition, there was substantial diversity in the culturally diverse groups (both ethnic and national diversity including white Americans, black Americans, Hispanic Americans, and foreign nationals compared with groups of all white Americans).

Watson, Kumar, and Michaelsen (1993) found that group heterogeneity appears to interfere initially with effective problem solving. This is consistent with prior research (e.g., Feldman et al., 1980; see Bettenhausen, 1991, for a review). However, this seems to be a short-run limitation. Cultural diversity becomes an asset over time on tasks that require a variety of viewpoints (as also found by Buller, 1986, and Janis, 1982). Time provides the opportunity for heterogeneous groups to resolve group process issues, such as difficulty in agreeing on what is important or members trying to control the group. Over time, members increase in their ability to use members' information resources (Watson, Kumar, & Michaelsen, 1993; Watson, Michaelsen, & Sharp, 1991).

This discussion about diversity in groups indicates that newly formed groups with substantial cultural diversity will be able to solve problems effectively. Over time, process and task proficiency even out between homogeneous and heterogeneous groups. This suggests the following interventions to enhance outcomes of culturally diverse groups (Watson, Kumar, & Michaelsen, 1993, p. 599):

- Data on group process should be collected regularly.
- Feedback on group process and performance should be provided regularly to group members.
- Time should be allowed for group members to discuss how things are going.
- The group should plan a course of action for increasing problem-solving effectiveness.
- In general, there should be a continuous and overt focus on group process and performance.

Perceptions of Group Variability.   Group members' perceptions of variability depend on the amount of information the members have about the similarity and differences among the members of the group. Kashima and Kashima (1993) found that observers perceived groups as more variable when there was more information about group member differences, even when less information indicated the same amount of variability. Also, groups were perceived to be less variable the more there was information about group member similarity. Since similarity and difference information did not interact, the two types of information seemed to have an additive effect on perceptions of group variability.

Research on perceived intragroup homogeneity generally finds that out-groups are perceived as less internally heterogeneous than in-groups (e.g., Linville & Jones, 1980). This is a result of the cognitive process of social categorization, a division of the world into "us" and "them" (Brown & Wootton-Millward, 1993). On the other hand, some evidence indicates the reverse phenomenon of in-group members being perceived as more homogeneous than out-group members, perhaps because such perceptions enhance social identity (Simon & Brown, 1987). Brown and Wootton-Millward (1993) suggested that in-group homogeneity may be especially prevalent during the initial stages of group formation, especially on dimensions important to the group's identity. This may also occur at other important transition points in the group's evolution. Out-group homogeneity may occur on dimensions that are central to the identity of the out-group. Brewer (1993) argued that the variability of in-groups, more than out-groups, is subject to motivational forces associated with the need for self-identity and differentiation from others. Brewer and Weber (1994) found that majority group members compare themselves to in-group members while minority group members compare themselves to out-group members.

The extent to which the group is open to new members may determine the tolerance of heterogeneity in the group. Specifically, tolerance of members to expressions of individualism in the group depends on the permeability of the group—that is, the ease with which new members can join the group. When group boundaries are difficult to permeate, members expect collective responses rather than individualistic responses from each other (Lalonde & Silverman, 1994). This is especially true for group members for whom social identity is important.

Increasing Group Heterogeneity. Processes of attraction, selection, and attrition suggest that people with similar personalities tend to be found in the same work setting (Schneider, 1987; George, 1990; George & James, 1993). Therefore, interventions may be needed to ensure group heterogeneity and then take advantage of it. Without such interventions, perceptual and self-selection processes are likely to result in homogeneous groups—a characteristic that may lead to easy group member agreement but little use of diverse ideas.

Group Structure and Productivity

Being a member of a group requires deciding how much effort to contribute. As individuals enter a group, they evaluate what is expected of them, the costs of participating at different levels of effort, and the rewards that accrue. Group members evaluate the worthwhileness of their individual contributions to the group in relation to their abilities and energy, likely outcomes, and the effort and abilities of the other group members. The information, support, and rewards they receive from their fellow group members, supervisors, or others (e.g., customers) about performance expectations and requirements are likely to influence the effort they expend. In addition to evaluating their own efforts relative to group and individual gain, they also influence the efforts of other group members. Thus, understanding this evaluation and influence process is important to understanding group members' insight and ways to affect it.

Social Loafing

Group design and structure determine individual effort. Factors that influence the extent of individual contributions include coordination of effort, fatigue, and ability. However, low motivation and productivity often occur when individuals pool their energy to form a collective product (Shepperd, 1993). A social dilemma arises when the behavior that seems best to the individual (i.e., to exert less energy) is in conflict with the interests of the group (to produce a high-quality product). This situation, known as *social loafing,* occurs when there is the potential for a "free ride" off the efforts of others or the threat that others will enjoy a free ride on one's own efforts. Social loafing may be less likely for individuals who are motivated to participate in the task. For instance, those high in need for cognition generate more ideas during group brainstorming than do those low in need for cognition, while those high and low in need for cognition generate the same high number of ideas in individual brainstorming (Petty, Cacioppo, & Kasmer, 1985; Cacioppo et al., 1986).

A related concept is the choice to volunteer for the benefit of the group. Volunteers generally incur more costs than other group members, even when their actions are successful (Murnighan, Kim, & Metzger, 1993). The decision to volunteer poses a dilemma: Group members can "volunteer to do more and gain less than the rest of the group, or they can hope that someone else will volunteer, knowing that if no one does, their group will not receive the benefits volunteering could produce" (Murnighan, Kim, & Metzger, 1993, p. 515). Murnighan and colleagues (1993) presented management students with a variety of scenarios similar to the following:

> You are in a waiting room with 99 strangers. A distinguished-looking individual comes up to you and says "I would be willing to pay many of you $200 if at least one of you is willing to accept $2. You may not talk about it or communicate with each other in any way. If at least one of you chooses $2, all of you will get what you asked for. If all of you ask for $200, none of you will get anything." If you were in this situation, what would you choose: $2 or $200? (p. 522)

The research showed that increasing volunteers' payoffs increased the number of volunteers, while increasing the payoffs for nonvolunteers increased the number of nonvolunteers. Fewer people volunteered as group size increased. The number of volunteers increased as the number required increased. People tended to volunteer less when work was involved (e.g., when the boss asked for someone in the group to work on the weekend). The researchers recognized that since actual interrelationships were not involved, the context may not have inspired much sympathy, empathy, or moral obligation. However, the results suggested the frailty of altruistic action.

Shepperd (1993, p. 69) cited a number of remedies to the dilemmas of social loafing and the volunteer's dilemma:

- Change the nature of the situation so there is no longer a conflict between the interests of the individual and the interests of the group.
- Open avenues for communication.
- Establish and emphasize norms for appropriate behavior.
- Establish a superordinate authority to punish defection from, and reward maintenance of, the group's good.
- Promote a sense of group cohesiveness or group identity.
- Make individual contributions noticeable so group members cannot "hide in the crowd"; hold each member accountable for a certain output, replacing group goals with individual goals.
- Make individual contributions indispensable (for instance, by monitoring and requiring a certain contribution from each individual).
- Appeal to altruistic concerns and a sense of duty.

Shepperd (1993) indicated that such remedies work because they enhance motivation levels by increasing expectancy of valued outcomes from contributing to the group. Incentives for contributing may be external (e.g., monetary) or internal (e.g., commitment, pride, challenge, or responsibility). They may be provided to each individual (by rewarding each individual separately), or they may be provided to the group as a whole (by recognition or honors for the group as a whole, or a special group reward, such as a group dinner).

A further strategy for avoiding social loafing is to make individual contributions indispensable so that each person's efforts are essential and unique. A related strategy is to convince group members that their efforts are needed because of the difficulty or challenge of the task and the low likelihood that their contributions will be duplicated by other group members.

Another strategy is to decrease or eliminate the costs of contributing by decreasing the physical costs (e.g., make group meetings convenient to attend) or by decreasing the psychological costs (e.g., instruct members that their co-workers will not reduce their efforts—which will work if each person's efforts are observable).

These strategies require the group leader to structure the task and incentives to reward individual and group effort. More than one strategy is likely to be needed simultaneously, so it is not uncommon to have a combination of group and individual rewards. This requires understanding how people perceive group expectations, mutual benefits, and mutual contribution.

Effects of Expectations on Perceptions of Group Performance

Preobservation performance expectations influence behavioral ratings of work groups. Martell and Willis (1993) studied subjects who were given positive or negative information about the group's performance prior to observing the same work group on videotape. Subjects who were led to believe that the group had performed well attributed more effective behaviors and fewer ineffective behaviors to the group. This occurred because of the decision criteria resulting from positive expectations. Subjects who had been provided with positive performance information adopted a more liberal decision criterion when judging the occurrence of effective work behaviors and a more conservative decision criterion when judging the occurrence of ineffective work behaviors. Performance expectations did not affect memory of behaviors one week after the observation. Thus, the expectation bias seemed to be introduced in the establishment of judgment criteria, not in the memory of effective versus ineffective behaviors. An open question is whether the same expectation biases influence perceptions of work groups in which people actually participate. That is, are people more liberal in their judgments of fellow members when they expect positive performance than when they expect negative performance, and how does this influence their interaction with the group?

Group Members' Self-Enhancement Bias

Recent research suggests that participation in groups produces a perceptual leniency bias in self-evaluations (Diehl & Strobe, 1991). Group members believe that the group's performance is better than that of other groups, while individuals performing the same task believe that their performance is much worse than others. This consistent finding emerged from a series of laboratory studies by Jourden and Heath (1993) using different tasks (creative, logical/analytic, and engineering/productivity) during which subjects could observe others' output. In one study, undergraduate business students were randomly assigned to three-person groups or to an individual performance condition. Their task was to construct the tallest possible freestanding tower by folding and in other ways working with a one-inch stack of newspapers. In another experiment, subjects worked on logic puzzles as individuals, dyads, or quadruples. In a third study, business students worked on a creative, brainstorming task (creating a list of new products). After completing the tasks, subjects ranked their performances. Actual performance accounted for less than half of the variance in performance perceptions, but less so when the product was clearly visible, as it was in the first study in the series.

This may explain the feeling in many organizations that group procedures are better than individual procedures. Jourden and Heath (1993) conjectured that the bias in favor of one's own group performance occurs because groups reduce anxiety, increase altruistic behavior, and increase commitment—that is, a group ethnocentrism effect (Blake & Mouton, 1962).

Interestingly, the finding of a negative self-bias for individual performers is contrary to the widely cited finding that individuals maintain large and systematically positive illusions about their performance as a means of maintaining a feeling of well-being (Taylor & Brown, 1988, cited in Jourden & Heath, 1993). Individual subjects in Jourden and Heath's (1993) research felt worse about their individual performance than did those participating in groups. This is a similar finding to Casey's (1993) discovery, described in Chapter 5, that negative feedback looms larger (gets more weight) than positive feedback, and that mixed feedback (positive and negative) results in less satisfaction with the feedback than does equal feedback. However, subjects self-enhance when predicting future self-evaluations. Jourden and Heath's experiments indicate that negative feelings resulting from performance observation may result in lower self-evaluations. Following control theory (Chapter 2), people may set high standards for themselves based on perceptions of others' performances (Nelson, 1993). The lower individual performance may be a way of expressing one's low performance satisfaction and defending what one predicts will be negative evaluations by others. Participating in a group apparently counters this tendency by bolstering positive feelings about the group's performance. These positive feelings may explain the popularity of group structures for accomplishing work in organizations.

Effects of Task Characteristics on Group Process and Outcomes

According to McGrath (1991), the nature of the task has a major effect on group process. The organization of work in the group determines group members' insights into the group process and resulting behavior. Behavior is also directed by goals and feedback—both of which may be directed to the individual or group as a whole. Therefore, an important part of understanding insight in group process is determining how task interdependence affects interpersonal perceptions and behavior.

Strauss and McGrath (1994) predicted that as tasks pose greater requirements for member interdependence, group performance will be better when communication media allow transmitting more social context cues. To test this prediction, they studied 72 three-person groups of undergraduate students working in either computer-mediated or face-to-face meetings on one of three 12-minute long tasks that had increasing levels of interdependence:

an idea-generation task (generating as many ideas as possible about ways to improve the quality of the physical environment), an intellective task (a complex logic problem similar to those found on graduate school entrance exams), and a judgment task (determining disciplinary actions for a fictitious case in which a college teaching assistant had accepted a bribe from the basketball team's star player to change the student's grade on an exam). The results showed higher productivity in the face-to-face than computer-mediated groups with greater discrepancies between media conditions for tasks requiring higher levels of coordination. There were few differences, however, in the quality of work completed, suggesting that social cues are more important for the amount of work done than for its quality. That is, social cues allow completing more of a given task in less time especially when the task requires member interdependence to generate outcomes. When interdependence is not required, as in a brainstorming task, the electronic medium prevents production-blocking mechanisms, such as evaluation apprehension, social loafing, and procedural mechanisms, such as only one person speaking at a time or a small number of vocal members dominating the group (Gallupe et al., 1994).

Saavedra, Earley, and Van Dyne (1993) studied the effects of task interdependence, goals (individual or group), and feedback (individual or group). Together, these elements constitute what Saavedra and colleagues (1993) termed *complex interdependence*. These elements determine performance requirements and direct group members' efforts toward achieving performance goals. Consider Saavedra, Earley, and Van Dyne's definition of each component (adapted from pp. 61–63):

Task Interdependence.   The degree to which group members must rely on one another to perform their tasks effectively given the design of their jobs. Thompson (1967) delineated a hierarchy of task interdependence based on the exchange of information or resources and increasing levels of dependence and coordination among group members. The hierarchy consists of the following four dimensions of increasing interdependence:

- *Pooled interdependence:* Each member makes a contribution to group performance without the need for direct interaction among members. The group members have similar roles, and each individual group member completes the whole task.
- *Sequential interdependence:* Here, one group member must act before another can act. Group members perform different parts of the task.
- *Reciprocal interdependence:* One group member's output becomes another's input and vice versa. Group members have different roles and specialties. Coordination is required since they perform different parts of the task in different order.
- *Team interdependence:* Group members jointly diagnose, problem solve, and collaborate to complete a task. They have the freedom to

design their own jobs. This requires mutual interaction and group discretion to decide the course of action. It imposes the greatest task demands.

Goal Interdependence. This refers to the interconnections among group members. Goals are expressed in terms of group or individual outcomes. Individual goals encourage group members to develop strategies that maximize individual performance. Consequently, they may engender competition and conflict. In contrast, group goals may improve the development of cooperative strategies and facilitate performance.

Feedback Interdependence. This refers to whether feedback is given to the group or to individuals. Group feedback provides information on how well members have implemented the task and suggests whether members should modify how they coordinate their work. Individual feedback directs members' attention to their own work effort as if group members did not depend on each other.

Compatibility of Goal, Feedback, and Task Interdependence. There is a compatibility among these task characteristics that can facilitate group process and outcomes. The greater the task independence, the more goals should be group-oriented and the more group feedback is beneficial.

Saavedra, Earley, and Van Dyne (1993) studied three-person groups of undergraduate students discussing recommendations for employees' merit bonus based on written performance descriptions. Each of the three types of interdependence (task, goal, and feedback) were manipulated in a $2 \times 2 \times 2$ factorial design. Performance quantity was measured by the total number of evaluations completed, and performance quality was measured by the total number completed correctly. Postdiscussion questionnaires measured group members' perceptions of conflict (e.g., "There was a lot of tension among people in our group") and strategy (e.g., "Our group was highly imaginative in thinking about new or better ways we might perform our task").

With respect to task interdependence, the study found that performance (quality and quantity) was significantly lower in the sequential condition than in the other conditions. Strategy was higher in the reciprocal and team conditions than in the pooled and sequential conditions. Conflict was higher in the reciprocal condition than in the other three conditions. Performance (quality and quantity) and strategy were higher in the group than in the individual goal condition. Conflict was higher in the individual condition than in the group goal condition.

The study revealed the importance of complex interdependence via the interactions among task, goal, and feedback interdependence. For instance, one significant interaction showed that for reciprocal and team interdependence, highest performance occurred for group goal and group feedback conditions. There also was evidence that task strategy and intragroup conflict mediated the relation of complex interdependence on group perfor-mance. Thus, complex interdependence increased group strategies, which in turn positively affected group performance. Also, coordination failures in reciprocal interdependent groups generated conflict, which in turn nega-tively affected group performance.

As a result of these findings, Saavedra, Earley, and Van Dyne (1993) offered the following recommendations for designing group processes to have a positive effect on performance by considering the interactive effects of task, goal, and feedback interdependence:

1. Use individual goals and individual feedback when task interdepen-dence is pooled such that group member works alone.
2. Use group goals and individual feedback when task interdependence is sequential such that each member performs a different task that provides input to another member's task.
3. Use group goals and group feedback when group members have con-siderable interaction and discretion over the work process (there is reciprocal or team interdependence).

Thus, the structure of the group's task and supporting mechanisms such as goals and feedback may influence group members' perceptions of the group process as well as their performance.

Social Process in Technological Systems: Defining the Collective Mind

Group members' recognition and communication of tightly linked interde-pendencies are crucial to the success of technologically complex tasks. So-cial processes and socialization of newcomers into the system are as critical to the system's success as the technology itself.

Weick and Roberts (1993) conceptualized "collective mind" to explain organizational performance in situations requiring nearly continuous oper-ational reliability. Collective mind is "a pattern of heedful interrelations of actions in a social system" (p. 357). These actions are heedful when they are combined intelligently (e.g., carefully, critically, and purposefully) rather than in a haphazard, unintelligent way. According to Weick and Roberts (1993), group members "construct their actions (contributions), understand-ing that the system consists of connected actions by themselves and others (representation), and interrelate their actions within the system (subordina-tion)" (p. 357).

Weick and Roberts (1993) give the example of flight operations on aircraft carriers—in particular, the process of a pilot landing an aircraft:

> This is not a solitary act. A pilot doesn't really land; he is "recovered." And recovery is a set of interrelated activities among air traffic controllers, landing signal officers, the control tower, navigators, deck hands, the helmsman driv-

ing the ship, etc. As the recovery of a single aircraft nears completion in the form of a successful trap, nine to ten people on the landing signal officer's platform, up to 15 more people in the tower, and two or three more people on the bridge observe the recovery and can waive the aircraft off if there is a problem. (p. 363)

The strength and maintenance of the interrelationships in such a system require "communities of practice" involving apprentices and experts. The socialization and education of inexperienced newcomers often resocializes and reeducates the insiders, strengthening the importance of heedful action.

The probability of errors decreases the more carefully the elements of the system are interrelated and tightly coupled—that is, the extent to which the interrelations are heedful and comprehension is mindful. Errors occur when interrelationships lose focus and break down. Individuals represent others in the system in less detail. Contributions are no longer shaped by anticipated responses. In such cases people may act deliberately but not with the required interrelationships in mind.

Thus, systems that are interactively complex are made safer by tight coupling when the mutually shared field is well developed. Accidents in technologically complex processes can occur when there is a breakdown of social relationships. As Weick and Roberts (1993) conclude, "Inadequate comprehension can be traced to flawed mind rather than flawed equipment" (p. 378). This dependency on social skills makes it easier for systems to lose mind rather than gain it, and they highlight the importance of communication and socialization to the maintenance of the system.

Tight coupling is difficult to accomplish when a recently formed, loosely structured group faces a life-threatening situation for which they have little or no preparation. Weick (1993) found such a situation in the Mann Gulch fire disaster of 1949, documented by Maclean (1992), in which thirteen young men from a group of sixteen "Smokejumpers" lost their lives. Maclean (1992) speculated on the organizational circumstances of the disaster:

The Smokejumpers have never had a fixed organization like the military, with the same squads and officers. . . . Since the cost of keeping separate crews intact during a hot fire season would be prohibitive, a list is posted of all the jumpers and "overhead" (foremen, squad leaders, and spotters), and when a man has been on a fire he is dropped to the bottom of the list and has to work his way back up. No one knows who or how many will be called next, especially since the number of jumpers dropped on a fire can vary from two men to several planeloads. You don't have to be an administrative genius to see in this organizational scheme of things the possibility of calamity in a crisis. (pp. 40–41)

Hellman led the crew across the gulch and started angling for the river, and, sure enough, it happened as it nearly always does when the second-in-command takes charge. The crew got separated and confused. (p. 65)

One event after another surprised the inexperienced crew. For instance, the foreman shouted to the men to drop their tools and subsequently lighted a fire that seemed to be in the middle of the only escape route. The foreman lay down in the ashes as an escape hole in the oncoming blaze while the others ran, unable to make sense of this action and unwilling to risk following the foreman's plea to join him.

Weick (1993) derives four lessons from his analysis to counter group vulnerability and build resilience: value improvisation (as when the leader discovered "a way out" by starting another fire); understand role distinctions; recognize one's inability to understand what is happening right now; and maintain respectful interaction in reporting honestly, respecting one's own perceptions and seeking to integrate them with the reports of others. In relation to respectful interaction, Weick (1993) wrote:

> If a role system collapses among people for whom trust, honesty, and self-respect are underdeveloped, then they are on their own. And fear often swamps their resourcefulness. If, however, a role system collapses among people where trust, honesty, and self-respect are more fully developed, then new options, such as mutual adaptation, blind imitation of creative solutions, and trusting compliance, are created. (p. 643)

Group relationships need to do more than stress coordination of action. They require "emotional ties that keep panic under control in the face of obstacles. Closer ties permit clearer thinking, which enables people to find paths around obstacles" (Weick, 1993, p. 647). Leaders should prepare their groups for tough times by focusing less on routine tasks and role separation and more on coordination and treating all group members as part of a single team.

This formulation of system integration highlights the importance of synchronization in groups. Also, it emphasizes the focus on coordinated team behavior, not individual action. Group members must perceive their behavior in relation to that of others. Moreover, they must develop a sense of the sequence of coordinated action and its effects, but not bound by rigid, impermeable role boundaries.

Interactions Produce Normative Expectations and Constraints: The Case of Self-Managing Teams

Barker (1993) studied an organizational shift from bureaucratic, hierarchical management to self-managing teams. He showed how the organization's members develop a system of value-based normative rules that control their actions more powerfully and completely than the hierarchical system. The rules become manifest through team members' interactions.

The move from supervisory to participatory structures is meant to enhance performance and efficiency by empowering the people who know the work best. Moreover, it assumes that motivation will be enhanced because team members control their own behavior. In self-managing teams, ten to fifteen workers gather and synthesize information, act on it, and take collective responsibility for those actions, rather than being told what to do by a supervisor (Barker, 1993). Norms and rules emerge from task functions and procedures, team goals, and top management's articulation of a value-based corporate vision. Team members are often cross-trained to perform many, if not all, of the tasks required by the team.

Barker (1993) found that control within self-managing teams emerged during the course of three to four years of operation. This extended time is necessary because the norms must pervade the entire organization, encompassing both within- and between-team relationships. Moreover, the evolution of lasting control mechanisms requires more than behavior synchronization for task completion, as in the group processes described by McGrath. Barker, who recognized that the emergence of control mechanisms in self-managing teams parallels the processes identified from the traditional literature on work-group norms and team development (e.g., Hackman, 1992), identified stages of development of control:

1. Teams form value consensus from top management's vision statement.
2. Team members develop emotional attachments to their shared values.
3. Teams form behavioral norms from the values enabling them to work effectively.
4. Older team members expect new members to identify with the norms and values and act in accordance with these value-based norms. Team members take on both supervisor and subordinate roles, monitoring and directing each other.
5. Teams' normative rules become more rationalized. Members enforce their rules with each other through peer pressure and behavioral sanctions.
6. Teams further objectify and formalize the rules and share these rules with each other. The work environment begins to stabilize. (adapted from Barker, 1993, p. 434)

The norms evolve in a way that is less apparent than bureaucratic control. Team members may not even be aware of how the system they created controls their actions. Team members' actions and interrelationships are guided by the value-based system they created, and they readily submit themselves to their own control mechanisms (for instance, a very strict and objective attendance policy that emerged in the case Barker studied). Uncommitted workers do not last in the system. Members who resist the team's control are made to feel unworthy as a "teammate."

Group Problem Solving

Understanding the individual in relation to the group first requires considering the nature of the group as a mechanism for solving problems. In their formulation of a group problem-solving model, Aldag and Fuller (1993) remind us of the elements of problem solving and outline the antecedents of group process and emergent group characteristics. The decision process starts with *problem identification* (including preliminary information search, survey of objectives, and problem definition) followed by *alternative generation* (which varies in terms of the number and quality of alternatives). The next major stage of group process is *evaluation and choice*. All this is a complex, interactive process requiring group members to do the following:

- Judge information quality.
- Allow the emergence of a preferred alternative.
- Follow decision rules (e.g., requiring consensus, which makes dissent difficult, versus adopting a majority decision, which makes dissent more acceptable).
- Decide to vote on priorities.
- Reconsider preferred and rejected alternatives.
- Evaluate the source of solutions.
- Develop contingency plans.
- Gather information about likely reactions and effects of the choice.

Continuing Aldag and Fuller's (1993) formulation, groups eventually develop their own identity. This may include a sense of vulnerability and the risks inherent in the task. These perceptions lie with each group member and may never be voiced explicitly. Member unanimity and facing opposing groups are other more objective characteristics—although these may have a perceptual quality as well. Elements of process that affect the group's character include how members respond to negative feedback, how they treat dissenters, and the use of self-censorship, which causes members to avoid certain topics, perhaps for fear of offending higher-status members. How these characteristics emerge will depend on the nature of the task (for example, its importance and urgency), how the group is structured (for instance, the leader's power and impartiality, prior group experience, and the decision-making context, including member's political motives, group norms of acceptable behavior, and degree of stress from external threat).

Groupthink

Aldag and Fuller (1993) contrasted these components of group problem solving with a more limited model that describes "groupthink." The groupthink phenomenon is the explanation given by Janis and Mann (1977) for some major public policy decision-making fiascoes, such as the Bay of Pigs invasion and the *Challenger* disaster. Groupthink, characterized by lack of vigilant search for information, distortion of the meanings of messages, selective inattention and forgetting, and rationalizing, is the group analogue of defensive avoidance or self-protection. It occurs when the group is dealing with emotional, affect-laden issues—what Janis and Mann termed "hot" cognitions as opposed to the "cold" cognitions of routine problem solving. Groupthink arises when there is a moderate to high level of group cohesion, a provocative situational context, and a history of partial leadership.

Aldag and Fuller (1993) view groupthink as only part of the story of group problem-solving: "[T]here is more to the performance of a football team than the absence of fumbles and interceptions, and there is more to group decision quality than the absence of error. A focus on negative outcomes of group process may divert attention from group synergies" (p. 54). For instance, groups can be more productive than the most productive member or the sum of the efforts of the group members working separately. Positive outcomes can emerge even from initially negative situations if the negative components are recognized and overcome.

Prescriptions for Group Effectiveness

Aldag and Fuller (1993) suggested that prescriptions for effective group functioning may be too limited or misguided. For instance, it may be naive simply to instruct leaders to be impartial. Facilitators and outside experts may be too costly. Recommendations to overcome group dysfunction may be too late—members may not perceive the need for them, or some members may manipulate the group for their own political ends. Rather, a more appropriate and systemic strategy is to assess and possibly alter organizational culture and change reward contingencies.

Group Feedback and Insight. The way group members or observers characterize groups is related to the nature of the feedback they receive about the group process and performance. People who are told that a group performed poorly report more instances of "poor" interaction processes, such as lack of willingness to hear other members' views (Guzzo et al., 1986; Aldag & Fuller, 1993; Saavedra, Earley, & Van Dyne, 1993).

Group feedback is likely to be effective in promoting enhanced group performance when the following conditions hold: the group members depend on each other to complete a task, the group members have differentiated roles and require coordination, group members are affiliation-oriented, and the feedback deals specifically with group process (i.e., interpersonal relations) targeted to how the group can work together more effectively (Nadler, 1979; London, 1988; Saavedra, Earley, & Van Dyne, 1993). Evaluative feedback assists group members in forming attributions about each other and about the group as a whole. The group feedback will be motivating if it increases the development of group goals and if the group receives assistance in using the feedback—for instance, how the information can be used in problem solving. Group feedback may contribute to cognitive outcomes, such as member acceptance of group goals and problems (Nadler, 1979). It may also contribute to affective outcomes, such as member attraction to the group. Behavioral outcomes of feedback may include staying with the group and increasing participation in group activities.

Studies of group process have focused on such topics as group superiority relative to individual performance, exaggerated group risk taking relative to individual risk-taking, group size and performance level relationships, and decision-making performance under varying degrees of procedural constraints (Davis, 1992). This section has tried to show another important area of group research: interpersonal judgment in groups and how such judgments affect decision processes and results. Interpersonal insight is important to group process, especially to group decisions that center on discussions of person perception in organizations, such as committees responsible for personnel selection or performance appraisal. Furthermore, organizations' reliance on groups for accomplishing tasks and making continuous improvements in work processes suggests the importance of members' perceptions of the group's performance. This is addressed next.

Group Members' Perceptions of Performance

Self–other comparisons in a work group may influence group members' evaluations of themselves and each other. In work groups, fellow members work in close proximity and therefore should be able to observe each other's task and interpersonal behaviors (Murphy & Cleveland, 1991; Saavedra & Kwun, 1993). They should be keenly interested in each other's performance, since the contributions of each group member affect the overall group outcome. Consequently, group members should be more able than observers to discriminate diverse behaviors, such as supervisors who are not present during all facets of group activity. In addition, better performers in the group may be more discriminating because they are more concerned that the group achieve a level of performance commensurate with their contribution. Lower-performing individuals may be less concerned or less willing to admit that they, along with some others in the group, are not performing as well as they could. A rating process that asks for self-ratings along with peer ratings may increase the raters' subjective involvement in the evaluation process and therefore cause them to exert greater cognitive effort in rating peers.

In several studies of self-managing groups of college business students working on class projects during a ten-week period, Saavedra and Kwun (1993) found that outstanding contributors were the most discriminating evaluators. This occurred when self-ratings were collected and when they were not. Self-ratings were higher than peer ratings. They speculated that the following cognitive factors are involved in peer ratings (adapted from Saavedra & Kwun, 1993, pp. 454–457):

- In ongoing groups, members (at least those who know they will be rating each other) are likely to form impressions of their co-workers' performance using "person categories" rather than memories of actual behavior.

- These impressions form automatically for observations of repetitive, frequent, or simple behaviors. Controlled (deep) processing occurs for unusual behaviors. (See Chapter 2's discussion of weak versus strong cognitive processing of social information.)
- Automatic processing could lead to biases that decrease variability among ratees because of the loss of information that occurs with unconscious processing.
- Such biases that stem from the use of impressions rather than behavior can be corrected by interventions that promote the active search for performance-related data. For instance, information processing is likely to increase when the personal relevance of the situation is heightened (Fiske, 1993). Personal relevance would increase when the rater's (i.e., the group member's) outcomes depend on the performance of his or her co-workers.
- Requiring self-ratings is a way to heighten personal relevance. This encourages the rater to use more cognitive effort in forming and recalling behaviors relevant to the performance of fellow group members. According to control theory (Chapter 2), people use social comparisons as a means of setting standards for self-evaluation. Further, social comparison theory indicates that people have a drive for self-evaluation and self-enhancement. These are equal and independent aspects of the comparison process. Self-enhancement is a way to increase one's self-esteem through social comparison. Therefore, on the one hand, the process of rating oneself may increase attention to group members' behaviors. On the other hand, this may lead to inaccurate processing of the information that results in inflated self-ratings.
- Self-enhancement and peer-rating biases stemming from the rater's relative performance may occur together. That is, group members who are motivated by self-enhancement evaluate themselves more leniently. However, they also discriminate more carefully between lower and higher peer performance.
- Outstanding contributors to the group are more likely to perceive group member differences in performance. They maintain a positive self-image by paying closer attention to their own positive behaviors. They recall those behaviors more closely and give those behaviors more weight in forming self-evaluations. These individuals perform and rate more effectively. Moreover, exceptional performance provides a rating vantage point that allows greater understanding of performance differentials in the group.
- Also, outstanding performers are likely to perceive the group as using its capabilities to the fullest extent. In comparison, below-average performers are likely to discount their relatively poor performance by attributing it to the group's not using its skills and knowledge to the fullest. This allows them to guard their self-image.

Saavedra and Kwun (1993) summarized their conclusions as follows:

First, a group performance setting fosters familiarity and promotes sufficient interpersonal contact to encourage the encoding of performance information into abstract impressions of co-workers rather than into behavioral records. Second, because personal interests in the form of performance ratings as well as self-esteem . . . are at stake, raters may be motivated to process performance information with a bias that enhances their relative performance in a group. Third, techniques designed to improve utilization of behavioral information through controlled cognitive processing (such as the self-rating instructions [used in the study]) do not seem to offset self-enhancement bias for mediocre performers. (p. 459)

Intragroup Conflict

Similar to individuals, groups try to stay alive, maintain some boundaries, and determine their own course of action over time (Sinnott, 1993). Working with others inevitably invokes some disagreement and often conflict. This can be functional for the group and for its members as individuals. However, making disagreements productive requires accepting multiple realities. This realization is necessary for synthesis to occur. Without this realization, someone in the group has to be "wrong," and misunderstandings are inevitable. The result is that relationships calcify and become rituals lacking in diversity and flexibility. Recognizing multiple realities, according to Sinnott (1993),

gives us a chance to welcome the inevitable conflict and freely play with the options of creating some different relationship . . . We are given a new power with this complex thinking tool—the power to see that we have some control over conflict. Knowing that we are not simply victims of external circumstances . . . is very liberating. Being in a conflict—and changing it to an intragroup opportunity—may provide the first opportunity a person, an organization, or a nation has to see that he, she, or it can think of a situation in fresh ways and make it into a new situation that works. This is the polar opposite of one combatant simply capitulating to another in the group. (p. 171)

Sinnott listed ways to become more comfortable with intragroup conflicts and to use them for group development. It appears that conflicts actually may induce an appreciation for diversity. These methods for transforming intragroup conflict into personal and group development include the following (from Sinnott, 1993, p. 172; italics in original):

• Purposely attempt to shift realities to some other reality about the problem.
• Consciously look forward to conflicts in the group.

- Consciously expect intragroup conflict as a routine experience.
- Consciously see ourselves as "all in this together."
- Posit that "no one is to blame for this problem."
- Assume that others act in the best way they know how (but that not all their actions need to be tolerated even if they mean well).
- Consciously face facts about the conflict, but don't assume that others see the same "facts."
- Create a story around the conflict . . . and let the story resolve itself at a higher level.
- Try to argue the position of an opponent in the conflict (convincingly!).
- Enlarge the "problem space" by redefining the problem or its parameters.
- Consciously shift the metatheory the group uses to frame the problem.
- Generate many "crazy" solutions to the conflict.
- Shift from focus on a concrete solution to focus on finding a good *process*.

Conclusion

This chapter has examined how people gain insight into, and contribute to, cooperative group work processes. Group members need insight into these emerging group processes in order to contribute to positive group outcomes. People gain insight in a task-group setting much as they do in a dyadic relationship. While this chapter has tried to show the underlying similarities in social cognitive processes, I have concentrated on how group structure and task demands influence interpersonal insight and help the individual contribute productively to the group. In a group, the patterns of communication and the rate and quality of task performance (entrainment and synchronization) emerge quickly in response to the effects of time pressure. Cues about roles and behavioral patterns are embedded in the face-to-face group interactions as the new group discusses how to proceed and initiates the task. Task interdependence supported by appropriate goals and feedback influences conflict and strategy emergence during the group process.

Many of the studies cited in this chapter are based on laboratory research that involved the use of undergraduate students who interacted in contrived group settings for relatively short periods of time. There were exceptions, for example, commentaries on actual group experiences by Weick (1993; Weick & Roberts, 1993) and Aldag and Fuller (1993) and Gersick's (1988) study of project teams. As noted in the preface to this book, this is common in social psychological research, and it suggests the need for more group research in real settings. Keep this in mind in evaluating the following conclusions:

1. Group members are able to quickly discern interaction patterns and cues. They develop a flow of interaction to suit the situation that is main-

tained even after the situation changes. Furthermore, newcomers to established groups quickly recognize group interaction patterns.

2. The cognitive theories of social information processing described in Chapter 2 can be applied to understand interpersonal insight in groups. Reflected feedback helps individuals position themselves in the group. Group members evaluate feedback in relation to their existing conception of self-efficacy in similar situations.

3. Group members both seek and convey expectations and reactions. Behaviors evolve into discernible patterns of interaction.

4. Group members' cognitions are important to group process, and organizations should be attentive to how strategies and likely outcomes are communicated. While group process and outcomes do not necessarily change the individual member's cognitions, the group is likely to be more averse to risks when half or more of the members frame decision alternatives in terms of gains; that is, they want to avoid risks that would bring about losses. On the other hand, focusing on possible losses may suit the organization well, depending on the circumstances, by encouraging more proactive and risky decisions by group members.

5. The cultural diversity of group members influences the effectiveness of group process and performance during the initial stages of the group's life. Homogeneous groups tend to be higher on process and performance measures, although these differences dissipate over time.

6. Perceptions of group heterogeneity may be influenced by the amount of information about group differences and similarities and by the relationship of the group to the perceiver (i.e., "out-groups" may be viewed as more heterogeneous than "in-groups"). Interventions may be needed to avoid self-selection biases, ensure group heterogeneity, and take advantage of it.

7. Interventions for enhancing outcomes of culturally diverse groups are applicable to any group process. They include regularly collecting and feeding back data on group process and performance, allowing members to discuss group process, and planning a course of action for increasing problem-solving effectiveness.

8. Group members evaluate the worthwhileness of their individual contributions to the group in relation to their abilities and energy, likely outcomes, and the effort and abilities of the other group members. Social loafing occurs when there is the potential for a "free ride." This may be avoided or overcome, for instance, by changing the situation so there is no longer a conflict between the interests of the individual and the interests of the group and by punishing defection from the group.

9. In general, group members have a positive bias in evaluating the performance of the group—a bias that is greater than that of individuals performing on their own. This may explain why group structures are favored for getting work done in organizations (e.g., the prevalence of committees, task forces, and teams that are often tied to special initiatives, such as quality improvement).

10. Task, goal, and feedback interdependence determine performance requirements and direct group members' efforts toward achieving performance goals. The interaction of these elements suggests ways to design groups to have a positive effect on performance. For example, individual goals and individual feedback enhance the performance when task interdependence is pooled (each member works alone). Group goals and individual feedback enhance performance when task interdependence is sequential (each group member performs a different task, but the tasks need to be coordinated). Group goals and group feedback enhance performance when task interdependence is reciprocal or there is considerable interaction and group discretion over work process.

11. Group interventions enhance motivation levels of group members by increasing their expectancy of valued outcomes. Groups eventually develop their own identity, which guides members' motivation. This identity may include a sense of vulnerability and of the risks inherent in the task, thereby weakening member motivation.

12. Groupthink is the lack of vigilant search for information, distortion of the meanings of messages, selective inattention and forgetting, and rationalizing. It is most likely to occur when the group is dealing with emotional issues.

13. Automatic processing of information about group process could lead to biases that decrease perceived variability of performance among fellow group members. These biases stem from the use of impressions rather than behavior. This can be corrected by promoting the active search for performance-related data. In general, outstanding contributors to the group will be more likely to perceive group member differences in performance.

14. Intragroup conflict can be a source of group development. This occurs if group members recognize and value different viewpoints. Group members need to realize that knowledge about themselves and others is subjective and requires probing and testing the environment to gain an understanding about alternative courses of action.

Chapter 8 extends this discussion by considering how interpersonal insight evolves during negotiations between individuals and within and between groups. These are situations in which conflict is endemic to the process and vested interests and personal vantage points are likely to influence behavior and ultimately conflict resolution.

8

Negotiation Processes

We hardly find any persons of good sense save those who agree with us.
François, duc de La Rochefoucauld, *Moral Maxim* 347

The last chapter considered interpersonal insight in cooperative groups—those charged with a task. The groups usually have a short deadline (McGrath, 1990). They have to start quickly and be productive almost immediately. They may, however, remain intact for some time, perhaps handling new assignments. The degree of cooperation or the smoothness with which the group becomes and remains productive may vary with the people involved and the type of task demands. Intragroup conflicts may arise, but cooperation is clearly the intended goal. This raises the question about what happens when cooperation is not the basis for group process—when the relationships are primarily adversarial or when the parties involved are concerned that their own interests will be sacrificed for the good of others. We learn about insight into conflict emergence and resolution by studying negotiation tasks.

Walton and McKersie (1991) distinguished between two types of negotiation: *distributive* (in which opposing parties perceive a win–lose situation) and *integrative* (in which both parties can win). Referring to insight in integrative bargaining they stated,

> Motivation to work on an agenda item as a problem assumes a certain type of insight-discovery of the integrative potential in the situation. Often the achievement of comparable motivation between the parties is primarily a problem of gaining similar or complementary perceptions of the problem area. Thus, if the key participants have a relatively long time horizon, they are more likely to perceive integrative potential and be more motivated to engage in problem solving. (p. 153)

This chapter considers the role of interpersonal insight in distributive and integrative bargaining. I begin by detailing the types of cues that initiate and direct insights. The way these cues are elicited and interpreted are often part of deliberate negotiation strategies. Feedback is considered a way for the parties to adjust their usual patterns of behavior and recognize which envi-

156

ronmental cues need to be monitored and which can be ignored. Categorization of feedback, attribution, and cognitive evaluation underlie insight in negotiations as they do in other interpersonal relationships. I examine how negotiator flexibility and movement changes as a result of these processes. Gender issues in negotiation are considered. I describe the negotiation situation in terms of the actions and behaviors of the negotiators and various interventions by mediators and agents. The chapter concludes with a discussion of negotiation processes within and between groups, with emphasis on group member motivation and compatibility.

Cues and Insights in Negotiations

Inferences about the other party in a negotiation are based partly on knowledge of the other party's costs and utilities (e.g., what would be gained and lost by a strike resulting from a breakdown in a labor negotiation). A party rarely has complete information, however, and there is a need to interpret a variety of cues about offers and behaviors throughout the negotiation process. In distributive bargaining, for instance, subtleties in communication suggest the degree of one party's commitment to a position. A statement of commitment has three tactical parts—the degree of finality of the commitment to a specific position, the degree of specificity of the position to which the commitment is made, and the consequence or threat to be associated with a positional commitment.

Negotiators have tactics to elicit cues and tactics to record and analyze reactions. The former include personal abuse, exaggerated impatience, and testing resistance points late in negotiations. The party's experience in similar negotiations (e.g., having been in the opponent's position) helps in making more valid inferences. In a long-running negotiation, or when the parties have negotiated with each other before, they "learn in various subtle ways to assess the position and intentions of the other person" (Walton and McKersie, 1991, p. 65). They also learn to modify the opponent's perceptions of utilities:

> If we assume that all the verbal and nonverbal behaviors of Party are being scanned by Opponent for clues about Party's utilities, then Party has two responses. He can be inscrutable, that is, behave in a minimal or irrelevant way, or he can disguise his utilities by deliberately misrepresenting them. (p. 67)

This leads to negotiation strategies that control the opponent's insights:

> It is especially important for Party to minimize clues early in negotiations rather than fashion misleading ones, to the extent that he has not already developed clear notions about what his ultimate resistance point is in these negotiations. (p. 67)

Walton and McKersie view the negotiation process as a mechanism for opposing parties to gather much of the information they need to test the appropriateness of their own positions. The process of controlling others' perceptions has many possible tactics and requires care. For instance, being careful not to sound off too early in an effort to resolve minor issues quickly is dangerous because such concessions weaken later bargaining power. There are risks in communicating misinformation; being oblique in one negotiation makes it hard to be accepted as a truthful reporter in the next negotiation. Also, inconsistency in information and position causes a loss of credibility. Verbal and nonverbal behavior is critical in interpreting positions in negotiations. Colorful and colloquial language, for instance, can force the opponent to reassess the cost and value of different issues.

The Role of Feedback

Neale and Bazerman (1991) considered insight through feedback as the mechanism for making good decisions in negotiations. They examined the role of cognitive biases in the ability of experts to make "good" decisions and the ability of negotiators to understand and incorporate feedback. Feedback provides the reason for negotiators to adjust their behavior and learn from experience, but feedback is likely to be biased or ambiguous. Also, the relationship between amount of experience and the validity of expert judgment is disappointingly low. Barriers that prevent negotiators from learning from experience include cognitive biases and inadequate cognitive processing, poor information-search techniques, inaccurate interpretation of information and feedback, and the use of unaided memory for coding, storing, and retrieving information. Interpreting information in negotiations may be affected by individual characteristics. For example, if the negotiator's self-esteem is involved in the outcome, he or she may find positive interpretations of ambiguous information more compelling or easier to believe. There are practical constraints on feedback use. For instance, outcomes may be delayed and not easily attributable to a particular action. Variability in the environment may degrade the reliability of feedback. There is likely to be no information about what the outcome would have been if another decision had been taken since most important decisions are unique and so provide little opportunity for learning.

Negotiation Scripts

Scripts are well-learned behavior patterns that represent typical reactions to sets of environmental stimuli under very specific circumstances. They summarize "a coherent sequence of events expected by the individual, involving him either as a participant or observer" (Abelson, 1976, p. 33, cited in Neale and Bazerman, 1991, p. 87). An effective strategic conceptualization of an interpersonal situation rests in knowing why the pattern of behaviors identified by the script is effective. Conceptual schemas identify important features of situations. For instance, a schema for negotiation might include information about bids, counteroffers, and cues about when bids and counteroffers are appropriate. Therefore, the schema indicates what information and events to monitor for feedback.

Thus, in the negotiation context, interpersonal insight is having an accurate representation of relevant scripts and schemas—that is, knowing which environmental cues need to be monitored and which can be ignored. Negotiators develop a strategic conceptualization that limits the universe of possible hypotheses to test during the trial-and-error phases of strategy acquisition. The feedback they receive needs to be sufficiently diagnostic to influence future behavior. The right perceptual set means that the feedback has diagnostic value (Neale & Northcraft, 1990). The wrong perceptual set interferes with a decision maker's ability to make good use of diagnostic feedback. Negotiators who have well-developed strategic conceptualizations do not rely on ritual, superstition, or luck. Further, they are less likely to be influenced by various biases. Experts and amateurs are both susceptible to biases. Expert negotiators, however, tend to recognize that both parties can win and are more able than amateurs to achieve agreements of greater joint value (Neale & Northcraft, 1986). This implies that strategic conceptualization should include a component that reduces the impact of cognitive biases. Also, diagnostic feedback is necessary to check the implementation of the strategic conceptualization. Experience without expertise limits negotiators' ability to transfer knowledge by conveying what they do. Insight, then, requires both the recognition of critical variables and the ability to transfer and apply them.

Emergence of Insight into Negotiation Processes

Negotiator perceptions are critical to negotiation processes and outcomes, as described here by Neale and Bazerman (1992):

> It may not be the objective, external aspects of the situation that directly affect negotiator judgment; instead, it may be the way that the negotiator perceives these features and uses those perceptions to interpret and screen information. . . . A negotiator's perceptual context includes the nature, origins, and use of . . . stereotypes, categorizations, norms, roles, schema, and scripts. . . . The framing of disputes invokes norms of behavior and orders the importance and relevance of available facts. (pp. 161–162)

Negotiators' orientations and expectations—that is, their frames of reference—are the way they make sense of the negotiation situation (Pinkley, 1990). Reframing allows alternative definitions of a situation emerge from a bargaining interaction (Putnam & Holmer, 1992). Positive frames generally lead to more completed transactions and higher profit from negotiations (cf. Putnam, 1990; Bazerman, Magliozzi, & Neale, 1985), while negative frames tend to increase conflict and the likelihood of impasse (Bazerman, 1984; Bazerman & Neale, 1983). Negotiators with more ambitious aspirations do better than those without, and low expectations of settlement prior to entering the negotiation increase the chances of impasse (White & Neale, 1994). Interpersonal relationships among negotiators affect their expectations, level of trust, perceptions of other negotiators' power, goals, values, feelings, and familiarity with one another. Various behaviors are used to establish these frames; for instance, role power is established from threats.

One way to define negotiator power is in terms of the alternatives available to the individuals if the parties fail to reach a negotiated settlement. Pinkley, Neale, and Bennett (1994) found that just having such an alternative increases the negotiator's value of the outcome (the value of the alternative if negotiation fails and the value of a joint outcome if negotiation succeeds). Also, the more valuable the alternative, the more benefits one perceives from the alternative and from a joint outcome, especially if the alternative is more attractive than the alternative available to the other negotiator.

Negotiators interpret conflicts according to three independent dimensions of conflict frames: (1) relationships versus task, (2) emotional versus intellectual, and (3) cooperate versus win (Pinkley, 1990). In a study of business students negotiating in pairs for sales territories, Pinkley and Northcraft (1994) coded subjects' descriptions of the conflict scenario before and after the negotiation in terms of these three dimensions. Disputants had higher monetary outcomes when they and their negotiating partners had relationship or cooperation frames. Those with intellectual frames were more satisfied with the negotiation, indicating that frames that relate to outcomes are not the same as those that relate to satisfaction with the outcome.

Negotiators shape issues through framing. They start the negotiation with a conceptualization of the problem, and this definition shifts during the negotiation (Putnam & Holmer, 1992). Arguments between negotiators affect the perceived significance and stability of positions. A negotiator's justifications for an argument shape the opposing negotiator's view of the position. Positions are shaped as multiple agendas are recognized and some issues emerge as more relevant than others. Reframing occurs as a negotiator develops a different field of vision for understanding agendas. This is a dynamic interaction process in which alternative meanings arise from discourse (Putnam & Holmer, 1992; Putnam & Geist, 1985).

Mutual disclosures occur as negotiating parties choose and articulate positions. This may be an arduous process, especially in distributive bargaining, during which parties may deliberately mislead each other in hopes of concessions from their opposition and higher gains for their side. Habitual or expected patterns may emerge that are easily categorized. However, some positions may be unexpected and need analysis, such as a major concession early in the bargaining. Attributions are made to explain the opposing party's actions as well as one's own. The parties interpret what is important to them and their constituents and estimate how the opposition is likely to react to various overtures and offers. Cognitive evaluations include the parties' goodwill and confidence in being able to resolve the conflict to their mutual benefit.

Negotiators influence each other's conflict frames. These frames also converge during the process of negotiation, and indeed the more the initial divergence between frames, the more the convergence during negotiation (Pinkley & Northcraft, 1994). This occurred for relationship and emotional conflict frames (Pinkley & Northcraft, 1994). However, there were no changes in the cooperate/win dimension.

While this approach to insight emergence in negotiations concentrates on verbal exchanges as cues to meaning, behavioral observation is a source of other cues. Relevant behaviors range from deliberate and obvious dramatizations (e.g., exaggerated yawning, or storming out of a negotiation session) to subtle gestures (e.g., taking notes on a particular subject). Such behaviors are notable when they diverge from expected or common behavior patterns.

Assessment for Feedback

Gilkey and Greenhalgh (1991) developed a comprehensive assessment program to provide an in-depth profile of executives and MBA students in a course on power and negotiation. The assessment included two hours of test batteries, another two hours doing group-administered projective tests (such as the well-known Rorschach test), and another hour in a face-to-face meeting with a clinical psychologist. Measures tapped such concepts as empathy, interpersonal orientation (interest in and reactions to others, taking others seriously—similar to self-monitoring), locus of control, and approach to conflict (competing, collaborating, compromising, accommodating, and avoiding). Feedback was provided to the participants in writing and in person by the clinician. The assessment was meant to be "a valuable teaching tool in expanding negotiators' awareness of the way they think and act. In addition to mobilizing their capacities for self-awareness, negotiators also learn to benefit from the feedback of peers and clinically-trained observers" (p. 285). The authors believed, consistent with the theme of this book, that self-awareness can create "the desire for change as the students become aware of alternative approaches to dealing with conflict that can allow them to use their individual strengths more fully" (p. 285).

The program also used behavioral exercises to feed back information about actual performance. (See Chapter 9's discussion of assessment centers as a development tool, and Resource Guide D for an outline of such a method.) Pairs of negotiators were videotaped doing a negotiation and then received an appraisal of their performance along with watching the tape. Thus, the executives had multiple opportunities to learn about their personalities and the effect of the latter on their negotiation behavior in a supportive, confidential setting.

Linking Consultation and Feedback

An important element of an effective dispute resolution system is consultation before negotiation and feedback after negotiation (Ury, Brett, & Goldberg, 1988). Consultation refers to an opportunity for one party (e.g., management in a labor dispute) to discuss a possible action affecting the other party (the union). This can prevent disputes that arise through misunderstanding and reduce the opposition that often results when decisions are made unilaterally. Also, consultation is a way to identify points of difference at the outset so they can be negotiated.

Postnegotiation feedback helps the parties learn from their dispute to avoid similar situations in the future. This is especially fruitful if the dispute is symptomatic of a broader, more pervasive problem that may affect others (e.g., a consumer dispute that may affect other consumers). An ombudsman may identify organizational procedures that cause disputes and suggest ways to avoid them (Ury, Brett, & Goldberg, 1988; Rowe, 1984). Ury, Brett, and Goldberg (1988) recommended establishing a regular forum for discussion so that the parties can consider issues that arise in disputes that cut across other aspects of relationships between the parties. Some firms have "common interest forums" in which union and management representatives meet regularly for such discussions (London, 1988).

Gender Issues in Negotiation

Men and women are likely to approach negotiation differently. Possible cultural, psychological, or biological antecedents of these differences are beyond the scope of this book. Here my focus is on the nature of the behavioral differences in negotiations. For instance, women who negotiate with other women tend to be more cooperative and use different forms of arguments than they do in mixed groups (Putnam & Jones, 1982). In general, men are oriented toward demonstrating separation and individuation as a motive for action, while women attempt to develop affiliation and relatedness to others (Kolb & Coolidge, 1991). After reviewing the literature on gender issues in negotiation, Kolb and Coolidge (1991) concluded that four themes explain the ways women frame and conduct negotiations (adapted from pp. 264–266):

1. *A relational view of others.* For women, their self-concept and perception of others are not in opposition. Rather, they are viewed in terms of mutual aid and support. Women attempt to create an environment in which people can come to know each other through expressions of emotion and feeling.
2. *Embedded view of agency.* Women view negotiations not as a separate game with its own set of rules and opportunities for individuation.

Rather, they view it within the context of other activities, and they expect that people will behave as they usually do. Therefore, they may have trouble realizing that negotiations are occurring.

3. *Control through empowerment.* The idea that power is accrued for oneself at the expense of others may be alien to women. Women emphasize the needs of the other person so as to allow that other person to feel powerful. They believe in mutual empowerment rather than competition.

4. *Problem solving through dialogue.* Women tend to engage others in the joint exploration of ideas. They expect that others will be active listeners. Women tend not to plan and strategize prior to action but instead are particularly able to adapt and grow as they learn through interaction.

These are fairly sweeping generalizations, and they certainly suggest that more research is necessary to prove their generalizability and underlying causes. Overall, these conclusions imply that distributive negotiation may be uncomfortable for women because it positions them in opposition to others. Women seem to prefer harmony and integration rather than win–lose situations with distributive rewards. However, women should be effective in learning about available alternatives and the priorities of others (Kolb & Coolidge, 1991, p. 269). Their disadvantage in distributive negotiations may be that they speak with qualifiers to demonstrate flexibility and a willingness to discuss, while men speak with confidence and self-enhancement, which suggest clarity and decisiveness. Kolb and Coolidge (1991, pp. 271–272) argued for the importance of recognizing the voice that women bring to negotiations. Moreover, women need to experiment with various modes of experience. There is a place for valuing this alternative voice—one based on a relational view of others, an embedded view of agency, a focus on empowerment, and problem solving through dialogue. This is especially valuable in integrative negotiations that seek a win–win solution.

Negotiator Flexibility

Negotiators need insight about each other's flexibility. Negotiating flexibility, according to Druckman (1993), is "a willingness to move from initial positions, and by an observed shift from rather rigid and tough bargaining postures toward an agreement. It is especially noticeable in the transition from negotiation impasses to successful solutions of the negotiation" (p. 236). Cooperation is "moving in the direction of others' positions or away from one's own initial position," while competition is "sticking to your own initial position in the hope that others will move toward that position, resulting in one's own position prevailing as the outcome of the negotiation" (Druckman, 1993, p. 237). Flexibility is evident in the verbal exchanges between negotiations and in their perceptions of their opponents and the situation. Indicators of flexibility include statements of commitment to positions, perceived incompatibility between positions, or descriptions of the situation as a win–lose contest or a problem-solving debate.

Ways to Increase Negotiator Flexibility

A negotiator's flexibility may be affected by the situation, including actions and behaviors of other negotiators and various interventions by mediators. Druckman (1993) outlined ways in which such situational factors influence negotiators' flexibility during different stages of the negotiation process (adapted from p. 241):

- During the prenegotiating planning period situational factors affecting flexibility include:
  —Willingness to study the issues from the perspective of other parties
  —Willingness to develop strategies from a unilateral perspective
- At the early periods when parties "set the stage" for the discussion to come:
  —Willingness to disaggregate issues, to consider the possibility of partial agreements should a comprehensive agreement not be possible, or to aim for a comprehensive agreement covering all issues
  —Amiable relationships
  —Increased responsibility of the negotiators and increased latitude for decision making
  —Holding many informal meetings outside the negotiating sessions
- During the give-and-take discussions:
  —Other negotiators make many concessions
  —Salient outcomes exist
  —Coalitions among weaker parties form to increase their influence
- During the final stage ("endgame"):
  —A deadline for concluding the talks exists
  —There is no attractive alternative to a negotiated agreement
  —A solution is suggested by a mediator

The Mediator as Information Processor and Impression Manager

Mediation refers to the assistance of a third party in solving a problem for two or more interacting parties (Wall & Lynn, 1993). Mediation is practiced in a variety of conflict-resolution situations, including labor–management negotiations, leader–subordinate relations, and community disputes. Mediation techniques and strategies require understanding person perception and helping the negotiating parties gain insight into each other's positions, motivation, and arguments. It entails using communications and knowledge of the effects of various types of information on the parties' perceptions of themselves and others. Mediators attempt to do the following (from Wall and Lynn (1993, p. 166):

• Clarify the situation.
• Make parties aware of relevant information.
• Rehearse each party in appropriate behavior.
• Clarify what parties intend to communicate.
• Act as a spokesperson for the weaker side.
• Help a party undo a commitment.
• Reduce tension.
• Summarize the agreement.
• Reward parties' concessions.
• Act as sounding board for positions and tactics.
• Threaten to quit or to bring in an arbitrator who will impose a solution.
• Convince a party that a proposal is salable to constituents.
• Bring third-party ultimatums to the negotiation.
• Exaggerate the costs of disagreement.
• Help parties save face.

Many of these tactics are ways to manage impressions and manipulate perceptions. These include coercion, reinforcement, face-saving (helping a party retain a positive image), and threats. Other tactics simply involve information processing—summarizing, clarifying, feeding back, and interpreting information.

Negotiator Perceptions of Mediators

Third-party mediators are often important in the resolution of conflict. For example, conflicts between subordinates often require the mediating intervention of the subordinates' manager. We assume that third parties are effective because disputants perceive them to be neutral. However, the mediator's impartiality may not be required for success. A mediator is never totally neutral anyway (Conlon & Ross, 1993; Forester & Stitzel, 1989). What is important is that the mediator ensures the representation of all affected parties. Partisan third parties have personal, political, or economic interests in settling a dispute that may favor one disputant over another or conflict with the interests of both disputants (Conlon & Ross, 1993). They may become involved because they have authority, as a manager does over two conflicting subordinates. However, the manager may be more closely affiliated with one party than another. Indeed, managers' preferences for a particular settlement may motivate their involvement in the intervention.

The third party's degree of partisanship may not be known by the conflicting parties. On the other hand, the disputants' perceptions of the third party's partisanship are likely to influence the disputants' behavior. Disputants may perceive a positive relationship between themselves and the third party. Alternatively, disputants may perceive an unfavorable relationship between themselves and the third party or a positive affiliation between their opponent and the third party (Murnighan, 1987, 1991). Disputants who perceive the third parties as neutral are more likely to view them as acceptable, trust their favorable suggestions, and follow their recommendations (Welton & Pruitt, 1987; Witmer, Carnevale, & Walker, 1991). A positive outcome from a partial third party who initially seemed to favor one's opponent may be viewed by the disputant with greater satisfaction than the same outcome from an impartial third party. This may occur because the disputant's expectations for a positive outcome were low and the disputant was relieved that the outcome was not negative (Lind & Lissak, 1985).

Conlon and Ross (1993) applied control theory (Kernan & Lord, 1991) to explain mechanisms that lead disputants to determine their subjective reactions to third parties, outcomes, and negotiation procedures. They hypothesized, "If positive affiliation heightens outcome expectations, then the larger discrepancies between these outcome expectations and disputants' actual outcomes in this condition will lead to lower outcome satisfaction ratings than under unfavorable affiliation, in which expectations are diminished and discrepancies are smaller" (p. 281). They showed that disputants who were unfavorably affiliated with the third party lowered their outcome expectations. As a result, their actual outcomes were closer to their initial expectations than were the outcomes for disputants who were favorably affiliated with the third party.

This section has described the role of the mediator and the importance of the disputants' perceptions of the mediator to the perceived success of the negotiated outcomes. In the next section I introduce another type of third party, the agent. The agent is intended to represent the interests of one party, yet an agent's multiple loyalties and professional obligations may interfere with this relationship and alter the representational role. Therefore, the role of the agent is likely to be very different than that of the negotiator.

Principal–Agent Relationships

Agents are those who act for, on behalf of, or as representatives of disputants or principals (Neale & Bazerman, 1992). An agent represents another party, the "principal," in negotiations with others. Therefore, the key distinguishing feature of the agent is that of representative, not unlike the negotiator or legislator representing constituency interests. The agent is usually a professional with certain expertise and standards that apply to the situation. Mitnick (1980) developed a theory of agency with respect to corporate political behavior. His concepts also apply at the individual level and demonstrate yet another key interpersonal relationship in organizations.

Agents are hired because they solve problems for principles, they get things for them that would be otherwise inaccessible, do things more efficiently or aggressively than by other means, have time to spend on an issue, or lend expertise and information to a situation or problem (Mitnick, 1993b).

The agent acts for, and attempts to benefit, the principal. An agent can reduce the principal's felt uncertainty and risk by providing expertise and experience in representing the principal's interests.

An agent may be internal or external to the organization. The organization—or, to be more exact, a manager in the organization—may hire an attorney, purchasing agent, executive search firm, or some other professional or service provider to represent the interests of the organization in negotiations with others. Large organizations also employ people on their central staffs to provide these services for the corporation (e.g., the legal services department or the human resources department). These centralized departments take into account the perspective of the entire organization as well as the interests of the departments using their services. In other cases, these services are decentralized, with departments having their own people acting as their agents—doing their own purchasing, recruitment, hiring, labor negotiating, financing, and so forth. An advantage to having these agents within the department or business unit is that they may have a better understanding of the interests and values of the department than would a central department or external agent. Moreover, they may have a stronger stake in the outcome of their work than they might if they have other clients.

Usually, we think of the principal as having choice in the selection of the agent. If desired outcomes are not forthcoming or principals believe their interests have not been represented adequately, they can dismiss the agent and hire someone else. In other cases the agent is imposed on the organization, as a judge or executor might be in the re-structuring of a bankrupt organization.

Agents, similar to mediators, may have little power to impose a solution to a dispute. Unlike mediators, however, agents may have a direct interest in the outcome of the dispute—as they would if they worked in the organization they represent, if they have other clients with similar interests, or if they have direct interests themselves (e.g., they have ownership in another enterprise with similar interests). They also are likely to feel a professional and ethical responsibility to accomplish the principal's goals. While negotiators may view third parties as neutral or acting in the best interest of the negotiators, agents may act against one or both of the principals. Or agents may feel conflicted by a concern for opposing principals, as a labor negotiator, perhaps a labor relations specialist, representing management may feel an affinity for the interests of the employees in the firm. So while the principal–agent relationship is likely to be cooperative as principal and agent band together to accomplish a goal, the relationship may not be smooth. Consequently, interpersonal perceptions are critical to the success of the process.

Problems with agency relations stem from a number of factors, including dynamics of social perception, motivation, and information processing:

> In seeking and processing information, . . . [agents] may infer a too simplistic causality for events; attribute change more to the environment than to the client organization; over-rely on dramatic or salient occurrences or coinci-

dences; over-rely on more available information; over-rely on past perceptions of the environment over present conditions; tend to ignore information
contrary to current perceptions and give excessive weight to consistent, apparently confirmatory evidence; allow their past personal commitments to
interpretations to influence present advice; and so on. (Mitnick, 1993a, p.
179)

Other problems stem from differences in interests or goals between the
agent and principal, differences in understandings of the issues or interpretation of information, differences in the levels of risk aversion of the principal and agent, and outside pressures on both the principal and the agent
(Getz, 1993). An agent may not act in the principal's interest because the
agent is not sure what the principal wants, disagrees with the principal's
interests, does not have the capability to act in the principal's interests, or
doesn't have the motivation to exert sufficient effort on behalf of the principal (Mitnick, 1984; Getz, 1993). An agent may represent multiple principals
at once, sometimes in the same negotiation. These principals may vary in
their values and aspirations. In some cases, as suggested previously, the
agent may have conflicting interests. Principals try to control these possible
problems by, for example, monitoring the agent, threatening to fire the agent,
working with multiple agents, giving feedback to the agent, and offering incentives for especially favorable outcomes (Getz, 1993).

Agent–Principal Compatibility and Complementarity

Agent–principal relationships develop as each member of the pair provides
the other with information about goals and expectations, values, and expressions of satisfaction with intermediate outcomes. The principal and agent
must have compatible goals and understand each other's interests. The relationship will be closer and more united the more similar the agent and
principal are in a number of respects, such as background, experience, and
values. On the other hand, the agent must complement the principal by adding value beyond what the principal can do alone. The agent's perspective
and experience are likely to be different than the principal's because of the
agent's professional expertise, knowledge of rules and regulations, and understanding about how decisions are made and how people are likely to react
to them. Hence, principal and agent may need to educate each other as well
as communicate frequently as the agent's work proceeds.

Both principal and agent engage in categorizing feedback, making attributions for unexpected events and behaviors, and revising their evaluations
of themselves and others. This process will depend on the amount and clarity of communication between agent and principal, the suddenness of
events, the degree of rapid response required, and the importance of the deal
under negotiation to the agent and the principal. My hypothesis is that
agent–principal relationships will be less productive the less information is
shared, the more confusing or conflicting the information, the more surpris-

ing the evolution of events, and the greater the need for rapid response. Principal and agent will devote more attention to the development of the relationship the more important the outcomes are for the principal and the more the agent stands to gain (e.g., money, additional business, enhanced reputation). Research is needed to study these principal–agent relationships, given the many service professionals who have a representational role.

Similar to negotiations, situations involving agents vary in the degree of competitiveness and combativeness. In some cases the agent is providing expertise to a primarily cooperative situation, such as hiring a new employee. In other cases the situation is more competitive, such as a distributive (win–lose) labor negotiation. This suggests the relevance of the agent's and negotiator's motivation to look out for themselves or maximize gains for all parties concerned. The next section examines motivational orientation and interpersonal relationships in group negotiation processes.

Intra- and Intergroup Negotiation Processes

At times during the life of a group, members may find it necessary to negotiate among themselves, perhaps for scarce resources, desirable roles and responsibilities, goals to pursue, or strategies for accomplishing a goal. Group members represent their own interests as well as what they perceive to be the interests of the group as a whole. Negotiations also occur between groups. These may be work groups competing for scarce resources or they may be negotiating teams, as in a large-scale labor negotiation. In this case, group members' insights about themselves, their fellow group members, and the members of the opposing team are relevant to the evolution of the negotiation process. Competition may arise within as well as between the groups.

Motivational Orientation and Group Member Insight

Motivational goals direct and limit behavior in negotiations. For instance, a competitive orientation prompts negotiating parties to maximize the difference between one's own and others' gains. An individualistic orientation involves maximizing only one's own gains. A variant of this is a cooperative orientation, which involves maximizing both one's own and others' gains. Having a representational role and responsibility, as does an agent or a negotiator in distributive negotiations, enhances the party's commitment and accountability to a client or constituency. However, it also slows the negotiation process and reduces member effectiveness (London, 1977; Haccoun & Klimoski, 1975).

Weingart, Bennett, and Brett (1993) argued for the superiority of a cooperative orientation in group negotiations, proposing that cooperative groups reach higher-quality decisions than groups whose members are individualistically oriented. Studying groups engaged in negotiating a possible joint venture, they found that cooperative groups were more trusting and argued less than individualistically oriented groups. Individualistically oriented group members were inclined to continue negotiating to improve their own outcomes at the expense of others even after an agreement had been identified that all group members could accept. In cooperative groups, further deliberations would not be beneficial because any future gains for one group member mean a loss for the others. Cooperative groups are more likely than individualistic groups to share information about the relative priority of issues.Moreover, cooperative groups are likely to have more accurate insight about the priorities of others in their group.

Effects of Negotiator Self-Esteem and Mood on Negotiation Behavior

Considerable work has focused on cognitive aspects of negotiation processes, rather than on understanding how motivational and affective processes influence negotiations. However, a study by Kramer, Newton, & Pommerenke (1993) investigated the impact of motivational and affected processes on negotiator judgments. They predicted that positive mood and the motivation to maintain high self-esteem would contribute to negotiator overconfidence and overly positive self-evaluations. In a laboratory study of negotiation dyads, they found that high self-esteem and positive mood (manipulated by watching a humorous videotape on corporate performance) positively affected both negotiators' confidence and optimism prior to negotiation and their postnegotiation evaluations of performance.

These results suggest why negotiators often fail to reach agreement. Kramer, Newton, and Pommerenke (1993) argued that self-enhancement biases that allow negotiators to maintain their self-esteem lead them to see themselves as more cooperative, fair, trustworthy, and flexible than others. As a result, they may overestimate their responsiveness to positive influence strategies and underestimate others' responsiveness. Also, self-enhancement biases may reduce negotiators' ability to learn from their experiences. Negotiators may fail to revise their expectations and perceptions as a negotiation proceeds. "Thus, the need to feel good about one's self may be gained at the price of developing more realistic assessments" (Kramer, Newton, & Pommerenke, 1993, p. 127). They suggest that an issue for future research would be to investigate whether expert negotiators compensate for self-enhancement tendencies. Another would be to determine whether negotiators who are made aware of this bias may be able to lessen its effects.

Intergroup Evaluations

Participating in negotiations can influence intergroup relations and group stereotypes. Specifically, the evaluations of others who are different than ourselves may be influenced by the outcome of negotiations with members of that group. People can be categorized into social groups in many ways, for instance, based on organizational membership, socioeconomic status, and ethnicity. People generally show favoritism to in-group members (i.e., those who share the same characteristics they have) and are negative toward out-group members (those who have different characteristics—groups of which they are not a member). Thompson (1993) found that negotiating with an out-group member increased the favorability of evaluations of the out-group. Negotiating with an in-group member increased in-group favoritism. This effect occurred only when the negotiation was integrative (i.e., both parties could reach a beneficial agreement) and not when it was distributive (both parties' goals could not be achieved). Those who expected to negotiate with out-group members thought they would obtain significantly lower outcomes, but they did not. There were no differences in the value of the actual outcomes for whose who negotiated with an in-group member compared with those who negotiated with an out-group member.

These results show that social contact can reduce prejudice even in competitive situations, unless negotiating parties are prohibited from making a profit (Thompson, 1993). Reaching a mutually profitable situation is the key to interpersonal favorability here. Moreover, it is not enough for the bargaining situation to contain the potential for integrative agreement in order for intergroup relations to improve. A mutually beneficial solution must be reached. Moreover, while people approach intergroup negotiation in a more competitive fashion than they approach intragroup negotiation, this negative expectancy does not prevent or decrease the ultimate quality of the negotiated settlement. (See the discussion of intragroup conflict at the end of Chapter 7.) In general, compromise may be achieved when each party is extremely cooperative and offers concessions from the start or when each party adopts a competitive stance and then agrees to a compromise (Thompson, 1993). Similarly, a highly integrative solution may be achieved when the parties have a high concern for each other's welfare as well as their own or when they relentlessly examine each alternative. Third-party interventions that prompt negotiators to discover creative solutions may be especially worthwhile when negotiators are members of different groups that perceive each other negatively (Thompson, 1993). Interventions that improve the likelihood of a win–win solution will improve the negotiator's perceptions of the opposing party's group.

Conclusion

This chapter has considered interpersonal insight in win–lose (distributive) and win–win (integrative) negotiations. We found that negotiator insights are derived from knowledge of what the opposing party would gain or lose as a result of various alternative solutions. This entails interpreting a variety of cues about offers and behaviors throughout the negotiation process. One way to gain such information is to test various positions to determine the opposing party's reactions. These ideas are developed further in the chapter to yield the following points:

1. Feedback allows negotiators to adjust their behavior and learn from experience. However, feedback is likely to be biased or ambiguous. Barriers that prevent negotiators from learning from experience include cognitive biases and inadequate cognitive processing, poor information search techniques, inaccurate interpretation of information and feedback, and the use of unaided memory for coding, storing, and retrieving information.

2. Insight is knowing which environmental cues need to be monitored and which can be ignored. Negotiators develop an idea about what hypotheses should be tested, and the feedback they receive guides their future behavior. Unfortunately, experienced negotiators may not be able to convey what they do, thereby reducing their ability to transfer their knowledge to others.

3. Negotiators make attributions that explain the opposing party's actions as well as their own. They interpret what is important to them and their constituents and estimate how the opposition is likely to react to various overtures and offers. They evaluate the opposing party's goodwill and develop a sense of confidence in being able to resolve the conflict to mutual benefit.

4. Women seem to bring a different perspective to negotiations than do men. In particular, they bring a relational view of others, an embedded view of agency, a focus on empowerment, and an attitude that problem solving can be accomplished through dialogue.

5. Situational factors influence flexibility during different stages of the negotiation process. For instance, a willingness to study the issues from different perspectives is important during the prenegotiation planning period. Willingness to consider partial agreements is important during the early periods when the stage is set for subsequent discussions. Making concessions and forming coalitions is important during give-and-take. Finally, having a deadline for concluding the talks facilitates the final stage.

6. Third-party mediators assist the negotiating parties in gaining insight into each other's positions, motivation, and arguments. Mediators use communications and knowledge of the effects of various types of information on the parties' perceptions of themselves and others. Benefits of mediation include clarifying what parties intend to communicate, having a spokesperson for the weaker side, helping a party save face in the process of undoing a commitment, and generally reducing tension.

7. While mediators try to ensure the representation of all parties in the negotiation, mediators are likely to have vested interests in settling the dispute. This is especially true of agents. However, mediators and agents may have more information about the dispute than one or both of the disputants. As such, they are a way of bringing expertise and experience to the negotiating table.

8. Motivational goals direct and limit behavior in negotiations. A competitive orientation prompts negotiating parties to maximize the difference

between one's own and others' gains. An individualistic orientation involves maximizing only one's own gains. A variant of this is a cooperative orientation, which involves maximizing both one's own and another's gains.

9 Cooperative groups reach higher-quality decisions than groups whose members are individualistically oriented. Thus, negotiators' motivation can be manipulated to enhance the outcome of the process.

10. The experience of negotiating with people who are different from ourselves may ultimately prompt us to view that group more favorably, especially if the parties achieve a mutually beneficial solution.

This chapter has shown that interpersonal insight depends on feedback, motivational orientation, and negotiation outcomes. As such, there are ways to facilitate negotiations through cognitive and affective processes that affect goals and interpretations of events and alternatives. Third parties are often useful in providing such facilitation. The next part of the book focuses on intervention strategies to induce and enhance self- and interpersonal insight.

III

Developing Insight

9

Insight-Induction Techniques
in Organizations

I have come to feel that the only learning which significantly influences behavior is self-discovered, self-appropriated learning.
                                        Carl R. Rogers, *On Becoming a Person*

The model of cognitive information processing and the analyses of how self
and interpersonal insight apply in organizations covered in earlier chapters
suggest methods for increasing insight. Clearly, salient feedback is essential
to the insight-induction process. The nature of the feedback and ways to
provide it are central to learning about oneself and others. However, the
individual must evaluate the feedback and make accurate attributions. For
this to occur (that is, for feedback to make a difference to the individual's
behavior and development), the feedback must be noticed. This may seem
obvious, but as our information-processing model indicates, it cannot be
taken for granted. If the feedback is new information that should redirect
behavior, recipients cannot simply categorize it as reinforcement of their
preconceived self-concept or stereotypes of other people. For the feedback
to be noticed, it must be distinct and not easily attributed to the environment. Facilitating mechanisms may be needed to assist the individual to engage in self-reflection, resist denial and other defense mechanisms, and understand the implications of the information for behavior change.

Perceptual psychology suggests that perceptions can be changed as a result of new experiences:

> Since perceptions are the product of experience, there is no more fruitful way
> of affecting or changing perception than through the medium of some kind of
> new experience. . . . This can be done in two ways. In the first place, it is
> possible to change perception by exploring our old experiences to discover
> new meanings from them. . . . Secondly, perceptions can be changed as a
> consequence of seeking new kinds of experience which will produce new
> kinds of perceiving. Perhaps one of the most important ways in which per-
> sons can assure new perceptions is through the deliberate breaking away from
> accustomed patterns. (Combs, Richards, and Richards, 1988, p. 288)

Seeking self-knowledge is a basis for, and motivator of, growth and improvement. Change occurs as people gain feedback, achieve self-awareness, and experience different relationships. Becoming aware of one's patterns of thought and behavior and the psychological defenses that maintain them precedes developing new ways of relating with others (Kahn & Kram, 1994). Kahn and Kram (1994) apply these ideas of personal learning to their internal authority models (discussed here in Chapters 6 and 7). For example, counterdependent people may become more interdependent when they work with a supervisor or team that values, reinforces, and encourages interdependence. While some people may fear knowing more about themselves, feedback that is verifiable, predictable, and controllable is difficult to deny (Whetten & Cameron, 1991, p. 53). Such information may come through a testing process from reliable authoritative sources (e.g., assessment centers) or from reliable self-assessment instruments.

I begin this chapter by considering the nature of learning in organizations as a rationale for supporting organizational programs that promote self- and interpersonal insight. Insight-induction methods discussed in the chapter include self-assessment, survey feedback, assessment centers, computerized assessment, socialization processes for new employees, and resocialization for displaced employees. These are not new methods, nor are they the only methods for insight induction I could have included, such as T-groups, sensitivity training, individual counseling, and mentoring. My purpose here is to show how such programs enhance self- and interpersonal insight. As such, managers and human resource professionals should view these techniques as having increased potential for facilitating the development of interpersonal relationships and processes. These programs should be designed in a way that maximizes feedback and self-reflection. Examples of actual tools and techniques are provided in the form of resource guides at the end of the book; these examples show how the methods can be designed to enhance insight induction. I devote the next chapter to upward and 360-degree rating and feedback programs as an insight-induction mechanism. These increasingly popular programs are important because they attempt to provide the individual with regular feedback from diverse sources. The process connotes the importance of different viewpoints to insight formation and the importance of developing insights that reflect the multidimensional nature of individual and organizational effectiveness.

Creating Learning Organizations

An organization must continually build the performance capability of its members. This is accomplished in large measure through insight into individuals and situations.

> The firm . . . is challenged to study, codify, and disseminate information and knowledge that affects its diverse clients, the problems those clients face and,

most significantly, the resources available to serve clients. Additionally, it is challenged not only to exchange existing information among its members, but also to generate and document new knowledge, for example, on environmental factors affecting clients and the implications of these, on whole new methodologies developed to provide services to clients, on experiences in one situation that might be applied to another, and on insights or creative ideas that break new ground for clients, practitioners, or the firm. (Morris, 1993, p. 182)

Learning organizations emphasize *generative learning*—that is, "an emphasis on continuous experimentation and feedback in an ongoing examination of the very way organizations go about defining and solving problems" (McGill, Slocum, & Lei, 1992, p. 5). An example of a learning organization is the Chaparral Steel Company, a highly successful firm incorporated in 1973 with the mission of becoming the international low-cost producer of high-quality steel products (Forward et al., 1991). Its organizational culture includes close attention to customer service and viewing employees as resources for development rather than as "labor costs." Moreover, the company maintains a strategy of being on the leading edge of technology. Learning is a critical and explicit element of the corporate values articulated by the firm's founders. These values include taking risks for achievement and success, welcoming the challenge to grow in knowledge and expertise, and being open to learn and to teach.

This example is in contrast to the usual defensiveness in learning. Argyris (1982) referred to this as "single-looped" learning—skill in protecting ourselves from the pain and threat of dealing with interpersonal conflict openly and honestly. This is contrasted with "double-looped" learning—skill in recognizing and articulating our underlying assumptions and beliefs, even if they are painful to ourselves and others. Single-looped learning results from defensive routines that insulate us from self-examination. The result is "skilled incompetence." Rather than resolve conflict, we contribute to it by suppressing what we are actually thinking and never communicating the generalizations that underlie our perceptions and behavior. For instance, a subordinate might assume that the supervisor prefers to speak rather than listen, so the subordinate sits and nods rather than voicing an opinion or raising issues for discussion. Or I may believe that my opponent in a negotiation is unable to understand my point of view; as a result, I never try to articulate the reasons for my viewpoint.

Argyris's concept of "action science" is moving people from single- to double-looped learning. This involves developing skills of reflection and inquiry. Skills of reflection allow us to slow down our own thinking processes so that we become more aware of how we form underlying assumptions and mind-sets and the way these influence our behavior. This requires understanding how we make leaps of abstraction when we move from direct observation to making a generalization without testing it. Such leaps of abstraction impede learning as erroneous assumptions are treated as fact.

Our inquiry skills affect how we obtain information in face-to-face inter-actions. More effective inquiry skills help us avoid making leaps of abstrac-tion. We need to learn and practice identifying our generalizations and ask-ing ourselves about the basis for these generalizations. Leaps of abstraction should be tested directly. This has to be done carefully, since direct ques-tions about another's behavior can put the individual on the defensive. For instance, asking your boss why he doesn't listen to others' opinions would be likely to invoke denial. But there are more productive ways to approach the subject. The subordinate could ask how he or she might help the super-visor by providing alternative opinions.

Not voicing what we think undermines our learning. We avoid issues out of a sense of politeness and a desire to prevent embarrassment. We often talk around subjects. As a result, conflicts fester and decisions are not im-plemented. Argyris refers to this as the gap between our "espoused theory" (what we say) and our "theory-in-use" (what we do). For example, I may profess to expressing my point of view no matter what (my espoused the-ory), but I may never openly disagree with my boss (my theory-in-use). My espoused theory may truly be my goal. The difficulty is not with the goal but in not being able to live up to it.

Argyris recommends that problems be faced directly and openly—that we "discuss the undiscussable." The desire to do this develops after we recognize that not doing so just makes things worse. We need to understand our own assumptions and question the data on which they are built. We need to recognize and evaluate our espoused theories and determine if we truly believe them. If we do and there is a gap between the espoused theory and theory-in-use, then we should try to resolve the tension produced by this gap. This requires living up to our beliefs—"walking the talk" in today's management jargon.

Building on Argyris's work, Peter Senge (1990) described the learning organization in his book *The Fifth Discipline*. Senge asserted that managers are natural advocates who become successful by debating forcefully and in-fluencing others. As they rise to more important positions, however, they confront increasingly complex and diverse issues that go beyond their ex-pertise and personal experience. They must learn to ask questions. "What is needed," according to Senge, "is blending advocacy and inquiry to pro-mote collaborative learning" (p. 198). This entails inquiring into the reason-ing behind others' views but also stating one's own point of view in a way that reveals one's assumptions and reasoning and invites others to inquire into them. "I might say, 'Here is my view and here is how I have arrived at it. How does it sound to you'" (Senge, 1990, p. 199).

Referring to their experience at MIT's Center for Organizational Learn-ing, Kofman and Senge (1993) concluded:

Building learning organizations, we are discovering, requires basic shifts in how we think and interact. The changes go beyond individual corporate cul-tures, or even the culture of Western management; they penetrate to the bedrock assumptions and habits of our culture as a whole. We are discovering that moving forward is an exercise in personal commitment and community building. (p. 5)

Kofman and Senge (1993) asserted that we have drifted into a culture that fragments our thoughts, requiring analytic decomposition rather than attention to the whole. We need an expanded view of the creative possibilities, and we need to experience and realize the wonder and joy of learning as a team.

The difficulty people have in recognizing generalizations is that single-looped learning is ingrained. We easily and routinely categorize responses in ourselves and others and do not take the time or exert the emotional effort to think or do otherwise. We may ascribe reasons for another's behavior and our responses, but we are reluctant to articulate these reasons and break the cycle. Doing so is not in our pattern of behavior or mind-set.

Becoming a double-looped learner takes initiative and courage. It requires a combination of aggressiveness and a spirit of inquiry. Senge (1990) offered guidelines for balancing advocacy and inquiry:

- When advocating your view:
    - *Make* your own reasoning *explicit* (i.e., say how you arrived at your view and the "data" upon which it is based).
    - *Encourage* others to explore your view (e.g., "Do you see gaps in my reasoning?").
    - *Encourage* others to provide different views (i.e., "Do you have either different data or different conclusions, or both?").
    - Actively *inquire* into others' views that differ from your own (i.e., "What are your views?" "How did you arrive at them?" "Are you taking into account data that are different from what I have considered?").
- When inquiring into others' views:
    - If you are making assumptions about others' views, state your assumptions clearly and acknowledge that they are assumptions.
    - State the "data" upon which your assumptions are based.
    - Don't bother asking questions if you're not genuinely interested in the other's response (i.e., if you're only trying to be polite or to show the others up).
- When you arrive at an impasse (others no longer appear to be open to inquiring into their own views):
    - Ask what data or logic might change their views.
    - Ask if there is any way you might together design an experiment that might provide new information.
- When you or others are hesitant to express your views or to experiment with alternative ideas:
    - Encourage them (or you) to think out loud about what might be making it difficult (i.e., "What is it about this situation, and about me or others, that is making open exchange difficult?").

—If there is mutual desire to do so, design with others ways of overcoming these barriers. (pp. 200–201; italics in original)

On the one hand, these recommendations make eminent sense. On the
other, if an individual acted this way consistently, he or she would never get
anything done. Senge's recommendations seem to require a person to be
unaffected by human limitations such as defensiveness, time pressure, and
emotion. The alternative would be to remove the human element from human behavior. Consequently, following these guidelines and more generally
striving for double-looped learning constitute an ambitious goal that cannot
be achieved instantly by following a few simple steps. However, incremental
progress is possible.

Adaptive and Generative Learners

Adaptive learners are willing to make incremental changes to enhance existing operations and activities. This works fine as long as things are relatively
stable. When they are not, adaptive learning can be dysfunctional if it per-
petuates behaviors that no longer work.

Generative learners know how to learn how to learn. This can result in
transformational changes—major shifts in behavior that emerge after self-
study and situational assessment. In Senge's view, generative learning helps
organizations to make sharp, transformational changes.

Generative learners are characterized by their behaviors of openness,
system thinking, empathy, creativity, and self-effectiveness (Senge, 1990;
McGill, Slocum, & Lei, 1992). Openness is being aware of a wide range of
perspectives in order to identify trends and generate choices. This requires
suspending the need for control and being open to different values, backgrounds, and experiences. Systems thinking means being able to see connections between issues, events, and data. Empathy is being sensitive to and
concerned for human nature; empathetic individuals are able to avoid or
repair strained relationships. Creativity is personal flexibility and a willingness to take risks. Self-effectiveness is having the feeling that one can and
should influence the world; people with a strong sense of self-effectiveness
have a keen sense of themselves—their strengths and weaknesses—and their
ability to solve problems and make things happen.

These concepts apply to organizational and individual learning. In large
measure, organizational changes do not occur without individual learning.
As people learn how to collect and use information about themselves and
their environments, they are learning how to learn. Applying this information to identify and implement directions for change then becomes a transformational process. The new habits involve learning how to learn, not new
behaviors or organizational strategies per se. When applied consistently,
learning mechanisms and outputs naturally suggest changes. Transformation
is anticipated and seen positively, rather than as a forced and emotionally
wrenching experience.

Following from the concept of the learning organization and generative learning as goals, the next sections consider methods for learning about oneself and others—methods for improving self- and interpersonal insight.

Self-Assessment

Self-assessment and self-evaluation are both ways of taking stock of oneself. Self-assessment is a person's view of his or her own capacities and abilities, while self-evaluation is judging the quality of these capacities and abilities. Self-assessment generally precedes self-evaluation.

Chapter 3 argued that self-assessment is the foundation for self-learning. Insight precedes behavior change, and self-examination is the basis for self-insight. Self-assessment methods lead the individual through a self-examination of competencies, abilities, skills, knowledge, interests, and behavioral and personality tendencies. Self-assessments are increasingly popular in career planning because of their cost-effectiveness compared with other methods such as assessment centers. They also eliminate worry about the security of the data and the inability of outside assessors to understand job requirements and organizational opportunities (Thornton & Byham, 1982, p. 357).

A major limitation of self-assessment is that people are inclined to avoid new knowledge about themselves as a self-protection mechanism. Seeking feedback is risky because new information may be negative and lead to feelings of inferiority or weakness. The desire for new self-knowledge is a necessary precursor to self-insight enhancement. Such information may best come from sources beyond self-reflection and self-report. However, self-assessment can be useful, especially when it asks about important information, such as self-observations of behaviors and characteristics that are important to the individual's job, organization, and career.

Consider the following reasons for understanding self-assessments (adapted from Ashford, 1989, p. 135):

1. Self-assessment recognizes the self as a source of feedback.
2. Self-assessment is important to self-regulation and goal achievement.
3. Self-assessment is important in increasingly turbulent organizational environments that require employees to sort out supervisory and peer preferences and evaluative criteria.
4. Self-assessment may have important strong effects. For instance, self-assessments have been related to depression, efficacy expectations, aspiration levels, persistence, effort, and performance.
5. Self-assessments help reduce ambiguity in the environment (e.g., about performance expectations and one's capability to meet these expectations).

An important part of self-assessment is evaluating comparative information in relation to one's self-evaluation. Comparative information allows calibrating one's own behavior and feelings. Thus, self-assessment processes should be accompanied by information about the environment (e.g., career opportunities and competency requirements for different types of career paths), standards of performance (what the organization expects), and how other people perform and feel (performance appraisal and attitude survey results averaged across employees). Self-assessment should guide people in identifying the ways they usually interpret and act in different situations (Wofford, 1994). They can compare their self-assessments to information about effective ways of behaving in the organization in a process that couples self-assessment, situational assessment, and training. They can then practice interpreting situational demands and effective behavior patterns.

Self-assessment questions can be both measurements and cues. They make salient behaviors and characteristics that otherwise might be overlooked. Thus, measurement reactivity can be used to induce insights.

The following are some guidelines for developing self-assessment procedures:

1. *Present information about the organization to indicate why the self-assessment is important.* For instance, state performance expectations, describe career paths, indicate where job opportunities will occur. Relate this information to individual requirements—characteristics needed to be successful and take advantage of the opportunities. This makes the self-assessment salient and links it to organizational strategies and objectives.

2. *Provide guidance on how to interpret the self-assessment results.* A score or average rating means little by itself. Present comparative statistics—that is, averages of how other people score on the same measure. Then offer guidance on how to use the results—that is, what the results imply for development and behavior change. Give the employee some ideas for courses or developmental experiences. Also, provide a means of seeking more information from other sources. Suggest that employees share the information with their supervisor.

3. *Embed self-assessment methods within the context of a career development program and/or a performance improvement program.* For instance, AT&T developed a "Managing for Excellence Library" that articulated dimensions of leadership expected in its managers in an increasingly competitive environment (London & Mone, 1994). The intention of the library was to communicate that managers have more discretion than ever before and that the organization counts on them to make necessary decisions that are responsive to customer needs. The emphasis was on mandating *what* should be accomplished (i.e., outcomes), *not* on specifying *how* things should be done (activities). The expected dimensions of leadership were simple: create challenging jobs, promote teamwork, and increase cooperation between groups. The company's philosophy was to provide the enabling resources and to empower managers to take responsibility for their own development.

Booklets in the library outlined these expectations and spelled out competencies associated with each leadership dimensions. Self-assessment material was offered to help individuals evaluate their level of competence. An educational curriculum offered by the corporation's training department tailored courses to each of the competencies. Methods for tracking improvement were provided.

Resource Guides A and B at the end of this book provide examples of these processes. Guide A is an outline of a human performance system that explains to employees how the organization supports their career development and how their career development fits within the goals and strategies of the organization. Guide B presents examples of a set of self-assessment instruments offered in relation to the human performance system. The self-assessments try to enhance the employee's understanding of the organization environment and what is required to be successful. The Resource Guides show how self-assessment, situational analysis, internal attributions, and self-evaluation can be designed into career development programs and performance improvement processes.

Given self-regulatory mechanisms and social learning through observation, modeling observed behaviors, and feedback, Thornton and Byham (1982) suggested that assessments be designed to give assessees more involvement in the assessment process. This includes involvement in "identifying dimensions to be assessed, making observations, comparing behaviors from different exercises, identifying strengths and weaknesses, and comparing assessment and job behaviors" (p. 413). This may increase their acceptance of the results, improve the accuracy of the assessment, and increase the likelihood of career planning and training based on assessment results. While their recommendations applied to assessment centers (described in a later section), they also apply to self-assessment methods.

Enhancing Self-Assessment Accuracy

Self-assessments are more likely to be accurate when they are based on objective, easily measured performance dimensions (e.g., number of units produced or communications ability) rather than on subjective or ambiguous dimensions (e.g., one's organizational sensitivity). In general, when self-ratings are compared with ratings by others, overestimation is more common than underestimation (Ashford, 1989).

Ashford's model of self-assessment. Ashford (1989, p. 144) outlined the following self-assessment outcomes:

- The degree of match between self- and other assessment
- How well a standard is being matched
- The level of aspiration for future behaviors
- Beliefs about the efficacy of achieving a standard
- The decision to devote energy to a goal
- Willingness to persist in achieving the goal

These outcomes may be derailed in several ways:

- Failure to assess progress on a relevant behavior dimension
- Assessment of progress on an irrelevant behavior dimension
- Not paying attention to a relevant cue
- Paying attention to an irrelevant dimension

These possible outcomes suggest several challenges to accurate self-assessment:

- Being able to gather information in an organizational reality characterized by randomness, conflictual cues, and ambiguity and chance (the "information problem")
- Obtaining information while protecting one's self-image as an autonomous and self-assured person (the "self-presentation problem")
- Obtaining accurate information necessary for survival without suffering costs to the ego (the "ego-defense problem")

An individual's self-esteem and early success or failure experiences are filters for interpreting later information. Individuals who need to defend their egos will selectively attend to or interpret information in a way that allows them to maintain a positive self-image.

Moreover, according to Ashford, there are several possibilities in self–other agreement: (A) Both self- and others' assessments are positive; (B) Both self- and others' assessments are negative; (C) Self-assessment is positive and others' assessment is negative; or (D) Self-assessment is negative and others' assessment is positive. Condition A will lead to favorable feelings of efficacy and will support persistent effort toward high aspirations. Condition B will do the reverse—lead to discouragement, procrastination, or lack of action. Condition C is self-delusion; if it persists, behaviors are likely to be dysfunctional. Condition D may also be dysfunctional if individuals set lower standards than they could achieve and do not try as hard as they should. The long-term cost of conditions C and D is that individuals lose the chance to do better. This has implications for the individual in foreclosing opportunities and implications for the organization in not making full use of available and capable human resources.

Organizational interventions may help avoid conditions B through D. Training or job placement may be ways to avoid negative self-image and prompt a positive self-view. However, this may take considerable time if the individual has been conditioned to a negative self-image. Conditions C and D may be overcome by a feedback program that encourages specific and frequent performance information and bases promotion and other rewards and personnel decisions on the feedback. To do otherwise makes the feedback irrelevant or at least only mildly salient.

Recognizing Possible Cultural Differences in Self-Assessments. A common finding in performance appraisal studies is that people tend to be lenient in rating themselves compared with supervisor and peer ratings (Harris & Schaubroeck, 1988). This may not be a universal pattern but may reflect a bias in Western culture. A study of Taiwanese workers found a "modesty bias" in self-ratings, with self-ratings lower than ratings obtained from supervisors (Farh, Dobbins, & Cheng, 1991). This may be explained by the relative emphasis placed on individualism in the United States and on collectivism in Taiwan, with Taiwanese workers being more likely to experience pressure to understate their own performance. Yu and Murphy (1993) extended this research by testing the extent to which the modesty bias observed in Taiwanese samples would be replicated in samples from the People's Republic of China. They studied Chinese blue-collar workers in three plants in and around Nanjing, one of the traditional centers of commerce and industry in China. Contrary to the modesty bias hypothesis, self-ratings showed a leniency bias; that is, self-ratings were higher than supervisor or peer ratings.

These results suggest that broad cultural factors do not explain a modesty bias. Yu and Murphy (1993) proposed that the modesty bias found in Taiwan may be due to more specific factors than global East–West differences in self-evaluation. The Taiwanese culture supports relatively high levels of deference to authority and as a consequence may be more conducive to modesty bias than are the cultures of other Eastern nations.

The next section examines sources of information from others as a method to enhance insight.

Survey Feedback

Survey feedback refers to feeding back attitude survey results to employees (London, 1988). The data may be collected by means of paper-and-pencil questionnaires, one-on-one interviews, or interviews with groups of employees (termed *focus groups*). The survey feedback report contains responses to items averaged across employees within different work groups, business units, or the entire organization. This is in contrast to upward or 360-degree feedback surveys, which provide specific information about target managers—that is, how the target manager is rated by his or her subordinates, peers, or customers. Survey feedback results may be disaggregated to determine the average responses within a work group and then reported to the manager of the group. However, the topics generally go beyond boss–subordinate relationships to include attitudes about a variety of facets of the organization such as pay, working conditions, career opportunities, and job challenge.

Survey feedback results may be reported to everyone through special bulletins. Work groups might meet with their supervisors to discuss the meaning of the results for the organization as a whole and the work group in particular (Solomon, 1976; Gavin & Krois, 1983).

The stages of survey feedback include the design of the survey method, the analysis of the data, conveying the results to employees and management, interpreting the results, determining courses of action based on the results, and developing methods for monitoring the success of these actions.

Lawler (1986) identified possible positive and negative outcomes that might result from a survey feedback program. *Positive* outcomes include improvements in work methods and procedures, attraction and retention of employees, higher quantity and quality of output, enhanced decision making (resulting from better communication), and smoother group process and problem solving (from enhanced attention to group process). Potential *negative* effects include costs to communicate and facilitate interpretation of results, the need for more support personnel to run the survey program, unrealistic expectations for organizational change, middle-management resistance to being evaluated (which occurs especially with upward-feedback targeted directly to the supervisor's performance), and lost time from group meetings first to complete the survey and then to discuss the results.

Implicit in the notion of survey feedback is the idea that the survey data will not only be collected but also fed back. The process of feeding back data (i.e., discussing the findings and deciding to act on them) is more important than the actual content and collection of the data (Nadler, 1976, 1977). Not feeding back the data can be counterproductive; failure to address issues raised by the survey may foster the belief that management is inattentive or lacks the power or will to deal with the issues.

Employee participation throughout the survey feedback process is important for acceptance of the results. London (1988, 1985b) used the term *employee-guided management* (EGM) to refer to guidelines for applying information from employees to establish management strategies. The process relies on principles of participative management and is based on survey feedback. EGM principles are presented in Resource Guide C.

Surveys should be a regular process in the organization—one that occurs annually or more often. Another method for inducing self-insight provides more intensive, in-depth information but may occur only once during a person's career. This is the assessment center. The next section considers this method as a source of information of insight in the career development process.

Assessment Centers

Assessment centers are used in many organizations to evaluate the potential of job candidates. The candidates may be prospective employees or current employees who aspire to another, usually higher-level, position. The benefit of the assessment center is that it collects and integrates diverse information about an employee. This information includes test performance and behavior on different exercises designed to simulate job requirements. So a sales assessment will have exercises that simulate sales situations and measure relevant knowledge of marketing. A managerial assessment center will include techniques that evaluate behavior on key situations faced by managers. Participants are observed by multiple assessors trained to code and evaluate behaviors demonstrated by the assessees. After the assessments are conducted, the results (narrative reports and test scores) are reviewed by the assessors in a group discussion called an integration session. The group then rates each dimension, usually trying to come to agreement, for instance, agreeing within one point on a five-point scale. The advantage of the assessment center method, then, is that multiple assessors and multiple, joblike methods combine to produce more reliable and valid results than can be obtained by any one method alone (Bray, Campbell, & Grant, 1974; Cascio & Silbey, 1979).

Assessment centers are designed to mirror job requirements and assess dimensions of behavior important to job performance (e.g., managerial skills for middle-management positions). They provide specific information about candidates' abilities and areas for skill development (Thornton & Byham, 1982, p. 357). Therefore, the design of the assessment center begins with the identification of performance dimensions to be assessed. For instance, in the case of predicting potential to advance to a higher level of management, a job analysis across a variety of jobs at that organizational level would reveal the important dimensions of performance. Or the intention may be to select a different type of manager as a way to induce culture change (e.g., managers who empower subordinates and encourage participation in decisions as opposed to managers who are bureaucratic and retain decision-making authority). In this case a "future job analysis" would be conducted by interviewing organizational leaders about the intended culture or strategy shift. The set of behavioral performance dimensions then guide the identification and design of the assessment methods.

Assessment centers have been criticized for several reasons. There is the danger that biases that pervade supervisor judgments of performance also pervade assessor judgments (Klimoski & Strickland, 1977). However, this can be overcome by good assessor training, not to mention supervisor training on how to rate subordinates' performance. Another potential problem is that the assessment center results may be used as the sole source of information for making decisions about employees. Moreover, the results can become a self-fulfilling prophecy if individuals who do poorly are not given a chance to be promoted. Proper procedures can ensure that the assessment center results are not used in these ways.

Assessee Insight and Performance

The extent to which assessees recognize the dimensions on which they are rated in an assessment center positively affects their performance (Kleinmann, 1993). That is, assessees who more accurately identify the rating dimensions evaluated during the assessment perform better. This implies that people who can discern elements of effective performance from understanding the situational requirements are able to identify the behaviors relevant for each rating dimension and perform these behaviors well. Conversely, people who are not able to discern the behavioral requirements for successful performance will not do as well.

On the one hand, this might be viewed as a weakness of assessment centers—that the rating dimensions are so transparent that assessees know what they need to do to be evaluated highly. On the other hand, assessees vary in their ability to discern these dimensions—just as they vary in their ability to know what is important in job behavior. However, this suggests that performance in an assessment center and, by extension, on the job, depends on both the individual's insight into situational demands and the individual's ability to meet these demands. So, not surprisingly, people who are successful in assessment centers have a high level of social skills (Kleinmann, 1993).

Developmental Assessment Centers

The assessment center is a reliable tool for obtaining information about people and a valid tool for making decisions about them (Thornton & Byham, 1982). However, perhaps because of the problems mentioned earlier, assessment centers are increasingly used for development purposes, sometimes solely for development of the participants rather than as input to help higher-level managers make decisions about them. These are *developmental assessment centers,* in which the information is fed back to the participants, usually by an assessor or a psychologist. The meaning of the results is reviewed and discussed, and guidance is offered for using the results to enhance strengths and, when possible, overcome weaknesses. This may include recommending training or different job assignments. (Some areas of performance, such as decision making, are difficult to teach, while others, such as communication skills, are more easily taught. As such, guidelines for development may recommend building on one's strengths rather than eliminating weaknesses.)

An assessment center focusing on career development was designed by London and Bray (1983; London, 1985a). Outlined in Resource Guide D, it includes a variety of tests and exercises centered around career goals and decisions. The assessment was designed for research purposes to measure career motivation components and understand situational factors affecting them. The dimensions assessed were the domains of career motivation: resilience, insight, and identity and their subcomponents. This idea was extended when the AT&T Company instituted a developmental assessment center for midlevel high-potential managers. The assessment, called "Insight," is used solely to give managers developmental feedback on their managerial skills and related behavioral tendencies. The results of the center are not used to make decisions about the managers. (The insight assessment center was introduced in Chapter 3.)

Other types of assessments are also aimed at development. Some are incorporated into training programs. One used in a leadership development program is called "Looking Glass, Inc." (Lombardo & McCall, 1982). Developed by the Center for Creative Leadership in Greensboro, North Carolina, this is a six-hour simulation that includes roles for twenty top-level managerial positions in a fictional company called Looking Glass. Participants receive feedback on their performance, with concentration on areas most relevant to their current job and career growth. The feedback from the simulation is supplemented by a 360-degree rating process conducted prior to attending the training. This provides input from the participants' subordinates, peers, and supervisor. The participants receive and interpret the results along with the simulation results as they begin their week-long leadership development program.

Computerized Assessment

Computerized assessment is the use of computers to present items customized to the assessee's ability, measure a variety of responses (e.g., time to respond to different situations), and, if appropriate, provide feedback at various points in time. Advancing personal computer technologies, including the incorporation of CD-ROM, allow displaying full-motion video with stereo sound to boot.

> [C]omputerized tests and assessments stand on the threshold of important advances in the evaluation of individual differences. New assessments examine response processes, performance on simultaneous tasks, and individual differences in non-academic skills such as administration and conflict management. . . . *the PC can present any form of social interaction that can be portrayed by actors and videotaped.* (Drasgow et al., 1993, pp. 164–165; italics in original)

Multimedia computer-based assessment clarifies information presentation, allowing people to see how others might react to their behavior and decisions. Repeating similar situations, the realism of interactive video, and the capability of varying the difficulty and complexity of the simulations, coupled with the opportunity for immediate and repeated feedback, can reduce the unwitting categorization or discounting of feedback information and the inaccurate attribution of conclusions about oneself or others. Precise data can be derived for assessment. For example, consider an in-basket exercise which asks the assessee to handle a variety of memos and other information requiring prioritization, responses, and decisions (Drasgow et al., 1993). Computerizing the material and response format permits a close examination of the process used by the assessee in making judgments. For example, the computer can calculate the amount of time devoted to important and unimportant issues. It can also determine whether the assessee responds to an issue before viewing other pertinent information. The results can be used to evaluate and make decisions about the assessee, provide feedback to the assessee, and deliver computer-based training based on the results.

Computerized assessment is most valuable for the assessment of skills not easily or inexpensively measured via traditional in-person exercises or paper-and-pencil tests (Drasgow et al., 1993). Combinations of computers, videos, and other media produce realistic simulations of social interactions that engage the assessee as part of the situation. This enhances the assessee's motivation to respond truthfully in a way that would reflect the assessee's actual behavior. Time sequencing and branching options move the assessee into different situations over time depending on initial responses. Of course, the situations are the same across assessees, producing reliability not available from in-person exercises which may have different dynamics each time they are run depending on the individuals being assessed. Thus, the assessee's behavior can be examined in the context of dynamic yet consistent social situations.

Drasgow et al. (1993) estimate that the hardware requirements for this type of assessment are relatively modest. It requires an inexpensive personal computer with a color monitor; a hard disk; 1 megabyte of memory; a laser disc player, videotape player, or CD-ROM; an amplifier; and stereo speakers. The production costs for developing the assessments have also decreased considerably with the availability of camcorders, videotape conversion processes to laser discs, and digital imaging (i.e., cameras that record pictures directly on floppy disks for through-the-computer viewing).

Drasgow et al.'s (1993) COMPAS computer program uses interactive video to replace traditional assessment centers as a means of measuring managerial skills. Each exercise measures a single skill. For instance, in an exercise that measures conflict-management skills, the assessee views scenarios of different conflict situations in a hypothetical organization. The interactive video stops at various points to ask the assessee which of several actions he or she would take. Drasgow et al. (1993) describe such an exercise:

> One scene begins with a young woman entering her manager's office. She is visibly upset, saying that she has been sexually harassed by a co-worker and she "just won't take it anymore." The screen freezes on the woman's face and a series of options are shown on the screen. The assessee is asked to choose the option that best describes the action he or she would take at this point if he or she were the manager. Suppose the option "Call the alleged offender into your office to get his side of the story" were selected. . . . the PC branches to a scene that portrays a likely outcome of the assessee's re-

sponse. . . . the action stops again and the assessee is asked to decide how he or she, as the manager, would respond to this development. (p. 192)

The laser disc stores five to fifteen scenarios, or about thirty minutes of continuous video. Different types of disputes are provided in the conflict-management assessment, each allowing the assessee two chances to choose the best response to the conflict. The first choice allows the respondent to affect what happens next. The scenarios were developed from critical incidents from job incumbents. Possible responses were developed and content analyzed, and the responses were then validated by examining their relation to other responses and other measures of conflict resolution as well as their relation to ratings of actual behavior.

Insight requires both self-learning and understanding the situation. After all, interpersonal situations occur within the context of the organization. Becoming a learning organization means that employees are aware of organizational goals and how people work together to accomplish them. Moreover, it means that individuals are able to make sense of interpersonal relationships. New employees, in particular, require this understanding to become productive members of the organization. For this reason, the next section considers socialization practices as an insight-induction mechanism.

Socialization Practices: Helping Newcomers Make Sense of Their Environment

Socialization is the process of learning the attitudes and behaviors required for an organizational position (Morrison, 1993a, 1993b). Socialization tries to target the direction of newcomers' insights and feelings about the organization.

The socialization process, coupled with early work experiences, alters the newcomers in such a way that attitudinal items take on a different conceptual meaning from one time to the next. Vandenberg and Self (1993) examined the commitment of 117 new employees in a bank. Measures were collected over three times (on the first day and on the three- and six-month employment anniversaries). While they found declining commitment, the interpretability of this finding was weakened by the discovery of pronounced changes in the relationships among facets of commitment. This replicated a similar discovery by Schaubroeck and Green (1989) that studies of newcomers' attitudes need to account for instability in measurement continua. This includes changes over time in the factor structure of the items, termed *gamma changes* by Golembiewski, Billingsley, and Yeager (1976), and in the meaning of scale points evidenced by changes in item variance called *beta changes; alpha changes* are mean differences in this terminology. These changes occur because newcomers develop an understanding about the organization and its constituent components during the first months of work.

In the process, they glean knowledge about organizational values and principles, and they develop an emotional attachment to the organization.

This research suggests that newcomers have a limited conceptual frame of the organization when they start employment. This may depend on the experience of the newcomers; a newly minted college graduate, for example, may have a less-developed conceptual framework of organizations than an individual in midcareer moving to another firm in the same industry. This points to the importance of the socialization process as a means of developing a conceptual framework to organize and evaluate one's perceptions of the work environment. This framework consists of scripts that explain common behavior patterns in the organization ("The way we do things around here").

Early socialization is critical. Indicators of socialization (social integration, task mastery, role clarity, and acculturation) that are measured after only two weeks on the job have been found to be highly predictive of the same measures three and six months later (Morrison, 1993a) despite the possibility of changes in meaning affecting scale factor structures referred to previously. Organizations engage in a number of tactics to enhance the socialization process, including new employee orientation programs, special assignments, probationary periods, and mentor programs (cf. Van Maanen & Schein, 1979).

Newcomers are active participants in seeking information and essentially orienting themselves to the organization. Research has examined how newcomers make sense of, and cope with, their new work setting (Louis, 1990; Falcione & Wilson, 1988). This sense-making process occurs as newcomers seek information, thereby reducing uncertainty and increasing mastery of their new environment (Morrison, 1993a; Miller & Jablin, 1991). Information seeking compensates for the often inadequate, or nonexistent, information from supervisors and co-workers. By requesting information, newcomers are able to clarify role expectations, obtain technical information, and glean performance feedback, thereby improving their task mastery. Moreover, by asking for information, they learn about norms that enhance their relationships with other workers and increase their integration into the society of the organization (Morrison, 1993a).

According to Morrison (1993a, p. 183), sources of socialization information include the immediate direct supervisor, a more experienced staff member, another new employee, a manager other than the immediate supervisor, someone outside the organization (e.g., a friend, family member, customer), or someone in a support function such as a secretary or personnel manager. In addition, new employees have a variety of ways to determine how people behave and what they value. Again according the Morrison (1993a, p. 183), they may pay attention to how others behave, socialize with people in the organization, observe what behaviors are rewarded, or consult memos, annual reports, or other written material. The kinds of information they may seek include *normative information* (the behaviors and attitudes that the organization values and expects), *technical information* (how to perform different aspects of the job), *referent information* (what is expected of you in your job), *performance feedback* (how well you are performing your job), or *social feedback* (the appropriateness of your social behavior at work; Morrison, 1993b).

In a study of 205 new accountants one, three, and six months into their jobs, Morrison (1993b) found that patterns of newcomers' information seeking varied by the type of information sought. "Newcomers sought technical information primarily by asking others and sought other types of information primarily through observation. Further, they sought technical information, information about role demands, and performance feedback mostly from supervisors but sought normative and social information mostly from peers" (p. 557). The study found that these patterns were stable over time and that information seeking was positively related to satisfaction and performance and negatively related to intentions to leave the organizations.

Newcomers are more likely to monitor the organization environment than they are to directly inquire about it. They do this to avoid the social costs of inquiry (e.g., feelings of embarrassment from appearing ignorant) (Morrison, 1993b). However, newcomers are more likely to ask their supervisors for technical information directly, perhaps because of its importance to job performance and the difficulty of attaining it through observation. When it comes to expectations about appropriate behaviors and the social context, people rely on peers for information. Over time, Morrison (1993b) found that newcomers sought less normative information and social feedback and searched for more information about job expectations and performance. This supports the idea that over time newcomers are less concerned about fitting in—possibly because they feel more established or more used to the new situation and people.

This research indicates an important link between interpersonal insight and the newcomer's information seeking. The socialization process is more successful (that is, results in higher performance and more satisfied employees) when the employees engage proactively in information seeking. Contrary to Morrison's (1993b) expectations, self-confidence did not influence newcomers' patterns of information seeking. People with low self-confidence could be expected to be more concerned about looking bad in the eyes of their supervisors than those with high self-confidence. Morrison (1993b) suggested that she might have found stronger effects if there had been more people in her sample with lower self-confidence.

Other research has found that formal socialization programs for orienting all newcomers in the same way increase organizational commitment but reduce role innovation (Allen & Meyer, 1990). Socialization practices that require newcomers to create their own roles (the "sink-or-swim" approach) or individualized socialization practices that provide unique learning experiences (for instance, on-the-job training) increase role innovation and reduce organizational commitment. This suggests that the organization's socialization strategies should depend on the mix of role innovation and commitment desired from newcomers. The more role innovation required, the more individuals need to be encouraged to be proactive in searching the environment for information and creating their own work structures and role relationships. The more individualized the socialization and the more open the organization is to role innovation, the more important the supervisor is to the socialization process—both in fostering learning and in accepting new ideas.

As discussed in Chapter 6, the quality of the supervisor–subordinate relationship arises early in the life of the dyad. When the new subordinate is also newly hired, the supervisor may be particularly attentive to the acclimation of the subordinate to the organization as well as to the work group. However, the quality of the relationship will depend on early perceptions of expectations, liking, and similarity (Liden, Wayne, & Stilwell, 1993). This suggests the importance of perceived similarity and liking to the socialization process. If the relationship does not get off to a favorable start, socialization is likely to break down. This is all the more reason why organizations need formal socialization programs. Moreover, they need programs that train supervisors to understand their role in the socialization process. Without such training, only subordinates with favorable leader–member exchange will receive adequate attention—attention based on initial liking, similarity, and mutually supportive expectations. Resource Guide E outlines a program for new employees and one for their managers as methods for enhancing new employees' organizational insight.

Evaluating oneself and the environment and considering the match between the two are also important during other career transitions. Retirement is one example of a transition that calls for a new understanding of roles, expectations, and opportunities; losing one's job in mid-career is another. Unless the individual can secure another very similar job in the same industry, he or she may need to learn new behaviors for an extensive job search. In some cases the person may have to be retrained for a new career. Unfortunately, old categories for defining oneself and old expectations for what it takes to get a job may interfere with this learning process. The next section describes the self-assessment and resocialization processes that may accompany job loss.

Resocialization and Retraining for Displaced Workers: Learning to Create Value

Career development initiatives should reflect opportunities created by environmental and organizational changes (Campbell, 1991; Hall, 1986; London & Stumpf, 1986). Within organizations, changes in career opportunities for current employees occur as new ventures are established and existing areas of business decline. Employees who are displaced by these changes seek new opportunities, perhaps after some retraining. Reemployment in an economic climate of limited job vacancies must go beyond traditional outplacement strategies such as counseling, résumé preparation, interview training, and networking. To be successful, displaced individuals must realize the need to create new opportunities for themselves within their own organizations or within other organizations or new ventures.

Career development in a difficult economic environment requires that current and displaced employees recognize these changes and participate in their evolution as a means of enhancing the likelihood of continuing employment. They should understand how organizational growth creates new opportunities and new determinants for career advancement. They should understand how to add value and in the process create jobs for themselves and others. Moreover, they should understand, and be able to cope with, the frustrations of the job creation and job search process. New directions in career development focus on "inplacement" within organizations for current employees and on esteem building, internships, and community action for displaced employees.

All this is easier said than done. It requires self-assessment, relinquishing old categories for information processing, and making internal attributions. These new attributions initially may be painful as the individual realizes the need to learn new skills and behavior patterns. Confidence will grow with a succession of small successes. Necessary support includes interpretation of the assessment results, training that develops skills and conveys knowledge for which there is demand, and chances to create value and opportunities by trying out these new skills on real job problems, perhaps during an internship. The following sections describe this new framework for career development for employees who stay with a changing organization and for employees who are laid off.

Inplacement

Current employees are not always prepared to meet the demands of a changing organization (Maitlen, 1994). Their skills may not be in line with market demands within or outside the organization. Moreover, new job opportunities are not always at the same organizational level or pay scale. These employees face the challenge of retraining and repositioning themselves in the internal job market, often into entrepreneurial activities. These individuals need to become acclimated to new work strategies and techniques and to learn how the current job market works.

Inplacement is a jobs-creation strategy through the establishment and encouragement of new ventures and internships within the organization (Maitlen, 1994). As such, it meets the needs of individuals for employment security and also meets the needs of organizations for continued profitability and shareholder value.

Inplacement requires keeping employees informed about changing opportunities and skill requirements. It begins with assessing skills, knowledge, and goals as a way to identify employees' current value. Retraining may be necessary to ensure employees have the capabilities required by the changing organizational demands. This may take the form of in-house

courses or university programs; the idea here is to create value through training and development. Internships may be established within the organization
by loaning employees to new ventures or different units where they can learn
new skills and operations. This gives employees an opportunity to learn and
demonstrate their value, and, in the process, they may create job opportunities for themselves and/or new opportunities for others through the growth
of a new segment of the business.

Next, consider career development for unemployed individuals with an
emphasis on the individual's role in the jobs-creation process. Several approaches, described in the following, cover training to support a positive
attitude and effective job search behaviors, learning experiences that demonstrate how individuals can show their capacity to add value to an organization and develop job opportunities, and groups of unemployed workers
joining forces to foster business initiatives and thereby create employment
opportunities in the community.

High-Risk Job Losers

Displaced workers' attributions for job loss affect their optimism about
reemployment, which in turn relates to their future employment success
(Prussi, Kinicki, & Bracker, 1993). Because individuals who blame themselves for a job loss are likely to experience negative affect and lower self-
esteem, intervention programs should focus on increasing unemployed
workers' self-efficacy and confidence in finding another job.

Caplan et al. (1989) conducted a field experiment on the effects of an
intervention that provides social support and job search skills to unemployed workers. Called the JOBS Project and conducted at the University
of Michigan, the workshop for laid-off workers was designed as a research
and evaluation initiative to test a preventive intervention for unemployed
persons. The intervention was designed to provide participants with social
support and a promotive learning environment to acquire job search skills
and at the same time to "inoculate" the participants against common setbacks that are part of the job-seeking process by helping them know what
to expect. The idea was to prevent the deterioration in mental health that
often results from unemployment and to promote high-quality reemployment, thus contributing to individual growth. The method transforms the
crisis of job loss into an opportunity for individual development and growth.
(See also Vinokur et al., 1991.)

The intervention, consisting of a week-long seminar, focuses on building
self-insight and insight into how the job search environment works. Topics
covered during the seminar include "discovering your own job skills and
thinking like an employer," "presenting your own job skills and thinking like
an employer," "finding job openings," "résumés, contacts and getting the
interview," and "planning for setbacks" (Curran, 1992). In addition to job
search skill training, the seminar highlights active learning methods that use
the knowledge and skills of the participants elicited during group discus-

sions. Participants are inoculated against setbacks by anticipating possible barriers and preparing solutions to overcome them (generating possible behavioral and cognitive responses, evaluating the effectiveness of the responses, and rehearsing and reevaluating the responses). As a means for trainers to gain the participants' trust and respect, trainers are encouraged to engage in moderate self-disclosure and encourage participants to do the same. Trainers also offer participants unconditional positive regard and specific positive feedback. In addition, social support is provided by the trainers' expressing empathy for the participants' feelings and fellow participants' demonstrating support for each other.

Another process that focused on increasing job search skills and building self-esteem was conducted in Israel by Eden and Aviram (1993). The intervention, based on the importance of interpersonal perception and feedback to the process of building self-esteem, was an eight-day workshop that met every other work day for two and a half weeks. A behavior-modeling process began with four- or five-minute-long videos demonstrating successful job search behavior. Each tape was followed by brief discussion of the behavior and then by role playing in small groups in which each participant rehearsed the behavior and got feedback from the others. The treatment resulted in increased general self-esteem and job search activity. Reemployment increased more for those people who were initially low in self-esteem, indicating the malleability of self-concept for low-self-esteem individuals. The results suggest the importance of social observation, behavior modeling, and feedback, especially for those weak in self-esteem.

In another study, unemployed professionals who were assigned to write about their thoughts and emotions surrounding their job loss were reemployed more quickly than those who wrote about nontraumatic topics or who did not write at all (Spera, Buhrfeind, & Pennebaker, 1994). Addressing one's emotions and cognitively reappraising one's situation may improve the quality of the job search process by reducing the stress of keeping feelings to oneself.

Job-Creation Strategies for Displaced Engineers

A recent retraining program for displaced engineers was conducted at SUNY–Stony Brook (Wolf et al., 1994). The premise of the program was that outplacement in today's difficult economic times needs to be more than the usual job search strategies such as writing a strong résumé, learning how to be interviewed, and networking. The unemployed engineers needed a new mind-set. The engineers expected that finding a job requires searching hard enough for an opening that matches their capabilities and interests. However, the severe economic and technological changes of recent years and their own lack of up-to-date experience required the engineers to recognize that they not only needed new knowledge and skills but also had to create job opportunities. They could create these opportunities by demonstrating their value to firms with problems. The program helped generate these opportunities.

In addition to offering course work for graduate-level university credit in the management of new technologies, the semester-long program was designed to engage participants in meaningful and difficult real-world problems so they would have a chance to demonstrate their value to companies. Internships (sometimes paid, sometimes unpaid) were used to place the unemployed engineers in work situations as quickly as possible while they learned the management of new technologies. Initial assessment data and outcome measures indicated strategies for helping displaced workers to understand that their employment security rests on their demonstrating value to new and existing enterprises.

Funded with federal money channeled through local government agencies, the program was designed for displaced engineers from the defense industry. The program helped the displaced workers demonstrate their worth to themselves and to local firms that could become prospective employers. The goal was to help the participants work with these firms to solve problems and in the process create new job opportunities. Two groups of displaced engineers participated in two separate programs. Each program focused on basic management skills (e.g., communications and business strategy) and the management of emerging technologies (such as computer-integrated manufacturing systems and electron microspectroscopy) and offered fifteen graduate-level credits over a six-month period. The first group (fifty-six participants) was exposed to a series of company representatives presenting costly problems faced by their firms. The purpose was to engage the participants in important, real-world issues that would allow them to demonstrate how they could add value to an enterprise. Managers from a variety of businesses visited classes to outline real problems—those with a dollar value of at least $200K. This level was chosen so that if the engineers had an impact on the problem, the result may create a job for themselves or others that would pay approximately $50K per year.

The second group (eighteen participants) engaged in unpaid internships in the firms, working on problems the organizations needed to solve. Here again the focus was on helping the managers understand how they could contribute to the organization—the hope being that the added value would lead to job creation. Successful participants adopted an entrepreneurial mind-set that they could apply in making a contribution to new and existing enterprises, thereby creating employment opportunities for themselves.

The program showed that the displaced engineers varied considerably in their attitudes about the job search process and their roles in job creation. Some expected to be handed a list of job opportunities and to be placed in the assignment where they were needed; this was the model they had followed for years in the bureaucratic environments of large defense contractors. Other participants were willing from the outset to learn new skills and prove their value. Some were willing to learn new skills and experiment with new behaviors, while others remained depressed and unable to risk new learning and new ventures. The results have implications for selection of displaced individuals for graduate-level retraining programs and for the design of programs that create opportunities by demonstrating worth.

Collective Job-Creation Strategies for Laid-Off Workers

Leana and Feldman (1994), considered collective and individual reemployment strategies, describing how individuals in communities hard-hit by plant closings banned together to create new employment and prevent existing organizations from closing. Analyzing survey data on individuals' reactions to job loss, they examined the variable "community activism" (Leana & Feldman, 1992). They outlined factors that predict propensity to engage in this collective form of coping, often involving unions, local government, and educational institutions. They described examples from communities hit by business downsizing and plant closings in which individuals joined together to pursue various job-creation strategies. These collective efforts ranged from stopping plant closings to attracting new employment to an area.

While gaining insight into the organization is important for newcomers and others in career transitions, expanding horizons is important for all employees—especially, perhaps, those with several years' experience in the same organization. The final section in this chapter describes more general ways to improve self- and interpersonal insight by enhancing observation skills. This will serve individuals well as they face increasingly demanding work requirements.

Observation Skills Training

Conger (1993) argued that new leadership development methods are needed to train managers in dimensions of leadership that are central to managing in a competitive environment. These dimensions center on interpersonal understanding and effectiveness (e.g., sensitivity to diversity, building communities of common interest, and managing decentralized units). Training methods will have to be more than receiving feedback on ratings, self-assessments of personality characteristics, or games and role-playing exercises in artificial situations. Training methods, such as simulations, need to be built around organizational issues that improve observation skills.

Boice (1983) described the value of feedback in training observers. Information about judgment correctness improves accuracy. Feedback reduces biases. Observation training includes increasing the involvement of trainee observers in the observational context, for instance, by learning to role-play each of the types they are asked to recognize. Ways to maximize the performance of observers include the following: (1) give observers prior experience in judging the topic and object of interest, (2) use good actors as subjects, (3) make the discriminations as discrete and defined with familiar terminology as possible, (4) select judges of at least normal intelligence and median age, (5) allow judges to see all of a subject, including the context that may have provoked his or her actions, and (6) allow observers sufficient time to observe (Boice, 1983).

Russo and Shoemaker (1992) defined metaknowledge as an appreciation of what we do know and what we do not know. "Metaknowledge concerns a higher level of expertise: understanding the nature, scope, and limits of our basic, or *primary knowledge*. Metaknowledge includes the uncertainty of our estimates and predictions, and the ambiguity inherent in our premises and world views" (Russo & Shoemaker, 1992, p. 11; italics in original). They argued that people can be taught to avoid perceptual and judgmental biases, such as confirmation bias (leaning toward one perspective and seeking support for our initial view and avoiding disconfirming evidence) and hindsight bias (believing that the world is more predictable than it really is because what happened often seems more likely afterward than it did beforehand).

Methods to increase insight might include training people to observe cues, interventions to increase cue salience, interventions to encourage perceptiveness (e.g., recording and feedback mechanisms), interventions to encourage self-disclosure and feedback, training to search for disconfirming evidence, training to ignore biases, training to develop useful heuristics (ways to conceptualize and process perceptions), learning insight-induction tools and techniques (e.g., brainstorming, data collection, flowcharts, root cause analyses), and self-monitoring training. Such training may not have lasting effects, as noted by Perkins (1981): "People often modify considerably the heuristics they are taught. But they may gain anyway by improving poor heuristics, learning to think about how they think, and in many other roundabout ways" (p. 206).

Frame-of-Reference and Rater-Error Training

Stamoulis and Hauenstein (1993) compared two types of rater training: *frame-of-reference training* and *rater-error training*. Frame-of-reference training is aimed at raters with idiosyncratic performance standards that bias their perceptions (Bernardin & Buckley, 1981). It gives raters feedback on the accuracy of their ratings as part of the training, in addition to lecture and discussion of job behaviors and rating dimensions. Stamoulis and Hauenstein (1993) describe the process:

> raters read a job description and discuss the duties and qualifications that they believe are necessary for job performance. The trainees are then given three vignettes comprising critical incidents that represent outstanding, average, and poor job performance. Trainees rate each vignette on behaviorally based rating scales and submit their justifications for each rating. The trainer

informs participants as to what the correct ratings are for each vignette and gives the rationale behind each rating. A final discussion focuses on any disparity between "correct" and "idiosyncratic" ratings. (p. 994)

The idea behind frame-of-reference training is that rating accuracy can be enhanced by providing raters with information about the effectiveness of different work behaviors and the relevant performance dimension for each behavior (Pulakos, 1986). Thus, raters develop a common theory of performance to evaluate employees (Sulsky & Day, 1992). In frame-of-reference training, raters are told they are to evaluate employee performance along separate dimensions. The dimensions are defined and relevant behaviors described and discussed. The trainer clarifies which behaviors are indicative of different performance levels. Raters practice by watching and evaluating ratees' performance on video. The trainer then provides feedback on each manager's ratings and explains the ratees' "true" scores. The underlying mechanism is that shared performance schema fostered by frame-of-reference training as a basis for information processing results in better recall for behavior performance information and hence more accurate ratings (Woehr & Roch, 1994). However, the success of this training may be limited if previously held contradictory theories of performance interfere with learning a new performance model (Sulsky, Day, & Lawrence, 1994).

In contrast, rater-error training helps raters learn a new response set, for instance, one that lowers mean ratings (less leniency) and lowers scale intercorrelations (less halo; Stamoulis & Hauenstein, 1993). Unfortunately, this may lower rater accuracy, for instance, if generally high ratings are justified.

In Stamoulis and Hauenstein's (1993) study, 160 college students rated videotaped vignettes of work performance before and after training. They found that frame-of-reference training improved the accuracy of rating dimensions, while rater-error training improved differentiation among ratees (that is, accuracy in judging overall ratee performance levels collapsed across dimensions).

A third training condition, known as *structure of training* served as a control for the structural similarities between frame-of-reference and rater-error training, such as presenting examples of typical job behaviors and rating dimensions, practice ratings, and discussions about ratings. This control condition produced results that were similar to the frame-of-reference training. (The major difference between the control and frame-of-reference training was that the latter provided trainees with examples of what is good, average, and poor job behavior in each job dimension and specific feedback on their rating accuracy.) This result indicates that raters may still improve dimensional accuracy from training that is limited to lecture and discussion of job behaviors and rating dimensions and rating practice. This is important because designers of training may have difficulty providing accurate behavioral examples to reflect the full range of performance on each rating dimension. (Such examples are time-consuming and expensive to develop.)

Stamoulis and Hauenstein (1993) suggested that two types of training will be beneficial when combined. One type of training should focus on increasing the correspondence between the variability in observed ratings and the variability in actual ratee performance. The second should provide raters with practice in differentiating among ratees, rather than focus on rating errors. Both types of training may be accomplished by lecture and discussion of job behaviors and rating dimensions, general performance examples, rating practice, and general rating feedback.

Conclusion

This chapter has described various methods for inducing self- and interpersonal insight based on the social information–processing concepts presented earlier in the book. Self-knowledge is a prerequisite for, and motivator of, growth and improvement. A parallel concept to self-knowledge is the learning organization. This encompasses methods to help organization members understand themselves and their environments and how they can function together more effectively. Insight-induction methods discussed in this chapter include self-assessment, survey feedback, assessment centers, computerized assessment, socialization processes, retraining, and observation skills training. A review of these methods suggests the following conclusions:

1. Learning organizations place emphasis on "generative learning"—that is, continuous experimentation and feedback for balancing advocacy and inquiry.

2. Organizational changes require individual learning. People "learn how to learn" as they discover how to collect and use information about themselves and their environments. This knowledge can help individuals and organizations accomplish transformational changes.

3. Adaptive learners make incremental changes to enhance existing operations and activities. Adaptive learning requires openness to a wide range of perspectives; being able to see connections between issues, events, and data; sensitivity to and concern for human nature; and having the feeling that one can and should influence the world.

4. Self-assessment and self-evaluation are the foundation for self-learning and behavior change.

5. Self-assessment entails comparing oneself to others (in line with the discussion in Chapter 2 of control and social comparison theories). Reasons for understanding self-assessments include realizing that we can be the source of our own feedback, self-regulation, and clear perceptions of the environment.

6. Ways to design effective self-assessment procedures include presenting information about the organization to indicate why the self-assessment is important, providing guidance on how to interpret the self-assessment results, and presenting comparative data. Resource Guide A is an outline for a career development program tailored to the organization. Resource Guide

B includes examples of self-assessment methods that support the career development program.

7. Employee attitude surveys can have positive outcomes (e.g., improved work methods and performance) and negative outcomes (e.g., costs of communicating and using the results and resistance from managers who feel threatened by the process). "Employee-guided management," outlined in Resource Guide C, establishes principles for involving employees in the design, implementation, and analysis of survey feedback.

8. Developmental assessment centers (see the sample outline in Resource Guide D) and computerized assessment may be used to establish a direction for enhancing one's strengths and overcoming one's weaknesses. The assessment center has the advantage of integrating a diverse set of information from a variety of sources to result in a comprehensive view of one's goals and/or capabilities.

9. Socialization is the process of learning the attitudes and behaviors required for an organizational position. The process helps new employees make sense of organization. Resource Guide E outlined a new employee orientation program and a program for supervisors of new employees.

10. Resocialization and retraining may be necessary for people experiencing major career transitions. This can occur within the organization (a concept called "inplacement") or outside the organization for those who have been laid off. The resocialization calls for individuals to recognize their need to create value and opportunities for themselves. This may be a new way of thinking for those accustomed to being assigned their next position.

11. Observation skills training includes increasing the involvement of employees in the observational context using multiple methods, such as learning to role-play each of the types participants are asked to recognize, discussing job behaviors and rating dimensions, reviewing performance examples, practicing rating, and receiving general feedback on rating accuracy.

The next chapter continues this review of insight-induction techniques by focusing specifically on 360-degree feedback. As already noted, this is an increasingly popular organizational intervention aimed at employee development and evaluation. It is of particular interest here because it draws on the perceptions of multiple observers to compare with self-assessments. As such, it relies on the cognitive processes discussed throughout this book.

10

Designing 360-Degree
Feedback Processes

Oh wad some power the giftie gie us
To see oursels as others see us!

Robert Burns

Nothing, indeed, is so likely to shock us at first as the manifest revelation of ourselves.

Havelock Ellis, *The Dance of Life*

Feedback is a key ingredient to the development of self- and interpersonal insight. This chapter focuses on 360-degree feedback (ratings from subordinates, peers, supervisors, and internal or external customers or clients) as a tool to enhance self-insight. This form of feedback is growing in importance as a process that contributes to individual and organizational development (Bernardin & Beatty, 1987; Hautaluoma et al., 1992; London, Wohlers, & Gallagher, 1990; London & Beatty, 1993; Dunnette, 1993; Tornow, 1993.) The complexity of organizational life for managers indicates the value of having input from people who have different expectations (Latham & Wexley, 1982; Tsui & Ohlott, 1988). Managers may have to respond in different ways to subordinates, peers, supervisors, and customers. Rapid organizational changes have forced managers to be attuned to the shifting expectations of these constituencies and to the need for continuous development to accomplish these shifts. Subordinates' perspectives are important given that boss–subordinate relationships are a primary part of managing—in many cases, the central relationship for the manager. Other perspectives are likely to be equally important but for different reasons. Peers' viewpoints focus on the manager's contribution to teamwork, while customers' viewpoints demonstrate the manager's responsiveness to the customer and the manager's contribution to customer satisfaction; 360-degree feedback is a way for organizations to call attention to these differing and changing roles.

The use of 360-degree feedback helps overcome the drawbacks of relying on supervisors as the sole source of performance review and feedback. Supervisors may avoid evaluating subordinates, for instance, because of low interpersonal trust or the desire to avoid a negative situation (Fried, Tiegs, & Bellamy, 1992). Supervisors are often uncomfortable giving feedback—whether positive or negative. They find giving negative feedback especially difficult because subordinates often become defensive, deny the problem altogether, or blame situational factors beyond their control, including the supervisor's unrealistic expectations and demands (Meyer, 1991). The 360-degree feedback process highlights the importance of self-assessment and employees' taking responsibility for their own development. The organization provides the rating process, feeds back the results in the form of a computer-generated report, and offers developmental opportunities. Managers must interpret the feedback results and use them to identify areas for improvement.

The 360-degree feedback survey may ask raters to report their observations of the manager's behaviors. This may be a report of the frequency of different behaviors or an evaluation of the behaviors—the extent to which they were done well. As an alternative, the survey may ask raters for their expectations of the manager—that is, what the manager should do (Moses, Hollenbeck, & Sorcher, 1993). Another format is to request two ratings for each behavior: what the manager does and what the manager should do. Asking the rater to evaluate observed behaviors assumes that the behaviors were observed often enough for the rater to recall their frequency and/or evaluate them. Asking for expectations leaves more to the rater's judgment but does not require that the behaviors have actually been observed. Moreover, ratings of expectations are a way for the raters to communicate what they expect, not simply report their view of what has occurred. Thus, managers can use the information about expectations to guide their behavior in the future. However, they have to evaluate their own competence and behavioral tendencies in light of the expectations, and they have to evaluate the reasonableness of the expectations.

Whether the rating process asks for expectations, reports of observed behaviors, or evaluations of behaviors will depend on the purpose for the process. Ratings of expectations will be important when there are communication difficulties between the manager and the various constituencies. Knowledge of others' expectations may be especially helpful for new managers. Ratings of behavior frequency and quality or favorability will be important when managers are more experienced in knowing the requirements of the job but perhaps are lax in focusing on their routine behavior and the effects of their actions. Behavior-based ratings will also be justified when the raters have had ample opportunity to observe the manager's behavior and performance.

Theoretically, asking for both behavioral observations and expectations determines the degree to which there is a performance gap between what is done and how much should be done. However, practically, the two ratings are likely to be correlated. This may occur because raters like to be consistent, so something that is not done well or is rarely done implies that more is necessary, and something done well implies that enough is being done. In addition, using the same method, such as the same type of rating scale, often results in a correlation called *common method bias*. The consequence is that the additional rating for each behavior does not contribute much added information beyond the first rating regardless of whether the first rating is an expectation or a behavioral observation.

The results of 360-degree ratings are usually provided to the managers for their use in making development plans, possibly as part of a training program (Van Velsor & Leslie, 1991; Cialdini, 1989). Part of the process may be training to help the recipients interpret and use the results—for instance, to establish development plans (Kaplan, 1993). In other cases, 360-degree feedback may be incorporated into performance evaluations for administrative purposes (e.g., merit pay and advancement decisions). Using 360-degree feedback for development alone, at least at the inception of the process, helps to alleviate concerns about the fairness and accuracy of the data; it does not eliminate these concerns, however, since subordinates may still say inaccurate things either to hurt the boss's feelings or to gain favor with (or "brownnose") the boss. Also, the organization may have to take pains to convince ratees of the confidentiality of the results—that is, that higher-level managers will not know the managers' individual results. Using the feedback for administrative purposes puts teeth into the process—that is, adds to its importance—but may lead to concerns about the reliability and accuracy of the method. Managers who are threatened most by the process, generally those who are concerned about the relationships they have with their subordinates or others, are likely to be the most vocal in expressing their distrust of the process. Using several waves of 360-degree feedback solely for development purposes is a good way to initiate the process. As raters and managers become familiar with it, the policy can be changed to incorporate the results into decisions about the managers rated. In general, managers are more accepting of 360-degree feedback when they believe the organization supports development efforts related to the appraisal dimensions and when the dimensions are perceived to be high-priority behaviors in the organization (Maurer & Tarulli, 1994).

This chapter reviews research on 360-degree and upward feedback (ratings from subordinates) and then provides suggestions for designing and implementing a 360-degree feedback program. (Major portions of the literature review come from Smither et al., 1993. Readers who want additional information about 360-degree feedback should see a special issue of the journal *Human Resource Management* edited by Tornow, 1993. Many of the papers in this issue are cited here.)

Review of Theory and Research

Early research on performance appraisal often compared traditional supervisor ratings to subordinate, peer, and self-ratings, for instance, examining the psychometric properties of subordinate ratings, the validity of self-evaluations, or comparing rating sources. (For reviews of these three types of studies see, respectively, Mount, 1984; Mabe & West, 1984; and Harris & Schaubroeck, 1988.) Convergent validity and leniency effects were found for supervisor and subordinate ratings (Mount, 1984). Other research has found clear distinctions between different sources of performance ratings (Borman, 1974; Klimoski & London, 1974; Holzbach, 1978; Mabe & West, 1982; Shrauger & Osberg, 1981). This research suggests that managers tend to maintain a favorable view of themselves, causing inflated self-ratings (Campbell & Lee, 1989; Farh, Dobbins, & Cheng, 1991; Klimoski & Brice, 1991). Yet self-ratings can be a valuable basis for beginning a performance appraisal discussion (Meyer, 1991).

Recent research has focused specifically on 360-degree feedback and more particularly on upward feedback (subordinates rating their immediate supervisor). Understanding moderators of self–subordinate agreement is important in calibrating results and guiding the use of multiple-source information in different situations. Self–observer differences have been found to be stable over time regardless of the type of rating (skill-based or personality-based), and self-perception seems to be a stable individual difference (Nilsen & Campbell, 1993). Agreement between self- and others' ratings is one possible index of self-objectivity or self-awareness (Wohlers & London, 1989; Yammarino & Atwater, 1993). It does not necessarily mean the individual is objective, however. As one of this book's reviewers noted, "Just because my wife and I think I am handsome doesn't mean I am." Nevertheless, agreement between our self-ratings and others' ratings of us is associated with enhanced individual and organizational outcomes (Hazucha, Gentile, & Schneider, 1993; Yammarino & Atwater, 1993). As a consequence, there is a growing body of research on the agreement between self- and subordinate ratings and demographic and organizational variables that affect agreement (Atwater & Yammarino, 1992; Becker & Klimoski, 1989; DeGregorio, 1991; McEvoy & Buller, 1987; Smither, Wohlers, & London, 1992; Van Velsor, Ruderman, & Phillips, 1991; Wohlers & London, 1989; London & Wohlers, 1991; Wohlers, Hall, & London, 1993; also, see Chapter 3 for a discussion of how self–other agreement suggests directions for development as well as a discussion of limitations of agreement indexes). For example, self–subordinate agreement has been found to be higher in line units than in staff units, possibly due to the higher task structure and performance clarity in line units (London & Wohlers, 1991). Other research found lower agreement in government organizations than in private corporations and the military (Wohlers, Hall, & London, 1993) and higher agreement in more supportive work settings than in less supportive settings (Yammarino & Dubinsky, 1992). An additional finding from two studies is that women tended be higher on self-awareness than men (London & Wohlers, 1991; Van Velsor, Taylor, & Leslie, 1993). (See Chapter 5's review of self–other agreement.)

There has been somewhat less research on the effects of 360-degree feedback on changes in managerial performance over time. An early study found that 360-degree feedback leads to subordinates' perceiving positive changes in the boss's subsequent behavior (Hegarty, 1974). A study that asked for first-line managers' reactions to 360-degree ratings one week after receiving feedback found that the managers were generally supportive of the subordinate appraisal, especially if they received feedback from both their subordinates and their higher-level manager (Bernardin, Dahmus, & Redmon, 1993). Other research has found that managers reported positive reactions to the process six months after receiving feedback (London, Wohlers, & Gallagher, 1990). Still other research has found that self–subordinate agreement and favorability toward the 360-degree feedback process were not related to supervisors' later reactions (Smither, Wohlers, & London, 1992). In another study, self–subordinate agreement increased one year after the first 360-degree feedback process was administered (London & Wohlers, 1991). A study of skill changes in managers discovered that 360-degree feedback resulted in skill increases and higher self–other agreement two years later (Hazucha, Gentile, & Schneider, 1993).

Smither and colleagues (1993) studied self-ratings and subordinate performance ratings for 1,472 managers in an international operations division of a large corporation at two points in time, six months apart. The study examined the effects of subordinate familiarity with the supervisor, participation of the manager in providing self-ratings, and changes over time on the favorability of ratings and the degree of self–subordinate agreement. Familiarity with the supervisor (time reporting to the supervisor and/or being co-located with the supervisor) resulted in more critical subordinate ratings. Managers who participated by providing self-ratings received higher subordinate ratings than did managers who did not provide self-ratings, suggesting that nonparticipating managers also didn't do much to support their subordinates. Managers who received feedback following wave 1 improved their performance from wave 1 to wave 2, whereas managers who did not receive feedback in wave 1 did not improve their performance over time. The difference between self-ratings and upward feedback declined for managers who received individualized feedback compared with those who received general (normative) information about how managers at their level on the average were rated by their subordinates. Subordinates were less likely over time to indicate that supervisors did not have an opportunity to demonstrate behaviors contained in the upward-feedback instrument. Also, managers were less likely over time to indicate that they did not have an opportunity to demonstrate behaviors presented in the rating instrument. These results indicate the importance of calibrating the effects of organizational circumstances, such as exposure to the manager, when interpreting upward-feedback results.

Theoretical Foundation

As covered in Chapters 2 and 5, several theories may explain the degree of agreement between subordinate and self-ratings and the effects of level of rating and agreement on changes in performance. Role theory and impression-management processes suggest reasons for agreement. Subordinates and their supervisors are likely to share common expectations about the supervisor's behavior (Biddle, 1979; Tsui & Ohlott, 1988); these expectations, however, may depend on the subordinates' relationships with the supervisor. Supervisors may behave differently with different subordinates, and in this way affect whether subordinates view their supervisors in the same way as the supervisors view themselves (Yammarino & Dubinsky, 1992). Familiarity, based on similarity and exposure, is likely to affect how much information supervisors disclose about themselves to subordinates, and such self-disclosures are likely to influence subordinate perceptions. The amount of time working together and length of tenure with the firm are also likely to influence having similar standards and expectations, which can also influence self–subordinate agreement.

In general, supervisors are likely to try to maintain an image that is congruent with their ideal self (Baumeister, 1982; Funder & Colvin, 1988; Morrison & Bies, 1991; Tedeschi & Norman, 1985; Villanova & Bernardin, 1989; Wayne & Kacmar, 1991). As such, supervisors are likely to portray themselves as favorably as possible with subordinates, especially if they care about the subordinates' perceptions of them. They are more likely to disclose information about themselves to subordinates with whom they work frequently and closely (Gardner, 1991; Taylor, 1979; Wortman & Linsenmeier, 1977). From the subordinates' perspective, greater familiarity with the supervisor is likely to contribute to greater differentiation and variability in 360-degree ratings.

Thus, self-image, expressed through impression management, self-disclosure, and role relationships, may explain agreement between self- and subordinate ratings. Self-image also may contribute to reactions to 360-degree feedback through information categorization and internal attribution processes (Beach, 1990; Mitchell & Beach, 1990; DeNisi, Cafferty, & Meglino, 1984; Feldman, 1981; Taylor, Fisher, & Ilgen, 1984). Information that is consistent with expectations will be easily categorized and ignored (Cronshaw & Lord, 1987). However, discrepant information is likely to draw attention. When supervisor ratings are lower than self-ratings, the manager will make an attribution. An external attribution is likely to be sought for negative information, while an internal attribution is likely to be sought for positive information. When negative information cannot be attributed easily to external causes (i.e., when it is based on objective data, such as reports of behaviors rather than judgments, or when subordinates agree among themselves), an internal attribution will be likely. An internal attribution is also likely for individuals who are high in self-esteem and internal control (Yammarino & Atwater, 1993). Other moderators of attribution may include the following: (1) social comparison information—if others received the same ratings, then an external attribution is likely; (2) role clarity—clear roles make it difficult for the manager to deny the importance of the results to themselves; and (3) use of the results—the use of the results for evaluation rather than just development increases the salience of the ratings and forces the manager to deal with the impact of negative results (Yammarino & Atwater, 1993).

As discussed in Chapter 2's review of control theory, social comparisons may play an important role in managers' reactions to 360-degree feedback. That is, reactions to feedback may depend not just on the favorability of the results but also on knowledge about how others did. Social comparison thus becomes part of the feedback. This helps calibrate the meaning of the feedback (Festinger, 1954; Tesser, 1988). Discovering that a "comparison other" (someone to whom we compare ourselves and to whom we see ourselves as similar) received a more favorable rating produces negative affect—perhaps jealousy, frustration, and lowered self-evaluation. Discovering that a comparison other received a more negative evaluation, on the other hand, produces a positive affect. In some cases, however, finding out that someone did better may provide a model for achievement and success, and so produce a positive feeling. Finding out that someone else did more poorly than ourselves may provide an example of failure that causes us to be frightened or at least wary. (See reviews of these points by Aspinwall & Taylor, 1993; Wood, 1989.)

Use of comparison information is a way to manage negative affect or mood (Aspinwall & Taylor, 1993). The choice of a comparison other may depend on mood. People may choose people for comparison who perform more poorly than themselves in order to raise their own negative affect (Wills, 1991). Negative mood may result naturally in the work setting in many ways—for instance, information about an organizational problem or a personal crisis.

In addition, self-esteem may determine how people process positive and negative social comparison information. Aspinwall and Taylor (1993) demonstrated that people high and low in self-esteem respond to comparisons in different ways when they are managing a negative mood. In their research, undergraduate students participated in a study of "how moods affect the way people think." The subjects were asked to recall a personal relationship that had made them feel happy or sad in the past. After completing some filler anagram tasks, they listened to a tape of a student who told a story of either success or failure at the university (inducing a more or less favorable comparison other). Measures of self-esteem were administered. During the experiment, the subjects were asked at several times to report their mood. The study found that comparing oneself with someone less favorable may bolster self-evaluations and increase expectations of success among people with low self-esteem who are experiencing negative mood. People with low self-esteem may have a greater need for self-enhancement and may be more sensitive to social comparison information because they are less certain of their own attributes. In addition, they expect a less favorable comparison.

Benefits of 360-Degree Feedback

The 360-degree feedback process builds on the value of feedback as a source of information to direct and motivate future managerial behaviors (Ashford,

1986); results are affected by interpersonal dynamics of customer–supplier relationships, self-presentation and disclosure, and impression management. Also, 360-degree feedback can be an organizational intervention that raises the salience of behaviors and relationships and increases employees' participation in decisions and development.

While there has been considerable research and theory on performance appraisal (downward evaluation and feedback), little attention has been given to 360-degree feedback. This section of the chapter is based on London and Beatty (1993). They apply image theory (Mitchell & Beach, 1990) to explain image formation and evaluation (raters gathering and interpreting information and managers' receiving and reacting to 360-degree feedback). The 360-degree feedback process is tied to the psychology of interpersonal relationships and the development of participative organizational cultures.

Similarity and Differences between 360-Degree Feedback and Performance Appraisal

Performance appraisal (with supervisors rating subordinates) and 360-degree feedback may request reports of behavior or judgments of performance. Both use rating scales, and both may be subject to the same biases, such as response consistencies, leniency, halo, and stereotyping (Borman, 1974). The rating scales may be the same for all ratings or may be customized to reflect the unique nature of each type of relationship. For instance, upward feedback is likely to include items that focus primarily on the boss–subordinate relationship.

There are some major differences, however, between performance appraisal and 360-degree feedback. Performance appraisal is conducted primarily for evaluation purposes and has organizational implications, such as pay treatment and opportunities for job assignments, transfer, and promotion. Secondarily, performance appraisal has a developmental component in that performance results should be fed back to subordinates with the intention of determining ways to improve weaknesses and enhance strengths. As such, performance appraisal is useful in development and career planning. Results of 360-degree feedback may also be input to evaluation, but, as discussed at the outset of the chapter, they are often used solely for developmental purposes. Managers may share the results with their supervisors if they are comfortable doing so; otherwise the supervisors would not have access to the information.

Advantages of Multiple Perspectives

Unlike performance appraisal, 360-degree feedback is not one-sided; instead, it recognizes the complexity of management and the value of input from multiple sources (Becker & Klimoski, 1989). For instance, subordinates are in an excellent position to view and evaluate many supervisory behaviors. Indeed, they may have more complete and accurate information about some behaviors than do supervisors. This is especially likely to be true of information about boss–subordinate relationships—for instance, the extent to which the manager structures the work, provides performance feedback, fosters a positive working environment, provides necessary resources, sends subordinates to training, and generally supports their development. The quality of boss–subordinate relationships is likely to be important to the success of the work group. Similar arguments can be made for ratings from peers and customers.

Ratings from multiple sources allow examination of the reliability of the information in relation to expected consistency or differentiation of behavior. When subordinates' capabilities and the demands of their jobs are fairly similar, the manager is likely to behave in the same way with most, if not all, subordinates. In such cases, subordinates should agree in their ratings of the manager. However, when subordinates' jobs and capabilities differ and subordinates' jobs are not interrelated, the manager is likely to behave differently with different subordinates. In these cases the range of ratings among the subordinates in the work group may be useful feedback along with the average favorability of results.

This applies to peer, customer, and supervisor relationships as well. Peers may agree with each other about evaluating a colleague because they observe the colleague in the same contexts. On the other hand, they may see the manager differently if they interact with the manager for different reasons at different times. The supervisor may also differ from peers and subordinates in opportunity and occasion to observe. Managers may behave differently with these constituencies because of how the managerial role and expectations differ in relation to each constituency. They may try to create different impressions, perhaps being more concerned about creating a favorable impression in the eyes of supervisors who control pay and promotional opportunities as well as resources than in the eyes of peers with whom they may be in competition for promotion. Relationships with subordinates may be concerned less with creating a favorable impression than with getting the work done to certain specifications, regardless of the impression created by behaviors and directives. Implementing 360-degree feedback, or a portion of it, may alter the importance of others' impressions and reactions to managerial behavior.

Spin-off Benefits

The 360-degree feedback approach has a number of potentially beneficial spin-offs for an organization. It calls attention to performance dimensions that otherwise might not have been viewed as important; as such, it is a way to convey organizational values. It may be an intervention to enhance two-way communications, increasing formal as well as informal communications. It may build more effective work relationships, increase opportunities for employee involvement, uncover and resolve conflict, and demonstrate top managers' respect for employees' opinions. It establishes an element of reciprocity between managers and their co-workers as sources of feedback and reinforcement.

Introducing a feedback system may encourage managers to set goals (Locke & Latham, 1990). This may be especially effective if the feedback includes normative information (i.e., a way to compare oneself with the "competition"; Locke & Latham, 1990). This will work well if the average level of performance is high; if it is low, managers may be satisfied with just meeting or slightly exceeding their co-workers' performance level (London & Smither, 1994). The more specific the data (e.g., the more it contains prescriptive or behavioral items), the more it is likely to lead managers to set specific and challenging goals (London & Smither, 1994). Furthermore, specific feedback will help managers determine the discrepancy between their goals and their performance. When 360-degree feedback is too vague or general (e.g., ratings of characteristics rather than behaviors), goal-setting theory and control theory predict that behavior change will not be likely.

Reactions to 360-degree feedback are likely to depend on an interaction between goals and self-evaluations. Consider the common situation in which managers believe their performance meets or exceeds their goals but co-workers disagree, rating them lower than the managers expected. The organization hopes that the 360-degree feedback will cause the managers to revise their self-evaluations and set goals to improve performance (London & Smither, 1994). However, this may not happen: managers in this circumstance may lower their self-evaluations (and performance goals), try to discredit or discount the feedback from co-workers, try to alter co-workers' opinions by means of impression-management techniques, develop a greater tolerance for discrepancy, or avoid the situation by directing their attention to other issues. Attribution and image theories suggest that the managers will seek an explanation for the feedback. The managers are likely to make external attributions for the disappointing results when there are no clear alternatives for improving performance (e.g., training). Thus, the effect of 360-degree feedback on future goals requires having support to help managers interpret the feedback accurately and consider constructive responses.

Use of 360-degree feedback may also contribute to other organizational initiatives to improve the quality of work processes. Quality-improvement programs focus on interpersonal relationships between and within groups. The 360-degree feedback process is consistent with, and promulgates, participative cultures; while managers may be evaluated on group outputs, information about managerial behaviors should help develop and ultimately improve these outputs.

Costs of 360-Degree Feedback

The potential costs of 360-degree feedback include time and money for implementation and preparation (e.g., explaining the purpose of the feedback program and training managers in how to use the feedback). It adds complexity to the appraisal administration process, requiring the distribution of forms to the right individuals and analyzing the data, possibly with the use of sophisticated computer programming and outside help. It imposes potential risks for the raters and may generate tension between the manager and others who provide ratings (Hautaluoma et al., 1992). It establishes expectations that behavior will change and may set up a potential conflict by highlighting the need to be different things to different people. It also provides a lot of information to integrate, creating a greater possibility for selective perception and information distortion. Because ratings are made by others who are significant to the manager, 360-degree feedback imposes increased pressure on the manager's self-concept and goals—making negative information all the more powerful and difficult to deny, especially when raters agree, or easy to distort or perceive selectively, especially when raters disagree.

Designing and Implementing a 360-Degree Feedback Program

This section, also based on London and Beatty (1993), offers guidelines for implementing 360-degree feedback. A number of approaches may be used to design the 360-degree feedback instrument, collect the data, and report and use the results (Bernardin & Beatty, 1987; London, Wohlers, & Gallagher, 1990). Here I consider the involvement of employees in the development of the items, the content and salience of the items rated, the inclusion of managers' self-assessments, the implementation procedure (e.g., training, the format of the instrument, and instructions), the use of the 360-degree feedback results (whether for evaluation and/or development), and the format and detail of the feedback. A sample 360-degree feedback survey is presented in Resource Guide F, which also includes a sample evaluation survey asking supervisors for their reactions to the process.

Item Content and Involvement of Employees in Program Design

As with performance appraisal, 360-degree feedback ratings should be made on performance dimensions that are relevant to the job; these dimensions may be derived from job analyses. In some cases, however, managers should be evaluated on desired behaviors, not necessarily on those that are typical or part of the current formal job design. For instance, the top executives of the organization may outline the types of leaders they want to reward and advance in the organization. This may be part of an organizational change effort (e.g., to make management more democratic or to increase employee empowerment). These behavioral elements can be captured on the feedback scales. Also, a group of employees may be asked to generate behavioral statements. Such involvement of employees and the link between 360-degree feedback and key strategies of the firm are ways to engender commitment to the 360-degree feedback process, communicate desired behaviors, and enhance the importance and value of the process to the organization (Maurer & Tarulli, 1994).

The 360-degree feedback ratings are made on a set of items that are likely to be familiar to the raters. The items may be general (for instance, asking about managers' characteristics and abilities) or specific (asking about behaviors that reflect boss–subordinate relationships or peer relationships). The question posed may request an evaluation (e.g., "How *well* does the manager . . . ?") or an estimate of frequency (e.g., "How *often* does the manager . . . ?"). The items are likely to reflect elements of leadership, work-group relationships, or boss–subordinate relationships that are easily understood and tied to experiences with the manager. They are the sorts of things one would expect to rate or be rated on. That is, they are consistent with organizational and personal values. Moreover, the raters have ample opportunity to observe the behaviors.

Implementation

The 360-degree feedback process itself must be clear, with participants understanding the procedure and the purpose of the results. Instructions should be clear. Employee briefings should be provided to explain the reason for the ratings, how the data will be aggregated, and how the results will be fed back. Also, as with performance appraisal, training should reduce rater biases by making employees aware of the types of errors people make (e.g., leniency, central tendency, and halo—rating all elements of performance alike).

Format. The specific rating format (number of scale points and wording of items) may not have much effect on rating accuracy, just as it does not in performance appraisal (DeNisi, Cafferty, & Meglino, 1984). Thus, the number of rating points on the scale may be a matter of the designer's preference. Having a midpoint, as on a five-point scale, may encourage more central tendency by making it possible for raters to provide middle-of-the-road ratings. A six-point scale has no midpoint, alleviating this problem, but raters using it may be offended that they cannot provide a neutral rating. The more scale points, the more likely there will be variability in the ratings.

Wording of items may be in terms of behavioral frequency, expectations, or evaluations, as discussed earlier. Ratings are likely to be more reliable when the items refer to objective or observable behaviors (e.g., meets with subordinates at least once a year to discuss their career goals) rather than individual qualities (e.g., trustworthy, responsive). Ratings of behavioral expectations produce a different type of information—that is, what the observer hopes will happen or judges could happen given the manager's prior behavior. In general, the focus of the items will depend on the purpose of the process, that is, the type of information the organization wants the process to convey to its managers. Of course, items should be clear and not double-barreled such that it is not clear what question they are asking. (An example of a double-barreled item is "The manager asks subordinates for input in making decisions that affect the department and in setting development plans for employees.")

Requiring Participation.   The administration of 360-degree feedback poses several alternatives. Managers may be required to have their groups participate in 360-degree feedback, or participation could be voluntary. Another aspect of participation is discussing results with subordinates after the manager receives the feedback; this may be up to the manager or may be specified in the operations procedures. Hautaluoma, Jobe, Visser, and Donkersgoed (1992) investigated employees' attitudes about various approaches to 360-degree feedback along with whether the feedback results should be used for development or evaluation. The employees were managers and 222 subordinates from two departments of a large firm in the photographic industry. Employees preferred an approach that incorporated the advantages of a formal policy requiring managers to use the process and a strong developmental purpose with no direct contact between manager and subordinate in discussing results. Also, exemplifying the importance of organizational context referred to earlier, employees who rated their trust in the company higher were more likely to perceive benefits of participation. In addition, they recognized that some of the main benefits from a 360-degree feedback process would be producing a sense of participation in important decisions, increasing beliefs of fairness about supervisors' evaluations, increasing accuracy of evaluations, and resolving conflicts.

Raters' Anonymity.   Care should be taken to ensure raters' anonymity. This means guarding the ratings, probably by having an outside consultant code and analyze the data and prepare feedback reports. Such reports are usually computer-generated, particularly if the survey is on an optically scanned sheet, on a computer disk, or on a computer program tied to a local area network or mainframe. Handwritten comments may require typing to disguise the handwriting. Managers should not receive subordinate ratings if there are too few peers or subordinates (e.g., four or fewer) since this might suggest the identity of the raters.

The importance of anonymity was demonstrated in a follow-up survey several months after 360-degree feedback had been provided to managers (London, Wohlers, & Gallagher, 1990). When asked in an interview, "Would you have rated your boss any differently if feedback had not been given anonymously," 24 percent of the fifty-three subordinates interviewed stated yes. See Resource Guide F for an example of such an evaluation survey. In an experimental field study of thirty-eight managers and their subordinates from an insurance company, managers who received feedback from subordinates who identified themselves viewed the upward appraisal process more positively than did managers in the condition in which subordinates did not identify themselves (Antonioni, 1994). However, subordinates produced inflated ratings and felt less comfortable when they identified themselves, suggesting the value of anonymous ratings. However, the recipients of the feedback should know that the raters were credible sources of information—for instance, peers and customers with whom they interact frequently. Feedback is evaluated more favorably when the source is credible than when the source is of doubtful credibility (Albright & Levy, in press). This does not mean, however, that the names of the raters should be disclosed.

Uses of Feedback

The uses of 360-degree feedback should influence the seriousness with which it is treated and how quickly it becomes an integral part of managing the organization. Some organizations incorporate 360-degree feedback results with performance evaluation. Alternatively, supervisor, subordinate, and/or peer feedback may be viewed as separate performance criteria, and managers may be expected to reach or exceed a given level of results on each. For example, managers may be expected to achieve a certain level of favorable ratings from their subordinates. If managers do not reach this level, they may be placed on a probation or "watch" list which requires them to show improvement the next year.

Another model is to use 360-degree feedback solely for development. Managers receive a report but are not required to share the results with their boss or their subordinates. Guidelines or counseling may be available to help support use of the data. This approach emphasizes the importance of development in the organization and may be a way to introduce 360-degree feedback as a part of the organizational culture. As suggested earlier, using peer and/or subordinate ratings for development only is likely to be less sensitive (less likely to put managers on the defensive and cause them to criticize the validity of the data) than using them for evaluation. Use for development only, however, may also decrease the application of the results since there is no requirement to respond to the feedback. A desirable initial strategy may be a two-step process, using 360-degree feedback for development during the first few years before using it as input to supervisory evaluations and decisions about pay and promotion.

Use of 360-degree feedback is likely to affect employees' attitudes about the feedback process and possibly the nature of the results. In the 360-degree feedback follow-up survey referred to earlier, 34 percent of the subordinates believed they would have rated their boss differently if the feedback had been intended for the manager's performance appraisal (London, Wohlers, & Gallagher, 1990).

Self-Assessment

The 360-degree feedback ratings may be accompanied by managers' self-ratings on the same items on which they are rated by their subordinates, peers, and/or customers. The inclusion of self-ratings should enhance the manager's attention to the results and his or her desire to use them to establish directions for development (Meyer, 1991; Bassett & Meyer, 1968).

While self-appraisals are often used for employee development (Campbell & Lee, 1988), performance appraisal research has shown that self-appraisals generally disagree with supervisor appraisals (Harris & Schaubroeck, 1988; Mabe & West, 1982). Disagreement between raters may be due to differences in attributional processes, with self-ratings subject to a strong self-serving bias (for instance, the tendency to attribute negative events to external causes and positive events to internal causes) (Levy & Foti, 1989; Levy, 1991). Providing self-rating results along with 360-degree feedback allows managers to compare their self-perceptions with how others see them. As such, it can force managers to reconsider their self-concepts in light of direct information about others' opinions about them; however, this still allows room for misinterpretation, discounting, or ignoring the results. The inclusion of self-ratings focuses attention on differences and similarities between self- and others' perceptions, identifies gaps in perceptions, and requires resolution (rationalization, changing self-perceptions, or altering behaviors).

Frequency of Feedback

It is common for 360-degree ratings to be made annually. Motorola's cellular telecommunications division uses it quarterly. Whatever the frequency, managers are not precluded from seeking informal feedback. Indeed, the introduction of a 360-degree feedback process may engender managers to seek feedback more frequently, although this hypothesis needs to be tested. The assumption is that, over time, employees and managers will become familiar with the 360-degree feedback process and see its effects on managers' development.

Report Format

The nature of the 360-degree feedback report may influence how the results are internalized and applied. Several report formats are possible: one is a narrative statement summarizing the results; another is a statistical summary with average ratings reported across the items, or perhaps average results for groups of items. Measures of average variation can also be reported to reflect agreement among subordinates (e.g., average range or variance). A more detailed report format would be an item-by-item report. The results might include the mean subordinate rating, the highest and lowest rating, the norm for the department or organization (the average rating for the item across managers rated), and the manager's self-rating. The more detailed the report, the more specific the information for guiding behavior change. Summarizing the information by averaging items across predetermined factors should produce more reliable and meaningful data. Resource Guide F includes a sample feedback report.

The more detailed the report, the more the interpretation required, and the greater the likelihood that the managers' biases will affect the interpretation. Also, the more detailed the report, the more the managers may focus on results that match their self-perceptions and ignore results that contradict their self-perceptions (Kahneman, Slovic, & Tversky, 1982; Fischoff, 1988). People are generally good at estimating measures of central tendency (e.g., Peterson & Beach, 1967), and this may extend to determining on average how well one is perceived by one's subordinates from detailed 360-degree feedback results. The more information that is presented and the more the task is potentially threatening to one's self-concept (because one fears negative results), the more judgments deteriorate and are subject to biases (Fischoff, 1988). Reports that summarize information based on statistically derived factor analyses should provide reliable data without losing distinguishing information. (See Chapter 3's discussion of how people are likely to react to feedback of different sorts and change their self-assessment as a result.)

Applications in Multinational Organizations

The study by Smither et al. (1993), discussed earlier in this chapter, also examined cultural differences in upward-feedback ratings. The following outlines their reasoning and reports their findings.

When multicultural organizations create a 360-degree feedback process, they try to use the one instrument, or at least a core set of items, accurately translated into applicable languages, for unit comparisons after averaging individual results within units. Furthermore, a common item set is a way to communicate important organizational behaviors that are expected and will be rewarded. Cross-cultural research on performance evaluations can be applied in training that prepares managers to make transitions to new cultures when they are transferred (Li, 1992; Domsch & Lichtenberger, 1991). It will also indicate the transportability of management techniques such as 360-degree feedback to a variety of organizational settings, as well as generate an improved understanding of subordinates' and managers' perspectives on supervisor performance (Adler, 1983; Arvey, Bhagat & Salas, 1991; Hofstede, 1980).

The concepts of good managerial performance and boss–subordinate relationships are likely to vary between cultures within the same company (Dowling, 1988; Hamada, 1991; Shama, 1993; Sundaram & Black, 1992). For example, face-to-face communications are a high priority for managers in some countries but not in others (Laurent, 1981; Derr, 1986). Such differences may be magnified depending on the culture in which the manager is currently working and the manager's background (foreign national or in-country national; Adler & Bartholomew, 1992). Other research suggests unique aspects of managerial performance in particular cultures. For example, management in China is dependent on developing warm relationships with co-workers, offering favors, and loosening the operating rules (Wall, 1990). Management success in Great Britain is associated with high self-confidence, assertiveness, and innovativeness (Cox & Cooper, 1989). Other research has found large gaps in attitudes about participative management between managers and their subordinates in a developing country, such as Bangladesh, with managers hesitating to accept worker participation and employees valuing participation but fearing victimization (Ali, Khaleque, & Hossain, 1992).

Self-ratings are generally more lenient than ratings from other sources (Harris & Schaubroeck, 1988). A study of Taiwanese workers, however, found a "modesty bias" in self-ratings, with self-ratings lower than ratings obtained from supervisors (Farh, Dobbins, & Cheng, 1991). Yu and Murphy (1993) failed to replicate this finding in samples from the People's Republic of China, discovering instead a leniency bias in self-ratings.

These studies were conducted within single cultures rather between cultures, which suggests the need for comparative research, such as that provided by Smither et al. (1993). Their results suggested possible cultural biases in subordinate expectations and self-evaluations. Supervisors located in Central and South America rated themselves more favorably than did supervisors in other locations. Self–subordinate agreement was higher (i.e., closer to zero) for managers located in North America and Europe than for managers located in Asia and the Pacific or Central and South America. These results could have been affected by different cultural expectations. For example, if subordinate expectations are especially high in Asian and Pacific locations, supervisors may be less likely to live up to these expectations and therefore receive less favorable ratings.

This was an exploratory study. Future research in this area should test specific, theory-driven hypotheses concerning cultural differences in self-ratings and upward feedback. Meanwhile, multinational organizations using upward-feedback surveys should recognize potential cultural differences and calibrate the meaning of the results accordingly. If data from initial administrations of 360-degree feedback show, for instance, that self-ratings are likely to be inflated, or conversely, that subordinates' ratings are more critical, this would suggest the need for training that encourages employees to guard against certain rating biases. In addition, knowledge of such cultural differences could help managers interpret their results and help higher-level executives interpret differences within or between organizational units that cut across cultures.

Conclusion

This chapter has reviewed theory and research underlying 360-degree feedback and its variants, principally upward feedback. The use of 360-degree feedback recognizes the potential value of feedback from multiple sources. I discussed the value of understanding moderators of self–subordinate agreement for calibrating 360-degree feedback results in different situations. Self-image, expressed through impression management, self-disclosure, and role relationships, may explain agreement between self- and subordinate ratings. Self-image also may contribute to reactions to 360-degree feedback through information categorization and internal attribution processes. Social comparison information provides standards for evaluating individual performance.

The discussion of uses of 360-degree feedback suggests the following conclusions:

1. The 360-degree feedback process involves several interlocking components: the uses of the data, the survey content and format, the report format, methods of distribution of results and facilitation of their use, and means of follow-up to assess progress.

2. Use of 360-degree feedback extends information from traditional supervisory performance appraisal. Performance appraisals are used mainly for evaluation purposes to make decisions about people. In contrast, 360-degree feedback is a way of tracking behavior and providing directions for development. Over time, and after multiple administrations, 360-degree feedback should be trusted as a reliable and valid indicator of performance—indeed, better than performance appraisal because it recognizes the importance of obtaining information from different perspectives.

3. Effective implementation of 360-degree feedback requires that participants understand the intended purpose of the results.

4. Implementation should be accompanied by training to explain the reason for the ratings, how the data will be aggregated, and how the results will be fed back.

5. Self-assessment is often built into the 360-degree rating process. As such, the feedback highlights the self–other comparison. This should increase the manager's attention to the results and his or her desire to use them to establish directions for development.

6. A 360-degree feedback process may cause managers to more frequently seek feedback on their own.

7. Reports of 360-degree feedback can be quite detailed, including for each item and each rating source (subordinates, peers, customers) the means, the range (low and high rating), the mean across all managers, and the self-rating. Facilitation may be needed to help managers interpret and apply the information.

8. International firms may want to use the same survey items for 360-

degree feedback across units in different cultures. In such cases, comparisons between countries should be conducted to understand different interpretations of items based on cultural values. A positive result in one culture might be negative in another.

This chapter concludes my review of insight induction with a special emphasis on 360-degree feedback. The next chapter summarizes the major findings about self- and interpersonal insight covered throughout the book. I review conclusions from earlier chapters to highlight how people learn about themselves and others in organizations and how such learning contributes to individual and organizational development.

11

Conclusions and Directions for Research and Practice

> I have come to feel that the only learning which significantly influences behavior is self-discovered, self-appropriated learning.
>
> Carl R. Rogers, *On Becoming a Person*

In this final chapter I summarize the major conclusions from the book and provide some directions for research and practice. My premise is that how we see ourselves and others is important to individual success and interpersonal and group performance. The book addressed how self- and interpersonal insights form, how they affect our behavior in organizations, how they can be measured, and how they can be developed to improve the quality of our decisions and the effectiveness of our actions.

Chapter 1 considered the meaning of the term *insight* and how it applies to perceptions of oneself and others. I described insight formation as a cognitive, social information–processing task. The information stems from self-observations and explicit and implicit feedback from others. Insight emergence is not just a cognitive process, however, behavioral and emotional components can be integrated with a cognitive interpretation for a more complete psychology of self- and interpersonal insight. Understanding insight formation helps us recognize the development of relationships between two people, the interaction among members in cooperative groups, and the behaviors and reactions of parties engaged in conflict and negotiation. In addition, insights can be induced by providing feedback, self-assessment, and training people in observation and self-assessment.

I examined the cognitive processes underlying the formation of interpersonal insights in Chapter 2. This included a discussion of the sources and types of information, especially the effects of feedback about one's performance on establishing self-insight. Cognitive theories of information showed how people acquire information about themselves and others, process that information in the formation of interpersonal insights, and then use the information to guide decisions and behavior. Information processing includes perception, interpretation, and use (e.g., in evaluating oneself and others or in deciding to take an action).

Continuing Chapter 2's line of reasoning, we "reflect" the feedback we receive about ourselves in the sense of seeing ourselves through others' eyes. Feedback that matches expectations is categorized in a rather shallow thought process. Information that diverges from expectations or is sudden and unusual requires an attribution. When self-perceptions are involved and the information is negative, the tendency will be to search for a cause outside ourselves. A strong situational circumstance is likely to lead to an external attribution. When the information does not match environmental characteristics, we attribute the cause to ourselves and we then decide the degree to which the internal attribution is good or bad. This is a cognitive evaluation process. We are more inclined to make self-attributions for positive feedback and external attributions for negative feedback. Insight occurs when we make an internal attribution that results in a reevaluation of our self-concept or our conception of others.

Control and social comparison theories suggest the relevance of comparative information for setting standards, evaluating information by comparing it with these standards, and using the discrepancy to set goals. Prospect theory suggests that frame of reference will affect interpretation of information. For instance, a lower initial expectation will lead to more positive evaluations, while a higher initial expectation will lead to being more critical. In addition, mood may further predispose an individual to be more attentive to direct and indirect feedback. Therefore, performance feedback should be framed in a positive way, as should explanations of the likelihood of success from positive opportunities. This does not mean misleading the individual but rather stating the same thing in a positive light (i.e., similar to saying the glass is half full rather than half empty).

In Chapter 3 I focused on self-assessment, viewing it as a foundation for self-learning and establishing realistic goals. Sometimes, however, self-knowledge can inhibit rather than facilitate personal improvement. People frequently evade personal growth and new self-knowledge in an effort to protect their self-esteem. Nevertheless, self-knowledge motivates professional growth and improvement. All people have a picture of themselves in relation to the environment based on reflection and attribution processes. Moreover, people have varying self-schemas to match different situations. Individual characteristics prompt people to be more self-aware. For example, self-monitoring increases self-insight, while self-protection and self-handicapping decrease it. Self-disclosure is a means to test reactions to self-concepts; some people, however, avoid self-disclosure just as they avoid direct feedback. Self-protection mechanisms, such as denial and self-promotion, insulate the individual from meaningful feedback and developing self-insight. Self-reflection can be encouraged by creating a reason for increased attention to one's own performance and to performance feedback.

I reviewed theory and research behind interpersonal insight in Chapter 4. Early person perception research investigated the recognition of emotion in others, the accuracy of appraisals of others' personalities, and the process by which personality impressions are formed. Heider (1958) theorized that attributions of others' behaviors to internal or situational causes depend on one's self-perceptions in relation to the object perceived. For instance, the degree of intimacy of contact between two people depends on the situation, how long the people have known each other, and individual differences, including similarity on a variety of demographic characteristics. Thus, the perspective of the observer is critical to understanding how people form insights about others. Individual characteristics affecting interpersonal insight include observation skills, environmental sensitivity versus self-focus (self-monitoring), and empathy. Insights about others emerge from observation of others and from others' self-disclosures.

Chapter 5 considered how we perceive others and how feedback from others influences our self-perceptions. Image theory was used to integrate cognitive, interpersonal, and organizational dynamics that influence rating and feedback reaction processes. The chapter presented a model that includes rater and ratee perceptual processes, showing the interrelationships between self-image and goals, such as impression management and expectancy confirmation, the performance environment, the nature of the rating and feedback program, rater image formation and evaluation, and ratee acceptance and behavioral reactions to feedback. The chapter also considered ways to study and enhance rater accuracy, such as ways to access and reward accuracy and managers' attention to performance feedback.

In the next three chapters I applied the theories of person perception and social information processing underlying self and interpersonal insight to the development of interpersonal relationships between two people, within groups, and in negotiation or conflict-resolution situations. Chapter 6 described the development of mutual expectations of goals and behaviors between two people. The interpersonal relationship is a developmental process that suggests the emergence of deeper insight over time as the relationship grows from openness and self-disclosure to mutual investment. Dyadic relationships develop through attribution, assessment, and expectations that take place before, during, and after exchanges. Interpersonal relationships are affected by impression-management strategies such as ingratiation, intimidation, supplication, and face-saving.

My focus in Chapter 7 was on how person perception and self-concept affect the way people gain insight into, and contribute to, cooperative group processes. Group members gain insight into interaction patterns and how they can contribute to the group effort. Patterns of communication and interaction emerge quickly in response to the effects of time pressure. Cues to these patterns are embedded in the face-to-face group interactions. Group members capture a sense of the needed flow of interaction, and this flow is maintained over time, even after the situation changes. Newcomers to established groups use reflected feedback to recognize and become part of these patterns. They evaluate feedback in relation to their existing conception of self-efficacy in similar situations. They seek and communicate expectations and reactions. Task interdependence coupled with appropriate goals and feedback direct group members' attention, increase their expected outcomes, and affect group performance. Intragroup conflict can be a source of group development if group members recognize and value different viewpoints as they gain information about themselves and their relationships with others.

Negotiation processes, covered in Chapter 8, deal with interpersonal insight in win–lose (distributive) and win–win (integrative) situations. Negotiator insights require interpreting a variety of cues about offers and behaviors throughout the negotiation process. Feedback is obtained and behavior is adjusted as alternative positions are tested. Barriers that prevent negotiators from accurately interpreting feedback include cognitive biases, inadequate cognitive processing, poor information-search techniques, and inaccurate interpretation of information. Negotiators make attributions that explain the opposing party's actions as well as their own. They judge what they and their constituents value, and they estimate how the opposition is likely to react to various offers. Openness to different perspectives, willingness to consider partial agreements, making concessions, and forming coalitions are important to the successful negotiation. Third-party mediators aid negotiating parties in gaining insight into each other's positions, motivations, and arguments through communications and knowledge of the effects of various types of information on the parties' perceptions of themselves and others. Another type of third party is the agent, called the "principal," who is hired to represent a negotiating party. Conflicts may emerge between agents and principals who hire them, indicating the importance of mutual insights in the evolution and success of this relationship.

After completing this review of insight in key interpersonal situations, I turned to ways for improving self- and interpersonal insight. Chapter 9 described examples of several insight-induction techniques and applied cognitive/information processing to explain how these methods work in organizations to generate self- and interpersonal insight. These techniques prompt awareness of feedback, self-reflection, attribution, and self–other evaluation. They help individuals resist denial and other defense mechanisms. Moreover, they promote the concept of the learning organization—an environment that supports continuous experimentation and feedback. Self-assessment methods rest on the assumption that obtaining self-knowledge is a prerequisite for, and motivator of, growth and improvement. Insight-induction methods discussed in this chapter and in the resource guides include self-assessment, survey feedback, assessment centers, computerized assessment, socialization processes, training to create opportunities and add value, and observation skills training.

In Chapter 10 and Resource Guide F, I focused on upward and 360-degree rating and feedback programs as increasingly popular ways to provide the individual with regular feedback from diverse sources. These methods build on the value of feedback as a source of information to direct and motivate future managerial behaviors and reduce uncertainty. Moreover, they recognize the importance of input from multiple sources that have different viewpoints and concerns about different aspects of performance. The 360-degree feedback approach is usually used to establish directions for performance improvement—often as a prelude to a training program. Once incorporated as a management technique, it is likely to be useful for making decisions about employees without threat and resistance. Designing a 360-degree feedback program entails considering the use for the survey data, the content and survey format, an explanation for employees, a report format, methods of distribution of results and facilitation of their use, and means of follow-up to assess progress. The 360-degree feedback results are affected by interpersonal relationships, self-presentation and disclosure, and impression management. The technique can be an intervention that highlights the salience of behaviors and relationships and increases employees' participation in decisions and development.

Directions for Research

Research should examine the validity of the basic information-processing model of insight acquisition and development outlined in Chapter 2. We want to know whether the model reflects how people actually think of themselves and others. This means examining sources of information and how information is sought, received, and processed. Both initial information-processing and deeper encoding processes should be analyzed. In addition, resulting behaviors should be studied. This model should be tested on how individuals perceive themselves and others in various group contexts.

The more specific processes of reflected feedback, image processing, and efficacy revision should also be explored. Multifactor experiments can manipulate feedback content, its fit with existing prototypes, and the uniqueness and associations of the information that guide attributions. Such research should identify feedback sources, study characteristics of feedback, explore existing categories and prototypes, create new prototypes and expectations, and study image matching and attributions. Alternative situations should be created to understand attribution processes (e.g., by varying the uniqueness of information). Self-efficacy should be measured and its relationship to feedback studied. Thus, such research should test the use of reflected appraisals, image processing (categorization and attribution processes), and cognitive evaluation (emergence of, and changes in, perceptions of efficacy).

Such research would enhance our understanding of interpersonal insight in different contexts. Thus, at least five streams of research are necessary, corresponding to a focus on insight about self, others, interactions between oneself and others and between others, task group processes, and negotiations.

Research Variables

Table 11.1 lists input, process, and output variables for research on insight emergence and recognition. Taking several variables from the list, consider how they might be a focus for research:

Cues and Clues.   This refers to information characteristics, such as amount, clarity, reliability, favorability, depth, source, characteristics of the source such as forcefulness, ease of acquisition, consistency with other information and with self-concept, and objectivity. The presumption is that the more information requires interpretation, the more it will be subject to perceptual biases (e.g., perceived selectively to enhance one's self-concept).

Task Demands.   This includes time requirements to generate a product in a group, work flow (e.g., synchronized versus sequential), and negotiation mode (e.g., distributive versus integrative). Specificity of demands creates cues that focus perceptions. For instance, sequential tasks may force role clarity. Synchronous tasks may require that members create the process first and then plan. This may lead to better mutual insight and understanding of the entire process (how one fits into the process and how the group members work together).

Rule Clarity.   Rule-based interactions require few interpersonal inferences. A hypothesis to be tested here is that the clearer and more specific the rules, the more accurate the perceptions of expectations and the faster people will conform to group norms.

Criteria for Evaluating Outcomes.   This refers to the evaluation criteria people apply to feedback information and the clarity of the criteria. The clearer the criteria, the more accurate the resulting attributions.

Importance of the Work and Outcome.   This encompasses the task and outcome significance to the individual and to others in the group or other parties. High incentives should influence cue salience and focus attention on efficacy attributions.

Self-Disclosure Tendencies.   People who disclose more about themselves should influence others' perceptions of them and increase the amount and favorability of feedback they receive about themselves.

Self-Monitoring Tendencies.   People who are high in self-monitoring attend to environmental characteristics. They should be highly attuned to task demands and behavior patterns and should more quickly adapt to these patterns. In contrast, the behavior of individuals who are low in self-monitoring should be influenced more by their existing behavioral tendencies.

TABLE 11.1 Variables for Research on Interpersonal Insight

I. Input Variables for Possible Manipulation
  A. Environment—Group Parameters
    1. Cues and clues
    2. Task demands
    3. Clarity of rules and norms for interaction
    4. Criteria for evaluating outcomes
    5. Importance of the work and outcome
  B. Individual
    1. Self-disclosure tendencies
    2. Self-monitoring tendencies
    3. Observation skills and, obversely, perceptual biases (induced or prevalent in subject)
    4. Empathy
    5. Need for cognition
  C. Group
    1. Composition of the participants in terms of similarity of experiences, motivations, and perceptions
  D. Individual–Group Interactions
    1. Consistency of information with self-concept
    2. Consistency of information with prototypes
    3. Uniqueness of the information
II. Process—Intermediate/Mediating Behaviors
  A. Frequency of different types of information and behaviors (e.g., expressions of preferences)
  B. Nonverbal behavior and language of opposing party
  C. Communication channels (type, number, openness)
  D. Creation of rules
  E. Biases influenced by overconfidence, self-inflation, desire to be like others, desire to make others like oneself (attributing one's own motives to others)
  F. Tactics to invoke action and test inferences (baiting, threatening, abusing)
  G. Degree of coordination, ensemble (symbiotic relationships and interpersonal comfort) among parties
  H. Agreement and accuracy of information content (e.g., accuracy in reporting others' preferences)
  I. Accuracy of stimulus–response contingency (consistency with prior occurrences and events)
  J. Information seeking/probing
  K. Response tactics to uncover or predict stimulus–response contingencies (e.g., abuse, threat in negotiations)
  L. Process characteristics (type and frequency of communication; discovery of integrative potential)
  M. Tactics for eliciting, recording, and analyzing cues about an opponent's strategy and resistance point
III. Outcomes
  A. Characteristics of the solution (innovation, time to completion)
  B. Similarity of perceptions of the parties
  C. Self-efficacy

Need for Cognition.   Chapter 2 suggested that the desire to engage in mind-ful information processing may be an individual difference variable. Re-search on the need for cognition has focused on the extent to which attitudes are formed through issue-relevant thinking and on the finding that individu-als who are more likely to think about and elaborate cognitively on issue-relevant information when forming attitudes have stronger attitude–behavior correspondence (Cacioppo et al., 1986). Research is needed to determine whether people who are high in need for cognition are likely to be more motivated than others to seek feedback about themselves, avoid mindless categorization, and integrate new information in a way that revises their self-image or their image of others.

Measurement

The theoretical perspectives described here suggest the need to capture feedback, reflections of feedback, categories (prototypes and expectations), the categorization process, the attribution process, efficacy, and the content of insights. These variables can be measured using self-reports (surveys, interviews) that are based on the respondent's retrospection and introspec-tion. Protocol or thinking-aloud methods can tap perceptions as subjects derive insights from observing others (e.g., on videotape). In addition, re-searchers can observe interactions using interaction process analysis meth-ods to record verbal and nonverbal behaviors and communications. These might include the following:

- Observation and recording of ensemble development with participant self-reflection and protocol analysis
- Observation of negotiation or other types of interactions—in person or on videotape
- Observation and process analysis of discussions about analyzing and modifying others' behavior
- Bootstrapping and modeling "mind maps"; tracing information streams; also referred to as protocol analysis or introspection (i.e., recording and content analyzing what people say they are doing while they are doing it)

Introspection.   This method may be quite important for studies of insight given the internal, cognitive nature of the concept. Perkins (1981) provided advice for using introspection to tap insights: "Introspective reports are most reliably obtained only with the help of good tactics, including careful instructions that warn against explaining or filling in, but encourage as con-tinuous a report as memory and other factors permit" (p. 38). There are many problems with thinking-aloud and retrospective methods—for in-stance, people will often report what they assume the researcher wants to hear. People tend to overexplain, interrupting the activity to provide a spec-ulative analysis of the activity, not a report of the thinking. Thinking aloud can be a more valuable research method when the subject is properly guided. Perkins (1981, p. 33) offers six principles as instructions for thinking aloud— the product of which would be tape-recorded for a later analysis by the researcher.

1. Say whatever's on your mind. Don't hold back hunches, guesses, wild ideas, images, intentions.
2. Speak as continuously as possible. Say something at least once every five seconds, even if only, "I'm drawing a blank."
3. Speak audibly. Watch out for your voice dropping as you become involved.
4. Speak as telegraphically as you please. Don't worry about complete sentences and eloquence.
5. Don't overexplain or justify. Analyze no more than you would normally.
6. Don't elaborate past events. Get into the pattern of saying what you're thinking now, not of thinking for a while and then describing your thoughts.

This section has considered variables that should be manipulated and measured by researchers. In the next section I suggest how these variables can be incorporated into research to understand self- and interpersonal insight.

Alternative Research Designs

Several research designs are possible for studying interpersonal insight emergence and recognition. An experimental design would call for the manipulation of variables such as those described previously and in Table 11.1. Initial research could manipulate the key variables identified earlier—that is, characteristics of feedback, prototypes, and uniqueness of feedback information to the individual or situation prompting an attribution. Dependent measures could be reflections of the feedback (the degree to which the information is noticed), interpretations of the feedback (categorization, attributions), the degree to which the feedback is viewed as insightful, and the perceiver's self-efficacy. The expectation would be that feedback that is noticed and leads to self-attributions would be perceived as insightful. Self-insights would be related to changes in self-efficacy. Feedback that is not noticed or that is categorized into expected prototypes would not be viewed as insightful. Moderators of these relationships may include subjects' observation skills, empathy, or self-monitoring. A general hypothesis is that people who have keen observation skills, who have strong empathy with others, and who are high in self-monitoring will be more likely to notice behaviors that require attributions and lead to understanding oneself, others, or relationships between oneself and others.

Other research could ask people to predict how they will be rated and compare their predictions with actual ratings. Another research design asks people to identify their perceptual model—that is, the weights they give to attributes in making judgments of themselves or others. Their weights can be compared with actual weights in making judgments or decisions. Moderators of insight-prediction accura~~cy~~ ~~s~~tudied, including individual differences, aspects of th~~e~~ ~~relation~~ships, and situational conditions, suc~~h~~ ~~f~~eedback, and ambiguity of

~~n~~ and how insights about ~~-~~flowing behavioral inter- ~~v~~ideotaped for later view- ~~t~~he group could be ma- ~~ta~~sk (sequential versus ~~partici~~pant and observers (e.g. ~~throu~~gh assignment of people to gr~~oups~~ ~~the~~ tape of the interaction and report introspectio~~n~~ ~~could~~ stop the tape whenever they believe they have an insight. At these times, they could be asked questions about the nature of the information, its meaning, whether they categorize it into a readily available prototype or norm, or whether they make an internal or external attribution. If subjects are told the questions before viewing the tape, this procedure may also be a method to induce insights as well as study them. To control for this confound, another group of subjects can be asked to stop the tape (or in other ways indicate the place on the tape) where an insight occurs to them.

Some Directions for Research on 360-Degree Feedback

As 360-degree feedback grows in popularity, research will be needed to improve and facilitate the process. Research is needed on different types of 360-degree feedback processes (e.g., different methods for its design and implementation and different rating and reporting formats). Differences between uses for development and evaluation should be studied. Investigations of 360-degree feedback in different organizational cultures are needed, exploring cultural differences in scale meaning and dimensional structure. The short- and long-term effects of 360-degree feedback on work-group relationships and organizational cultures should be studied. The effects of varying interpersonal relationships and characteristics on rater agreement and manager acceptance of feedback should be examined. Research is needed on image formation and acceptance processes. Managers' self-concepts and raters' prototypes of managers and leaders should be identified. Ways to clarify and differentiate these images should be investigated (e.g., by involving subordinates, peers, customers, and managers in generating relevant behaviors to be rated). Practitioners should experiment with interventions to improve the acceptance of 360-degree feedback processes and results. In addition, the long-term effects of 360-degree feedback on management style and behavior change should be investigated. Finally, multiple criteria of 360-degree feedback success should be measured, including employees' acceptance of the process, managers' acceptance and use of results, managers' change in behavior, and changes in work group and organizational relationships.

Guidelines for Practice

I set the stage for this book in the first four chapters by outlining the major cognitive theoretical positions behind self- and person perception that influence the development of interpersonal relationships. Chapters 5 through 7 applied the theory to dyadic, group, and negotiation relationships. In the next two chapters I described programs aimed at enhancing self- and interpersonal insight. In this final section, from London (in press), I try to encapsulate how the theory and research on self- and interpersonal insight drive practice.

How we view ourselves and others—what is termed here *interpersonal insight*—is important to the effectiveness of key interpersonal processes in organizations. Individual biases often obscure information processing, however, and bog down organizational initiatives. Unfortunately, human resource programs often do not take these cognitive processes into account.

Consider problems faced by many human resource executives. One may be communicating organizational strategy and corresponding performance expectations. Another may be ensuring that human resource systems work together to prompt employees to closely examine their self-concepts in relation to organizational requirements. Still another may be designing interventions that improve cooperative relationships and promote conflict resolution. Too often, programs that address these issues occur in isolation. They are based on what the organization wants to accomplish, or on what is popular (Johns, 1993). They may be based on economic and sociological models that drive efforts to improve quality, reduce costs, or develop a strong organizational culture centered on a common mission. Or they are based on theories of individual motivation, group dynamics, or organizational processes (e.g., about leadership or structure).

What is missing is how people process information, apply it to themselves, and learn about social interactions that are the foundation of organizational functioning and success. The cognitive approach I take in this book adds another dimension to understanding how individuals react to the work environment. It is an approach that cuts across a variety of human resource efforts aimed at enhancing organizational functions. Recognizing the underlying cognitive processes common to key interpersonal situations in organizations can help link, integrate, and create more effective human resource programs. Social information processing can cause individuals to change their self-image and behavior and enhance interpersonal relationships. Human resource programs such as assessment, feedback, and training can be improved by building on how we process information about ourselves and others.

Cognitive information processing has been applied to performance appraisal (e.g., Ilgen, Barnes-Farrell, & McKellin, 1993). Other human resource programs, such as self-assessment, attitude surveys, feedback, and development planning, assume cognitive processes occur, but they do not delineate them. That is, the cognitive components and their relationships are not used as a basis for program design. Nor do they show how the underlying cognitive components are related to interpersonal dynamics. In this book I have extended the application of cognitive information processing to the emergence of self-insight and the development of important interpersonal processes—specifically, one-on-one relationships, group dynamics, and negotiations. I summarized major cognitive processes in the form of a four-step insight-formation process and how human resource executives can use this process to understand how interpersonal situations operate and can be improved. As such, the book has described how human resource programs can be designed so that they deliberately enhance self- and interpersonal insight. In this last section I outline principles for practice, describe training for improved insight, and, finally, propose a human performance system that uses the cognitive insight-formation model to integrate and strengthen human resource programs.

Some Guiding Principles

Consider some of the major research-supported principles arising from the theoretical discussions:

- Feedback from others influences self-perceptions.
- The process of collecting and providing feedback highlights the salience of the issues or behaviors about which the feedback is provided.
- Feedback needs to be strong, consistent, and salient to the situation (i.e., have consequences for receiving or not receiving valued outcomes) for it to matter.
- People's self-observations match how they believe others see them but not how others actually see them.
- Self-observations are as important as feedback in influencing self-perceptions.
- Observations about others, however, are likely to be more accurate than self-observations.
- People tend to categorize information into preexisting images, thereby not changing their self-concept.
- Information that is discrepant with the preexisting image is attributed to internal or external causes.
- Discrepant, negative information is likely to be attributed to external causes.

- Information consistency or interventions to force self-reflection can increase the likelihood that discrepant negative information is attributed to internal causes.
- Internal attributions may require means to force awareness and avoid automatic categorization of feedback.
- The way in which feedback and developmental opportunities are framed (i.e., stated in a positive or negative light) affects feelings of loss or gain. Negative frames put people on the alert and lead to more negative decisions.
- Interpersonal relationships and associated performance are multidimensional. As a result, information should come from multiple sources.
- Self- and interpersonal insight are important to the development of relationships between two individuals, in cooperative groups, and in conflict and negotiation situations.

Guidelines for Insight Induction

The following are guidelines for insight induction based on these principles. The guidelines are listed under each element of the cognitive information–processing model.

Sources of Feedback. Methods are needed to engender self-assessment and feedback from a variety of the relevant sources. This suggests the following guidelines:

- Train employees in self-observation.
- Offer methods to assist self-assessment, such as inventories and rating scales as part of career development and performance improvement programs.
- Provide opportunities for self-assessment and reflection on dimensions important to the organization.
- Train all employees in observation skills and ways to give positive and negative feedback.

New Frames that Prevent Unwitting Categorization of Information. Categorization can be avoided by having balanced feedback from diverse sources. Thus guidelines include the following:

- Train employees to give positive and negative feedback.
- Train employees to try different strategy structures when they face unfamiliar situations.
- Ensure that feedback comes from many sources, including subordinates, peers, supervisors, customers, and suppliers.
- Ensure that feedback is constructive—that is, specific and behavioral.
- Frame feedback and information about developmental opportunities in a positive light.

Attribution Processes. Making an attribution requires comparing oneself to others to determine the uniqueness of the feedback. Also, attribution processes suggest a tendency for people to attribute negative results to external factors. This suggests the following guidelines:

- Provide comparative information on the performance of peers or relevant others.
- Start feedback sessions by asking for self-assessment as a way to avoid defensiveness and generate self–other comparisons.
- Ensure that feedback is not critical or threatening. The goal should be to avoid defensiveness and denial.

Reevaluation of Self-Concept or Conception of Others. For feedback to lead to a renewed self-concept and a recognition of needed developmental experiences, it should be more than a onetime event. Employees should be encouraged to seek and discuss feedback with others, and feedback should be related to the important organizational processes that require effective interpersonal relationships, making the following guidelines:

- Do not limit feedback to formal performance appraisal and feedback programs. It should be given frequently and soon after the occurrence of the behavior in question. It should be given with reference to observations of interpersonal relationships in one-on-one, group, and negotiation situations.
- Encourage and train employees to discuss their own performance with others. They should learn to request feedback from subordinates, peers or group members, customers, and supervisors.
- Offer specific directions for change, assuming change is necessary.

Developing an Integrated Human Performance System

The guidelines for practice based on the cognitive model and the suggestions for insight induction can be applied to form a comprehensive set of human resource programs called a *human performance system.* Such a system was developed for several of AT&T's business units. (See Chapter 9 and Resource Guide A for an outline of such a program. Also, see London & Mone, 1994, for a more detailed description of a series of human performance programs to meet evolving organizational strategies.) AT&T recognized that the success of an organization depends in large part on all employees' recognizing the organization's objectives and their role in achieving these objectives. In turn, this requires that employees understand their own capabilities and motivation and the expectations that others have of them. Moreover, they need to understand how to build effective relationships in one-on-one relationships and group settings. In addition, they have to know how to resolve conflicts that prevent individuals and groups from working with each other effectively to accomplish a common goal. That is, self- and interpersonal insight are the foundations of smooth and productive work functions.

Increasingly, human resource departments are expected to generate policies and programs that support the strategies of the organization. These programs need to recognize and support self- and interpersonal insight, which requires understanding the cognitive processes involved in self- and other perception. An integrated human performance system reinforces organizational strategies in all elements of managing human performance, including assessment, goal setting, training, appraisal, feedback, compensation, and career development. Also, all these elements should strengthen self- and other perception.

A human performance system begins by identifying the general performance dimensions that are important to the organization. (Later, performance dimensions specific to different job families can be identified and incorporated into the programs.) The key performance dimensions may be based on job analysis and performance evaluations of model performers. In addition, the dimensions may include components of behavior and performance that are not common in the organization but that the organization wants to establish. For instance, a defense contractor attempting to diversify may want its engineers to acquire marketing skills, or a once-successful business attempting to rebound by entering new markets may want its managers to learn entrepreneurship. A large bureaucratic organization facing cost cutting may want its low-level employees to handle more responsibility and to be empowered to make more decisions on their own.

The key performance dimensions then lead to an analysis of competency requirements. These may be knowledge, skills, or abilities. They may also be motivational and attitudinal, indicating the extent to which individuals must want to learn new behaviors and accept new goals. The organization's strategies, performance dimensions, and competency requirements form the basis for program design. Elements of the program may be outlined in written form for communication to all employees. Orientation programs and supervisory training support the effort.

Overall, the program follows my cognitive model by providing a frame of reference for employees to interpret information about themselves and others in relation to the organization's goals and expectations. Unconscious categorization of feedback is decreased and attributions are encouraged. Individuals are prompted to think about the extent to which their behavior and learning match the organization's expectations for today and the future. The human resource programs drive a reevaluation and development of one's self-concept and perceptions of interpersonal situations.

A cornerstone philosophy of the program is that employees are responsible for their own development; the organization (including the immediate supervisor) provides the enabling resources. In addition, development has multiple goals: to improve in one's current job, to acquire the skills needed to perform the job in the future given changing organizational requirements and expectations, and to prepare for a new job.

Human Performance System Components. The following major components of an integrated human performance system are listed under the elements of the cognitive model they support:

Sources of Feedback

- Self-assessment methods for review of the performance dimensions and competencies
- Methods for collecting feedback from broader sources (e.g., questions to ask subordinates, peers, and customers)
- An upward-feedback or 360-degree feedback program
- A performance appraisal program that assesses employees on the key performance dimensions

New Frames That Prevent Unwitting Categorization of Information

- An overview of organizational changes and requirements
- Definitions of performance dimensions (important behaviors) and key competencies
- Guidelines for feedback and compensation

Attribution Processes

- Guidelines for competency discussions with one's supervisor
- Information about career opportunities in the organization (where the jobs are likely to be and what the requirements will be for these jobs; for example, functions that are growing, those that are declining, and those that are remaining stable)
- A "supervisor as coach and developer" training program

Reevaluation of Self-Concept or Conception of Others

- A goal-setting process (for job and career goal setting) whereby supervisors work with subordinates to share perceptions and set goals for improvement (A focus on areas for improvement, which may include current strengths, is likely to be more productive than expecting people to share their weaknesses, especially in this era of corporate downsizing.)
- An annual development planning process for establishing training plans and career goals
- A training curriculum that offers short courses and self-administered learning (e.g., computer-based self-paced learning and written job aids) to learn about and enhance one's capabilities and observation skills
- A reinforcement system that rewards employees for participating in development activities and rewards supervisors for making accurate appraisals, conducting constructive performance reviews, and, in general, paying attention to their subordinates' development

Recognizing that these elements of the human performance system work through different cognitive processes, each system component can be designed to strengthen the associated cognitive process. For instance, assessment methods can be tested to ensure the behavioral dimensions assessed are clear, observable, and objective so that self-reflection is meaningful and difficult to escape. Organizational objectives can be stated in terms of clear performance dimensions against which to compare feedback and self-assessment. Therefore, performance information cannot be categorized in a way that results in denying or ignoring the results. Instead, thought is needed to determine the cause of the information and the extent to which performance results are internally determined. Guidelines, counseling, and planning processes can encourage meaningful use of internal attributions, leading to development and new ways of thinking about oneself. Also, human performance systems can be designed around different interpersonal processes, or can be designed to include multiple interpersonal processes. Thus, performance dimensions can include group and negotiation behaviors. Feedback processes can assess these behaviors, and planning and developmental experiences can enhance them.

Conclusion

This final chapter has reviewed the findings from previous chapters, offered directions for research, and suggested guidelines for practice. Throughout the book, I have viewed self- and interpersonal insight as the foundation of self-efficacy and interpersonal effectiveness. Accurate self-concepts, those that reflect reality and agree with others' perceptions, are likely to encourage the individual to engage in meaningful development activities. Accurate perceptions of others and of interpersonal relationships are likely to encourage behaviors that contribute to the development and productivity of these relationships.

Now for a final set of conclusions:

1. Research is needed on insight about self, others, and interpersonal relationships.

2. This research should test the basic information-processing model of insight acquisition and development, covering the processes of reflected feedback, image processing, and the reevaluation of self- or other's efficacy.

3. Variables for research include characteristics of individuals, interpersonal relationships, and the situation. These variables can be categorized as indexes of input, process, and outcomes of the general insight-formation process.

4. Measures need to capture feedback, reflections of feedback, categories, the categorization process, the attribution process, efficacy judgments, and the content of insights.

5. Relevant research methods include observation, protocol analysis and introspection, and survey measures of perceptions and attitudes.

6. This research will become a basis for individual and organizational development. Research-supported principles for practice can then be derived. Some principles listed earlier suggest how feedback from others influ-

ences self-perceptions and the process of collecting and providing meaningful feedback.

7. These principles can be translated into methods for insight induction, such as opportunities for self-assessment, training in self- and other observation, and methods that provide comparative information on others' performance. They can also be used to structure interventions to facilitate group process and conflict resolution.

8. These ideas can be incorporated into human resource programs, which should be integrated to form a human performance system for improved management. The system encompasses a cycle from goal setting through training and development methods to improve interpersonal processes to outcome assessment.

Thus, self- and interpersonal insight can be fostered by self-assessment, observation skills, feedback, reflection, and evaluation. Cognitive processes and social information are at the heart of meaningful insight development. Situational conditions can modify others' reactions, be the source of clear feedback, and overcome categorization, stereotyping, and avoiding or denying reality. Insight research can guide career development, assessment processes, socialization practices, retraining that helps employees learn how to create value and opportunities, survey feedback programs, and negotiation mediation. Overall, interventions to induce insight and facilitate interpersonal processes can enhance individual and organizational development and effectiveness.

Resource
Guides

A

Outline for a Self-Directed Career Development Process

This Resource Guide offers ideas for how self-insight can be fostered by a structured, self-paced career development process. This type of process is not uncommon. Self-help career counseling books are readily available to the public, and organizations often develop similar materials tailored to the firm and its employees. This guide shows how such materials support the basic components of insight formation by encouraging reflected feedback, categorization avoidance, accurate attribution, and cognitive evaluation. (The following introductory points are from London, in press.)

The guidelines for conducting and interpreting self-assessments coupled with input from salient others are the means for reflected feedback. Announcing the program in connection with evolving organizational strategies and initiatives suggests to employees the need to take notice. Evaluating employees on participation in development and having supervisors who take development seriously are other forms of support for self-reflection.

Once employees recognize that this is serious business and begin to participate in the process, they need help to understand the results and not deny, dismiss, or otherwise categorize them in ways that prevent constructive actions. Providing social comparison information and information about corporate directions and career opportunities is one way to do this. Seeing that others are different than oneself makes an external attribution more difficult. So does seeing clearly that one's knowledge, skills, and experiences are not needed—or are needed in one area of the business but not another. The goal is for the employee to think, "Yes this is me, and I better do something about it!" The result is a reevaluation of self-concept, formulating plans for development, and implementing these plans.

The career development program requires employees to take responsibility for their own development. The organization provides the resources, including information about career opportunities, supervisory support, and materials. Self-assessment is key to the success of the program. Also, the program tries to enhance the employee's understanding of the organizational environment and what is required to be successful. Therefore, the program encourages self-reflection and evaluation based on the relationship between organizational requirements and self-evaluation.

The development modules described here are a comprehensive series of guidelines to support the employee's job mastery, professional development, and career development. The modules should help the employee do the following: determine competency requirements for the job and professional development; examine career opportunities and career interests; identify competency requirements for job, professional, and career development; assess competencies associated with job, professional, and career development; prioritize competency needs; plan development, participate in training and on-the-job developmental experiences; and track progress. Although this is meant to be a useful model for practitioners, it would be expensive to develop and use in its entirety and should be adapted to fit an organization's requirements. Also, some elements of the program require considerable self-control on the part of the supervisor—for instance, in not using employees' competency assessment results for performance appraisals.

Eight modules are suggested. Each would be published in booklet form:

Module 1. *Job and Career Development: Process Overview*

This introductory module describes the organization's commitment to employee development. It recognizes that having experienced, motivated management development is critical to being a world-class organization. Experience and motivation stem from continuous attention to learning and development. *Continuous learning and development* refers to:

1. *Doing better on your current job.* For people who are new to their job, this means achieving job mastery by learning required skills and knowledge, correcting weaknesses, and/or enhancing strengths. For more experienced employees, this entails anticipating and preparing for job changes. Changes in job requirements may result from new technology, new procedures, or different assignments and responsibilities.

2. *Professional development.* Professional development means going beyond job mastery to ensure that the employee is up-to-date on professional practices. This may involve continuous learning in areas such as finance, business, telecommunications, management information systems, and supervision.

3. *Planning and preparing for career changes in line with career interests and opportunities in the company.* The process of preparing for other jobs is appropriate for all employees to varying degrees. They should concentrate on their career development after they have achieved job mastery and have a plan for continued professional development. However, once this has occurred, career planning should occur jointly with continuous learning for job and professional development.

Additional parts of this first module provide an overview of the other modules. The other modules are described in the following.

Module 2. *Competency Assessment Process and Methods*

This module offers a process for employees to assess their competencies in areas that are important to the organization today and for the future. As such, the competency assessment helps identify areas for job and career development. This guideline helps employees formulate a competency assessment tool that makes sense for them—one that measures competencies relevant to current job, profession, and career interests. Employees are asked to follow a five-step process:

1. Determine the extent to which they need to focus on job, professional, and career development.

2. Use the tool *Assessment to Identify Key Competencies*. This supplementary module helps employees identify the competencies that are important for job, professional, and career development.

3. Adapt the module entitled *Assessment to Identify Development Needs*. This is an achievement rating format for employees to rate how frequently and how well they perform the behaviors associated with each key competency. Employees can ask their boss, co-workers, and/or subordinates to evaluate the behaviors as well.

4. Invite these other people to complete the competency rating form and return it to a clerk for confidential coding.

5. Analyze results. Employees should meet with their supervisor to discuss results. Information is provided in the module about how others rate themselves and are rated by their supervisor, peers, subordinates, and customers on common competencies. The results are input for building a development plan.

Module 3. *Achieving Job Mastery: A Continuing Learning Process through Job Development Planning*

This booklet outlines ways to consider what the employee needs to do to improve in the current job. It also addresses what the employee needs to do to prepare for anticipated changes in the current job (for instance, new technology, new accounting systems or procedures, or new clients) and what the employee needs to do for continuous professional development. Planning for career development is a separate activity that comes together later to form an integrated development plan.

Module 4. *Career Planning and Development Process*

This module describes the purpose for career planning. It includes self-assessment forms for employees to evaluate their job preferences, values, and career motivation. Also, it outlines how to integrate the results of competency assessments with additional information about preferences and interests to form career development plans. More details about this module are included below.

Module 5. *Development Planning Form*

This is a form to be completed by the employee and signed by the supervisor. It indicates career goals for the next five years (e.g., target next jobs) and development plans for the coming year (e.g., courses to take, new responsibilities and assignments to undertake).

Module 6. *Adaptation Tool: Customizing to Department Needs*

This module considers how the other modules can be adapted to meet individual needs. For instance, the first module, *Job and Career Development: Process Overview,* allows the individual to decide which of the following are important to development now? Doing better on the current job: anticipating and preparing for changes in the current job, professional development, and planning and preparing for job changes in line with career interests and opportunities in the organization. Knowing this will guide the content of the subsequent parts of the development process. It will determine the types of competencies assessed, the opportunities that are sought, and the development activities that are planned. Some people will focus equally on job, professional, and career development. Others will vary in the emphasis they place on each of these areas for development.

Module 7. *Supervisor Guide to Support Job and Career Planning*

While employees are ultimately responsible for their own developmental planning and participation in developmental experiences, the supervisor applies organizational policies and resources to provide the enabling resources. As such, an important component of a supervisor's performance as a manager is the extent to which the supervisor coaches and develops his or her subordinates. This module explains the role of the supervisor as coach and developer. It asks supervisors to be prepared to work through the career development modules with subordinates—in particular, to help them face up to their results and understand what they mean in light of career opportunities for the present and the future.

Supervisors are requested not to use the competency assessment results for performance appraisal. The results should be a guide for development planning. Using them for performance appraisal could lead to inflated or otherwise inaccurate assessments that would undermine their diagnostic value. Development plans are linked to appraisal in that the supervisor should evaluate employees on how well they set and achieve development goals.

Module 8. *Follow-up Guide: Methods for Reflection and Reassessment*

Development planning needs to be followed by action. Action should be followed by an evaluation of progress. This, in turn, should lead to revising or redirecting development plans. This module explains this process to supervisors and employees.

Specifically, the module states that supervisors are expected to provide feedback and encouragement, allow an employee to demonstrate acquisition of the new skill or knowledge, and assess the degree to which the objectives of the plan were met. Subordinates who meet their development objectives should be praised and rewarded. Subordinates who have not met their development objectives should explain why. This calls for a discussion of the reasons for not meeting the goals and of ways to correct any problems (for example, establishing more reasonable goals or choosing developmental experiences that are more readily available). Progress may be rewarded with interesting work or assignments, praise and public recognition, higher salary, more responsibility and accountability, more autonomy, higher appraisal ratings, and encouragement of continuing development. Supervisors should recognize that these development modules represent an annual cycle and should prepare to support competency assessment and development planning at least once a year. Provide feedback and follow-up frequently, at least every six months.

For employees, the module indicates that they should be concerned about their own process. They should try keeping a development journal in which they record developmental experiences and what they learned. They should adhere to the development plan, and be prepared to reassess their competencies and revise their development plan at least annually.

Program Design Options

Design features of the modules may include the following: the modules may be printed in a pull-out format; This assumes graphics experts will help in the design and production. Each module may be in the form of a brochure or trifold, allowing additional modules to be added easily and cheaply (e.g., modules on goal setting, appraisal, compensation, recruiting). Reference may be made in these modules to more detailed materials available in the organization, perhaps a performance management handbook. Some supporting materials may be summarized in a brochure format, such as a trend analysis describing company changes and emerging job and career opportunities.

An Example

The following is an excerpt from the fourth module on career planning. The sections included here are the introduction to the module and an outline of its components. The material emphasizes the employee's role in self-assessment and understanding. The module addresses the employee and explains what the employee should expect from the program.

Module 4: *Career Planning and Development Process*

The purpose of this Development Module is to help you make the most of your career.

What Is a Career?

The definition of a career will vary from person to person. For some it is simply a sequence of jobs over the course of one's working life. For others it is a single job. For still others it is meeting their long-range dreams, interests, and motivation, such as desires for achievement and success. *Career goals* may be interpreted in terms of advancement, increased earnings, increased responsibility, acquiring more expertise, more influence, and increased contribution to the organization's success. These valued outcomes come from working hard and performing well.

Need for Self-Insight

The outcomes you care about depend on your values, interests, motivation, education, and capabilities. Career planning requires self-reflection to gain insight into your values, interests, personality, and capabilities. The second development module, *Competency Assessment Process and Method,* will help you increase your awareness of your capabilities in areas that are important to the organization. Here we focus on helping you reflect on your career-related values and interests. We also help you combine these insights with information about your capabilities and the needs of the organization to establish career plans.

Everyone should have a career plan. However, people who are concerned about mastering their current job will have less detailed career plans than people who have achieved a level of mastery and expertise on their current job. Also, career planning is an annual process. This means that you should reevaluate your career interests and goals annually in relation to the training and job experiences you have had during the course of the year and changing opportunities within the company.

Over time, your increased knowledge and expertise grow in value to the firm. You are valuable to the organization for at least two main reasons: The first is *meeting immediate business needs*. To do this you must master your current job, be ready for changes in this job, and be concerned about your development as a professional. The second is your *long-term value*. This goes beyond doing well in your current job. It includes your commitment and loyalty to the firm, your functionally related experiences, and your ability to meet the company's future needs in other assignments. This requires *career planning and development*.

Career planning requires knowing what's important to your department and the organization. First, review what is important and of interest to you. Then determine potentially fruitful directions for career development within the organization. Read company publications about what departments, functions, and business units are growing, contracting, or remaining stable [the employee is referred to specific company documents]. Then consider your competencies in relation to likely opportunities.

There are three major considerations in choosing a career goal:

1. Determining what opportunities are available. (Knowing the functions and job families in the organization will help you here. These are described briefly below and again in the *Career Planning Self-Reflection Guide* [see Resource Guide B in this book].)

2. Determining whether you have the capabilities to pursue a career goal—and what capabilities you need to acquire. (The *Competency Assessment* provides a way to evaluate your capabilities on the organization competencies. The *Self-Reflection Guide* helps you apply those competencies along with other self-insights in selecting a career goal.)

3. Determining your work and career preferences, interests, values, and motivation. The *Career Planning Self-Reflection Guide* offers several tools to help you assess your behavior preferences, interests, values, and motivation.

Some people believe they have an excellent understanding about themselves and what they want from a career. Others need some guidance in thinking about what they want. The assessments in the *Self-Reflection Guide* ask you to think about whether you want the elements common to jobs and a career in the organization.

Each self-reflection tool contains instructions to help use the results in establishing your career goals. The tools can be used separately or together. They don't have to be used in any special sequence. If you have further interest in using this career assessment in relation to the other assessments, transfer your results to the *Putting It All Together* section.

Six self-assessments are offered:

1. The *Behavior Preferences Assessment*
2. The *Career Interests Assessment*
3. The *Job Characteristics Preference Assessment*
4. The *Work Environment Preference Assessment*
5. The *Career Values Assessment*
6. The *Career Motivation Assessment*

Here's an overview of each, including how it can help you:

1. The *Behavior Preferences Assessment* helps you think about your preferences for the leadership/managerial competencies. These competencies fall into the categories of managing interpersonal relationships, communication skills, achieving business results, individual style, and business environment knowledge. These are all positive behaviors, but not everyone prefers a position that requires being high on all of them. For instance, some people would prefer to have a job that requires public speaking. This is a way for you to think about which competencies you enjoy most and whether you want to work in a way that emphasizes some or all of the competencies.

Knowing your behavioral preferences is valuable because it helps you think about the managerial activities you will be doing and whether these are things you enjoy. These are activities that are important to many jobs here. The results of your *Behavior Preference Assessment* should be compared with requirements of various career goals and jobs. In making a career goal decision, you should also think about other aspects about yourself, including your competencies, interests, values, and motivation.

2. The *Career Interests Assessment* asks you to rate how interested you are in each of the functional/technical competencies important to positions here. Recall that the competency assessment tool provides a way to evaluate how good you are now on the competencies and how much training you need to develop them further. Here you consider the degree to which you are interested in them, since your career plans should be based on your interests as well as your capabilities.

Knowing your interests is valuable because it helps you think about the technical aspects of jobs. Given the diversity of job options, there are some functions that will be of particular interest to you and others that will not. Being aware of your interests in different technical and functional positions will help you select a meaningful career goal.

3. The *Job Characteristics Preference Assessment* asks you to consider the job characteristics you prefer. There are many types of jobs in the organization that vary considerably. Job characteristics refers to the nature of the work that you do, for instance, its complexity, whether it deals more with numbers or people, and the degree you have to determine what to do yourself.

Knowing your preferences for different job characteristics will help you choose a career goal with elements you will enjoy. You should apply the results of this assessment to your review of job opportunities. Completing the assessment not only will tell you something about yourself but also will inform you about relevant job characteristics. Without doing this assessment, you might not consider these factors thoroughly enough when selecting a career goal.

4. The *Work Environment Preference Assessment* asks you to consider the type of work environment you prefer. The work environment refers to the conditions under which the work is done, for example, whether you work in a group or alone and the extent to which you have to meet deadlines.

Knowing your preferences for different work environments will help you choose a career environment that is most suitable to your needs. The assessment will highlight aspects of the environment that are important to you and that you might not consider specifically unless you stop to complete such an assessment. It may also suggest ways you can create an environment you prefer—or at least help structure such an environment to the extent you have discretion over job components.

5. The *Career Values Assessment* asks you to consider the values that are important to you and that you hope will be met by your career goals. Values are attributes of the job, or opportunities that the job provides, that have special meaning to you. Examples of values are security, money, collegiality, friendships, opportunities to continue learning, advancement, convenience, contribution to organization, challenge, excitement, role clarity, order/structure, influence over others, power, knowing how well you are doing, responsibility, autonomy, control over work, being respected, leisure, and family.

Knowing what you value will help you choose a career goal that is consistent with your values. Recognizing your career values will help you evaluate your likely comfort with, and desire for, the outcomes and conditions associated with different career goals.

6. The *Career Motivation Assessment* helps you think about three major components of your career motivation: the direction you wish to follow (your career identity), how much you believe you know about yourself and the work environment (career insight), and your desire to achieve and overcome career barriers (career resilience).

- Knowing your **career identity** will allow you to determine if a particular career goal is the direction you want to pursue—that is, whether it is consistent with the way you see yourself.
- Knowing your **career insight** will help you determine if you have all the information about yourself and the environment to make a meaningful and realistic career choice.
- Knowing your **career resilience** will help you predict whether you can withstand and overcome barriers you may confront with a particular career goal. In selecting a goal, you should inquire about likely barriers and difficulties and consider whether you have the desire to achieve, the willingness to take risks, and the persistence required for success.

A summary guide called *"Putting It All Together"* helps you compare career alternatives with your competencies (from the *Competency Assessment*), behavior preferences, interests, values, and motivation. The summary guide helps you think about the match between career alternatives and your competencies, behavior preferences, interests, values, and motivation. You can also use the summary guide to help select career alternatives after reviewing the types of positions available in the organization. The summary guide concludes with a description of these positions.

Career Options

At this point the Career Development Module continues with a section that details the kinds of jobs available in terms of different job functions. Some brief job descriptions are provided to help the employee conceive what it would be like to work in the area. An example follows:

You are an expert in information management systems in the organization's **Financial Systems and Practices** Department.

You know sophisticated PC software applications for data management and analysis. You work on network communications, system linkages, and security management in connection with financial databases and operations. You are a recognized expert in these areas of MIS and are called on by your department to help solve difficult problems in the management and analysis of financial information. Competencies required for this position and others in Financial Systems and Practices include general accounting, programming, interpersonal skills, excellent written and oral communications skills, finance, planning, project management, and knowledge of computer systems (e.g., on-line systems and data processing).

Questions for Self-Reflection and Discussion with Your Supervisor

Career planning should begin by **defining your career goals.** Consider the following questions and suggestions for interpreting your responses:

—What are your major interests? What are your major career-related values? What components of career motivation do you want to improve? You can answer these questions by completing the assessments in the *Self-Reflection Guide*.

—What types of jobs do you like doing? The *Self-Reflection Guide* includes ways for you to think about your career preferences (see the *Behavior Preference Assessment,* the *Job Characteristics Assessment,* and the *Work Environment Assessment*).

—Given your preferences, interests, values, and motivation, what are some possible career goals? Rank order them or list the top three or four. (It might help to limit your career horizon to the next five years.)

—For each career objective, list how it reflects your career preferences, interests, values, motivation, and capabilities.

The *Self-Reflection Guide* helps you interpret the results of you self-assessments. The *Putting It All Together* section in the *Guide* has a way to determine if a particular career goal is right for you.

—Where in the organization would you like to work? You can answer this question only if you know what jobs are in the organization beyond your current position and department.

The *Career Planning Module* and the *Self-Reflection Guide* have some useful descriptive information about the organization.

—Do your goals require relocating?
—Do you have the skills and knowledge to achieve your goals? The *Competency Assessment* will help you answer this.
—Are your goals realistic and attainable with respect to your competencies, preferences, interests, and likely opportunities? Once again, refer to the *Self-Reflection Guide*'s *Putting It All Together* section to answer this.

Next, consider what **support** and **resources** you need to achieve your career goals:

—What types of training, education, or coaching are needed?
—What possible jobs or sequences of jobs would prepare you for your career goals? (List these jobs and when they should occur.)
—Include your career goals and plans to achieve these goals in completing the *Development Planning Form*. Talk to your supervisor about what you expect from him or her to help you achieve your goals. Agree to have a follow-up meeting six months from now to review how well your plan is working. Schedule the meeting now.

Recording Development Plans

• The Performance Appraisal Form completed by your supervisor has a space for your development plans. The response should be related to the results of your performance appraisal.
—If the appraisal indicates low performance, then movement to a different job or remedial training may be indicated.
—If the appraisal indicates average performance, development plans may suggest new and different job experiences or advanced training to enhance current job performance.
—If the appraisal indicates that you are exceeding expectations or have outstanding performance, then development plans may focus on ways to increase job challenge and maximize your accomplishments. This may be through a new or expanded job assignment, possibly, although not necessarily, a job at a higher organizational level.
• The Career Planning section of the Development Form should be an extension of the development information on the performance appraisal. The career planning form asks you and your supervisor to agree on your . . .
—recommended developmental objectives (competencies to be developed through training and job experiences)
—the specific developmental activities to be undertaken
—the time frame for completion of these activities

—responsibilities (who will do what—for instance, who will arrange for the training, who will evaluate your progress and how often, who will initiate a job change if appropriate)

• Expand the development form by including the following details:

—your next job options (list up to three possible next jobs, including for each the probable business unit, department, function, and target date for a move to that job)

—your mobility (whether you are willing to relocate to a different geographic location, when you would be willing to move, and any restrictions you have)

—possible time lines (indicating jobs or work functions for a series of positions during the next five years)

—general comments that you or your supervisor want to make

—a copy of your latest résumé attached to the development planning form. This will force you to have an updated resume. It is a way to encapsulate your accomplishments to date, and will be available if you need it to apply for another position.

• The Development Planning form, and the Career Planning section in particular, will be a valuable guide to you and your supervisor to indicate when you should take various classes, be assigned certain job projects, and prepare for a job change.

• In addition, copies of the form will be available to the management in your department to calibrate the degree of turnover planned for the department as a whole and to evaluate whether managers are acting on their commitments to develop their subordinates.

B

An Example of a Self-Reflection Guide

The *Self-Directed Career Development Process* outlined in Resource Guide A is a series of modules. The guide details one of these modules, the *Career Planning and Development Process,* which offers a number of assessment tools. Employees need a clear conception of what they want from their careers to evaluate and select career options. The module helps them think about their career preferences, interests, values, and motivation. Each self-assessment contains a guide to help use the results in establishing their career goals. The tools can be used separately or together. Note that the tools are designed to be vehicles to promote self-reflection at any given time. The results are not necessarily stable over time or predictive of specific performance criteria.

Here I offer an example of one of these tools, the *Behavioral Preferences Assessment*. It shows how the employee can be led through the self-reflection process to interpret and apply information. The behaviors are fairly general but were written to apply to managers in the finance department of a large company. Other behaviors might be used in other contexts.

While the items are meant to be clear and distinctive, this is not necessarily intended to be a psychometrically sound instrument. It is merely a tool to help people think about their preferences and apply them to the job and organizational context. It may lead them to ideas about different behaviors and work environments. Also, this tool should be used in conjunction with other self-assessment instruments as well as input from others. It's the combination of this information that is intended to inform the career planning and development process.

Self-assessment tools such as this help employees avoid inaccurate self-categorization and make accurate attributions about the meaning of their behavioral preferences. The format of choosing one behavior over another forces employees to formulate their preferences. The categories of behaviors referred to in the scoring are a way for employees to structure their thinking about their jobs and the types of behaviors that are important in different contexts. The guidelines for interpreting responses try to prevent employees from making faulty assumptions about the importance of their behavioral preferences to the organization.

257

Note that the tool addresses the employee, just as it would in the actual document.

Behavior Preferences Assessment

This assessment asks you to think about the extent to which you prefer jobs that require the organization's leadership/managerial competencies. These competencies fall into the categories of managing interpersonal relationships, communication skills, achieving business results, individual style, and business environment knowledge. These are all positive behaviors, but not everyone prefers a position that requires being high on all of them. For instance, some people would prefer to have a job that requires public speaking. This is a way for you to think about which competencies you enjoy most and whether you want to work in a way that emphasizes some or all of the competencies.

For each of the following pairs of statements, check the one that best reflects your behavior preferences. Note that while you are asked to check only one item in each pair, both items may be important things to do, and you may indeed do both. Your response here indicates the choice that you prefer the most.

1. _____ (a) Relying on subordinates and co-workers to be accountable for work that is important
   _____ (b) Relying on yourself, not others, to do important work

2. _____ (a) Managing diverse work groups and teams (e.g., selecting team members, gaining team member commitment)
   _____ (b) Being part of a group but not being responsible for managing the group

3. _____ (a) Working with people who have the same type of background as you do, and so they share the same interests, values, and ways of doing things
   _____ (b) Working with people who come from different backgrounds, and so they have different interests, values, and ways of doing things

4. _____ (a) Having to find a variety of sources of information to do your job
   _____ (b) Having a clear, single source of information to do your job

5. _____ (a) Being able to act the way you always do around others
   _____ (b) Adjusting your behavior to the behavior of others

6. _____ (a) Avoiding or minimizing conflict
   _____ (b) Surfacing and resolving conflict

7. _____ (a) Expressing your ideas, feelings, and opinions to others
_____ (b) Being able to keep your ideas, feelings, and opinions to yourself

8. _____ (a) Writing memos, letters, and documents that describe analyses and express conclusions
_____ (b) Not having to do a lot of writing

9. _____ (a) Talking to people one-on-one, not in front of groups
_____ (b) Speaking in front of groups and large audiences

10. _____ (a) Setting your work goals and objectives yourself
_____ (b) Setting your goals and objectives based on what others need

11. _____ (a) Making tough decisions—those that are difficult or unpopular, have to be made quickly, or have to be made with little information
_____ (b) Making decisions that are routine, where there are clear choices and guidelines for what needs to be done

12. _____ (a) Doing regular, predictable work that does not require planning far ahead
_____ (b) Prioritizing work and establishing a schedule for getting work done on time

13. _____ (a) Analyzing problems that have clear solutions and known effects
_____ (b) Analyzing problems that have uncertain solutions and broad ramifications

14. _____ (a) Trying actions that are innovative but somewhat risky
_____ (b) Taking actions that have been applied successfully before

15. _____ (a) Setting goals based on what you know you can accomplish
_____ (b) Setting goals that stretch your capabilities

16. _____ (a) Constantly seeking tasks that provide new and different experiences
_____ (b) Trying to work on tasks on which you have ample prior experience

17. _____ (a) Working in an environment that is unstructured, changing, uncertain, and unpredictable
_____ (b) Working in an environment that is structured, unchanging, certain, and predictable

18. _____ (a) Knowing what's important yourself without having to get input from many other people
_____ (b) Listening to others to find out what's important to your job and department

19. _____ (a) Keeping up with continuously changing developments and knowledge in your area of financial expertise
    _____ (b) Keeping up with knowledge in telecommunications as well as finance

20. _____ (a) Knowing the company—its business plans, structure, and policies—along with your specialty area in finance
    _____ (b) Concentrating on your specialty in finance—its intricacies, regulations, and advances

21. _____ (a) Having a broad understanding of global economics (such as fiscal policy, monetary policy, and material supply and demand) that go beyond your job
    _____ (b) Understanding elements of economics that relate directly to your job

22. _____ (a) Understanding the needs of those departments and managers who use the outputs of your work
    _____ (b) Understanding global customers and market behaviors that go beyond your job

23. _____ (a) Tracking the specific financial indicators that are important to the departments you serve
    _____ (b) Tracking the broad financial indicators that are important to the company as a whole regardless of the department you are in

24. _____ (a) Keeping up with the company's major product lines and services—including what they are and their profitability
    _____ (b) Knowing the details of the company's products and services that are important to your job

25. _____ (a) Demonstrating ethical behavior at all times, such as maintaining confidentiality of information and avoiding conflicts of interests
    _____ (b) Worrying less about ethical behavior and more about being effective on the job

Recording and Interpreting Your Behavior Preferences

The pairs of items are based on the Leadership/Managerial Competencies important for a multinational organization community. These fall into five categories: managing interpersonal relationships, communication skills, achieving business results, individual style, and business environment knowledge. Record your answers on the following form and then consider their meaning. In each category give yourself one point for each of the responses indicated.

Managing Interpersonal Relationships

    1a _____
    2a _____
    3b _____
    4a _____
    5b _____
    6b _____

The closer your score is to six, the more you prefer a career goal that is consistent with the managing interpersonal relationships competencies.

People who have a score of six or close to six prefer a job that allows them to energize and empower others, build and manage teams, understand and value cultural diversity, build information networks, respond to people in a way they can understand, and raise and resolve conflict.

People who have a one or close to one prefer to rely on themselves rather than others, be part of a group but not the manager of the group, not having to search for information, be themselves around others rather than adjusting behavior to others' needs, and minimize conflict.

Communication Skills

    7a _____
    8a _____
    9b _____

The closer your score is to three, the more you prefer a career goal that is consistent with the communication skills competencies.

People who have a score of three prefer jobs that require public speaking, writing, and making presentations.

People who have a score of less than three prefer jobs that allow them to keep their thoughts to themselves, do little writing, and communicate with others one-on-one rather than in front of groups.

Achieving Business Results

    10b _____
    11a _____
    12b _____
    13b _____
    14a _____

The closer your score is to five, the more you prefer a career goal that is consistent with the achieving business results competencies.

People with a score of four or five prefer jobs where their objectives are based on what others need (e.g., a customer focus) and that require them to make tough decisions, plan, think strategically (that is, deal with problems that have uncertain solutions and broad ramifications, and be innovative.

People with a one or two prefer jobs that allow them to set objectives for themselves, make decisions that have clear choices and guidelines, do predictable work that requires little planning or prioritizing, analyze problems that have clear solutions and known effects, and take actions that are tried-and-true rather than experimental.

Individual Style

    15b _____
    16a _____
    17a _____
    18b _____

The closer your score is to four, the more you prefer a career goal that is consistent with the individual style competencies.

People with a score of four prefer jobs that allow them to set goals that stretch their capabilities, constantly seek learning experiences, work in an ambiguous environment, and listen to others to determine what is important to their job and department.

People with a score of one prefer jobs that allow them to set goals based on what they know they can accomplish, perform tasks on which they have ample prior experience, work in structured and stable environments, and focus on what they believe is important, not what others say.

Business Environment Knowledge

    19b _____
    20a _____
    21a _____
    22b _____
    23b _____
    24a _____
    25a _____

The closer your score is to seven, the more you prefer a career goal that is consistent with the competencies related to knowledge of the business environment.

People with a score of seven or close to it prefer jobs that require keeping up with continuously changing developments in the industry; understanding the company's business plans, organizational structure, and policies; understanding global economics; understanding global customers and markets; tracking financial indicators of the success of the whole company; knowing the firm's products and services; and being a role model for global business ethics.

People with a score of one or close to it prefer jobs that allow them to concentrate on their own area of functional expertise rather than on the industry in general or the company's broad business objectives, understand elements of economics that relate directly to their jobs, understand the needs of departments that use the outputs of their work rather than the firm's global markets, track the specific financial indicators that are important to the departments they serve, keep up with the products and services in which they are involved on a regular basis, and worry less about ethical behavior and more about being effective on the job.

C

Employee-Guided Management and a Sample Survey Feedback Report

Throughout this book I emphasize the value to organizations of implementing programs that give people feedback about their performance. The design and implementation of these programs need to be done in a way that enhances the likelihood that the information will be used. Employees who give and receive the feedback need to feel that the process is important—that it fits with the goals and expectations of the organization and that it is relevant to them in doing their work and in having a successful career.

Attitude surveys are a commonly used method for tracking employees' feelings about the organization and their management. This serves as feedback to managers about issues that are of concern to employees, including their supervision. Upward and 360-degree feedback is a type of employee attitude survey that asks for an evaluation of a particular manager; the report directly addresses the behavior and performance of the manager. (This technique is reviewed in Chapter 10, and components of the method are described in Resource Guide F.)

In contrast, an employee attitude survey usually summarizes the results across all employees in the organization or in particular departments. This is known as *survey feedback*. The report addresses how employees feel about management in general, not about a particular manager. All managers in the department receive the same feedback report. Communicating the results, involving employees in discussing their meaning in their unit, and suggesting ways to overcome the problem become organizational development interventions in and of themselves. The process engenders participation and commitment to the organization while it focuses on problems. It encourages managers to take employees seriously, listen to what they have to say, and act on their input. Employees are quick to recognize which managers ignore or dismiss the results and those who engage their department in confronting and resolving problems.

Employee-guided management (EGM) is a set of guidelines for using information from employees to establish management strategies (see Chapter 9). The process relies on principles of participative management and is based on survey feedback. This Resource Guide first presents the major elements of EGM (adapted from London, 1988, pp. 255–266). The outline puts survey feedback within the larger context of organizational change. Moreover, it tries to capture the major arguments for adopting such a program in a way that makes the process engaging. It also provides a comprehensive picture of all the elements from survey design through feedback and evaluation of the program.

Then a sample feedback report is presented. Unlike a qualitative report derived from an attitude survey, this report is based on a series of focus groups. The qualitative data—that is, employees' stated impressions and ideas—are summarized by a consultant and provided to management. Part of a larger intervention to increase employee involvement in the organization, the report demonstrates how clear and pointed employee opinions can be fed back to management and used to take actions for improved organizational performance.

I. *Principles for Employee-Guided Management*

1. *Conditions for Effectiveness*

- EGM is more effective when those who will use the process design it and have control, responsibility, and authority over each component.
- Participation in design and implementation should be voluntary.
- EGM works best in an environment that already has a tradition of employee participation (although EGM is a way to engender and support participative management).
- EGM is more acceptable to the organization's management the lower the costs and the higher the potential benefits—monetary and psychological. Such benefits should be delineated.

2. *Objectives of the Program*

- Reasons for introducing EGM include organizational diagnosis (discover what's going on—what problems may exist), obtain information about a particular problem, enhance long-term organizational health, highlight interpersonal processes.
- Feedback may reduce uncertainty; correct errors; signal the importance of various goals; provide comparative information for calibrating standards, behaviors, and goal accomplishment; and reinforce positive behavior and limit or extinguish negative behavior.
- The purpose of the EGM process should be clear and specific so that appropriate data-collection methods will be chosen and the right questions will be asked.
- The purpose should be realistic so that employees' expectations will be realistic.

3. *Type of Information Sought*

- The questions addressed should be under the control of the employees or the managers who will receive the feedback.
- The issues addressed by the survey should be important to the work group. This is essential since asking the questions makes them salient. Focusing on low-importance issues detracts attention from critical areas.
- The information collected should be specific and aggregated to the level of the individual who has responsibility for the issues addressed. The more general the information, the less recipients know how the results apply to them.
- Survey data should be collected regularly and frequently. A work-group leader may administer a brief attitude survey once a month or once every three months. An organization may administer a comprehensive organization-wide survey annually.

4. *Sources of Information*

- Employees may be both sources and recipients of information.
- Data may be collected from subordinates, peers, supervisors, and/or oneself.

5. *Data-Collection Methods*

- Available methods differ in a number of ways. They affect the amount and depth of information that can be collected and whether the results are quantitative (averaged responses to numerical scales) or qualitative (narrative reports derived from interviews).
- If possible, more than one data-collection method should be used.
- A method should yield accurate and salient information. Some methods generate *signs* of what is important—as indicators of satisfaction suggest some underlying cause. If this is not recognized, the index may become an end in itself (e.g., "We need to improve employee satisfaction!") without focusing on the true underlying cause.
- Employees receiving the survey results should delve below the surface to understand and ultimately control the phenomena in question.
- The data should be collected, analyzed, and fed back as quickly as possible to maintain interest and a sense of immediacy.

6. *Feedback*

- Feedback should be given to those who are accountable for the data and who have control over factors affecting it.
- Recipients should participate actively in the feedback process—for example, by asking questions and discussing the meaning of the results.

- The favorability of the results and the self-confidence of the recipients affect the acceptance of the feedback. Positive results allow focusing on recipients' competence and personal control to avoid complacency in the future. Negative or average results are more likely to be denied or ignored. They should be fed back by beginning with strong points and emphasizing what rewards are likely to result by overcoming weaknesses. Confident, resilient recipients can confront negative results more easily than individuals with a poor self-image.

7. *Using the Information*

- Using the data requires integration and interpretation, generating and evaluating alternative courses of action, deciding on courses of action, and determining a way to monitor the effects of that action.
- EGM works best when those who provide the information receive feedback and are responsible for doing something about the results.
- Recipients' desire to respond to feedback increases when the issues addressed are under their control, the costs of action are low in relation to possible benefits, and the issues are sufficiently salient and the benefits sufficiently high to make action worthwhile.
- There should be minimum delay between feedback and action.

8. *Monitoring Strategies*

- EGM should be monitored and evaluated to answer the following questions: Has a clear purpose been identified and agreed to by the parties involved? Is the information collected salient to the purpose? Is it reliable and sufficient? How is feedback provided? Is it complete? Is there assistance for interpretation? Are action strategies based on the feedback? Are they carried out? Are the actions effective?

9. *Outcomes*

- The outcomes should be close to the variables measured in the survey feedback process. For instance, asking about perceived career opportunities and doing something to enhance them may not directly affect organizational performance outcomes, such as profitability, that are affected by numerous other factors.

10. *The Role of the Consultant*

- A consultant often plays an indispensable role in designing and conducting an EGM effort.
- The most effective consulting role is probably that of nondirective counselor. Rather than seek to influence by expressing a particular viewpoint, the consultant should clarify and reflect the views of the

employees who are participating in each stage of the processes. As such, the consultant is a catalyst helping to overcome barriers.

II. *Sample Feedback Report*

The following is an excerpt from a consultant's feedback report generated from a series of focus groups. The report concludes with some recommendations for action. The intention of the process was to provide the organization's full-time professional staff with insight into the attitudes of the part-time employees. This was important because of the organization's reliance on part-time employees. The organization had about 40 full-timers and 250 part-timers.

This report was part of a larger organizational intervention that began with these focus groups. Next steps included a meeting of all full-time staff to discuss their perceptions of part-timers and then to review the focus-group interview report. Then an employee attitude survey was developed for administration to all employees. The results were fed back to all employees.

A variety of actions were taken to address issues emerging from this process. These actions didn't wait for the process to be complete—that is, for all data to be collected, a report written and distributed, and discussion groups held to review the results. Rather, actions were taken as solutions seemed evident. As actions were taken, they were announced to all employees and associated with the survey feedback process by means of a logo (a graphic representing a group of smiling people). This signified that actions were taken as a result of employee input.

Introduction

This report is based on seven focus groups with five to ten part-time employees per group. Overall, the group sessions were lively discussions, with most members participating actively. The mood was upbeat, and several groups ended their sessions with participants saying how much they enjoyed having a chance to express their opinions.

Brief Summary.   A key issue seemed to be the need for frequent and clear communication to avoid misperceptions and misunderstandings. Indeed, this was at the heart of many of the complaints and areas for improvement— for example, dissatisfaction with various rules, restrictions in dress, and limitations in work hours. Issues involving interpersonal relationships (e.g., the "caste system" separating full-time and part-time employees) and fairness in applying rules also boil down to communication (*how* people communicate as well as *what* they say). Two other themes, which are related to improved two-way communication, are the desire for more involvement in decision making and the desire for more training and information about events and changes.

The Report. Participants were promised confidentiality. Therefore, this report integrates information across the groups. Of course, sources of quotes are not identified. The quotes are close approximations of what was said. My goal was to reproduce as accurately as possible the thoughts and feelings of the group members. Some statements are generalizations. They may give the appearance of a pervasive problem while the issue occurs only sometimes. The all-employee survey will assess the frequency and strength of these problems. The report is organized by topic.

Topics

Supervisor–subordinate relationships
Opportunities for involvement
Group meetings
Performance appraisals
Rules/bureaucracy/structure
Feelings of inequity and unfair treatment
General atmosphere
    Part-time versus full-time employees
Pet peeves and suggestions
Positives about working in the organization
Recommendations
    Meetings
    Training
    Job aids
    Enhanced communication

[The following is a sample of each of these topics.]

Supervisor–Subordinate Relationships

There were very few complaints about supervisors. Communication was generally good, and supervisors were viewed as helpful. However, supervisors could be sticklers for rules and regulations, and were sometimes perceived as unfairly applying these rules. Occasionally supervisors reprimand part-timers in the presence of others. Some supervisors may be too ready to complain about problems in areas other than their own. Some comments from employees follow:

"Communication is good with my own supervisor, but not with other supervisors."

"Some supervisors go off the deep end when something goes wrong."
"In general, supervisors are accessible."

Opportunities for Involvement

"Part-timers are not asked for their opinions on matters that involve them
in their work areas."

Group Meetings

Some supervisors hold frequent meetings. Others do not. When asked, the
part-time employees indicated that they would like more meetings—for instance, regular (e.g., monthly) meetings with their immediate supervisor.
These should be both group meetings and one-on-one meetings as appropriate.

"The part-timers don't get together enough. Maybe only once a year to
hear about the summer schedule."

Performance Appraisals

Employees indicated that while performance appraisals are supposed to occur annually in some form, they often don't occur at all.

"It would be nice to know when we are doing a good job. You certainly
hear about it when you don't."

Rules/Bureaucracy/Structure

Overall, there was the perception that there are too many rules. Moreover,
rules are set without adequate communication. For instance, curt memos
are posted. Some memos are distributed, some are not. Memos are not explained. Consequently, people don't read them.

"Some departments have meetings with two or three people at a time to
explain new rules and procedures. But for the most part, we find out information later."

Feelings of Inequity and Unfair Treatment

Rules and processes differ between departments. Sometimes this is justified
because of different department requirements. Other times, it seems to be
arbitrary, based on favoritism, or a function of the mood and personality of
the supervisor. Supervisors appear to vary in their administration of policies. Rules appear to change to suit the person. People in one department
can do one thing, and those in another department can do something else.

General Atmosphere

The part-time employees feel increasingly constrained and regulated. There is also a general fear of repercussions for doing something wrong. Channels of communication are perceived to be overly bureaucratic and hierarchical.

"Lately, the atmosphere has been tense."

"When part-timers know their job, they move you. They don't want you to feel comfortable."

• *Part-time versus full-time employees*

Many participants in the interviews reported feeling that "no one cares about part-timers."

"Being a part-timer is synonymous with being a nobody."

There appear to be separate rules for part- and full-time employees.

"There is a definite caste system here."

Part-timers are not respected. Full-time employees will whisper about the part-timers in their presence. This is "bad manners" and demonstrates "lack of respect."

"Everything is broken down into full-timers and part-timers. Even work desks are arranged to separate full- from part-time employees."

Some Pet Peeves and Suggestions

The following is a mix of concerns and issues. Some focus on ideas for improved operations. Others focus on rules and benefits. Others are just statements of attitudes or perceptions.

—"It's hard to get to know people because there is so much change."

—"15 minute breaks are nice, but they are really 10 minutes by the time you get to the break room and prepare to return. They should give you a minute or two more."

[Many other quotes were included.]

Some Positives

Everyone is committed. Despite some problems, this is an excellent place to work.

"We have fun among ourselves."

"It is a nice place to work."

"Today there is still a lot of flexibility in time scheduling. This is the best part about working here."

Recommendations [Ideas generated by the consultant]

A. *Meetings*

—Ways of holding information meetings should be identified and encouraged as a way to increase two-way communication. These include . . .

• Meetings with supervisors and immediate subordinates (which require multiple meetings to ensure all part-time employees are covered)

- All-organization meetings (primarily to convey information)
- "Skip-level" meetings with the director (without the presence of middle managers) to allow employees to express their opinions

B. *Training*

—Supervisory training may be a way to ensure that communication increases and negative attitudes are minimized. Topics could include:

- Giving performance feedback (positive and negative)
- Conducting meetings/conveying information
- Managing problem performers
- Understanding how supervisory behavior affects employee attitudes and productivity
- The role of the supervisor as developer and coach
- Requesting input/engendering participation and involvement
- Understanding differences and managing diversity (older versus younger employees, part-time versus full-time employees, professional versus nonprofessional employees)
- "Owning the problem": Part-time employees would like to "own the problems" that come to them, but this is not part of their jobs. Yet they don't want to say "it's not my problem." A program on responding to patrons might help. The organization might formulate an initiative on being responsive to patrons and "owning the problem" until the patron's problem is solved or until the patron is directed to the best person to solve the problem.

C. *Job aids*

—A "job aid" is a written document that serves as a resource and reference on procedures and information. Job aids can be an inexpensive substitute for training. Topics could include:

- New employee orientation or guidelines for new employees. This would cover important rules and their rationale. Topics would include scheduling procedures, behavioral expectations, and an overview of different positions in the organization.
- Ordering procedures (and how they differ between departments)

—There is a need for a resource to give people up-to-date information—for instance, a newsletter or bulletin. Perhaps such a publication already exists. If so, its mode of communication and method of distribution should be analyzed.

D. *Enhanced communication*

—Be sure to report the results of this survey and indicate how the results are used. (Employees recalled not ever hearing anything about the last survey.)

—Provide an explanation for new rules as they emerge. Review existing rules and determine if it would help to write a summary description and rationale.

—Recognize how the treatment of older part-time employees versus students affects attitudes and performance. Also, recognize that different groups have different expectations. Train supervisors in understanding and managing these differences.

—Hold more meetings like the focus groups. As one employee stated, "I've been sitting on these feelings so long, it's good to have a chance to vent."

D

Outline for a Two-Day
Career Motivation Developmental
Assessment Center

In the preface to this book I described two streams of research I have been involved in that led me to consider further the concepts of self- and interpersonal insight. One stream was research on upward and 360-degree feedback. The other was research on career motivation—in particular, *career resilience* (self-confidence, achievement motivation, and willingness to take risks), *career insight* (career goal clarity, self-knowledge, and knowledge of the organization), and *career identity* (the direction of one's career goals). I presumed that meaningful career identity could not emerge without a solid foundation of career insight. (See London, 1983, 1985a, for a complete review of the underlying theory and definition of dimensions.)

The initial method Douglas Bray and I used to measure the components of career motivation was an assessment center (London & Bray, 1983). This method was chosen because it provides in-depth qualitative and quantitative information about the individual's background, personality, needs, and interests. Multiple assessees observe and evaluate the individual, reviewing test results and responses to behavioral decision exercises and interviews. The information is integrated by reviewing all the reports and test scores and rating the individual on the career motivation dimensions.

This technique has been adapted in insight assessment centers, as described in Chapters 3 and 9. These centers are generally used to assess mid- to executive-level managers, and they serve as a foundation for career and development planning. A narrative report and the assessor ratings on the dimensions are fed back to the individuals assessed but not to their supervisor. The feedback is explained in depth by a professional, probably an industrial and organizational or clinical psychologist. Help is offered in using the information to establish career goals, seek further assessment, and/or make development plans.

The assessment center outlined here provides information important to career development. It does not deal with elements of performance capability, although other assessments centers do (cf. Thornton & Byham, 1982). The components of such skill-assessment centers could be designed into an assessment oriented to career development. Assessment exercises that require such skills as communications, leadership, organization, and decision making would be needed in this case. (See Bray, Campbell, & Grant, 1974, for the design of one of the original assessment centers to measure managerial performance potential.) The following outline of the career motivation assessment center was reported by London (1985a, pp. 52–54).

Note that a number of the measures are standardized forms. Others, particularly the decision exercises, were designed especially for the assessment. Also, note that the assessors included two psychologists and one graduate student intern in psychology. Other psychologists were involved in integrating the data.

Note, too, that there are many different ways to construct such an assessment center. The combination of tests and exercises outlined in the following is just one example. The components selected depend on the type of individuals to be assessed, the nature of career decisions they are likely to confront, and the depth of information the organization wants to provide. Using the assessment center is a way to highlight to the participants the importance of career planning. Their participation encourages them to match the company's investment of resources with a personal investment in self-reflection.

The assessment dimensions measured by the exercises are listed after the outline. These are generally evaluated during an integration session. After reviewing the reports and test scores for a given individual, the assessors rate the person on each of the dimensions, usually on a five-point scale from 5 = high to 1 = low. The assessors then review their judgments on each dimension and try to reach agreement within one point.

Assessment Center Outline

Preassessment mailing: Personal history form and background questions

Day 1

Projectives
Thematic Apperception Test (60 mins.): Participants write a story about each of six picture cards. The cards describe what is happening in the picture, what led up to the events, and what the outcome will be. The pictures are suggestive of career-related issues (e.g., a young person talking to an older person, possibly to obtain advice).
Rotter Incomplete Sentences Test (30 mins.)
Company-Related Incomplete Sentence Test (30 mins.)
The responses to these measures were analyzed by a clinical psychologist, who prepared a narrative report of their meaning.

Intellectual Abilities

School and College Ability Tests (80 mins.): A timed test of quantitative and verbal ability.

Personality Measures

Edwards (60 mins.): Total of 225 forced-choice items measuring fifteen personality variables originating from a list of manifest needs, such as achievement, deference, order, autonomy, and affiliation.

Sarnoff (10 mins.): Eighteen items measuring need for upward mobility, need to advance and get ahead, and value of money and position.

Expectations Inventory (25 mins.): Fifty-six statements describing the situation in which a manager might find himself or herself five years later.

Background

Interview (120 mins.): A semistructured interview covering four major areas: (1) A brief account of the person's life up until graduation from high school. (2) The person's college years. (3) The person's current life, including work and nonwork. (4) The person's perceptions of the company and his or her career so far. [Note, all assessees were recent college graduates and relatively new hires to the company—generally within their first year of employment.]

Day 2

Personality Measures

Guilford Zimmerman Temperament Survey (50 mins.): Measures ten personality constructs: general activity, restraint, ascendance, sociability, emotional stability, objectivity, friendliness, thoughtfulness, personal relations, and masculinity.

[See London, 1985a, for the list of other personality inventories used, taking an additional 80 minutes.]

Career Interests

Strong-Campbell Vocational Interest Blank (30 mins.): Asks the person 325 questions that elicit preferences (likes, dislikes, or indifferences) concerning various occupations, school subjects, activities, amusements, and types of people.

Fact-Finding Exercise, Career Projectives, and Cases

The Fact-Finding Exercise (30 mins.): Participants are given three hypothetical job choices: assistant branch manager of a bank, staff member in the new services development department of the bank, or assistant product manager in a consumer products company. The participant then has an opportunity to question a resource person (an assessor) about the alternatives. The assessor evaluates the participant's decision process.

Career Projectives (Management Apperception Test) (30 mins.): Six pictures focusing on career-related topics. Each picture was used as a basis for discussion between the participant and the assessor.

Six Cases (40 mins.:) Each case asked the participant to advise a character in the case about a life-career decision. Issues dealt with different problems faced by men and women in balancing work and family; career stagnation; advantages and disadvantages of advancement; women supervising men; and equal employment opportunity. An assessor questions each participant on his or her reaction to each case.

Career and Life Expectations Measures

Future Time Line (25 mins.): The participant listed positive and negative events he or she expected will happen at different times in the future. Separate lists were made for career, family, and self-development.

Ideal Business Day (10 mins.): The participant was given a blank page from one day on a calendar and requested to indicate what he or she would be doing each hour of the day on an ideal job.

What You Want in Life (15 mins.): Asked the participant to list what he or she wanted most from life and a career.

Expectations Discussion (55 mins.): A semistructured interview covering career and life goals for the next five years, in such areas as family, spare-time activities, personality, financial matters, health, career, relations with supervisors and peers, training, and job performance.

Career Motivation Dimensions Under the Domains of Career Resilience, Insight, and Identity (adapted from London & Mone, 1987, pp. 56–59)

Career resilience: The ability to adapt to changing circumstances, even when the circumstances are discouraging or disruptive.

Belief in oneself: The degree to which one is confident of one's ability to perform well. Evident from conveying self-assurance, easily adjusting to changes, expressing ideas even when they are unpopular, and trying to promote career progress.

Need for achievement: The degree to which one desires to excel in one's work. Evident from trying hard on all tasks, taking the initiative to do what is needed to achieve career goals, and seeking assignments that require learning new skills.

Willingness to take risks: The degree to which one is able to take actions with uncertain outcomes. Evident from expressing ideas even when the ideas are contrary to those of one's boss, being unafraid to let others know when they have made mistakes, going out on a limb for something one believes in, and being innovative in doing one's job.

Working independently or cooperatively as needed: The degree to which one is comfortable working either alone or with a group, depending on the demands of the task. Evident from making decisions or working effectively either as an individual or as a member of a team, and being able to complete whole assignments independently and being able to contribute effectively to a group assignment.

Career insight: The ability to be realistic about oneself and one's career and to put these perceptions to use in establishing goals.

Establishing career goals: The degree to which one has thought about one's career objectives and planned how they can be achieved. Evident from having a specific, realistic career goal and a plan for achieving it, being willing to alter goals as career interests and circumstances change, and welcoming job changes and assignments that enhance career opportunities.

Knowing one's strengths and weaknesses: The degree to which one has determined one's strong and weak points, especially with respect to career objectives. Evident from seeing oneself as others do, having a clear perception of one's ability to accomplish a task, and using feedback from others to learn about oneself.

Career identity: The extent to which one defines oneself by work.

Job involvement: The degree to which one is willing to immerse oneself in activities related to the job. Evident from working hard, even if it means frequently working long days and weekends, treating the job as more important than other activities in one's life, and considering the job to be fascinating.

Organization involvement: The degree to which one is willing to immerse oneself in organizational activities. Evident from expressions of pride in working for the firm, and associating one's personal success with the company's success ("I feel successful when the company does well.").

Professional involvement: The degree to which one is willing to immerse oneself in the activities of a professional association or in other ways demonstrate dedication to the profession. Evident from seeing oneself as a representative of the profession, being active in a professional organization, and encouraging others in the field to join the professional organization.

Need for advancement: The degree to which one desires to be promoted. Evident from wanting to advance as rapidly as possible, and having advancement as a major career goal.

Need for recognition: The degree to which one wants to be recognized for one's accomplishments. Evident from valuing words of recognition from one's boss, looking forward to the prestige that comes with advancement, and wanting to be recognized for good performance.

Need for leadership: The degree to which one desires to be in a leadership role. Evident from desiring a position of leadership, emerging as the leader in group situations, and wanting to hold an elective office in an organization.

E

Outline for a New Employee Orientation Program

Chapter 9 indicated that organizations try to enhance employees' insight into the work environment. This is especially important for new employees, who need to be clear about what they are expected to do and how they contribute to the organization's goals. This helps them form categories for interpreting information, making accurate attributions, and evaluating their behavior and performance in relation to organizational requirements. Socialization is often accomplished at least in part by an orientation program. Such a program should be designed to enhance insight and encourage comparisons of one's self-concept with organizational expectations and others' behavior.

Orientation programs inculcate and indoctrinate employees into the organization's culture, perhaps a culture that reinforces continuous learning and development, teamwork, and supportive supervision. These are the goals of the programs for new managers and supervisors of new managers outlined in the following. Only a bare outline is presented to show the structure and major components of such programs.

I. *Orientation Program for New Managers*

Who Will Attend

All new management hires and all recent promotees

When

Ideally first day on the job or within the first two weeks.

Need for the Program

New hires and new managers don't see the whole picture. They don't know how their job and department fit into the organization. Many new hires are unsure about their roles and job responsibilities during the first weeks with the company. Many new hires and new managers don't know what is expected of them as managers.

Goals for the Program

Allow new managers to meet other new managers (give them an opportunity to network and socialize with each other), hear from more experienced managers, become familiar with the top managers, clarify the company's expectations of them, learn about development opportunities, and highlight the link between them and the company's future.

Ten Modules

The program is organized into a number of segments.

1. *Explaining the organization*—goals, structure, functions, and people.
2. *An examination of the department's role in the organization.*
3. *Brief overview of common departmental procedures.*
4. *Corporate values guiding management and career development.* These might include customer satisfaction through sensitivity and responsiveness, teamwork, quality, employee development opportunities, and continuous learning.
5. *Employee development opportunities in the organization.* This is a review of courses, tuition support, job transfer and promotion policies and procedures, career paths, and development planning processes.
6. *Continuous learning.* Employees are told that they should take responsibility for their own job, professional, and career development. They are requested to work with their supervisor to set development goals and plans that relate to their capabilities and career interests and to the firm's needs. They are told that their supervisor will provide the support and resources to make your plans a reality.
7. *Supervisors' expectations and support.*
8. *Types of management jobs and roles* (supervision, staff support, liaison to business units, responding to clients, managing financial processes, belonging to a team, being a "quality champion" promoting Total Quality Management).
9. *Job mastery, professional development, career opportunities.* This means doing better on your current job, professional development, and preparing for career changes in line with career interests and opportunities in the organization. (See Resource Guide A for an explanation of this distinction within the context of a career development program.) Development is not a onetime event but a regular

process that occurs throughout the year. It has several components: (1) assessment of competence, job requirements, and career goals; (2) development discussions and establishing a development plan; (3) taking action through training and on-the-job experiences; and (4) tracking progress.

10. *Conclusion: Future trends; World Class Vision for the organization.* Emphasize that "This is the place to be!!".

Video Resources

Several videos should be made for the program: (1) video by the CEO describing the organization and its goals; (2) video of current employees and managers, describing their work; (3) video of the CEO and other top managers describing the philosophy of employee development in the organization; and (4) video of supervisor panel or interviews with individual supervisors describing their expectations and experiences with new managers. These videos should be supplemented by in-person presentations from one or more executives and experienced managers.

II. *Program for Supervisors of New Managers*

Supervisors need to understand that new managers require support for understanding their jobs, knowing what they don't know and what they must learn to achieve job mastery, developing job structure is an important part of managing—that is, working with subordinates to create meaningful jobs and work group relationships and developing subordinates is an important part of managing. Also, supervisors need to recognize that they will be evaluated on how well they develop their subordinates. Moreover, they should understand that basic principles of good managing (e.g., setting performance goals with subordinates, appraising performance, giving feedback, and linking appraisal to compensation) are especially important for new employees.

Who Will Attend

All supervisors of new management hires

When

Prior to assuming responsibility for a new hire; scheduled when a vacancy announcement is circulated and a new hire is sought.

Need for the Program

Too often new hires and new managers don't see the whole picture; they don't know how their job and department fit into the organization. Many new hires are unsure about their roles and job responsibilities during the first weeks with the company. Further, many new hires and new managers don't know what is expected of them as managers.

Supervisors need to understand why continuous employee development is central to being a world-class organization. Supervisors don't understand their role in management development. Supervisors don't take a hand in structuring jobs for new managers. Supervisors often don't take an active role in explaining job and corporate expectations to new managers. Supervisors need to understand how they contribute to the socialization of new employees in the company.

Goals for the Program

Show the power of good management; describe how to design a "mastery path" that provides new managers with support for learning their jobs and working with subordinates to create meaningful jobs and work group relationships; take an action learning approach since developing subordinates is an important part of managing, and managers will be evaluated on how well they develop subordinates; and develop an understanding of learning styles (experiment, reflection, reasoning) and ways to promote individual and team learning.

Seven Modules

The program is organized into seven segments.

1. *Power of good management.* This covers at least four basic principles of good management: help subordinates set performance goals, appraise performance periodically, provide frequent performance feedback, and reward accomplishments. Carrying out these principles contributes to employee development. New employees require attention to performance management and job mastery. Experienced and proficient employees require attention to their professional development and long-term career goals.

2. *Structuring work assignments.* Job challenge stems from using a variety of skills, autonomy, feedback, doing a whole and complete task, and task significance.

3. *Designing a mastery path.* Mastery paths specify levels of competency and provide directions for training and on-the-job learning. Mastery paths for specific job families specify the required level of skill development and accomplishment to perform the job. It is expected that employees will achieve this level of competence after a certain amount of training and job experience—usually after one year to eighteen months on the job. Mastery paths indicate the training curriculum, the types of job experiences needed over time to gain mastery, and the supervisor's role in evaluating performance and coaching the subordinate along the way.

Steps for establishing a mastery path for a new employee include the following: (1) Specify competency requirements of the job (part of the process of preparing the job description, evaluating job candidates, and making a selection). (2) Establish early performance objectives (for first three months) and review with the new manager; include training and developmental assignments. (3) Have monthly meetings to evaluate progress and do some coaching. (4) At the end of month 3, conduct the first mastery assessment (evaluate the newcomer's proficiencies and decide on the next training and developmental assignments. (5) Continue monthly feedback and coaching. (6) Conduct six-month review; set performance and development objectives for the next six months; continue monthly performance review meetings. (7) In the first annual appraisal; establish additional mastery goals as needed by the individual and required by the position. Mastery may take six months to a year for some positions and as long as eighteen months to two years for others.

4. *Meeting immediate business need while supporting long-term development.* There are three targets for development: job improvement, professional development, and career development. Development occurs throughout the year. [Similar message to the one presented to new managers in the ninth module of new manager orientation above.]

5. *Action learning for individual and team learning.*

6. *Supervisor and co-workers as role models and mentors.* An important component of managers' performance is the extent to which they coach and develop their subordinates. Managers should appraise subordinates on setting goals, provide feedback and encouragement, allow employees to demonstrate acquisition of the new skill or knowledge, and assess the degree to which the objectives of the plan were met.

F

360-Degree Feedback Methods

The following are examples of 360-degree feedback surveys. As I stated in Chapter 10, the feedback survey is a way to emphasize to the raters and the managers who are rated the importance of certain behaviors to the manager's job. These behaviors can be tied to organizational strategies, such as goals to enhance quality, improve communication, increase customer satisfaction, and enhance career development. The survey also highlights the importance of receiving feedback from different sources of information.

The first sample is an upward feedback survey. It asks specifically about the boss-subordinate relationship and highlights the support the boss provides for the subordinate's development. The next survey includes items for peers to rate each other with items focusing on cooperation and communication. The third sample is a customer survey. It requests two ratings for each item—what should happen (i.e., a rating of expectations, as recommended by Moses, Hollenbeck, & Sorcher, 1993) and perceptions of behavior.

Note that an instrument can be designed that has a common set of items rated by all sources. This would allow managers to compare how they are viewed by different constituencies. However, different forms for different constituencies can focus on behaviors that are specific to that relationship. Also, note that the surveys included here can be reformulated for self-ratings, for instance, by asking the manager to rate "the extent to which you do the following" or "how satisfied you are with your performance in the following areas." The self-rating scale should be the same as the scale used by the other raters (i.e., whether satisfaction, expectations, or behavioral observations).

Many scale formats are possible, and several different ones are included here. Another format is to have raters simultaneously rate and rank peers and themselves on the same scale. For instance, Klimoski and London (1974) used a 20-point scale. Group members were asked to list their own name and each of their peers' names next to a letter and place the letter corresponding to each name on the appropriate place on the scales (one 20-point scale for each behavior rated, as indicated below). Multiple letters could be placed on the same point. The method forced raters to compare themselves to their peers and compare their peers to each other in a deliberate way. A disadvantage of this method is that it is more difficult to code than other formats, and it may be hard to computerize if the survey uses optically scanned forms, on-line computer ratings, or input on a computer disk that is returned for analysis—although software could be developed for this.

Sample 20-point scale (Letters stand for names of peers; "a" represents the self-rating.)

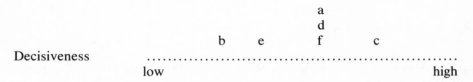

A sample feedback report is also provided that demonstrates the richness of information available. This form contains the average and range of subordinate ratings, the self-ratings, and the average rating managers across the department for each item. A separate form would be available to report similar information for peer and customer ratings. The information is conveyed item-by-item rather than averaged across items or groups of items (i.e., scores for factors of items). This is done to maximize the diagnostic value of the feedback. However, all this is quite a bit for any manager to absorb. Guidelines for interpreting the information would be helpful, and some firms offer training sessions to help managers use the information. Such guidance is a way to help the manager reflect on the feedback, avoid categorizations that dismiss or rationalize the data, make correct attributions, and establish a plan to alter behavior. This information could be supplemented by career counseling based partly on the feedback. The repeated use of the feedback survey is another way to make the information more acceptable and user friendly by becoming a regular part of the way the organization operates. Moreover, it is a way for the manager to track the effects of behavior changes on raters' perceptions.

Finally, there is a sample survey and results reporting supervisors' reactions to the feedback process sometime after receiving the feedback. While not an indication of actual use of the feedback results and behavior change, the survey is a way to measure how the process is perceived and how it can be improved.

I. Sample Upward Feedback Survey
(Items adapted from Wohlers & London, 1989)

Instructions: An important aspect of leadership is the management of people. This survey focuses on your satisfaction with the relationship you have with your supervisor. Use the numeric scale below to rate your supervisor.

Indicate the number that best describes your rating. Use "N" to indicate you have had insufficient opportunity to accurately gauge your degree of satisfaction. Your responses will be averaged with those of other subordinates who also report to your supervisor.

Scale: 1 = Very dissatisfied
2 = Dissatisfied
3 = Somewhat dissatisfied
4 = Somewhat satisfied
5 = Satisfied
6 = Very satisfied
N = No opportunity to observe

_____ 1. Jointly sets performance objectives with you.
_____ 2. Supports you in developing your career plans.
_____ 3. Motivates you to do a good job.
_____ 4. Gives you authority to do your job.
_____ 5. Provides the support necessary to help you do your job (e.g., advice, resources, or information).
_____ 6. Understands the work to be done within your work group.
_____ 7. Is available to you when needed.
_____ 8. Encourages innovation and creativity.
_____ 9. Holds employees accountable for meeting performance objectives.
_____ 10. Keeps commitments.
_____ 11. Allows adequate training time for you.
_____ 12. Provides ongoing performance feedback.
_____ 13. Provided a useful performance appraisal within the past year.
_____ 14. Conducts productive staff meetings.
_____ 15. Demonstrates trust and confidence in you.
_____ 16. Treats you with dignity and respect.
_____ 17. Informs you about issues affecting you.
_____ 18. Balances the work load fairly.
_____ 19. Communicates the reasons for his/her actions.
_____ 20. Supports and backs you up.
_____ 21. Has the subject matter knowledge to do the job.
_____ 22. Fairly evaluates your job performance.
_____ 23. Represents the group effectively to others (e.g., to clients, management, or at meetings).
_____ 24. Ensures that you get credit/recognition for your work.
_____ 25. Encourages open, two-way communication.
_____ 26. Modifies his/her position based on feedback from you (e.g., ideas, plans, or solutions).
_____ 27. Provides opportunities for you to develop new skills.
_____ 28. Strives for quality in spite of time pressure.

II. Peer Survey

Instructions: An important aspect of management is relationships with peers—the people who report to the same supervisor you do. This survey focuses on important aspects of peer relationships. Here you are asked to rate (*name provided*). Use the numeric scale below to indicate the extent to which this person performs each of the following behaviors. Use "N" to indicate you have had insufficient opportunity to make a judgment. Your responses will be averaged with other peers in your work group.

Scale: 1 = Not at all
         2 = To a small extent
         3 = To a moderate extent
         4 = To a great extent
         5 = To a very great extent
         N = No opportunity to observe

_____   1. Is a team player.
_____   2. Is cooperative.
_____   3. Communicates clearly.
_____   4. Shares ideas.
_____   5. Informs me of decisions affecting my work group.
_____   6. Treats me with respect.
_____   7. Asks for my opinion.
_____   8. Let's me know when there is a problem in my department.
_____   9. Is willing to listen.
_____ 10. Seems to be in competition with me.
_____ 11. Doesn't give others a chance to speak at group meetings.
_____ 12. Suggests ways to improve the operations of the total department.

III. Customer Survey

*(Portion of longer survey excerpted
from London & Beatty, 1993, pp. 362–363)*

	Level of Service that *Should* be Provided						Level of Service You Received					
Services Provided												
COMMUNICATION												
Tells when service will be performed	5	4	3	2	1	NA	5	4	3	2	1	NA
Listens to customer	5	4	3	2	1	NA	5	4	3	2	1	NA
Seeks feedback	5	4	3	2	1	NA	5	4	3	2	1	NA
RELIABILITY												
Provides service that is promised	5	4	3	2	1	NA	5	4	3	2	1	NA
Dependable	5	4	3	2	1	NA	5	4	3	2	1	NA
Consistent in service delivery	5	4	3	2	1	NA	5	4	3	2	1	NA
RESPONSIVENESS												
Prompt service	5	4	3	2	1	NA	5	4	3	2	1	NA
Answers my questions	5	4	3	2	1	NA	5	4	3	2	1	NA
Meets deadlines	5	4	3	2	1	NA	5	4	3	2	1	NA
Takes quick actions to problems	5	4	3	2	1	NA	5	4	3	2	1	NA
Returns phone calls	5	4	3	2	1	NA	5	4	3	2	1	NA
COOPERATION												
Helps customer reach shared goals	5	4	3	2	1	NA	5	4	3	2	1	NA
Willing to help	5	4	3	2	1	NA	5	4	3	2	1	NA
Easy to do business with	5	4	3	2	1	NA	5	4	3	2	1	NA
Willing to deal with special requests	5	4	3	2	1	NA	5	4	3	2	1	NA

IV. *Sample Feedback Report*

	Self-Rating	Mean Sub-ordinate Rating	Range		Number of Subordinates Responding to Item	"Norm"[1]
			Low	High		
1. Jointly sets performance objectives with you.	5	3	1	4	7	3
2. Supports you in developing your career plans.	4	4	2	4	8	4
3. Motivates you to do a good job.	6	5	3	6	8	4
4. Gives you authority to do your job.	5	4	3	5	8	3
5. Provides the support necessary to help you do your job (e.g., advice, resources, or information).	6	4	2	5	7	4
6. Understands the work to be done within your work group.	6	5	3	6	8	5
7. Is available to you when needed.	5	3	1	5	7	4
8. Encourages innovation and creativity.	5	2	1	4	7	3

[1]Norm is the average of subordinate ratings for the item across all managers in the unit.

Results Interpretation Guide

An interpretation guide would ask the manager receiving the report to compare his or her self-ratings to the average subordinate ratings. In the Sample Feedback Report, the self-ratings tend to be higher than the subordinate ratings—not an unusual finding. The manager would be asked to consider the range of subordinate ratings. In this case, there is a wide range on each item. This information in combination with the average suggests the amount of disagreement. For instance, if the average rating was high but there was still a wide range of ratings, this would indicate that one or two people provided low ratings. On the other hand, if the range was low, then most subordinates agree. Areas where there is high agreement (low range) and low average ratings need the most work.

The number of responding subordinates is an indication of the representativeness of the results across the work group. Data would not be presented if four or less subordinates responded to an item. This is especially important if there were only four or less subordinates in the group. These managers would not receive the upward feedback at all since it might be possible for the manager to guess who provided what ratings. (The subordinates may still participate in the process so their ratings could be averaged in with the others as part of the normative data.) Even in large groups, managers may try to guess who the outliers are (e.g., the one person who provided a low rating to an item).

The "norm" provides a comparison to how managers overall were perceived by their subordinates. In this case, the manager rated seems to be typical. This doesn't mean there isn't room for improvement. In fact, it suggests that the same training and development programs may apply to many managers in the department. Therefore, while top management may not receive the results for each individual manager, the norms suggest interventions that might be valuable for the department as a whole.

The guide would include information about training and developmental experiences available that would be useful for each category of items.

V. *Survey of Supervisors'*
Reactions to Upward Feedback Process
(Data collected six months after feedback)

Scale: 1 = Strongly disagree
         2 = Disagree
         3 = Neutral
         4 = Agree
         5 = Strongly agree

		RANGE	MEAN
1.	I have been able to use the feedback to improve my performance as a supervisor.	1–5	2.5
2.	The upward feedback report was worthwhile.	3–5	3.5
3.	The upward feedback process worked well.	3–5	3.5
4.	My subordinates' evaluation of me was reported confidentially to me only and not to any library administrators.	3–5	4.5
5.	The responses from my subordinates were anonymous; I could not identify any specific subordinate's response.	3–5	4.5
6.	My subordinates' ratings were consistent with my self-evaluation.	2–5	4
7.	I would like the library to provide training in some of the areas in which I was rated weakest.	2–5	4
8.	I have met or intend to meet with my subordinates to discuss the feedback results.	1–5	2.5
9.	I have met or intend to meet with my supervisor to discuss the feedback results.	1–3	2
10.	I learned something about myself I didn't already know.	2–5	3
11.	The results were helpful to me in setting goals for my career development.	2–4	2.5
12.	The upward feedback process should be made a regularly recurring (e.g. annual, biannual) process.	2–4	3

References

Abelson, R. P. (1976). Script processing, attitude formation and decision making. In J. S. Carroll & J. W. Payne (Eds.), *Cognition and social behavior*. Hillsdale, NJ: Erlbaum.

Adler, N. J. (1983). Cross-cultural management research: The ostrich and the trend. *Academy of Management Review, 8,* 226–232.

Adler, N. J., & Bartholomew, S. (1992). Managing globally competent people. *Academy of Management Executive, 6,* 52–65.

Albright, M. D., & Levy, P. E. (in press). The effects of source credibility and performance rating discrepancy on reactions to multiple raters. *Journal of Applied Social Psychology.*

Aldag, R. J., & Fuller, S. R. (1993). Beyond fiasco: A reappraisal of the groupthink phenomenon and a new model of group decision processes. *Psychological Bulletin, 113,* 533–552.

Ali, M. R., Khaleque, A., & Hossain, M. (1992). Participative management in a developing country: Attitudes and perceived barriers. *Journal of Managerial Psychology, 7,* 11–16.

Allen, N. J., & Meyer, J. P. (1990). Organizational socialization tactics: A longitudinal analysis of links to newcomers' commitment and role orientation. *Academy of Management Journal, 33,* 847–858.

Altman, I., & Taylor, D. A. (1973). *Social penetration: The development of interpersonal relationships*. New York: Holt, Rinehart and Winston.

Anderson, L. R. (1987). *Self-monitoring and performance in nontraditional occupations. Basic and Applied Social Psychology, 8,* 85–96.

Anderson, L. R. (1990). Toward a two-track model of leadership training: Suggestions from self-monitoring theory. *Small Group Research, 21*(2), 147–167.

Anderson, L. R., & Thacker, J. (1985). Self-monitoring and sex as related to assessment center ratings and job performance. *Basic and Applied Social Psychology, 6,* 345–361.

Antonioni, D. (1994). The effects of feedback accountability on upward appraisal ratings. *Personnel Psychology, 47,* 349–356.

Arbib, M. A., & Hesse, M. B. (1986). *The construction of reality*. Cambridge: Cambridge University Press.

Argyris, C. (1982). *Reasoning, learning and action: Individual and organizational*. San Francisco: Jossey-Bass.

Arvey, R. D., Bhagat, R. S., & Salas, E. (1991). Cross-cultural and cross-national issues in personnel and human resources management. In K. M. Rowland & G. R. Ferris (Eds.), *Research in personnel and human resources management.* (Vol. 9), (pp. 367–407). Greenwich, CT: JAI Press.

Ashford, S. J. (1986). Feedback seeking in individual adaptation: A resource perspective. *Academy of Management Journal, 29,* 465–487.

Ashford, S. J. (1989). Self-assessments in organizations: A literature review and integrative model. *Research in Organizational Behavior, 11,* 133–174.

Ashford, S. J., & Cummings, L. L. (1983). Feedback as an individual resource: Personal strategies of creating information. *Organizational Behavior and Human Performance, 32,* 370–398.

Ashford, S. J., & Northcraft, G. B. (1992). Conveying more (or less) than we realize: The role of impression-management in feedback-seeking. *Organizational Behavior and Human Decision Processes, 53,* 310–334.

Ashford, S. J., & Tsui, A. S. (1991). Self-regulation for managerial effectiveness: The role of active feedback seeking. *Academy of Management Journal, 34*(2), 251–280.

Aspinwall, L. G., & Taylor, S. E. (1993). Effects of social comparison direction, threat, and self-esteem on affect, self-evaluation, and expected success. *Journal of Personality and Social Psychology, 64,* 708–722.

Atwater, L. E., Roush, P., & Fischthal, A. (1992). The impact of feedback on leaders' performance and self-evaluations. SUNY-Binghamton, School of Management, Working Paper 92-220. Cited in Yammarino & Atwater (1993).

Atwater, L. E., & Yammarino, F. J. (1992). Does self-other agreement on leadership perceptions moderate the validity of leadership and performance predictions? *Personnel Psychology, 45,* 141–164.

Balzer, W. K., Doherty, M. E., & O'Connor, R., Jr. (1989). The effects of cognitive feedback on performance. *Psychological Bulletin, 106,* 410–433.

Balzer, W. K., Sulsky, L. M., Hammer, L. B., & Summer, K. E. (1992). Task information, cognitive information, or functional validity information: Which components of cognitive feedback affect performance? *Organizational Behavior and Human Decision Processes, 53,* 35–54.

Bandura, A. (1977). *Social learning theory.* Englewood Cliffs, NJ: Prentice-Hall.

Bandura, A. (1982). Self-efficacy mechanisms in human agency. *American Psychologist, 37,* 122–147.

Barker, J. R. (1993). Tightening the iron cage: Concertive control in self-managing teams. *Administrative Science Quarterly, 38,* 408–437.

Barnes-Farrell, J. L. (1993). Contextual variables that enhance/inhibit career development opportunities for older adults: The case of supervisor-subordinate age disparity. In J. Demick & P. M. Miller (Eds.), *Development in the workplace* (pp. 141–154). Hillsdale, NJ: Erlbaum.

Barnes-Farrell, J. L., L'Heurèux-Barrett, T. J., & Conway, J. M. (1991). Impact of gender-related job features on the accurate evaluation of performance information. *Organizational Behavior and Human Decision Processes, 48,* 23–35.

Barr, S. H., & Conlon, E. J. (1994). Effects of distribution of feedback in work groups. *Academy of Management Journal, 37,* 641–655.

Barrick, M. R., & Mount, M. K. (1991). The big five personality traits and job performance: A meta-analysis. *Personnel Psychology, 44,* 1–26.

Barrick, M. R., & Mount, M. K. (1993). Autonomy as a moderator of the relationships between the big five personality dimensions and job performance. *Journal of Applied Psychology, 78,* 111–118.

Bass, B. M., & Yammarino, F. J. (1991). Congruence of self and others' leadership ratings of naval officers for understanding successful performance. *Applied Psychology: An International Review, 40,* 437–454.

Bassett, G. A., & Meyer, H. H. (1968). Performance appraisal based on self-review. *Personnel Psychology, 21,* 421–430.

Bateman, T. S., & Organ, D. W. (1983). Job satisfaction and the good soldier: The relationship between affect and employee "citizenship." *Academy of Management Journal, 26,* 587–595.

Baumeister, R. F. (1982). A self-presentational view of social phenomena. *Psychological Bulletin, 91,* 3–26.

Bazerman, M. H. (1984). The relevance of Kahneman and Tversky's prospect theory on organizational behavior. *Journal of Management, 10,* 333–343.

Bazerman, M. H., Magliozzi, T., & Neale, M. A. (1985). The acquisition of an integrative response in a competitive market. *Organizational Behavior and Human Performance, 34,* 294–313.

Bazerman, M. H., & Neale, M. A. (1983). Heuristics in negotiation: Limitations to dispute resolution effectiveness. In M. H. Bazerman & R. J. Lewicki (Eds.), *Negotiating in organizations* (pp. 51–67). Beverly Hills, CA: Sage.

Beach, L. R. (1990). *Image theory: Decision making in personal and organizational contexts.* New York: Wiley.

Beach, L. R., & Mitchell, T. R. (1990). Image theory: A behavioral theory of decision making in organizations. In B. Staw & L. L. Cummings (Eds.), *Research in organizational behavior* (Vol. 12), (pp. 1–41). Greenwich, CT: JAI Press.

Beck, A. T. (1987). Cognitive models of depression. *Journal of Cognitive Psychotherapy, 1,* 5–37.

Becker, T. E., & Klimoski, R. J. (1989). A field study of the relationship between the organizational feedback environment and performance. *Personnel Psychology, 42,* 343–358.

Bee, H. (1992). *The journey of adulthood* (2nd ed). New York: Macmillan.

Behling, O., & Eckel, N. L. (1991). Making sense out of intuition. *Academy of Management Executive, 5*(1), 46–54.

Bem, D. J. (1972). Self-perception theory. In L. Berkowitz (Ed.), *Advances in social psychology* (Vol. 1), (pp. 1–62). New York: Academic Press.

Berger, S. M. (1977). Social comparison, modeling, and perseverance. In J. M. Suls & R. L. Miller (Eds.), *Social comparison processes: Theoretical and empirical perspectives* (pp. 209–234). Washington, DC: Hemisphere.

Bernardin, H. J., & Buckley, M. R. (1981). Strategies in rater training. *Academy of Management Review, 6,* 205–212.

Bernardin, H. J., & Beatty, R. W. (1987). Can subordinate appraisals enhance managerial productivity? *Sloan Management Review, 28*(4), 63–73.

Bernardin, H. J., Dahmus, S. A., & Redmon, G. (1993). Attitudes of first-line supervisors toward subordinate appraisals. *Human Resource Management, 32,* 315–324.

Berscheid, E., Snyder, M., & Omoto, A. M. (1989). Issues in studying close relationships: Conceptualizing and measuring closeness. In C. Hendrick (Ed.), *Review of personality and social psychology.* (Vol. 10), *Close relationships* (pp. 63–91). Newbury Park, CA: Sage.

Bettenhausen, J. L. (1991). Five years of group research: What have we learned and what needs to be addressed? *Journal of Management, 17,* 345–381.

Beyer, J. M. (1981). Ideologies, values, and decision making in organizations. In P. C. Nystrom & W. H. Starbuck (Eds.), *Handbook of organizational design* (Vol. 2). New York: Oxford University Press.

Biddle, C. (1979). *Role theory: Expectations, identities, and behaviors.* New York: Academic Press.

Bigoness, W. J. (1976a). Effect of applicant's sex, race, and performance on employers' performance ratings: Some developmental procedures and formats. *Journal of Applied Psychology, 61,* 75–79.

Bigoness, W. J. (1976b). Effect of applicant's sex, race, and performance on employers' performance ratings: Some additional findings. *Journal of Applied Psychology, 61,* 80–84.

Billig, M. (1987). *Arguing and thinking: A rhetorical approach to social psychology.* Cambridge: Cambridge University Press.

Bishop, G. (1985). *Gems of New Jersey.* Englewood Cliffs, NJ: Prentice-Hall.

Blake, R. R., & Mouton, J. S. (1962). Overevaluation of own group's product in intergroup competition. *Journal of Abnormal and Social Psychology, 64,* 237–238.

Blakely, G. L. (1993). The effects of performance rating discrepancies on supervisors and subordinates. *Organizational Behavior and Human Decision Processes, 54,* 57–80.

Blau, P. (1964). *Exchange and power in social life.* New York: Wiley.

Bobko, P., & Colella, A. (1994). Employee reactions to performance standards: A review and research propositions. *Personnel Psychology, 47,* 1–29.

Boice, R. (1983). Observational skills. *Psychological Bulletin, 93,* 3–29.

Borman, W. C. (1974). The rating of individuals in organizations: An alternative approach. *Organizational Behavior and Human Performance, 12,* 105–124.

Bowers, K. S. (1984). On being unconsciously influenced and informed. In K. S. Bowers & D. Meichenbaum (Eds.), *The unconscious reconsidered.* New York: Wiley.

Bray, D. W., Campbell, R. J., & Grant, D. L. (1974). *Formative years in business: A long-term AT&T study of managerial lives.* New York: Wiley.

Brewer, M. B. (1993). Social identity, distinctiveness, and in-group homogeneity. *Social Cognition, 11,* 150–164.

Brewer, M. B., & Weber, J. G. (1994). Self-evaluation effects of interpersonal versus intergroup social comparison. *Journal of Personality and Social Psychology, 66,* 268–275.

Brief, A. P., & Hollenbeck, J. R. (1985). An exploratory study of self-regulating activities and their effects on job performance. *Journal of Organizational Behavior, 6,* 197–208.

Brockner, J., Derr, W. R., & Laing, W. N. (1987). Self-esteem and reactions to negative feedback: Toward greater generalizability. *Journal of Research in Personality, 21,* 318–333.

Brooks, L. (1974). Interactive effects of sex and status on self-disclosure. *Journal of Counseling Psychology, 21,* 469–474.

Brouwer, P. J. (1964). The power to see ourselves. *Harvard Business Review, 42,* 156–165.

Brown, M. T. (1989). A cross-sectional analysis of self-disclosure patterns. *Journal of Mental Health Counseling, 11,* 384–395.

Brown, R., & Wootton-Millward, L. (1993). Perceptions of group homogeneity during group formation and change. *social Cognition, 11,* 126–149.

Bruner, J. S., & Tagiuri, R. (1954). The perception of people. In G. Lindzey (Ed.), *Handbook of social psychology* (Vol. 2). Cambridge, MA: Addison-Wesley.

Buda, R., Reilly, R. R., & Smither, J. W. (1990). The influence of indirect knowledge of prior performance on evaluations of present performance: The generalizability of assimilation effects. Paper presented at the Fifth Annual Conference of the Society for Industrial and Organizational Psychology, Miami Beach.

Buller, P. F. (1986). The team-building, task performance relation: Some conceptual and methodological refinements. *Group and Organization Studies, 10,* 147–168.

Burke, M. J., Brief, A. P., & George, J. M. (1993). The role of negative affectivity in understanding relations between self-reports of stressors and strains: A comment on the applied psychology literature. *Journal of Applied Psychology, 78,* 402–412.

Byrne, D. (1971). *The attraction paradigm.* New York: Academic Press.

Cacioppo, J. T., Petty, R. E., Kao, C. F., & Rodriguez, R. (1986). Central and peripheral routes to persuasion: An individual difference perspective. *Journal of Personality and Social Psychology, 51,* 1032–1043.

Caldwell, D. F., & O'Reilly, C. A. (1982). Boundary spanning and individual performance: The impact of self-monitoring. *Journal of Applied Psychology, 67,* 124–127.

Campbell, D. J., & Lee, C. (1988). Self-appraisal in performance evaluation: Development versus evaluation. *Academy of Management Review, 13,* 302–314.

Campbell, J. D., & Fehr, B. (1990). Self-esteem and perceptions of conveyed impressions: Is negative affectivity associated with greater realism: *Journal of Personality and Social Psychology, 58,* 122–133.

Campbell, R. J. (1991). HR development strategies: In K. N. Wexley (Ed.), *Developing human resources* (pp. 1–34). Washington, DC: The Bureau of National Affairs.

Caplan, R., Vinokur, A., Price, R., & van Ryn, M. (1989). Job seeking, re-employment, and mental health: A randomized field experiment in coping with job loss. *Journal of Applied Psychology, 74,* 759–769.

Carver, C. S., Peterson, L. M., Follansbee, D. J., & Scheier, M. F. (1983). Effects of self-directed attention on performance and persistence among persons high and low in test anxiety. *Cognitive Therapy and Research, 7,* 333–354.

Carver, C. S., & Scheier, M. F. (1981). *Attention and self-regulation: A control-theory approach to human behavior.* New York: Springer.

Carver, C. S., & Scheier, M. F. (1982). Control theory: A useful conceptual framework for personality—social, clinical, and health psychology. *Psychological Bulletin, 92,* 111–135.

Cascio, W. F., & Silbey, V. (1979). Utility of the assessment center as a selection device. *Journal of Applied Psychology, 64,* 107–118.

Casey, J. T. (1993). Self-enhancement and loss aversion in self-assessment of performance. Unpublished manuscript, W. A. Harriman School for Management and Policy, SUNY–Stony Brook.

Chapdelaine, A., Kenny, D. A., & LaFontana, K. M. (1994). Matchmaker, matchmaker, can you make me a match? Predicting liking between two unacquainted persons. *Journal of Personality and Social Psychology, 67,* 83–91.

Cherniss, C. (1980). *Staff burnout.* Beverly Hills, CA: Sage.

Cialdini, R. (1989). Indirect tactics of image management: Beyond basking. In R. A. Giacalone & P. Rosenfeld (Eds.), *Impression management in the organization* (pp. 45–56). Hillsdale, NJ: Erlbaum.

Cleveland, J., & Berman, A. (1987). Age perceptions of jobs: Convergence of two questionnaires. *Psychological Reports, 60,* 1075–1081.

Cleveland, J., & Landy, F. (1983). The effects of person and job stereotypes on two personnel decisions. *Journal of Applied Psychology, 68,* 609–619.

Combs, A. W., Richards, A. C., & Richards, F. (1988). *Perceptual psychology: A humanistic approach to the study of persons.* Lanham, MD: University Press of America.

Conger, J. A. (1993). The brave new world of leadership training. *Organizational Dynamics, 21*(3), 46–58.

Conlon, D. E., & Ross, W. H. (1993). The effects of partisan third parties on negotiator behavior and outcome perceptions. *Journal of Applied Psychology, 78,* 280–290.

Copeland, J. T. (1993). Motivational approaches to expectancy confirmation. *Current Directions in Psychological Science, 2,* 117–121.

Cox, C. J., & Cooper, C. L. (1989). The making of the British CEO: Childhood, work experience, personality, and management style. *Academy of Management Executive, 3,* 241–245.

Craik, K. J. W. (1943). *The nature of explanation.* Cambridge: Cambridge University Press.

Crick, N. R., & Dodge, K. A. (1994). A review and reformulation of social information-processing mechanisms in children's social adjustment. *Psychological Bulletin, 115,* 74–101.

Cronbach, L. J. (1955). Processes affecting scores on "understanding of others" and "assumed similarity." *Psychological Bulletin, 52,* 177–193.

Cronbach, L. J. (1958). Proposals leading to analytic treatment of social perception. In R. Tagiuri & L. Petrullo (Eds.), *Person perception and interpersonal behavior* (pp. 353–3579). Stanford, CA: Stanford University Press.

Cronshaw, S. F., & Lord, R. G. (1987). Effects of categorization, attribution, and encoding processes on leadership perceptions. *Journal of Applied Psychology, 72,* 97–106.

Curran, J. (1992). *Jobs: A manual for teaching people successful job search strategies.* Ann Arbor: Michigan Prevention Research Center, Institute for Social Research, University of Michigan.

Davey, G. C. L. (1993). A comparison of three cognitive appraisal strategies: The role of threat devaluation in problem-focused coping. *Personality and Individual Differences, 14*(4), 535–546.

Davis, J. H. (1992). Some compelling intuitions about group consensus decisions, theoretical and empirical research, and interpersonal aggregation phenomena: Selected examples, 1950–1990. *Organizational Behavior and Human Decision Processes, 52,* 3–38.

Deaux, K. (1979). Self-evaluation of male and female managers. *Journal of Sex Roles, 5,* 571–580.

Deci, E. L., & Ryan, R. M. (1990). A motivational approach to self: Integration in personality. *Nebraska Symposium on Motivation, 38,* 238–288.

DeGregorio, M. B. (1991). An investigation of the influence of self–other feedback congruence on feedback acceptance. Paper presented at the Sixth Annual Meeting of the Society for Industrial and Organizational Psychology, St. Louis.

deJung, J. E., & Kaplan, H. (1962). Some differential effects of race of rater and ratee on early peer ratings of combat aptitude. *Journal of Applied Psychology, 46,* 370–374.

DeNisi, A. S., Cafferty, T. P., & Meglino, B. M. (1984). A cognitive view of the performance appraisal process: A model and research propositions. *Organizational Behavior and Human Performance, 33,* 360–396.

Derr, C. B. (1986). *Managing the new careerists.* San Francisco: Jossey-Bass.

Diehl, M., & Strobe, W. (1991). Productivity loss in idea-generating groups: Tracking down the blocking effect. *Journal of Personality and Social Psychology, 61,* 392–403.

Dobbins, G. H., & Russell, J. M. (1986). The biasing effects of subordinate likeableness on leaders' responses to poor performers: A laboratory and a field study. *Personnel Psychology, 39,* 759–777.

Doise, W. (1978). Actions and judgments: Collective and individual structuring. In H. Brandstatter, J. Davis, & H. Schuler (Eds.), *Dynamics of group decisions.* Beverly Hills, CA: Sage.

Domsch, M., & Lichtenberger, B. (1991). Managing the global manager: Predeparture training and development for German expatriates in China and Brazil. *Journal of Management Development, 10,* 41–52.

Dowling, P. J. (1988). International HRM. In L. Dyer (Ed.), *Human resource management: Evolving roles and responsibilities* (pp. 228–258). Washington, DC: The Bureau of National Affairs.

Drasgow, F., Olson, J. B., Keenan, P. A., Moberg, P., & Mead, A. D. (1993). Computerized assessment. *Research in Personnel and Human Resources Management, 11,* 163–206.

Driskell, J. E., Olstead, B., & Salas, E. (1993). Task cues, dominance cues, and influence in task groups. *Journal of Applied Psychology, 78,* 51–60.

Druckman, D. (1993). The situational levers of negotiating flexibility. *Journal of Conflict Resolution, 37,* 236–276.

Duarte, N. T., Goodson, J. R., & Klich, N. R. (1994). Effects of dyadic quality and duration on performance appraisal. *Academy of Management Journal, 37,* 499–521.

Dunegan, K. J. (1993). Framing, cognitive modes, and image theory: Toward an understanding of a glass half full. *Journal of Applied Psychology, 78,* 491–503.

Dunnette, M. D. (1993). My hammer or your hammer? *Human Resource Management, 32,* 373–384.

Earley, P. C. (1994). Self or group? Cultural effects of training on self-efficacy and performance. *Administrative Science Quarterly, 39,* 89–117.

Earley, P. C., & Erez, M. (1991). Time-dependency effects of goals and norms: The role of cognitive processing on motivational models. *Journal of Applied Psychology, 76,* 717–724.

Eden, D., & Aviram, A. (1993). Self-efficacy training to speed reemployment: Helping people to help themselves. *Journal of Applied Psychology, 78,* 352–360.

Eder, R. W., & Ferris, G. R. (Eds.). (1989). *The employment interview: Theory, research, and practice.* Newbury Park, CA: Sage.

Eder, R. W., Kacmar, K. M., & Ferris, G. R. (1989). Employment interview research: History and synthesis. In R. W. Eder & G. R. Ferris (Eds.), *The employment interview: Theory, research, and practice* (pp. 17–31). Newbury Park, CA: Sage.

Edwards, J. R. (1992). A cybernetic theory of stress, coping, and well-being in organizations. *Academy of Management Review, 17,* 238–274.

Ekman, P. (1992). An argument for basic emotions. *Cognition and Emotion, 6,* 169–200.

Ellis, S., & Kruglanski, A. W. (1992). Self as an epistemic authority: Effects on experiential and instructional learning. *Social Cognition, 10,* 357–375.

Falcione, R. L., & Wilson, C. E. (1988). Socialization processes in organizations. In G. M. Goldhaber & G. A. Barnett (Eds.), *Handbook of organizational communication* (pp. 151–169). Norwood, NJ: Ablex.

Farh, J. L., Dobbins, G. H., & Cheng, B. S. (1991). Cultural relativity in action: A comparison of self-ratings made by Chinese and U.S. workers. *Personnel Psychology, 44,* 129–147.

Farh, J. L., Werbel, J. D., & Bedeian, A. G. (1988). An empirical investigation of self-appraisal-based performance evaluation. *Personnel Psychology, 41,* 141–156.

Favero, J. L, & Ilgen, D. R. (1989). The effects of ratee prototypicality on rater observation and accuracy. *Journal of Applied Social Psychology, 19,* 932–946.

Feldman, J. M. (1981). Beyond attribution theory: Cognitive processes in performance appraisal. *Journal of Applied Psychology, 66,* 127–148.

Feldman, J. M., Sam, I. A., McDonald, W. F., & Bechtel, G. G. (1980). Work outcome preference and evaluation: A study of three ethnic groups. *Journal of Cross-Cultural Psychology, 11,* 444–468.

Felson, R. B. (1985). Reflected appraisal and the development of self. *Social Psychology Quarterly, 48,* 71–78.

Fenigstein, A., & Abrams, D. (1993). Self-attention and the egocentric assumption of shared perspectives. *Journal of Experimental Social Psychology, 29,* 287–303.

Ferris, G. R., Judge, R. A., Rowland, K. M., & Fitzgibbons, D. E. (1994). Subordinate influence and the performance evaluation process: Test of a model. *Organizational Behavior and Human Decision Processes, 58,* 101–135.

Ferris, G. R., Yates, V. L., Gilmore, D. C., & Rowland, K. M. (1985). The influence of subordinate age on performance ratings and causal attributions. *Personnel Psychology, 38,* 545–557.

Festinger, L. (1954). A theory of social comparison processes. *Human Relations, 7,* 117–140.

Fischoff, B. (1988). Judgement and decision making. In R. J. Sternberg, & E. E. Smith (Eds.), *The psychology of human thought* (pp. 155–187). New York: Cambridge University Press.

Fisicaro, S. A., & Lance, C. E. (1990). Implications of three causal models for the measurement of halo error. *Applied Psychological Measurement, 14,* 419–429.

Fiske, D. W., & Taylor, S. E. (1991). *Social cognition* (2nd ed.). New York: McGraw-Hill.

Fiske, S. T. (1982). Schema-triggered affect: Application to social perception. In M. S. Clarke & S. T. Fiske (Eds.), *Affect and cognition: The 17th annual Carnegi symposium* (pp. 65–76). Hillsdale, NJ: Erlbaum.

Fiske, S. T. (1993). Controlling other people: The impact of power on stereotyping. *American Psychologist, 48,* 621–628.

Fiske, S. T., & Neuberg, S. L. (1990). A continuum of impression formation, from category-based to individuating processes: Influences of information and motivation on attention and interpretation. In L. Berkowitz (Ed.), *Advances in experimental and social psychology* (Vol. 23), (pp. 1–74). San Diego, CA: Academic Press.

Fiske, S. T., Neuberg, S. L., Beattie, A. E., & Milberg, S. J. (1987). Category-based and attribute reactions of some information conditions of stereotyping and individuating processes. *Journal of Experimental and Social Psychology, 23,* 399–427.

Fogel, A. (1993). *Developing through relationships: Origins of communication, self, and culture.* Chicago: University of Chicago Press.

Forester, J., & Stitzel, D. (1989). Beyond neutrality: The possibilities of activist mediation in public sector conflicts. *Negotiation Journal, 5,* 251–264.

Forgas, J. P. (1994). Sad and guilty? Affective influences on the explanation of conflict in close relationships. *Journal of Personality and Social Psychology, 66,* 56–68.

Forward, G. E., Beach, D. E., Gray, D. A., & Quick, J. C. (1991). Mentofacturing:

A vision for American industrial excellence. *Academy of Management Executive, 5*(3), 32–44.

Fried, Y., Tiegs, R. B., & Bellamy, A. R. (1992). Personal and interpersonal predictors of supervisors' avoidance of evaluating subordinates. *Journal of Applied Psychology, 77*, 462–468.

Fulk, J., Brief, A. P., & Barr, S. H. (1985). Trust in manager and perceived fairness and accuracy of performance evaluation. *Journal of Business Research, 13*, 301–313.

Funder, D. C. (1987). Errors and mistakes: Evaluating the accuracy of social judgment. *Psychological Bulletin, 101*, 75–90.

Funder, D. C., & Colvin, C. R. (1988). Friends and strangers: Acquaintanceship, agreement, and the accuracy of personality judgment. *Journal of Personality and Social Psychology, 55*, 149–158.

Gabarro, J. J. (1978). The development of trust, influence, and expectations. In A. G. Athos & J. J. Gabarro (Eds.), *Interpersonal behavior: Communication and understanding in relationships*. Englewood Cliffs, NJ: Prentice-Hall.

Gabarro, J. J. (1979). Socialization at the top: How CEO's and their subordinates evolve interpersonal contracts. *Organizational Dynamics, 3*, 2–23.

Gabarro, J. J. (1990). The development of working relationships. In J. Galegher, R. E. Kraut, & C. Egido (Eds.), *Intellectual teamwork: Social and technological foundations of cooperative work* (pp. 79–110). Hillsdale, NJ: Erlbaum.

Galbraith, J. R. (1977). *Organization design*. Reading, MA: Addison-Wesley.

Gallupe, R. B., Cooper, W. H., Grise, M. L., & Bastianutti, L. M. (1994). Blocking electronic brainstorms. *Journal of Applied Psychology, 79*, 77–86.

Gangestad, S., & Snyder, M. (1985). To carve nature at its joints: On the existence of discrete classes in personality. *Psychological Review, 92*, 317–349.

Gardner, W. L., III. (1991). The impact of impression management on the performance appraisal process. Paper presented at the Sixth Annual Meeting of the Society for Industrial and Organizational Psychology, St. Louis.

Gardner, W. L., III. (1992). Lessons in organizational dramaturgy: The art of impression management. *Organizational Dynamics, 21*(1), 33–46.

Gavin, J. F., & Krois, P. A. (1983). Content and process of survey feedback sessions and their relation to survey responses: An initial study. *Group and Organization Studies, 8*, 221–247.

George, J. M. (1990). Personality, affect, and behavior in groups. *Journal of Applied Psychology, 75*, 107–116.

George, J. M., & James, L. R. (1993). Personality, affect, and behavior in groups revisited: Comment on aggregation, levels of analysis, and a recent application of within and between analysis. *Journal of Applied Psychology, 78*, 798–804.

Gersick, C. J. G. (1988). Time and transition in work teams: Toward a new model of group development. *Academy of Management Journal, 31*, 9–41.

Gersick, C. J. G. (1989) Marking time: Predictable transitions in task groups. *Academy of Management Journal, 32*, 274–309.

Getz, K. A. (1993). selecting corporate political tactics. In B. M. Mitnick (Ed.), *Corporate political agency: The construction of competition in public affairs* (pp. 242–273). Newbury Park, CA: Sage.

Gibbons, F. X., & Gerrard, M. (1991). Downward comparison and coping with threat. In J. Suls & T. A. Wills (Eds.), *Social comparison: Contemporary theory and research* (pp. 317–345). Hillsdale, NJ: Erlbaum.

Gibson, J. J. (1982). Reasons for realism. In E. Reed & R. Jones (Eds.), *Selected essays of James J. Gibson* (pp. 411–412). Hillsdale, NJ: Erlbaum.

Gifford, R. (1994). A lens-mapping framework for understanding the encoding and decoding of interpersonal dispositions in nonverbal behavior. *Journal of Personality and Social Psychology, 66,* 398–412.

Gilkey, R. W., & Greenhalgh, L. (1991). The role of personality in successful negotiating. In J. W. Breslin & J. Z. Rubin (Eds.), *Negotiation theory and practice* (pp. 279–290). Cambridge, MA: Program on Negotiation Books.

Gist, M. E., & Mitchell, T. R. (1992). Self-efficacy: A theoretical analysis of its determinants and malleability. *Academy of Management Review, 17,* 183–211.

Goethals, G., & Darley, J. (1977). Social comparison theory: An attributional approach. In J. M. Suls & R. L. Miller (Eds.), *Social comparison processes: Theoretical and empirical perspectives* (pp. 259–278). Washington, DC: Hemisphere.

Goldstein, W. M., & Mitzel. (1992). The relative importance of relative importance: Inferring other people's preferences from relative importance ratings and previous decisions. *Organizational Behavior and Human Decision Processes, 51,* 382–415.

Golembiewski, R. T., Billingsley, K., & Yeager, S. (1976). Measuring change persistency in human affairs: Types of change generated by OD designs. *Journal of Applied Behavioral Science, 12,* 133–157.

Gouldner, A. W. (1960). The norm of reciprocity: A preliminary statement. *American Sociological Review, 25,* 161–178.

Graen, G. (1976). Role making processes within complex organizations. In M. D. Dunnette (Ed.), *Handbook of industrial and organizational psychology* (pp. 1201–1246). New York: Rand McNally.

Graen, G., & Scandura, T. A. (1987). Toward a psychology of dyadic organizing. In L. L. Cummings & B. M. Staw (Eds.), *Research in organizational behavior* (pp. 175–208). Greenwich, CT: JAI Press.

Greenberg, J. (1990). Organizational justice: Yesterday, today, and tomorrow. *Journal of Management, 16,* 401–434.

Greenwald, A. G., & Pratkanis, A. R. (1984). The self. In R. S. Wyer & T. K. Skrull (Eds.), *Handbook of social cognition* (Vol. 3), (pp. 129–178). Hillsdale, NJ: Erlbaum.

Guzzo, R. A., Wagner, D. B., Maguire, E., Herr, B., & Hawler, C. (1986). Implicit theories and the evaluation of group process and performance. *Organizational Behavior and Human Performance, 37,* 279–295.

Haccoun, R. R., & Klimoski, R. J. (1975). Negotiator status and accountability source: A study of negotiator behavior. *Organizational Behavior and Human Performance, 14,* 342–359.

Hackman, J. R. (1992). Group influences on individuals in organizations. In M. D. Dunnett & L. M. Hough (Eds.), *Handbook of industrial and organizational psychology* (2nd ed.). (Vol. 3), (pp. 199–267). Palo Alto, CA: Consulting Psychologists Press.

Hackman, J. R. (Ed.). (1990). *Groups that work (and those that don't): Creating conditions for effective teamwork.* San Francisco: Jossey-Bass.

Hakel, M. D. (1974). Normative personality factors recovered from ratings of personality descriptors: The beholder's eye. *Personnel Psychology, 27,* 409–421.

Hakel, M. D., & Schuh, A. J. (1971). Job applicant attributes judged important across seven diverse occupations. *Personnel Psychology, 24,* 45–52.

Hall, D. T. (1986). An overview of current career development theory, research, and practice. In D. T. Hall and Assoc. (Eds.), *Career development in organizations* (pp. 1–20). San Francisco: Jossey-Bass.

Hamada, T. (1991). *American enterprise in Japan*. Albany: State University of New York Press.

Hamner, W. C., Kim, J. S., Baird, L., & Bigoness, W. J. (1974). Race and sex as determinants of ratings by potential employers in a simulated work sampling task. *Journal of Applied Psychology, 59*, 705–711.

Harris, M. M., & Schaubroeck, J. (1988). A meta-analysis of self-manager, self-peer, and peer-manager ratings. *Personnel Psychology, 41*, 43–62.

Hastie, R., & Park, B. (1986). The relationship between memory and judgment depends on whether the judgment task is memory-based or on-line. *Psychological Review, 93*, 258–268.

Hautaluoma, J. E. (1991). Employee reactions to different 360-degree feedback methods. Unpublished manuscript, Colorado State University.

Hautaluoma, J. E., Jobe, L., Visser, S., & Donkersgoed, W. (1992). Employee reactions to different upward feedback methods. Paper presented at the Seventh Annual Meeting of the Society for Industrial and Organizational Psychology, Montreal.

Hazucha, J. F., Gentile, S. A., & Schneider, R. J. (1993). The impact of 360-degree feedback on management skills development. *Human Resource Management, 32*, 325–352.

Heatherton, T. F., Polivy, J., Herman, C. P., & Baumeister, R. F., (1993). Self-awareness, task failure, and disinhibition: How attentional focus affects eating. *Journal of Personality, 61*, 49–59.

Hegarty, W. H. (1974). Using subordinate ratings to elicit behavioral changes in managers. *Journal of Applied Psychology, 59*, 764–766.

Heider, F. (1958). *The psychology of interpersonal relations*. Hillsdale, NJ: Erlbaum.

Heilman, M. E., Kaplow, S. R., Amato, M. A. G., & Stathatos, P. (1993). When similarity is a liability: Effects of sex-based preferential selection on reactions to like-sex and different-sex others. *Journal of Applied Psychology, 78*, 917–927.

Heilman, M. E., Lucas, J. A., & Kaplow, S. R. (1990). Self-derogating consequences of preferential selection: The moderating role of initial self-confidence. *Organizational Behavior and Human Decision Processes, 46*, 202–216.

Henry, R. A., & Sniezek, J. A. (1993). Situational factors affecting judgments of future performance. *Organizational Behavior and Human Decision Processes, 54*, 104–132.

Herriot, P. (1989). Attribution theory and interview decisions. In R. W. Eder & G. R. Ferris (Eds.), *The employment interview: Theory, research, and practice* (pp. 97–110). Newbury Park, CA: Sage.

Higgins, E. T., Roney, C. J. R., Crowe, E., & Hymes, C. (1994). Ideal versus ought predilections for approach and avoidance: Distinct self-regulatory systems. *Journal of Personality and Social Psychology, 66*, 276–286.

Hill, T., Lewicki, P., Czyzewska, M., & Boss, A. (1989). Self-perpetuating development of encoding biases in person perception. *Journal of Personality and Social Psychology, 57*, 373–387.

Hofstede, G. (1980). *Culture's consequences: International differences in work-related values*. Beverly Hills, CA: Sage.

Holland, J. H., Holyoak, K. J., Nisbett, R. E., & Thagard, P. R. (1986). *Induction: Processes of inference, learning, and discovery*. Cambridge, MA: MIT Press.

Holzbach, R. (1978). Rater bias in performance ratings: Superior, self, and peer ratings. *Journal of Applied Psychology, 63,* 579–588.

Howard, A., & Bray, D. W. (1981). Today's young managers: They can do it, but will they? *The Wharton Magazine, 5*(4), 23–28.

Hoyle, R. H. (1993). Interpersonal attraction in the absence of explicit attitudinal information. *Social Cognition, 11,* 309–320.

Hurley, A. E. (1993). The effects of self-esteem and source credibility on self-denying prophecies. Unpublished manuscript, Harriman School for Management and Policy, SUNY–Stony Brook.

Ilgen, D. R., Barnes-Farrell, J. L., & McKellin, D. B. (1993). Performance appraisal process research in the 1980s: What has it contributed to appraisals in use? *Organizational Behavior and Human Decision Processes, 54,* 321–368.

Ilgen, D. R., Fisher, C. D., & Taylor, M. S. (1979). Consequences of individual feedback on behavior in organizations. *Journal of Applied Psychology, 64,* 349–371.

Isen, A. M. (1984). Toward understanding the role of affect in cognition. In R. S. Wyer & T. K. Skrull, *Handbook of social cognition,* (Vol. 3), (pp. 179–236). Hillsdale, NJ: Erlbaum.

Jackson, S. E., Brett, J. F., Sessa, V. I., Cooper, D. M., Julin, J. A., & Peyronnin, K. (1991). Some differences make a difference: Individual dissimilarity and group heterogeneity as correlates of recruitment, promotions, and turnover. *Journal of Applied Psychology, 76,* 675–689.

Janis, I. L. (1982). *Groupthink.* New York: Houghton Mifflin.

Janis, I. L., & Mann, L. (1977). *Decision making: A psychological analysis of conflict, choice, and commitment.* New York: Free Press.

Janz, J. T. (1982). Initial comparisons of patterned behavior description interviews versus unstructured interviews. *Journal of Applied Psychology, 67,* 577–580.

Janz, J. T. (1989). The patterned behavior description interview: The best prophet of the future is the past. In R. W. Eder & G. R. Ferris (Eds.), *The employment interview: Theory, research, and practice* (pp. 158–168). Newbury Park, CA: Sage.

Janz, J. T., Hellervik, L., & Gilmore, D. C. (1986). *Behavior description interviewing: New, accurate, cost effective.* Newton, MA: Allyn & Bacon.

John, O. P., & Robins, R. W. (1994). Accuracy and bias in self-perception: Individual differences in self-enhancement and the role of narcissism. *Journal of Personality and Social Psychology, 66,* 206–219.

Johns, G. (1993). Constraints on the adoption of psychology-based personnel practices: Lessons from organizational innovation. *Personnel Psychology, 46,* 569–592.

Johnson-Laird, P. N. (1983). *Mental models.* Cambridge: Cambridge University Press.

Johnson-Laird, P. N., & Oatley, K. (1989). The language of emotions: An analysis of a semantic field. *Cognition and Emotion, 3,* 81–123.

Johnson-Laird, P. N., & Oatley, K. (1992). Basic emotions, rationality, and folk theory. *Cognition and Emotion, 6,* 201–223.

Jones, E. E., & Berglas, S. (1978). Control of attributions about the self through self-handicapping strategies: The appeal of alcohol and the role of underachievement. *Personality and Social Psychology Bulletin, 4,* 200–206.

Jones, E. E., Rhodewalt, F., Berglas, S., & Skelton, J. A. (1981). Effects of strategic self-presentation on subsequent self-esteem. *Journal of Personality and Social Psychology, 41,* 407–421.

Joplin, J. R. (1993). Developing effective leadership: An interview with Henry Cisneros, Secretary, U.S. Department of Housing and Urban Development. *Academy of Management Executive, 7*(2), 84–92.

Jourden, F. J., & Heath, C. (1993). Performance illusions in groups and individuals. Paper presented at the 1993 annual meeting of the Academy of Management Meeting, Atlanta.

Judge, T. A. (1993). Does affective disposition moderate the relationship between job satisfaction and voluntary turnover? *Journal of Applied Psychology, 78,* 395–401.

Judge, T. A., & Ferris, G. R. (1993). Social context of performance evaluation decisions. *Academy of Management Journal, 36,* 80–105.

Judge, T. A., & Locke, E. A. (1993). Effect of dysfunctional thought processes on subjective well-being and job satisfaction. *Journal of Applied Psychology, 78,* 475–490.

Jussim, L. (1991). Social perception and social reality: A reflection-construction model. *Psychological Review, 98,* 54–73.

Jussim, L., Soffin, S., Brown, R., Levy, J., & Kohlhepp, K. (1992). Understanding reactions to feedback by integrating ideas from symbolic interactionism and cognitive evaluation theory. *Journal of Personality and Social Psychology, 62*(3), 402–421.

Kahn, W. A. (1993). Caring for caregivers: Patterns of organizational care-giving. *Administrative Science Quarterly, 38,* 539–563.

Kahn, W. A., & Kram, K. E. (1994). Authority at work: Internal models and their organizational consequences. *Academy of Management Review, 19,* 17–50.

Kahneman, D., Slovic, P., & Tversky, A. (1982). *Judgment under uncertainty: Heuristics and biases.* New York: Cambridge University Press.

Kahneman, D., & Tversky, A. (1979). Prospect theory: An analysis of decision under risk. *Econometrica, 47,* 263–291.

Kahneman, D., & Tversky, A. (1982). The psychology of preferences. *Scientific American, 246,* 162–170.

Kaplan, R. E. (1993). 360-degree feedback PLUS: Boosting the power of coworker ratings for executives. *Human Resource Management, 32,* 299–314.

Karl, K. A., & Kopf, J. M. (1993). Will individuals who need to improve their performance the most volunteer to receive videotaped feedback? Paper presented at the annual meeting of the Academy of Management, Atlanta.

Kashima, E. S., & Kashima, Y. (1993). Perceptions of general variability of social groups. *Social Cognition, 11,* 1–21.

Kelley, H. H. (1967). Attribution theory in social psychology. In D. Levine (Ed.), *Nebraska Symposium on Motivation.* (Vol. 15), (pp. 192–238). Lincoln: Nebraska University Press.

Kelley, H. H. (1972). Attribution theory in social interaction. In E. Jones, D. E. Kanouse, H. H. Kelley, R. E. Nisbett, S. Valins, & B. Weinere (Eds.), *Attribution: Perceiving the causes of behavior.* Morristown, NJ: General Learning Press.

Kelly, G. A. (1955). *The psychology of personal constructs.* New York: Norton.

Kelly, J. R., Futoran, G. C., & McGrath, J. E. (1990). Capacity and capability: Seven studies of entrainment of task performance rates. *Small Group Research, 21,* 283–314.

Kelly, J. R., & McGrath, J. E. (1985). Effects of time limits and task types on task performance and interaction of four-person groups. *Journal of Personality and Social Psychology, 49,* 395–407.

Kelly, J. R., & McGrath, J. E. (1988). *On time and method*. Newbury Park, CA: Sage.

Kenny, D. A., & DePaulo, B. M. (1993). Do people know how others view them? An empirical and theoretical account. *Psychological Bulletin, 114*, 145–161.

Kernan, M. C., & Lord, R. G. (1991). An application of control theory to understanding the relationship between performance and satisfaction. *Human Performance, 4*, 173–185.

Klein, H. J. (1989). An integrated control theory model of work motivation. *Academy of Management Review, 14*, 150–172.

Kleinmann, M. (1993). Are rating dimensions in assessment centers transparent for participants? Consequences for criterion and construct validity. *Journal of Applied Psychology, 78*, 988–993.

Klimoski, R. J., & Brice, T. S. (1991). The nature and impact of self-appraisals in a manufacturing environment. Paper presented at the Sixth Annual Conference of the Society for Industrial and Organizational Psychology, St. Louis.

Klimoski, R. J., & Inks, L. (1990). Accountability forces in performance appraisal. *Organizational Behavior and Human Decision Processes, 45*, 194–208.

Klimoski, R. J., & London, M. (1974). Role of the rater in performance appraisal. *Journal of Applied Psychology, 59*, 445–451.

Klimoski, R. J., & Strickland, W. J. (1977). Assessment centers—Valid or merely prescient? *Personnel Psychology, 30*, 353–361.

Kofman, F., & Senge, P. M. (1993). Communities of commitment: The heart of learning organizations. *Organizational Dynamics, 22*(2), 5–23.

Kolb, D. M., & Coolidge, G. G. (1991). Her place at the table: A consideration of gender issues in negotiation. In J. W. Breslin & J. Z. Rubin (Eds.), *Negotiation theory and practice* (pp. 261–277). Cambridge, MA: Program on Negotiation Books.

Kramer, R. M., Newton, E., & Pommerenke, P. L. (1993). Self-enhancement biases and negotiator judgment: Effects of self-esteem and mood. *Organizational Behavior and Human Decision Processes, 56*, 110–133.

Kruglanski, A. W. (1992). On methods of good judgment and good methods of judgment: Political decisions and the art of the possible. *Political Psychology, 13*, 455–475.

Kruglanski, A. W., & Mayseless, O. (1990). Classic and current social comparison research: Expanding the perspective. *Psychological Bulletin, 108*, 195–208.

Kulik, C. T., & Ambrose, M. L. (1993). Category-based and feature-based processes in performance appraisal: Integrating visual and computerized sources of performance data. *Journal of Applied Psychology, 78*, 821–830.

Kumar, K., & Beyerlein, M. (1991). Construction and validation of an instrument for measuring ingratiatory behaviors in organizational settings. *Journal of Applied Psychology, 76*, 619–627.

Lalonde, R. N., & Silverman, R. A. (1994). Behavioral preferences in response to social injustice: The effects of group permeability and social identity. *Journal of Personality and Social Psychology, 66*, 78–85.

Lance, C. E., LaPointe, J. A., & Fisicaro, S. A. (1994). Tests of three causal models of halo rater error. *Organizational Behavior and Human Decision Processes, 57*, 83–96.

Lance, C. E., LaPointe, J. A., & Stewart, A. M. (1994). A test of the context dependency of three causal models of halo rater error. *Journal of Applied Psychology, 79*, 332–341.

Landy, F. J., Barnes-Farrell, J. L., & Cleveland, J. N. (1980). Perceived fairness and accuracy of performance evaluation: A follow-up. *Journal of Applied Psychology, 65,* 355–356.

Larrick, R. P. (1993). Motivational factors in decision theories: The role of self-protection. *Psychological Bulletin, 113,* 440–450.

Larson, J. R., Jr. (1984). The performance feedback process: A preliminary model. *Organizational Behavior and Human Performance, 33,* 42–76.

Latham, G. P. (1989). The reliability, validity, and practicality of the situational interview. In R. W. Eder, & G. R. Ferris (Eds.), *The employment interview: Theory, research, and practice* (pp. 169–182). Newbury Park, CA: Sage.

Latham, G. P., & Wexley, K. N. (1982). *Increasing productivity through performance appraisal.* Reading, MA: Addison-Wesley.

Laurent, A. (1981). Perceived determinants of career success: A new approach to organizational analysis. In K. Trebesch (Ed.), *Organizational development in Europe.* Bern, Switzerland: Houpt.

Lawler, E. E., III. (1986). *High involvement management.* San Francisco, CA: Jossey-Bass.

Lawrence, B. S. (1988). New wrinkles in the theory of age: Demography, norms, and performance ratings. *Academy of Management Journal, 31,* 309–337.

Lazarus, R., & Folkman, S. (1984). *Stress, appraisal, and coping.* New York: Springer.

Leana, C., & Feldman, D. C. (1992). *Coping with job loss: How individuals, organizations, and communities respond to layoffs.* New York: Lexington.

Leana, C., & Feldman, D. C. (1994). Collective job creation strategies for laid-off workers. Presented at the annual meeting of the Society for Industrial and Organizational Psychology, Knoxville.

Leary, M. R. (1983). *Understanding social anxiety.* Beverly Hills, CA: Sage.

Lennox, R., & Wolfe, R. (1984). Revision of the self-monitoring scale. *Journal of Personality and Social Psychology, 46,* 1349–1364.

Levenson, R. W., & Ruef, A. M. (1992). Empathy: A physiological substrate. *Journal of Personality and Social Psychology, 63*(2), 234–246.

Levy, P. E. (1991). Self-appraisal and attributional judgments. Paper presented at the Sixth Annual Meeting of the Society for Industrial and Organizational Psychology, St. Louis.

Levy, P. E., & Foti, R. J. (1989). Reactions to performance feedback as a function of attributional and performance discrepancies. Paper presented at the annual meeting of the American Psychological Association, New Orleans.

Li, L. C. (1992). The strategic design of cross-cultural training programmes. *Journal of Management Development, 11,* 22–29.

Lichtenstein, M., & Scrull, T. K. (1987). Processing objectives as a determinant of the relationship between recall and judgment. *Journal of Experimental Social Psychology, 23,* 93–118.

Liden, R. C., Martin, C. L., & Parsons, C. K. (1993). Interviewer and applicant behaviors in employment interviews. *Academy of Management Journal, 36,* 372–386.

Liden, R. C., Wayne, S. J., & Stilwell, D. (1993). A longitudinal study on the early development of leader-member exchanges. *Journal of Applied Psychology, 78,* 662–674.

Lind, E. A., & Lissak, R. I. (1985). Apparent impropriety and procedural fairness judgments. *Journal of Experimental Social Psychology, 21,* 19–29.

Linville, P. W., Fischer, G. W., & Salovey, P. (1989). Perceived distributions of the characteristics of in-group and out-group members: Empirical evidence and a computer simulation. *Journal of Personality and Social Psychology, 57,* 165–188.

Linville, P. W., & Jones, E. (1980). Polarized appraisals of out-group members. *Journal of Personality and Social Psychology, 38,* 689–703.

Locke, E. A., & Latham, G. P. (1990). *A theory of goal setting and task performance.* Englewood Cliffs, NJ: Prentice-Hall.

Locke, E. A., Motowidlo, S. J., & Bobko, P. (1986). Using self-efficacy theory to resolve the conflict between goal setting theory and expectancy theory in organizational behavior and industrial/organizational psychology. *Journal of Social and Clinical Psychology, 4,* 328–338.

Lombardo, M. M., & McCall, M. W., Jr. (1982). Leader on line: Observations from a simulation of managerial work. In Hunt, J. G., Sekaran, U., & Schriescheim, C. A. (Eds.), *Leadership: Beyond establishment views* (pp. 50–67). Carbondale: Southern Illinois University Press.

London, M. (1977). Effects of information heterogeneity and representational roles on group member behavior and perceptions. *Journal of Applied Psychology, 62,* 76–80.

London, M. (1983). Toward a theory of career motivation. *Academy of Management Review, 8,* 620–630.

London, M. (1985a). *Developing managers.* San Francisco: Jossey-Bass.

London, M. (1985b). Employee guided management: Steps for involving employees in decisions and actions. *Leadership and Organization Development Journal, 6,* 3–8.

London, M. (1988). *Change agents: New roles and innovation strategies for human resource professionals.* San Francisco: Jossey-Bass.

London, M. (1993). Relationships between career motivation, empowerment, and support for career development. *Journal of Occupational and Organizational Psychology, 66,* 55–69.

London, M. (in press). Interpersonal insight in organizations: Cognitive models for human resource development. *Human Resource Management Review.*

London, M., & Beatty, R. W. (1993). 360-degree feedback as competitive advantage. *Human Resource Management, 32,* 353–372.

London, M., & Bray, D. W. (1983). An assessment center to study career motivation. *Career Center Bulletin, 4*(1), 8–13.

London, M., & Mone, E. M. (1987). *Career management and survival in the workplace.* San Francisco: Jossey-Bass.

London, M., & Mone, E. M. (1994). Managing marginal performance in an organization striving for excellence. In A. K. Korman (Ed.), *Human resources dilemmas in work organizations: Strategies for resolution* (pp. 95–124). New York: Guilford.

London, M., & Smither, J. W. (1994). Can 360-degree feedback change self-awareness and behavior? Theory-based applications and directions for research. Working Paper, SUNY–Stony Brook.

London, M., & Stumpf, S. A. (1982). *Managing careers.* Reading, MA: Addison-Wesley.

London, M., & Stumpf, S. A. (1986). Individual and organizational career development in changing times. In D. T. Hall and Assoc. (Ed.), *Career development in organizations* (pp. 21–49). San Francisco: Jossey-Bass.

London, M., & Wohlers, A. J. (1991). Agreement between subordinates and self-ratings in 360-degree feedback. *Personnel Psychology, 44,* 375–390.

London, M., Wohlers, A. J., & Gallagher, P. (1990). 360-degree feedback surveys: A source of feedback to guide management development. *Journal of Management Development, 9,* 17–31.

London, M., & Wueste, R. A. (1992). *Human resource development in changing organizations.* Westport, CT: Quorum.

Lonergan, B. J. F. (1957). *Insight: A study of human understanding.* New York: Longmans, Green.

Lord, R. G. (1985). Accuracy in behavioral measurement: An alternative definition based on raters' cognitive schema and signal detection theory. *Journal of Applied Psychology, 70,* 66–71.

Lord, R. G., & Hanges, P. J. (1987). A control systems model of organizational motivation: Theoretical and applied implications. *Behavioral Science, 32,* 161–178.

Louis, M. R., (1980). Surprise and sense making: What newcomers experience in entering unfamiliar organizational settings. *Administrative Science Quarterly, 25,* 226–251.

Louis, M. R. (1990). Newcomers as lay ethnographers: Acculturation during socialization. In B. Schneider (Ed.), *Organizational climates and cultures* (pp. 85–129). San Francisco: Jossey-Bass.

Luft, J. (1969). *Of human interaction.* Palo Alto, CA: National Press Books.

Luft, J. (1970). *Group processes: An introduction to group dynamics.* Palo Alto, CA: National Press Books.

Luft, J., & Ingham, H. (1955). The Johari Window, a graphic model of interpersonal awareness. In *Proceedings of the Western Training Laboratory in Group Development.* University of California, Los Angeles, Extension Office.

Mabe, P. A., & West, S. G. (1982). Validity of self-evaluation of ability: A review and meta-analysis. *Journal of Applied Psychology, 67,* 280–296.

Macan, T. H., & Dipboye, R. L. (1990). The relationship of interviewers' preinterview impressions to selection and recruitment outcomes. *Personnel Psychology, 43,* 745–768.

Maclean, N. (1992). *Young men and fire.* Chicago: University of Chicago Press.

Macrae, C. N., Milne, A. B., & Bodenhausen, G. V. (1994). Stereotypes as energy-saving devices: A peek inside the cognitive tool box. *Journal of Personality and Social Psychology, 66,* 37–47.

Maddi, S. R. (1980). *Personality theories: A comparative analysis.* Homewood, IL: Dorsey Press.

Maier, N. R. F. (1970). *Problem solving and creativity in individuals and groups.* Belmont, CA: Brooks/Cole.

Maitlen, B. R. (1994). Workforce challenges in the year 2000: The concept of inplacement. Paper presented at the annual meeting of the Society for Industrial and Organizational Psychology, Knoxville.

Mandler, G. (1990). A constructivist theory of emotion. In N. S. Stein, B. L. Leventhal, & T. Trabasso (Eds.), *Psychological and biological approaches to emotion* (pp. 21–43). Hillsdale, NJ: Erlbaum.

Mano, H. (1994). Risk-taking, framing effects, and affect. *Organizational Behavior and Human Decision Processes, 57,* 38–58.

Markus, H., & Kunda, Z. (1986). Stability and malleability of the self-concept. *Journal of Personality and Social Psychology, 51,* 858–866.

Markus, H., & Smith, J. (1981). The influence of self-schemata on the perception of others. In N Cantor & J. F. Kihlstrom (Eds.), *Personality, cognition, and social interaction* (pp. 233–262). Hillside, NJ: Erlbaum.

Martell, R. F., & Borg, M. R. (1993). A comparison of the behavioral rating accuracy of groups and individuals. *Journal of Applied Psychology, 78,* 43–50.

Martell, R. F., & Willis, C. E. (1993). Effects of observers' performance expectations on behavior ratings of work groups: Memory or response bias? *Organizational Behavior and Human Decision Processes, 56,* 91–109.

Maslow, A. H. (1962). *Toward a psychology of being.* Princeton, NJ: D. Von Nostrand.

Matarazzo, J. D., & Wiens, A. N. (1972). *The interview: Research on its anatomy and structure.* Chicago: Aldine-Atherton.

Maurer, T. J., & Tarulli, B. A. (1994). Acceptance of peer and upward performance appraisal systems: Considerations from employee development, job analysis, and leadership. Unpublished manuscript, Georgia Institute of Technology.

McCall, M. W., & Lombardo, M. M. (1983). *Off the track: Why and how successful executives get derailed.* Technical Report No. 21. Greensboro, NC: Center for Creative Leadership.

McCauley, C., & Lombardo, M. (1990). Benchmarks: An instrument for diagnosing managerial strengths and weaknesses. In K. E. Clark & M. B. Clark (Eds.), *Measures of leadership* (pp. 535–545). West Orange, NJ: Leadership Library of America.

McEvoy, G. M., & Buller, P. F. (1987). User acceptance of peer appraisals in an industrial setting. *Personnel Psychology, 40,* 785–797.

McGill, M. E., Slocum, J. W., Jr., & Lei, D. (1992). Management practices in learning organizations. *Organizational Dynamics, 21*(1), 5–16.

McGrath, J. E. (1990). Time matters in groups. In J. Galegher, R. E. Kraut, & C. Egido (Eds.), *Intellectual teamwork: Social and technological foundations of cooperative work* (pp. 23–61). Hillsdale, NJ: Erlbaum.

McGrath, J. E. (1991). Time, interaction, and performance (TIP): A theory of groups. *Small Group Research, 22*(2), 147–174.

Meyer, H. H. (1991). A solution to the performance appraisal feedback enigma. *Academy of Management Executive, 5,* 68–76.

Miller, V. D., & Jablin, F. M. (1991). Information seeking during organizational entry: Influences, tactics, and a model of the process. *Academy of Management Review, 16,* 92–120.

Mills, C. W. (1940). Situated actions and vocabularies of motive. *American Sociological Review, 5,* 904–913.

Mitchell, T. R., & Beach, L. R. (1990). ". . . Do I love thee? Let me count . . ." Toward an understanding of intuitive and automatic decision making. *Organizational Behavior and Human Decision Processes, 47,* 1–20.

Mitchell, T. R., Hopper, H., Daniels, D., George-Falvy, J., & James, L. R. (1993). Predicting self-efficacy and performance during skill acquisition. Paper presented at the annual meeting of the Academy of Management, Atlanta.

Mitchell, T. R., & Wood, R. E. (1980). Supervisor responses to subordinate poor performance: A test of an attributional model. *Organizational Behavior and Human Performance, 25,* 123–138.

Mitnick, B. M. (1980). *The political economy of regulation: Creating, designing, and removing regulatory forms.* New York: Columbia University Press.

Mitnick, B. M. (1984). Agency problems and political institutions. Paper presented at the annual research conference of the Association for Public Policy Analysis and Management, New Orleans.

Mitnick, B. M. (1993a). Agents in analysis: The advisory role in public affairs management. In B. M. Mitnick (Ed.), *Corporate political agency: The construction of competition in public affairs* (pp. 169–186). Newbury Park, CA: Sage.

Mitnick, B. M. (1993b). Strategic behavior and the creation of agents. In B. M. Mitnick (Ed.), *Corporate political agency: The construction of competition in public affairs* (pp. 90–124). Newbury Park, CA: Sage.

Morris, L. E. (1993). Learning organizations: Settings for developing adults. In J. Demick & P. M. Miller (Eds.), *Development in the workplace* (pp. 179–197. Hillsdale, NJ: Erlbaum.

Morrison, E. W. (1993a). Longitudinal study of the effects of information seeking on newcomer socialization. *Journal of Applied Psychology, 78,* 173–183.

Morrison, E. W. (1993b). Newcomer information seeking: Exploring types, modes, sources, and outcomes. *Academy of Management Journal, 36,* 557–589.

Morrison, E. W., & Bies, R. J. (1991). Impression management in the feedback-seeking process: A literature review and research agenda. *Academy of Management Review, 16*(3), 522–541.

Morrison, E. W., Vancouver, J. B. (1993). The effects of source attributes on feedback seeking. Paper presented at the annual meeting of the Academy of Management, Atlanta.

Moses, J., Hollenbeck, G. P., & Sorcher, M. (1993). Other people's expectations. *Human Resource Management, 32,* 283–298.

Motowidlo, S. J. (1986). Information processing in personnel decisions. In K. M. Rowland & G. R. Ferris (Eds.), *Research in personnel and human resources management.* (Vol. 4), (pp. 1–44). Greenwich, CT: JAI Press.

Mount, M. K. (1984). Psychometric properties of subordinate ratings of managerial performance. *Personnel Psychology, 37,* 687–701.

Murnighan, J. K. (1987). The structure of mediation and intravention: Comments on Carnevale's strategic choice model. *Negotiation Journal, 2,* 351–356.

Murnighan, J. K. (1991). *The dynamics of bargaining games.* Englewood Cliffs, NJ: Prentice-Hall.

Murnighan, J. K., Kim, J. W., & Metzger, A. R. (1993). The volunteer dilemma. *Administrative Science Quarterly, 38,* 515–538.

Murphy, K. R., & Cleveland, J. N. (1991). *Performance appraisal: An organizational perspective.* Needham Heights, MA: Allyn & Bacon.

Murphy, S. T., & Zajonc, R. B. (1993). Affect, cognition, and awareness: Affective priming with optimal and suboptimal stimulus exposures. *Journal of Personality and Social Psychology, 64,* 723–739.

Nadler, D. A. (1976). Using feedback for organizational change: Promises and pitfalls. *Group and Organization Studies, 1,* 177–186.

Nadler, D. A. (1977). *Feedback and organization development: Using data based methods.* Reading, MA: Addison-Wesley.

Nadler, D. A. (1979). The effects of feedback on task group behavior: A review of the experimental research. *Organizational Behavior and Human Performance, 23,* 309–338.

Nathan, B. R., & Alexander, R. A. (1985). The role of inferential accuracy in performance ratings. *Academy of Management Review, 10,* 109–115.

Neale, M. A., & Bazerman, M. H. (1991). *Cognition and rationality in negotiation.* New York: Free Press.

Neale, M. A., & Bazerman, M. H. (1992). Negotiator cognition and rationality: A behavioral decision theory perspective. *Organizational Behavior and Human Decision Processes, 51,* 157–175.

Neale, M. A., & Northcraft, G. B. (1986). Experts, amateurs, and refrigerators: Comparing expert and amateur decision making on a novel task. *Organizational Behavior and Human Decision Processes, 38,* 105–117.

Neale, M. A., & Northcraft, G. B. (1990). Experience, expertise, and decision bias in negotiation: The role of strategic conceptualization. In B. Sheppard, M. Bazerman, & R. Lewicki (Eds.), *Research in negotiation in organizations.* (Vol. 2). Greenwich, CT: JAI Press.

Neisser, U. (Ed.). (1994). *The perceived self: Ecological and interpersonal sources of self knowledge.* New York: Cambridge University Press.

Nelson, T. D. (1993). The hierarchical organization of behavior: A useful feedback model of self-regulation. *Current Directions in Psychological Science, 2,* 121–126.

Neuberg, S. L. (1989). The goal of forming accurate impressions during social interactions: Attenuating the impact of negative expectancies. *Journal of Personality and Social Psychology, 56,* 374–386.

Nilsen, D., & Campbell, D. P. (1993). Self-observer rating discrepancies: Once an over-rater, always an over-rater? *Human Resource Management, 32,* 265–282.

Nisbett, R. E., & Wilson, T. D. (1977). Telling more than we know: Verbal reports on mental processes. *Psychological Review, 84,* 231–259.

Noe, R. A., Noe, A. W., & Bachhuber, J. A. (1990). Correlates of career motivation. *Journal of Vocational Behavior, 37,* 340–356.

Norman, W. T. (1963). Toward an adequate taxonomy of personality attributes: Replicated factor structure in peer nomination personality ratings. *Journal of Abnormal and Social Psychology, 66,* 547–583.

Organ, D. W. (1988). *Organizational citizenship behavior: The good soldier syndrome.* Lexington, MA: Lexington Books.

Padgett, M. Y., & Ilgen, D. R. (1989). The impact of ratee performance characteristics on rater cognitive processes and alternative measures of rater accuracy. *Organizational Behavior and Human Decision Processes, 44,* 232–260.

Pelham, B. W. (1991). On confidence and consequence: The certainty and importance of self-knowledge. *Journal of Personality and Social Psychology, 60,* 518–530.

Pennebaker, J. W. (1990). *Opening up: The healing power of confiding in others.* New York: Morrow.

Perkins, D. N. (1981). *The mind's best work.* Cambridge, MA: Harvard University Press.

Peterson, C. R., & Beach, L. R. (1967). Man as an intuitive statistician. *Psychological Bulletin, 68,* 29–46.

Petty, R. E., Cacioppo, J. T., & Kasmer, J. A. (1985). Individual differences in social loafing on cognitive tasks. Paper presented at the meeting of the Midwestern Psychological Association, Chicago.

Phillips, A. P., & Dipboye, R. L. (1989). Correlational tests of predictions from a process model of the interview. *Journal of Applied Psychology, 74,* 41–52.

Pinkley, R. L. (1990). Dimensions of conflict frame: Disputant interpretations of conflict. *Journal of Applied Psychology, 75,* 117–126.

Pinkley, R. L., & Northcraft, G. B. (1994). Conflict frames of reference: Implications for dispute processes and outcomes. *Academy of Management Journal, 37,* 193–205.

Pinkley, R. L., Neale, M. A., & Bennett, R. J. (1994). The impact of alternatives to settlement in dyadic negotiation. *Organizational Behavior and Human Decision Processes, 57,* 97–116.

Powers, W. T. (1973a). *Behavior: The control of perception.* Chicago: Aldine.

Powers, W. T. (1973b). Feedback: Beyond behaviorism. *Science, 179,* 351–356.

Prussia, G. E., Kinicki, A. J., & Bracker, J. S. (1993). Psychological and behavioral consequences of job loss: A covariance structure analysis using Weiner's (1985) attribution model. *Journal of Applied Psychology, 78,* 382–394.

Pulakos, E. D. (1986). The development of training programs to increase accuracy with different rating tasks. *Organizational Behavior and Human Decision Processes, 38,* 76–91.

Putnam, L. L. (1990). Reframing integrative and distributive bargaining: A process perspective. In B. H. Sheppard, M. Bazerman, & R. Lewicki (Eds.), *Research on negotiation in organizations.* (Vol. 2), (pp. 3–30). Greenwich, CT: JAI Press.

Putnam, L. L., & Geist, P. (1985). Argument in bargaining: An analysis of the reasoning process. *Southern Speech Communication Journal, 50,* 225–245.

Putnam, L. L., & Holmer, M. (1992). Framing, reframing, and issue development. In L. L. Putnam & M. E. Roloff (Eds.), *Communication and negotiation* (pp. 128–155). Newbury Park, CA: Sage.

Putnam, L. L., & Jones, T. S. (1982). Reciprocity in negotiations: An analysis of bargaining interaction. *Communication Monographs, 49,* 171–191.

Raimy, V. C. (1948). Self-reference in counseling interviews. *Journal of Consulting Psychology, 12,* 153–163.

Rand, R., & Wexley, K. (1975). A demonstration of the Byrnes similarity hypothesis in simulated employment interviews. *Psychological Reports, 36,* 535–544.

Reed, E. (1991). James Gibson's ecological approach to cognition. In A. Still & A. Costall (Eds.), *Against cognitivism: Alternative foundations for cognitive psychology* (pp. 171–197). New York: Harvester Weatsheaf.

Reichers, A. E., & Schneider, B. (1990). Climate and culture: An evolution of concepts. In B. Schneider (Ed.), *Organizational climate and culture* (pp. 5–39). San Francisco: Jossey-Bass.

Reilly, B. A., & Doherty, M. E. (1989). A note on the assessment of self-insight in judgment research. *Organizational Behavior and Human Decision Processes, 44,* 123–131.

Reilly, B. A., & Doherty, M. E. (1992). The assessment of self-insight in judgment policies. *Organizational Behavior and Human Decision Processes, 53,* 285–309.

Reilly, R. R., Warech, M. A., & Reilly, S. (1993). The influence of self-monitoring on the reliability and validity of upward feedback. Paper presented at the annual meeting of the Society for Industrial and Organizational Psychology, San Francisco.

Reisman, J. M. (1990). Intimacy in same-sex friendships. *Sex Roles, 23,* 65–82.

Rice, R. W., McFarlin, D. B., & Bennett, D. E. (1989). Standards of comparison and job satisfaction. *Journal of Applied Psychology, 74,* 591–598.

Ridley, C. R. (1986). Diagnosis as a function of race pairing and client self-disclosure. *Journal of Cross-Cultural Psychology, 17,* 337–351.

Robbins, T. L., & DeNisi, A. S. (1994). A closer look at interpersonal affect as a distinct influence on cognitive processing in performance evaluations. *Journal of Applied Psychology, 79,* 341–353.

Rogers, R. R. (1959). A theory of therapy, personality, and interpersonal relationships, as developed in the client-centered framework. In S. Koch (Ed.), *Psychology: A study of a science.* (Vol. 3), (pp. 184–256). New York: McGraw-Hill.

Rosen, B., & Jerdee, T. (1988). Managing older workers' careers. *Research in Personnel and Human Resources Management, 6,* 37–74.

Rosenfeld, L. B., Civikly, J. M., & Herron, J. R. (1979). Anatomical and psychological sex differences. In G. J. Chelune (Ed.), *Self-disclosure: Origins, patterns, and implications of openness in interpersonal relationships* (pp. 80–109). San Francisco: Jossey-Bass.

Rosenthal, R., & Rubin, B. R. (1978). Interpersonal expectancy effects: The first 345 studies. *Behavioral and Brain Sciences, 3*, 37–415.

Ross, A. O. (1992). *The sense of self: Research and theory.* New York: Springer.

Ross, M. (1989). The relation of implicit theories of the construction of personal histories. *Psychological Review, 96*, 341–357.

Rousch, P. E., & Atwater, L. E. (1992). Using the MBTI to understand transformational leadership and self-perception accuracy. *Military Psychology, 4*, 17–34.

Rowe, M. P. (1984). The non-union complaint system at MIT: An upward-feedback mediation model. *Alternatives to the High Cost of Litigation, 2*, 10–13.

Russell, J. A. (1994). Is there universal recognition of emotion from facial expression? A review of the cross-cultural studies. *Psychological Bulletin, 115*, 102–141.

Russo, J. E., & Schoemaker, P. J. H. (1992). Managing overconfidence. *Sloan Management Review, 33*(2), 7–17.

Saavedra, R., Earley, P. C., & Van Dyne, L. (1993). Complex interdependence in task-performing groups. *Journal of Applied Psychology, 78*, 61–72.

Saavedra, R., & Kwun, S. K. (1993). Peer evaluation in self-managing work groups. *Journal of Applied Psychology, 78*, 450–462.

Salancik, G. R., & Pfeffer, J. A. (1978). A social information processing approach to job attitudes and task design. *Administrative Science Quarterly, 23*, 224–253.

Salvemini, N. J., Reilly, R. R., & Smither, J. W. (1993). The influence of rater motivation on assimilation effects and accuracy in performance ratings. *Organizational Behavior and Human Decision Processes, 55*, 41–60.

Sanders, M. M. (1993). Situational constraints through the cognitive looking glass: A reinterpretation of the relationship between situations and performance judgments. *Human Resource Management Review, 3*, 129–146.

Schachter, S. (1964). The interaction of cognitive and physiological determinants of emotional state. In L. Berkowitz (Ed.), *Advances in experimental social psychology.* (Vol. 1), (pp. 49–82). New York: Academic Press.

Schaubroeck, J., & Green, G. (1989). Confirmatory factor analytic procedures or assessing change during organizational entry. *Journal of Applied Psychology, 74*, 892–900.

Scheier, M. F., & Carver, C. S. (1983). Two sides of the self: One for you and one for me. In J. Suls & A. G. Greenwald (Eds.), *Psychological perspectives on the self.* (Vol. 2), (pp. 123–157). Hillsdale, NJ: Erlbaum.

Schkade, D. A., & Kilbourne, L. M. (1991). Expectation-outcome consistency and hindsight bias. *Organizational Behavior and Human Decision Processes, 49*, 105–123.

Schmit, M. J., & Ryan, A. M. (1993). The big five in personnel selection: Factor structure in applicant and nonapplicant populations. *Journal of Applied Psychology, 78*, 966–974.

Schneider, B. (1987). The people make the place. *Personnel Psychology, 40*, 437–453.

Schneider, D. J. (1973). Implicit personality theory: A review. *Psychological Bulletin, 79*, 294–309.

Schneider, D. J. (1981). Tactical self-presentations: Toward a broader conception. In J. T. Tedeschi (Ed.), *Impression management theory and social psychological research* (pp. 23–40). New York: Academic Press.

Senge, P. M. (1990). *The fifth discipline: The art and practice.* New York: Doubleday.

Shama, A. (1993). Management under fire: The transformation of managers in the Soviet Union and Eastern Europe. *Academy of Management Executive, 7,* 22–35.

Shanon, B. (1991). Alternative theoretical frameworks for psychology: A synopsis. In A. Still & A. Costall (Eds.), *Against cognitivism: Alternative foundations for cognitive psychology* (pp. 237–263). New York: Harvester Weatsheaf.

Sharp, G. L., Cutler, B. L., & Penrod, S. D. (1988). Performance feedback improves the resolution of confidence judgments. *Organizational Behavior and Human Decision Processes, 42,* 271–283.

Sharpe, D., & Adair, J. G. (1993). Reversibility of the hindsight bias: Manipulation of experimental demands. *Organizational Behavior and Human Decision Processes, 56,* 233–245.

Shepperd, J. A. (1993). Productivity loss in performance groups: A motivation analysis. *Psychological Bulletin, 113,* 67–81.

Sherif, C. (1976). *Orientation in social psychology.* New York: Harper & Row.

Shotter, J. (1991). The rhetorical-responsive nature of mind: A social constructionist account. In A. Still & A. Costall (Eds.), *Against cognitivism: Alternative foundations for cognitive psychology* (pp. 55–80). New York: Harvester Weatsheaf.

Shrauger, J. S., & Osberg, T. M. (1981). The relative accuracy of self-prediction and judgments by others in psychological assessment. *Psychological Bulletin, 90,* 322–351.

Shrauger, J. S., & Schoeneman, J. (1979). Symbolic interactionist view of self-concept: Through the looking glass darkly. *Psychological Bulletin, 86,* 549–573.

Simon, B., & Brown, R. (1987). Perceived intra-group homogeneity in minority-majority contexts. *Journal of Personality and Social Psychology, 53,* 703–711.

Simon, H. A. (1987). Making management decisions: The role of intuition and emotion. *Academy of Management Executive, 1,* 57–64.

Sinclair, R. C., Hoffman, C., Mark, M. M., Martin, L. L., & Pickering, T. L. (1994). Construct accessibility and the misattribution of arousal: Schachter and Singer revisited. *Psychological Science, 5,* 15–19.

Sinnott, J. D. (1993). Use of complex thought and resolving intragroup conflicts: A means to conscious adult development in the workplace. In J. Demick & P. M. Miller (Eds.), *Development in the workplace* (pp. 155–175). Hillsdale, NJ: Erlbaum.

Slovic, P., & Lichtenstein, S. (1971). Comparison of Bayesian and regression approaches to the study of information processing in judgment. *Organizational Behavior and Human Performance, 6,* 649–744.

Smelser, N. J., & Erikson, E. H. (1980). *Themes of work and love in adulthood.* Cambridge, MA: Harvard University Press.

Smith, S. S., & Kihlstrom, J. F. (1987). When is a schema not a schema? The "big five" traits as cognitive structures. *Social Cognition, 5,* 26–57.

Smither, J. W., London, M., Millsap, R. E., Salvemini, N., Reilly, R. R., & Vasilopoulos, N. L. (1993). A longitudinal study of upward feedback and self-evaluations in a multi-national organization. Paper presented at the annual meeting of the Society for Industrial and Organizational Psychology, San Francisco.

Smither, J. W., Reilly, R. R., & Buda, R. (1988). Effect of prior performance information on ratings of present performance: Contrast vs. assimilation revisited. *Journal of Applied Psychology, 74,* 143–151.

Smither, J. W., Wohlers, A. J., & London, M. (1992). Effects of leader agreement and type of feedback on reactions to upward feedback. Paper presented at the annual meeting of the Society for Industrial and Organizational Psychology, Montreal.

Snyder, M. (1974). Self-monitoring of expressive behavior. *Journal of Personality and Social Psychology, 30,* 526–537.

Snyder, M. (1981). *Cognitive processes in stereotyping and intergroup behavior.* Hillsdale, NJ: Erlbaum.

Snyder, M. (1987). *Public appearances, private realities: The psychology of self-monitoring.* New York: W. H. Freeman.

Snyder, M. (1992). Motivational foundations of behavioral confirmation. In M. Zanna (Ed.), *Advances in Experimental Social Psychology.* (Vol. 25).

Snyder, M., & Gangestad, S. (1986). On the nature of self-monitoring: Matters of assessment, matters of validity. *Journal of Personality and Social Psychology, 51,* 125–135.

Snyder, S. M., & Haugen, J. A. (1990). Why does behavioral confirmation occur? A functional perspective. Paper presented at the annual meeting of the American Psychological Association, Boston.

Snyder, M., Tanke, E. D., & Berscheid, E. (1977). Social perception and interpersonal behavior: On the self-fulfilling nature of social stereotypes. *Journal of Personality and Social Psychology, 35,* 656–666.

Snygg, D., & Combs, A. W. (1950). The phenomenological approach and the problems of "unconscious" behavior. *Journal of Abnormal and Social Psychology, 45,* 523–528.

Solomon, R. J. (1976). An examination of the relationship between a survey feedback technique and the work environment. *Personnel Psychology, 29,* 583–594.

Spera, S. P., Buhrfeind, E. D., & Pennebaker, J. W. (1994). Expressive writing and coping with job loss. *Academy of Management Journal, 37,* 722–733.

Stamoulis, D. T., & Hauenstein, N. M. A. (1993). Rater training and rating accuracy: Training for dimensional accuracy versus training for ratee differentiation. *Journal of Applied Psychology, 78,* 994–1003.

Steele, C. M., Spencer, S. J., & Lynch, M. (1993). Self-image resilience and dissonance: The role of affirmational resources. *Journal of Personality and Social Psychology, 64,* 885–896.

Steiner, D. D., Rain, J. S., & Smalley, M. M. (1993). Distributional ratings of performance: Further examination of a new rating format. *Journal of Applied Psychology, 78,* 438–442.

Stinson, L., & Ickes, W. (1992). Empathic accuracy in the interactions of male friends versus male strangers. *Journal of Personality and Social Psychology, 62*(5), 787–797.

Storms, M. D. (1973). Videotape and the attribution process: Reversing actors' and observers' points of view. *Journal of Personality and Social Psychology, 27,* 165–175.

Strauss, S. S., & McGrath, J. E. (1994). Does the medium matter? The interaction of task type and technology on group performance and member reactions. *Journal of Applied Psychology, 79,* 87–97.

Street, R. L. (1986). Interaction processes and outcomes in interviews. *Communication Yearbook, 9,* 215–251.

Stryker, S., & Statham, A. (1985). Symbolic interactionism and role theory. In G. Lindzey & E. Aronson (Eds.), *The handbook of social psychology* (3rd ed.). (Vol. 1), (pp. 311–378). New York: Random House.

Suls, J. (Ed.) (1982). *Psychological perspectives on the self.* (Vol. 1). Hillsdale, NJ: Erlbaum.

Summers, D. A., Taliaferro, J. D., & Fletcher, D. J. (1970). Subjective vs. objective descriptions of judgment policy. *Psychonomic Science, 18,* 249–250.

Sundaram, A. K., & Black, J. S. (1992). The environment and internal organization of multinational enterprises. *Academy of Management Review, 17,* 729–757.

Surber, C. F. (1985). Measuring the importance of information in judgment: Individual differences in weighting ability and effort. *Organizational Behavior and Human Decision Processes, 35,* 156–178.

Sulsky, L. M., & Day, D. V. (1992). Frame-of-reference training and cognitive categorization: An empirical investigation of rater memory issues. *Journal of Applied Psychology, 77,* 501–510.

Sulsky, L. M., Day, D. V., & Lawrence, D. (1994). Schema change and negative transfer: A potential boundary condition on the effectiveness of frame-of-reference training. Paper presented at the Ninth Annual Conference of the Society for Industrial and Organizational Psychology, Nashville.

Tagiuri, R., & Petrullo, L. (Eds.), (1958). *Person perception and interpersonal behavior.* Stanford, CA: Stanford University Press.

Taylor, D. A. (1979). Motivational bases. In G. J. Chelune (Ed.), *Self-disclosure: Origins, patterns, and implications of openness in interpersonal relationships* (pp. 110–150). San Francisco: Jossey-Bass.

Taylor, S. E., & Brown, J. D. (1988). Illusion and well-being: A social psychological perspective on mental health. *Psychological Bulletin, 103,* 193–210.

Taylor, S. M., Fisher, C. D., & Ilgen, D. R. (1984). Individuals' reactions to performance feedback in organizations: A control theory perspective. In K. M. Rowland & G. R. Ferris (Eds.), *Research in Personnel and Human Resources Management, 2,* 81–124.

Tedeschi, J. T., & Norman, N. (1985). Social power, self-presentation, and the self. In J. T. Tedeschi (Ed.), *Impression management theory and social psychological research* (pp. 293–322). New York: Academic Press.

Tedeschi, J. T., & Reiss, M. (1981). Verbal tactics of impression management. In C. Antaki (Ed.), *Ordinary explanations of social behavior* (pp. 271–326). London: Academic Press.

Tesser, A. (1988). Toward a self-evaluation maintenance model of social behavior. In L. Kerkowitz (Ed.), *Advances in experimental social psychology.* (Vol. 2), (pp. 181–227). San Diego: Academic Press.

Tesser, A., & Campbell, J. (1982). Self-definition and self-evaluation maintenance. In J. Suls (Ed.), *Psychological perspectives on the self.* (Vol. 2), (pp. 1–31). Hillsdale, NJ: Erlbaum.

Thompson, J. D. (1967). *Organizations in action.* New York: McGraw-Hill.

Thompson, L. (1993). The impact of negotiation on intergroup relations. *Journal of Experimental Social Psychology, 29,* 304–325.

Thornton, G. C., III, & Byham, W. C. (1982). *Assessment centers and managerial performance.* New York: Academic Press.

Tice, D. M., & Baumeister, R. F. (1990). Self-esteem, self-handicapping, and self-presentation: The strategy of inadequate practice. *Journal of Personality, 58,* 443–464.

Tindale, R. S., Sheffey, S., & Scott, L. A. (1993). Framing and group decision-making: Do cognitive changes parallel preference changes? *Organizational Behavior and Human Decision Processes, 55,* 470–485.

Tornow, W. W. (1993). Perceptions or reality: Is multi-perspective measurement a means or an end? *Human Resource Management, 32,* 221–230.

Tsui, A. S., & Ohlott, P. (1988). Multiple assessment of managerial effectiveness: Interrater agreement and consensus in effectiveness models. *Personnel Psychology, 41,* 779–803.

Tversky, A., & Kahneman, D. (1981). The framing of decisions and the psychology of choice. *Science, 211,* 453–458.

Ury, W. I., Brett, J. M., & Goldberg, S. B. (1988). *Getting disputes resolved.* San Francisco: Jossey-Bass.

Vallacher, R. R., Nowak, A., & Kaufman, J. (1994). Intrinsic dynamics of social judgment. *Journal of Personality and Social Psychology, 67,* 20–35.

Van Maanen, J., & Schein, E. H. (1979). Toward a theory of organizational socialization. In B. M. Staw (Ed.), *Research in organizational behavior.* (Vol. 1), (pp. 209–264). Greenwich, CT: JAI Press.

Van Velsor, E., & Leslie, J. B. (1991). *Feedback to managers.* Vol. 1, *A Guide to rating multi-rater feedback instruments.* Report 149. Greensboro, NC: Center for Creative Leadership.

Van Velsor, E., Ruderman, M. N., & Phillips, A. D. (1991). Enhancing self-objectivity and performance on the job: The developmental impact of feedback. Paper presented at the annual meeting of the Society for Industrial and Organizational Psychology, St. Louis.

Van Velsor, E., Taylor, S., & Leslie, J. B. (1993). An examination of the relationships between self-perception accuracy, self-awareness, gender and leader effectiveness. *Human Resource Management, 32,* 249–264.

Vandenberg, R. J., & Self, R. M. (1993). Assessing newcomers' changing commitments to the organization during the first 6 months of work. *Journal of Applied Psychology, 78,* 557–568.

Villanova, P., & Bernardin, H. J. (1989). Impression management in the context of performance appraisal. In R. A. Giacalone & P. Rosenfeld (Eds.), *Impression management in the organization* (pp. 299–313). Hillsdale, NJ: Erlbaum.

Vinokur, A. D., van Ryn, M., Gramlich, E. M., & Price, R. H. (1991). Long-term follow-up and benefit-cost analysis of the Jobs Program: A preventive intervention for the unemployed. *Journal of Applied Psychology, 76,* 213–219.

Vohra, A. (1986). *Wittgenstein's philosophy of mind.* London: Croom Helm.

Wall, J. A. (1990). Managers in the People's Republic of China. *Academy of Management Executive, 4,* 19–32.

Wall, J. A., & Lynn, A. (1993). Mediation: A current review. *Journal of Conflict Resolution, 37,* 160–194.

Walton, R. E., & McKersie, R. B. (1991). *A behavioral theory of labor negotiations: An analysis of social interaction systems* (2nd ed.). Ithaca, NY: Institute for Labor Relations Press.

Warner, R. M. (1988). Rhythm in social interaction. In J. E. McGrath (Ed.), *The social psychology of time: New perspectives* (pp. 63–88).Newbury Park, CA: Sage.

Watson, W. E., Kumar, K., Michaelsen, L. K. (1993). Cultural diversity's impact on interaction process and performance: Comparing homogeneous and diverse task groups. *Academy of Management Journal, 36,* 590–602.

Watson, W. E., Michaelsen, L. K., & Sharp, W. (1991). Member competence, group interaction, and group decision making: A longitudinal study. *Journal of Applied Psychology, 76,* 803–809.

Wayne, S. J., & Ferris, G. R. (1990). Influence tactics, affect, and exchange quality in supervisor-subordinate interactions: A laboratory experiment and field study. *Journal of Applied Psychology, 75,* 487–499.

Wayne, S. J., & Kacmar, K. M. (1991). The effects of impression management on the performance appraisal process. *Organizational Behavior and Human Decision Processes, 48,* 70–88.

Weick, K. E. (1979). *The social psychology of organizing* (2nd ed.). Reading, MA: Addison-Wesley.

Weick, K. E. (1993). The collapse of sensemaking in organizations: The Mann Gulch disaster. *Administrative Science Quarterly, 38,* 628–652.

Weick, K. E., & Roberts, K. H. (1993). Collective mind in organizations: Heedful interrelating on flight decks. *Administrative Science Quarterly, 38,* 357–381.

Weingart, L. R., Bennett, R. J., & Brett, J. M. (1993). The impact of consideration of issues and motivational orientation on group negotiation process and outcome. *Journal of Applied Psychology, 78,* 504–517.

Welton, G. L., & Pruitt, D. G. (1987). The mediation process: The effects of mediator bias and disputant power. *Personality and Social Psychology Bulletin, 13,* 123–133.

Werner, J. M. (1994). Dimensions that make a difference: Examining the impact of in-role and extra-role behaviors on supervisory ratings. *Journal of Applied Psychology, 79,* 98–107.

Westcott, M. R. (1968). *Toward a contemporary psychology of intuition.* New York: Holt, Rinehart and Winston.

Whetten, D. A., & Cameron, K. S. (1991). *Developing management skills* (2nd ed.). New York: Harper Collins.

White, S. B., & Neale, M. A. (1994). The role of negotiator aspirations and settlement expectancies in bargaining outcomes. *Organizational Behavior and Human Decision Processes, 57,* 303–317.

Wills, T. A. (1991). Similarity and self-esteem in downward comparisons. In J. Suls & T. A. Wills (Eds.), *Social comparisons: Contemporary theory and research* (pp. 51–78). Hillsdale, NJ: Erlbaum.

Witmer, J. M., Carnevale, P. J., & Walker, M. E. (1991). General alignment and overt support in biased mediation. *Journal of Conflict Resolution, 35,* 594–610.

Woehr, D. J., & Feldman, J. (1993). Processing objective and question order effects on the causal relation between memory and judgment in performance appraisal: The tip of the iceberg. *Journal of Applied Psychology, 78,* 232–241.

Woehr, D. J., & Roch, S. (1994). The effect of frame-of-reference training on rating accuracy and behavioral recall. Paper presented at the Ninth Annual Conference of the Society for Industrial and Organizational Psychology, Nashville.

Wofford, J. C. (1994). An examination of the cognitive processes used to handle employee job problems. *Academy of Management Journal, 37,* 180–192.

Wofford, J. C., & Goodwin, V. L. (1990). Effects of feedback on cognitive processing and choice of decision style. *Journal of Applied Psychology, 75,* 603–612.

Wohlers, A. J., & London, M. (1989). Ratings of managerial characteristics: Evaluation difficulty, co-worker agreement, and self-awareness. *Personnel Psychology, 42,* 235–260.

Wohlers, A. J., Hall, M. J., & London, M. (1993). Subordinates rating managers:

Organizational and biographical correlates of self/subordinate agreement. *Journal of Occupational and Organizational Psychology, 66,* 263–275.

Wolf, G., Casey, J. T., Pufahl, J., & London, M. (1994). Job creation strategies for displaced engineers. Paper presented at the annual meeting of the Society for Industrial and Organizational Psychology, Knoxville.

Wood, J. V. (1989). Theory and research concerning social comparisons of personal attributes. *Psychological Bulletin, 106,* 231–248.

Wortman, C. B., & Linsenmeier, J. A. W. (1977). Interpersonal attraction and techniques of integratiation in organizational settings. In B. M. Staw & G. R. Salancik (Eds.), *New directions in organizational behavior* (pp. 133–178). Chicago: St. Clair Press.

Wyer, R. S., Budescheim, T. L., Lambert, A. J., & Swan, S. (1994). Person memory and judgments: Pragmatic influences on impressions formed in a social context. *Journal of Personality and Social Psychology, 66,* 254–267.

Yammarino, F. J., & Atwater, L. E. (1993). Understanding self-perception accuracy: Implications for human resources management. *Human Resource Management, 32,* 231–249.

Yammarino, F. J., & Dubinsky, A. J. (1992). Supervisor-subordinate relationships: A multiple level of analysis approach. *Human Relations, 45,* 575–600.

Yu, J., & Murphy, K. R. (1993). Modesty bias in self-ratings of performance: A test of the cultural relativity hypothesis. *Personnel Psychology, 46,* 357–363.

Zalesny, M. D., & Ford, J. K. (1990). Extending the social information processing perspective: New links to attitudes, behaviors, and perceptions. *Organizational Behavior and Human Decision Processes, 47,* 205–246.

Zalesny, M. D., & Highhouse, S. (1992). Accuracy in performance evaluations. *Organizational Behavior and Human Decision Processes, 51,* 22–50.

Zammuto, R. F., London, M., & Rowland, K. M. (1982). Organization and rater differences in performance appraisal. *Personnel Psychology, 35,* 643–658.

Index